C000094968

Iris

Flower of the Rainbow

Iris

Flower of the Rainbow

In ancient Greek mythology Iris was the messenger of the gods. Granddaughter of the earth goddess Gaea and the sea god Pontus, she travelled on the arc of the rainbow bearing messages between earth, sea and sky. Our modern iris flowers still echo the glowing spectrum of Iris's aerial pathway and the rainbow's symbolic message of hope, as re-created here.

Graeme Grosvenor

Photography Jim Frazier and Graeme Grosvenor

Kangaroo Press

ACKNOWLEDGMENTS

We wish to thank the following:

Barry Blyth of Tempo Two Nursery, Pearcedale, Victoria, for his assistance and comments in preparation of the text.

Keith Keppel for his particular assistance when we were in the USA.

The Schreiner family for their assistance while we were in the USA. In particular, thanks to David Schreiner and Ray Schreiner for assistance with the photography.

Perry and Kitty Dyer — good friends and willing chauffeurs.

Lorena Reid for the help given while in her garden in Oregon.

Members of the Italian Iris Society for assistance in Italy. Members of the British Iris Society for assistance while in England and numerous members of the American Iris Society, in California, Texas, Oklahoma, Oregon and Washington State, too many to mention individually, but the hospitality, assistance and general access to gardens was so much appreciated. Members of the New Zealand Iris Society, and our good friends Ian and Helen Gear from Heritage Horticulture.

Helen Grosvenor for her assistance and unflagging enthusiasm, for typing the text and for her constructive criticism.

John Taylor for his contribution to the text, for his comments and criticisms and his overview of the whole plot.

Densey Clyne for her contributions to the illustrations and her assistance in selecting the colour plates.

Pauline Payne and Marcus Payne for their assistance in selecting the colour plates.

Tom and Ellen Abrego, Chehalem Gardens, Dundee, Oregon, for assistance and the use of their garden.

Duane and Joyce Meek, D & J Gardens, Silverton, Oregon, for assistance and use of their garden.

Cooley's Gardens, Silverton, Oregon, for assistance and use of their garden, with special thanks to Rick and Larry Ernst.

Terry and Barbara Aitken, Salmon Creek Gardens, Vancouver, Washington, for assistance and the use of their garden.

Roberta Shoop, Portland, Oregon, for access to her garden and permission to photograph the iris of the late George Shoop.

Roger Nelson, Brooks, Oregon, for assistance and the use of his garden.

Ann Barbetti, Florence, Italy, for assistance while in Italy.

GRAEME GROSVENOR
JIM FRAZIER

Cataloguing-in-Publication data

Grosvenor, Graeme. 1936–

Iris: flower of the rainbow

Bibliography
Includes index.
ISBN 0 86417 777 1
1. Iris (Plant). 2. Iris (Plant) Varieties I. Frazier, Jim. II. Title.

584.38

10 9 8 7 6 5 4 3 2

© Graeme Grosvenor (text), Graeme Grosvenor and Jim Frazier (photography) 1997

Reprinted 1998
First published in Australia in 1997 by Kangaroo Press
an imprint of Simon & Schuster Australia
20 Barcoo Street, East Roseville NSW 2069

A Viacom Company
Sydney New York London Toronto Tokyo Singapore

All rights reserved. No part of this publication may be reproduced, stored in a retrieval system, or transmitted, in any form or by any means, electronic, mechanical, photocopying, recording or otherwise, without the prior permission of the publisher in writing.

'Ribands' (Grosvenor, 1994)

CONTENTS

INTRODUCTION

This book is the culmination of a rainbow tour, organised by Iris, goddess of the rainbow, who has led me on a journey encompassing three continents, over a dozen countries and spanning a 30-year period. It has been a journey of love, often mingled with frustration and near disaster as most love affairs are, but ultimately the rewards have been overwhelming. It is a journey that has certainly changed and often dominated my life and that of my family. Many new friendships and worldwide acquaintances have been formed, many objectives have been achieved and now it is time to record the journey, verbally and visually.

Of all the jewels in the floral kingdom, it is the iris which shines brightest for form and colour. It is this fascination with form and colour which has led me on my journey. There is an artistic streak in all of us, a desire for expression often latent, often suppressed and very often frustrated. Pursuit of the goddess Iris has allowed me to use those small talents I have to express myself in colour and form. I cannot produce art works as did Monet or Van Gogh, but I can paint pictures with my iris. I can enjoy the spring cavalcade of colour in my own garden and the gardens of others and I can spend the cold and somewhat dull winter days planning these pictures for myself and others to enjoy.

There is no other flower that offers the diversity of colour and colour patterns and there is no other flower that offers the wide range of growing conditions, which allows me to say that there is an iris for every position in every garden. There are iris that will grow in shade, iris that require full sun and all the variations in between. There are iris that like rich, high-nutrient soils, there are those more easily catered for, there are iris for hot, dry positions, iris for cold, wet positions, there are those that like well drained soils, those that enjoy bog conditions and a plethora of iris for water gardens. Some iris will not tolerate alkaline conditions while others relish a higher pH. Indeed there is an iris for every position in every garden and it is the chore of gardeners to ensure that their precious plants are grown to their highest potential. I have no argument with those among us who respond to, or even invite, a challenge and there is a perverse streak in many of us

that pushes us to try to achieve the difficult; even the impossible. In younger days, I enjoyed such a challenge but am now content to grow those varieties which I can grow well and leave the challenges to be met elsewhere. Indeed, part of my initial joy in growing iris in the warm, temperate Sydney climate was to prove to the 'experts' that, in spite of what they said or wrote, tall bearded iris could be grown well in and around Sydney. That point proved, I set about a breeding campaign to develop more and more bearded iris that were at home in our less than perfect growing conditions. I have now gone full circle in my thinking, and believe that one should concentrate on growing those plants most suitable for the environment. And then I think — what if I had never taken up this challenge nearly 30 years ago? How many gardeners would never have had the pleasure of growing these beautiful flowers, had it not been for experimentation?

Now, I say categorically, tall bearded iris can and do grow well in Sydney, and in other warm, humid climates but they do grow better in colder, less humid climates. I can recommend to gardeners in warm, semitropical climates that, for best results and ease of achievement, they will find Louisiana iris very rewarding. I have learned that growing iris, of all types, is different in Sydney than in western New South Wales, that growing iris is different in Victoria, in South Australia, in Tasmania, in Queensland and in Western Australia. I have learned that growing iris in Australia is different from growing iris in New Zealand, or in Italy, or in the United Kingdom, or in France, or in Germany, or in Austria or in Holland. I have learned that not only is there a great difference in growing iris here from growing them in the United States of America, but that in the USA growing habits and performance and hence cultural requirements are far different in Oregon from those in California.

Through all of this I wish to make one significant point and that is that cultural habits and requirements for growing beautiful iris will be unique to the area in which you live. Differences between one area and another may only be slight, but vary they will. It is not my aim to prescribe how to grow perfect iris for your conditions, but to lay down certain guidelines that have

THE GENUS IRIS

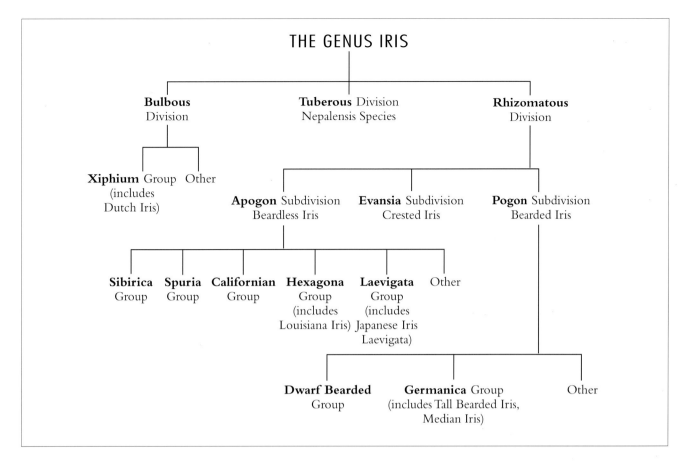

Figure 1. The genus Iris

been developed over a long, long period by many talented and devoted gardeners.

I wish to question the importance of whether it is truly significant to note that bearded iris 'grow better' in Oregon, USA than they do in Louisiana, USA, and that Louisiana iris 'grow better' in Queensland, Australia than they do in Tasmania, Australia. What we do know is that bearded iris grown in pots in standing water will not grow as well as Louisiana iris given the same conditions (and this applies anywhere in the world); likewise Louisiana iris grown high and dry in raised beds with rhizomes uncovered, will suffer, no matter what the climatic conditions.

I wish to explore the 'optimum' climatic conditions, the 'optimum' growing conditions and the 'optimum' cultural practices for those iris which are in cultivation. By all means, take up the challenge of growing iris under difficult conditions, if you wish. The gardening world will be the richer for your successes and failures but, if you want maximum reward for minimum effort, grow only those iris which are most suitable for your climate and conditions. Be warned! Nature has a habit of making fools of the most expert of experts and Iris, goddess of the rainbow, is a fickle lover. Seasonal variations play a major part in iris bloom and performance and your most ardent attention can sometimes go unrewarded while, in another season,

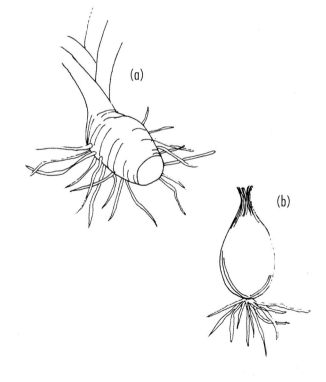

Figure 2. (a) rhizome, (b) bulb

nature's bountiful harvest is there for the taking, perhaps with a minimum of effort. Such are the joys and frustrations of growing iris.

In writing this book I wish to make a practical, cultural statement and I wish to help those among us with an interest in iris to grow them to the fullest potential, but this is only part of my ambition. The book is to be a statement of personal experience and of the experiences of others and a statement at a point in time. It can be nothing else. We can reflect on the past, we can anticipate the future, but what is — is now. I am fully aware that many of the iris grown 30 years ago are no longer in cultivation and that the giant strides in iris hybridisation and development that have been made in the last 30 years will continue, and be amplified in the next 30 years. There are, however, those iris which have stood the test of time and there are those that I anticipate will continue to do so. Is it really important that those iris, recommended as the paragons of perfection now, will no longer be so in five, ten, twenty or so years? I think not! What is important, is that, while this is a picture of the iris scene now and that the scene will change and hopefully develop, there is pleasure and information for all iris lovers and would-be lovers between these covers.

Much has been written about the genus *Iris* and iris species. Nothing has surpassed William Rickatson Dykes' legendary book *The Genus Iris,* first published in 1913, if one is interested in the classification and grouping of iris species — more than two hundred of them. In his preface to *The Genus Iris,* Dykes states, 'In publishing this book on Irises, I am fully aware that it is not yet possible to give a complete account of the Iris genus'. Not much has changed in that regard in over 80 years but, in many ways, the iris world has been revolutionised. I have no desire to replicate Dykes' mammoth volume nor do I wish to enlarge on it as a treatise on species. This has been done and done very well for all who are interested, by more scholarly people than I. What I do wish to do is to describe to you the great advancements that have been made in the genus iris over the last 80 years. I am not decrying nor am I denigrating the use of species iris in the garden, they certainly have their place, but I strongly disagree with those experts who praise the use of species to the detriment of the many thousands of hybrid cultivated varieties and who justify their stand by saying that hybrids fall from favour as newer cultivars are developed. There is no debating the truth of that observation, but that should not deter us from growing and enjoying the best available at any point in time. Progress will only beget further progress, just as success breeds success. This volume contains evidence of the success of many highly talented men and women who have brought the iris to what it is today, and it is dedicated to those equally talented hybridisers who will take the iris into the 21st century.

I only hope that this book will encourage more gardeners to grow and enjoy these beautiful flowers; that it will encourage those who do grow them to grow their iris better, increase their collections and pleasure from them and encourage others to do so; and that it will encourage new hybridisers to take up service as loyal and devoted servants of the goddess of the rainbow.

THE IRIS FAMILY

Like any aristocratic family with its roots deeply in the past, the iris has a well documented family tree.

No one knows for certain how many 'species' of iris there are, and indeed the term 'species' is often very loosely and incorrectly used — I have often heard the word 'species' used for all beardless (apogon) iris, obviously a loose and incorrect reference to the immense popularity of the bearded (pogon) iris and the fact that beardless iris 'differ' from the bearded. This definition ignores the vast differences that exist between many of the beardless iris.

So what does give an iris the rank of species and entitles it to the prestige of being noted as *I.*? For the purpose of this book, a species iris will be defined as an iris which has characteristics not shared by other iris and hence can be defined as botanically distinct. Where the fine line between species and naturally occurring hybrids lies is not under discussion here and I freely admit that changing terminology in an ever-changing world is a problem.

Let us, however, start at the beginning with the definition of a genus and clarify that this is a book about the genus, *Iris.* A genus is a unit of classification of plants (or animals) with structural characteristics in common. The genus *Iris* is characterised among other things by having its floral parts and reproductive parts in sets of three.

While this is an over-simplification of a complex issue, it will give us a common ground for understanding. Once we know what an iris looks like we can then begin to look at those differences, some very obvious and some rather obscure, which will distinguish members of the genus *Iris* from other members. The first division then is into subgenus, with iris being classified as bulbous, tuberous or rhizomatous. In other words, we classify iris as to whether they grow from bulbs, tubers or rhizomes. A true bulb produces its growth and flowers and is completely absorbed in this annual process. After flowering, a bulb is replenished and built up for flower production in the following year. Increase is achieved by the production of bulblets as offshoots of the main bulb and, properly nurtured, the bulbs will flower the following season.

A rhizome produces its growth and flowers without the absorption of its tissue and after flowering dissipates its energy into the production of young rhizomes for next year's bloom. Once it has flowered a rhizome will not flower again. A third division of iris into those which grow from tuberous rootstocks, while of botanical interest, is of little significance to the normal gardener as these rare iris from Nepal are not in general cultivation.

Having divided the genus according to how its members grow and increase it is worthwhile to discuss the bulbous iris as an entity in themselves and to further subdivide the rhizomatous iris into three sections, apogoniris (beardless iris), Evansia (crested iris) and pogoniris (bearded iris). It is within these sections that we allocate the rank of species to those iris with sufficient differences to distinguish them from others.

Having determined the characteristics which give an iris species status, there is a further 'non-botanical' discrimination that I wish to make. Many species are confined to their natural habitat or, if in general cultivation, have been basically ignored by man in his attempts to interact with nature to produce new and diverse plants. These species will be of interest to collectors and enthusiasts and as such are worthy of recognition in a book on iris. Other species, while having distinct differences, do have sufficient genetic similarity to enable man-made crosses to be effected, and hence the development of hybrids. For the purposes of this book a hybrid will be defined as a plant developed from mixed ancestors. This is a somewhat loose definition and a more precise statement would be that a hybrid is produced from the crossing of two species. The more precise statement does not, however, cover the vast number of seedlings which can be obtained once the two species have been crossed and further generations are produced, and it is easier to talk of hybrids as being humanly produced. This is not to ignore the existence of 'natural hybrids' where species, in their wild state, have been cross-pollinated naturally — by the elements, insects or birds. The delineation between species and natural hybrids can be very difficult and many botanists will not agree on the status of some iris. I do not wish to enter into this debate. I do wish to develop the main thrust of this book into the realm of cultivated garden plants of the genus *Iris*. It is therefore without apology that this book will emphasise those species which have been most developed by man and further emphasise those hybrids which are most accessible to the home gardener. Fashions and trends will change, further developments will be made, but there is an enormous range of outstanding cultivars of iris now in commercial production.

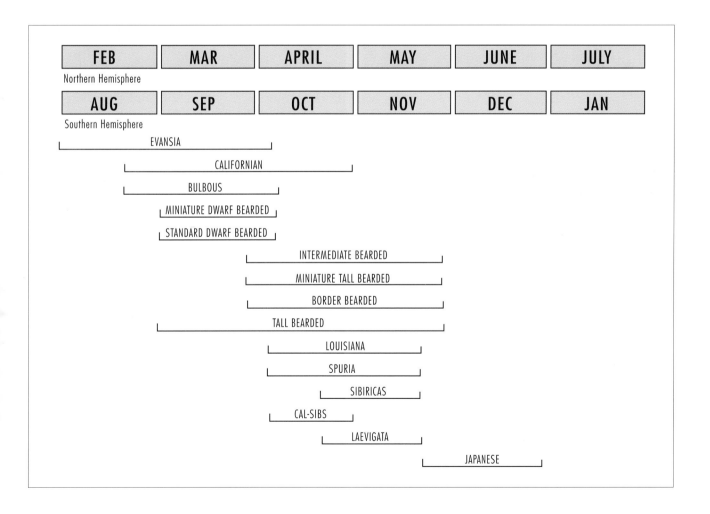

Figure 3. Bloom period

I.kochii

I. pallida

I. pallida variegata commonly known as 'Zebra'

CHAPTER 1

BEARDED IRIS –
POGON IRIS

The pogon subdivision of the rhizomatous iris is characterised by the conspicuous hairy append-ages or beards attached to the upper part of the falls. It has long been accepted that the pogon or bearded iris are classified according to the height of the flowering spike and this is the best and least confusing way to approach the subject.

◆ Miniature dwarf bearded iris have spikes which range in height up to 20 cm.
◆ Standard dwarf bearded range in height from 20 cm to 40 cm.
◆ Intermediate bearded iris range in height from 40 cm to 70 cm.
◆ Miniature tall bearded iris range in height from 40 cm to 70 cm.
◆ Border bearded iris range in height from 40 cm to 70 cm.
◆ Tall bearded iris are taller than 70 cm.

While this classification is very effective in pin-pointing the numerous hybrids now available to gardeners, it is not a natural way to classify the species. However, for simplicity, each type of iris listed above will be discussed in sequence with a combined discussion of species and hybrids which both fit the classification limits and could be of cultural interest. I have avoided discussion of those rare and often doubtful species of even more doubtful garden value

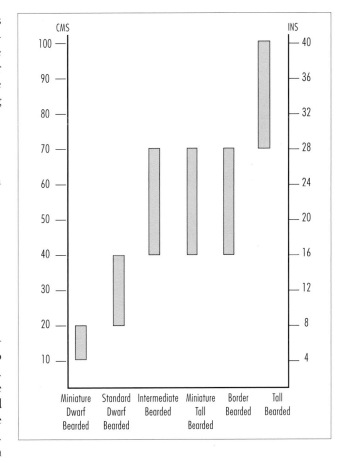

Figure 4. Height classification of bearded iris

and have concentrated on species and cultivars which could be obtained and grown under suitable conditions.

To avoid further confusion, there will be a further chapter on aril iris. These iris are bearded but are characterised by an aril or collar, usually white, on one end of the seed. They intercross with the other bearded iris to produce hybrids described simply as 'arilbred' iris.

BEARDED IRIS SPECIES

Miniature dwarf bearded iris (MDB)

The miniature dwarf bearded iris are characterised by having flowering spikes reaching less than 20 cm in height. Hybrids that are readily available to the gardening public have been derived after many generations of intercrossing with a starting point of up to 17 species which fit the height classification. These species are *I. alexeenkoi*, *I. astrachanica*, *I. attica*, *I. balkana*, *I. barthii*, *I. binata*, *I. bosniaca*, *I. chamaeiris*, *I. furcata*, *I. griffithii*, *I. mellita*, *I. pseudopumila*, *I. pumila*, *I. reichenbachii*, *I. scariosa*, *I. aurica* and *I. timofejewii*. Several of these are of doubtful species status, many are rare or unknown in general cultivation, and most are of insignificant value as garden plants.

I. chamaeiris grows to heights between 8 cm and 20 cm and is native to France, Italy, Spain and Switzerland. It is a very hardy iris, easy to cultivate and rewarding to grow. This iris requires full sun, good drainage and is very suitable for rock gardens. It is variable in form with the falls often tucked, giving an imbalance in appearance between standards and falls. Colour is also variable from white through shades of blue and purple and also through shades of yellow. Beards are usually yellow but here again the colour varies. Falls often carry a large spot which produces a two-tone or two-colour effect. In the bitones/bicolours the falls are darker than the standards. *I. chamaeiris* sets seed readily and can be propagated from seed or by division.

I. pumila produces a single bloom on spikes from 1.5 to 10 cm in height. Most are in the lower height range. This iris is diverse in its habitat and is found in the former Soviet Union, through Europe in Austria, Hungary, Czechoslovakia, the former Yugoslavia, Romania and Bulgaria. Because of its vast range, *I. pumila* varies considerably in form, size, colour, height and in other aspects. It is, however, characterised by its dwarf form and height and single, unbranched spike. It is shorter than *I. chamaeiris* and blooms up to two weeks earlier, in early spring. It is a little more difficult to grow and even more

demanding of perfect drainage. The colour range is extensive and flowers are characterised by an oval fall spot. Blooms come in shades of yellow, blue through violet and purple to black with maroon and ruby red shades also found. There are true bicolours in both the amoena and variegata pattern while there is often an overlay of other colours and sometimes veining in the falls. Beards are in various colours, yellow predominating and the beards also are often bicoloured or bitoned.

I. reichenbachii will grow to heights of 30 cm. Although less important as a garden plant or in hybridising than the previous two species, it is a dwarf species of significance. It is widespread in its natural habitat through Serbia, Bosnia, Bulgaria, Macedonia, Ukraine and Transylvania. This is a hardy iris, easy growing and quick to multiply. It is free flowering and, while lacking the individual beauty of *I. pumila*, it does make a colourful massed display. Yellow is the predominant colour but shades of violet and purple are found. There is often a haft pattern in shades of blue. *I. reichenbachii* usually carries two blooms to a spike and it blooms in early spring, after *I. pumila*.

Standard dwarf bearded iris (SDB)

I. aphylla will grow up to 30 cm in height. It is a native of Germany, Poland, Hungary, Bohemia and Russia. Flowering spikes are multibranched and carry many blooms producing a bunched mass of colour in early spring. Flowers are dark violet in colour with some variation according to location. These flowers are poorly substanced and often overcrowded. *I. aphylla* is hardy but requires full sun and good drainage for best performance.

I. subbiflora is native to Spain, Portugal and Tangiers. It is closely related to *I. aphylla* but is less hardy than that species. Spikes reach 23 cm in height and flowers are dark blue with variations on white, purple, light blue and some with striping.

Miniature tall bearded (MTB)

Miniature tall bearded iris are defined as 40–70 cm tall with height plus width of the flowers being not more than 15 cm. They are borne on slender stems and are required to have spikes to harmonise with the flower size.

I. cengialti is native to the European Southern Alps. It reaches 50 cm in height, has green foliage and lavender blooms. It is a close relative of *I. pallida* and is similar in appearance though somewhat smaller. This iris requires a sunny position, good drainage and an alkaline soil.

I. illyrica has dull green foliage and blue flowers. It is closely related to *I. cengialti* and both these iris could be feasibly included with *I. pallida*.

I. variegata is an important species which is native to Germany, Austria, Hungary, Czechoslovakia, Romania and the former Yugoslavia. This iris reaches 40 cm in height, bears only two flowers on a branched spike and has flowers reaching 6–7 cm in diameter.

Flower colour is variable with yellow standards and falls which can have blue veins blending to brown, and golden yellow beards. Variation in the falls, with forms having red-brown to red fall veining often blending to form patches with yellow rims, has led to the modern terminology of variegata being used to describe an iris with yellow standards and darker falls in the red to brown tones.

There is also a white with violet veining form called *I. amoena*. This again has led to accepted terminology where an amoena is described as an iris with white standards and blue to purple falls. Modern breeding has seen the development of iris with white standards and many differently coloured falls. The term amoena continues to be used with the improvisation of adding the fall colour. Thus a yellow amoena has white standards and yellow falls, an apricot amoena has white standards and apricot falls and so on.

Border bearded iris (BB)

Border bearded iris are iris which have flowering spikes less than 70 cm in height. They are, in general, shorter growing iris with general attributes similar to tall bearded iris as distinct from miniature tall bearded iris which, as already described, form an entirely different class.

I. alberti is a native of Russia, Turkestan, Kazakstan and Uzbekistan. Spikes are branched and reach 70 cm in height. Flowers are dull blue-violet with green to brown stripes. Beards are white with yellow tips. This iris, though somewhat unattractive, is of interest because it is early blooming, vigorous, inclined to rebloom and both hardy and disease resistant. While of little garden value it has an importance for hybridisers because of its many positive attributes.

I. imbricata is a native of Armenia and Caucasia. It is similar in size and growth to *I. alberti* but is more rounded in shape. Flowers are rich yellow while some of blue colouration have been found. It is less hardy and less vigorous than *I. alberti* though equally prolific.

I. junonia is a native of Turkey. It grows to 60 cm in height, has a branched stem and carries lavender-blue flowers with white beards tipped yellow. This iris could be identical with *I. mesopotamica*.

Tall bearded iris

Tall bearded iris have flowering spikes of 70 cm or more in height. The spikes are erect and the flowers 10–18 cm in size. These are the last of the bearded iris to bloom, in mid to late spring.

I. croatica is a native of Croatia. It is a tall-growing, hardy, free-flowering tetraploid species with non-descript dark violet flowers slightly bitoned and carrying white to yellow beards. This iris is of value because of its toughness and its readiness to hybridise with other tall bearded iris

I. cypriana comes from Cyprus. It is similar to *I. mesopotamica* but has large, light blue flowers with white beards. It is a tetraploid species and of value for hybridising.

I. kashmiriana, also known as *I. bartoni,* comes from Kashmir, India, Baluchistan, Afghanistan and Nepal. Flowers are strongly fragrant and white in colour, sometimes in shades of cream with green veins and lavender. It is similar to *I. albicans* and *I. florentina* but has flaring falls. It is not overly hardy but, as a white tetraploid, is of hybridising value.

I. mesopotamica comes from the near east and has lavender-blue flowers. It is a tetraploid and of value to hybridisers.

I. pallida, also known as *I. glauca* and *I. odoratissima,* is a native of the European Alps, Crimea and Dalmatia. It grows to 100 cm in height with broad blue-green sword-like foliage. Stiff, rigid spikes are poorly branched but carry large, well-formed and very fragrant light lavender-blue flowers with up to eight blooms on the spike. *I. pallida dalmatica* is very similar, with blooms more of a lilac blue. This is a significant species much used by hybridisers and part of the basic foundation of modern tall bearded iris breeding. *I. pallida* is a worthwhile garden subject. It is vigorous and hardy if given a sunny position with good drainage. This is the iris well known for the production of orris root — the fragrant dried rhizomes being used to manufacture perfume. Large fields of *I. pallida* used in this industry are to be seen in the vicinity of Florence, where they put on a spectacular carpet of blue in May each year. On each of my two visits to Italy, in May the sight of the *I. pallida* fields has been a highlight. The species is also cultivated in the Italian Iris Society garden in Florence, where the annual Premio Firenze is held.

I. pallida variegata is a variegated foliage form of the species and is a spectacular garden plant which is ornamental for eight months of the year, with its grey-green and yellow-white foliage. There is a rarer form with green and white foliage. Flowers are identical with the species.

I. germanica is that all-encompassing name under which most species bearded iris are incorrectly listed. This iris, or rather group of irises, is not a true species but an extended family of early hybrids which have naturalised in many countries in a variety of forms and colours.

There is little doubt that this family of iris hybrids has been derived from the true species by natural selection from naturally pollinated iris. Very obviously

'Baghdad Boy'
(Tim Blyth, 1989)

'Le Flirt' (M. Harding, 1988)

'Jazzamatazz' (Heidi Blyth, 1986)

these iris are undemanding, easy-care plants but they are of dubious garden value. Some iris given species ranking are:

I. *flavescens*, a yellow form, free flowering and hardy. It is probably from *I. pallida* x *I. variegata*.

I. *florentina*, a white iris, easily cultivated and used in the production of orris root for perfume. It has largely been replaced by *I. pallida*, var 'Dalmatica' for this use.

I. *germanica* var 'Atropurpurea' is a purple form.

I. *kochii* is a dark violet to purple form.

I. *sambucina*, also known as *I. concolor* and *I. neglecta*, is another hybrid, probably from *I. pallida* x *I. variegata*. It is of importance because of its bitone flowers in shades of lilac and violet with the standards lighter in colour than the falls. The term neglecta has become commonly used in modern terminology for any iris in shades of blue through violet and purple with standards in shades lighter than the falls.

I. *squalens* is another early hybrid with dull violet-grey standards and violet-purple falls. It is of importance to hybridisers because of its ruffled petal edges.

In a fascinating report published in the January 1994 *Bulletin of the American Iris Society* (number 292), Maretta Colasante discusses the taxonomic status of bearded iris found growing naturally in Italy. This article further reinforces my contention that, as classification is always in a state of flux, the allocation of species status to any iris clone can be questionable. There is need of a scientific review of the genus *Iris* and this will possibly revise much of the material presented here.

Colasante states that the bearded iris need to be identified by macroscopic and microscopic characteristics with these being the distinguishing elements in allocating species status:

1. Time and length of flowering period in the same cultural environment and altitude.
2. Deciduous or evergreen leaves.
3. Colour and morphology of the leaves, especially at the apex.
4. Branching of the stems.
5. Number and arrangement of the flowers on the stem.
6. Size and ratio of the perianth elements.
7. Form, number and disposition of the spathes and bracts.
8. Morphology of pollen.

Colasante goes on, in light of the above, to separate as species: *I. marsica*, a violet species with three to four scented flowers on spikes to 80 cm; *I. revoluta*, a dark violet species with two to four scented flowers on spikes to 70 cm; and *I. setina*, a violet purple bitone with four or more flowers on spikes to 40 cm.

These iris all have chromosome count 2n-40 and studies would indicate that I. germanica (chromosome count 2n-44) is probably a derivative of the species listed above and others with chromosome count 2n-40.

While this is of little interest to the average home gardener, or even the advanced irisarian, it is of scientific interest and helps to vindicate my approach to the definition of *I. germanica*.

DWARF BEARDED IRIS
(INCLUDING MDBS AND SDBS)

With spikes reaching a maximum of 40 cm, the dwarf bearded iris are ideal for planting in rockeries or as an edging or foreground planting in the normal garden or perennial border. If we ignore the Evansia iris, which mostly flower in late winter, and the Reticulatas, which have a similar bloom period, it is the dwarf bearded iris which really begin the spring iris season. They will usually begin to bloom in the middle of September in Southern Hemisphere gardens and March in Northern Hemisphere gardens, with exact blooming period depending on so many different factors.

These iris are very easy to grow, very quick to multiply and require little attention once established. Their main requirements are full sun, good drainage, neutral to slightly alkaline soil and some winter cold. They enjoy a rich, well-fertilised soil with potash essential for optimum results, but are somewhat forgiving if neglected. It is only in areas where there are four to six weeks of cold, frosty winter days and nights that these iris flourish and in areas with mild winters, bloom will not be satisfactory.

The miniature dwarf bearded iris with flowering spikes up to 20 cm high and minimal branching are the first to flower, but are quickly followed by the standard dwarf bearded iris which reach from 20 to 40 cm in height and flower on branched spikes carrying more blooms and hence extending the bloom season.

Both miniature and standard dwarf bearded iris can be planted or lifted and divided anytime after flowering in early spring, but they certainly perform better if planted or divided early, particularly in colder areas. For this reason, planting from late spring to early autumn is recommended.

Cultivation

My personal experience with dwarf bearded iris has been varied. In coastal, temperate Sydney they grew well but flowering was spasmodic with no bloom at all following mild winters. Once moved 250 km west to the cold winters of the Hillview property these iris really performed brilliantly. Here they relished the conditions where winter is long and cold — over two months of −6°C to 4°C minimum temperatures, regular frosts and many days with minimum temperatures below zero and maximum temperatures less than 10°C. While individual blooms last only one or two days, bloom is prolific and by careful selection of cultivars bloom can be obtained over an extended period of several weeks.

Fertilising with a complete rose food and the possible addition of extra potash straight after flowering is beneficial and these iris can be virtually left alone apart from weeding and cleaning up spent foliage until late winter, when they benefit from a light feeding again with additional potash. They are easy care and very rewarding. Remember that more harm can be done by over fertilising than by under fertilising. Best results will be obtained by giving a lot of attention to the careful selection of quality performers in the many available colours.

Recommended cultivars

There are thousands of dwarf bearded iris that have been catalogued and sold over the years. I cannot hope to see all of them in flower, let alone grow them all, but from my experience and that of other growers I have compiled a list of recommended varieties. These all have outstanding characteristics to recommend them and a selection from this list will give a great basis for any collection. I recognise that, in time, outstanding new cultivars will become available and that there are many cultivars not mentioned that would be equally suitable or, in some cases, superior to those listed.

Colour patterns of great diversity are available and indeed, there are colour patterns in the dwarf bearded iris not found in the taller irises, while all the self colours and most of the colour patterns of the taller irises can be found in the dwarf bearded.

Nearly all the dwarf bearded iris listed will flower on spikes reaching 30 cm to 35 cm in height under normal garden conditions with good cultivation. As with all iris, some will perform better than others in any particular situation.

‘Angelic Mist’ (Blyth, 1994) Beautiful soft pastel pink with the faintest plicata marks on the edge of the falls. White beards, tangerine in the throat.

‘Anjaya’ (Blyth, 1987) This is a pretty little iris with lilac standards, rose-ruby falls, and blue-violet falls.

‘Annies Dress’ (Niswonger, 1990) Very lovely maroon-red with blue beards which makes a great massed display.

‘April Elation’ (Nichols, 1989) Blue as a colour in dwarf bearded is not as common as in the tall bearded. This is a nice blue with a blue beard.

‘Ashanti’ (Blyth, 1984) Unusual colour of gold with an olive-green overlay on the falls.

‘Baghdad Boy’ (Tim Blyth, 1989) This has a popular colour combination of cream standards and white falls marked red. It is an excellent grower.

‘Bay Ruffles’ (Warburton, 1985) This is one of my favourite dwarfs in a shimmering light blue. It is well formed and prolific.

‘Bedford Lilac’ (Jones, 1991) Clean flax blue-lilac with a deeper spot on the falls.

‘Bee’s Knees’ (Blyth, 1994) Pink standards with a lavender flush and gold edge. Creamy white falls with a pink edge and lavender flush. Some brown lines around the white beard tipped bronze. This iris has a sweet perfume and is a favourite.

‘Bisbee’ (Spence, 1988) Showy iris in creamy tan with a russet brown spot and veins on the falls.

‘Black Star’ (Warburton, 1984) Great contrast for the lighter colours as it is a dark violet colour.

‘Blue Neon’ (Black, 1989) Very attractive orchid bitone with smoky orchid standards and blended violet falls with bright blue beards.

‘Blue Line’ (Jones, 1987) This is a most unusual colour combination of white with a blue beard. It is very attractive.

‘Bright Chic’ (Shoop, 1990) Great colour combination of bright yellow with a red beard.

‘Bright Vision’ (Shoop, 1983) This iris is a personal favourite in glowing apricot pink. It is a colour standout.

‘Broad Grin’ (Lankow, 1987) Wide ruffled dwarf in creamy pink with darker hafts and midribs.

‘Bunny Hop’ (Black, 1988) Great colour! White standards, yellow falls, blue beards. This is a very strong grower.

‘Camarilla’ (Blyth, 1989) Soft flesh pink with a deeper area around blue beards.

‘Cavort’ (Blyth, 1994) Very early flowering light orange.

‘Chanted’ (Blyth, 1990) Great iris in mid-pink with a smoky cast and beautiful lavender-blue beards. Vigorous, prolific and a personal favourite.

‘Chantilly Dancer’ (Blyth, 1994) Lavender pink standards with a violet infusion. Creamy white falls stitched lavender pink. White beards tipped tangerine. New and lovely.

'Honey Wind'
(Blyth, 1990)

'Marscay' (Blyth, 1989)

'Michael Paul' (Jones, 1979)

'Taja' (Blyth, 1990)

'Cherry Child' (Blyth, 1994) Very dark burgundy to cherry black standards. Falls are darker, near black, and edged the standard colour. Tangerine beards. This is one of the best dark dwarfs.

'Chortle' (Blyth, 1992) Lemon-ochre standards, old gold falls overlaid red-brown and lavender beards. This is a very attractive dwarf.

'Chubby Cheeks' (Black, 1985) One of the widest and best-formed dwarfs in white with a blue band.

'Cimarron Rose' (Nichols, 1990) Very, very vigorous dark rose to red blend with a deeper fall spot.

'Classy Babe' (Miller, 1990) Ruffled, pale coral pink with a deeper fall spot and white beards. Beautiful iris, well named.

'Comma' (Innerst, 1989) Yellow standards, garnet-red falls with a gold rim and overlay. Bright and colourful.

'Cool Satin' (Ritchie, 1987) Soft, smooth, pale sea lavender violet.

'Cream Cake' (Niswonger, 1990) Lovely colour combination of white standards infused lemon and lemon falls edged white. Vigorous iris of distinction.

'Crownette' (Blyth, 1992) Creamy apricot with a violet infusion in the standards. Lavender beards. Grows and flowers well.

'Cuban Cutie' (Dyer, 1979) An older dwarf but of interest for its brown bitone colour. Very vigorous.

'Cuddle Me' (Blyth, 1994) This is a soft pastel pink and white. Standards are pastel pink over white with a blue-pink cast. Falls are paler pink with a white area around pale blue tipped tangerine beards.

'Cuddle Up' (Hager, 1993) Lovely salmon pink with tangerine beards.

'Dark Rings' (Gatty, 1993) Wide and ruffled white stitched blue.

'Dark Vader' (Miller, 1987) This is one of the best dwarfs, very rich in colour and excellent in bloom. It is a dark blue-purple and black bitone with bushy blue beards.

'Delicate Pink' (Palmer, 1984) Its name well describes the soft colouring of this iris.

'Dicky Bird' (Hager, 1993) Wine-red standards, dark red falls edged wine and red-purple beards provide a delightful colour combination. I don't think it was named after the famous English cricket umpire, but . . . you never know!

'Dot' (Innerst, 1989) Soft cream with green-yellow shoulders.

'Electric Dreams' (Blyth, 1988) Vigorous lavender with an olive-green overlay. It sounds dull but is really very vibrant.

'Esoteric' (Blyth, 1991) Creamy beige standards with a pink cast and cream falls with a white area around tangerine beards tipped lavender. This is a personal favourite.

'Fairy Footsteps' (Blyth, 1985) Very pale plicata in white edged pale blue. This is a most vigorous iris.

'Fire Island' (Sindt, 1989) White with yellow hafts and fiery tangerine beards.

'Flitters' (Blyth, 1994) Pink with a champagne hue and brown signal.

'For Fun' (Blyth, 1993) Cream base with violet plicata marks and white beards, tangerine in the throat.

'Ghost Party' (Blyth, 1994) Sweetly fragrant, smoky pink and lavender bitone with a violet line flash below tangerine beards. Unique.

'Gigolette' (Blyth, 1990) Well named as it is a dwarf reminiscent of the tall bearded iris 'Gigolo'. Creamy apricot base with a rosy tan edge. Vigorous.

'Gypsy Passion' (Palmer, 1990) Pale pink standards and lavender-orchid falls.

'Hafnium' (Innerst, 1987) The dove grey colour would not appeal to everyone, but provides contrast in the garden. Very vigorous.

'Hi Honey' (Blyth, 1989) Pink standards and pink-tan falls edged pink with violet beards.

'Hi Sailor' (Gatty, 1983) Lovely small one in white with a blue spot on the falls.

'Honey Haze' (Blyth, 1992) Creamy pastel lemon with tangerine beards tipped white.

'Honey Wind' (Blyth, 1990) Large flowers in rich golden tan. This is a personal favourite in these tones.

'Huddle' (Innerst, 1987) Gold standards and dark red falls banded gold.

'In Heaven' (Blyth, 1992) Rich apricot standards, slightly lighter falls with a large central cinnamon area and tangerine beards.

'In Jest' (Blyth, 1994) Creamy lemon with a white central area in the falls and tangerine beards overlaid blue.

'Inflamed' (Innerst, 1982) Very bright and colourful yellow with a red-brown spot on the falls. This is a personal favourite.

'Jade Mist' (Dyer, 1979) Smoky blue with green veins and blue midribs. A subdued but nice older one.

'Jazz Man' (Nichols, 1983) Lemon gold with deeper hafts and orange beards.

'Jazzamatazz' (Heidi Blyth, 1986) Cream standards, red falls edged cream and gold beards.

'Jazzaroo' (Blyth, 1988) Brassy yellow standards and rim around ox-blood red falls.

'Jesse Lee' (Lankow, 1987) Lovely ruffled light blue self. This is a very pretty iris.

'Jiansada' (Blyth, 1985) Brown and violet bicolour.

'Joan Moritz' (Hagberg, 1990) Yellow standards, blue falls with a yellow rim. Unique colour.

'Joyce McBride' (Jones, 1981) Ruffled plicata with a white ground edged violet.

'Jungle Warrior' (Aitken, 1989) Smoky orchid and tan bicolour.

'Kandi Moon' (Blyth, 1986) Bright coral pink.

'Kiwi Slices' (Niswonger, 1990) Chartreuse with a burgundy spot and grey-blue beards. Subdued but nice.

'Le Flirt' (M. Harding, 1988) Tall for a dwarf but nice. Creamy white plicata stitched blue. This iris makes a lovely clump display.

'Learn' (Innerst, 1990) Clear pink colouration makes this a standout in the garden.

'Lemon Rings' (Aitken, 1983) Lemon yellow with a deeper spot and halo on the falls. Very pretty.

'Lesson' (Innerst, 1990) This is an attractive, ruffled light blue bitone.

'Lilac 'n Ice' (Blyth, 1993) Lavender lilac standards with white around mid ribs. White falls with a lavender lilac edge. Lavender beards, tangerine in the throat.

'Little Louie' (Black, 1985) Vigorous slate-lavender of subdued colouring.

'Live Jazz' (Lankow, 1986) Pink and coral orange bitone with coral beards.

'Making Eyes' (Blyth, 1982) This older iris with cream standards and red-violet falls edged cream retains its popularity and deservedly so.

'Marscay' (Blyth, 1989) Buff standards infused violet and burgundy falls with electric blue beards that light up the flower.

'Melodic' (Blyth, 1991) Peach pink with a blue-rose thumbprint on the falls. Very colourful.

'Merry Dance' (Blyth, 1992) Ice blue with a rose-brown area on half the falls and lavender-blue beards.

'Michael Paul' (Jones, 1979) Older iris but still one of the nicest in rich purple. This is a personal favourite.

'Mini Song' (Blyth, 1992) Smoky orchid to rose pink standards. Falls are creamier with a lavender flash below lavender and tangerine beards. Beautiful colour combination.

'Mister Roberts' (Willott, 1979) Older iris but retains its popularity for its brilliant golden-yellow colour.

'Moocha' (Paul Blyth, 1988) Maroon standards and lemon falls stitched maroon.

'Moon Dawn' (Blyth, 1991) Subtle blend of grey, tan and rosy brown with a blue beard.

'My Sheba' (Hager, 1987) Very lovely light peach-pink including the beards.

'Nancy Alane' (Jones, 1981) Purple standards and edge around maroon falls.

'Nimble Toes' (Heidi Blyth, 1987) Very vigorous white edged blue with a red beard.

'Noble Toff' (Blyth, 1994) Rich dark violet with an even darker thumbprint on the falls. Tangerine and lavender beards.

'Oh Jay' (Lankow, 1988) Rich orange-yellow.

'Orange Tiger' (Jones, 1988) Smooth, vivid orange with rich orange-red beards.

'Over Easy' (Lankow, 1990) Quality dwarf with pure white standards and canary yellow falls.

'Pal Sam' (Gatty, 1987) A plicata in cream with purple stitching.

'Pale Star' (Jones, 1986) Very pale blue self.

'Party Talk' (Blyth, 1993) Standards are pink with a violet cast, falls are pink with rosy pink ray pattern. Violet beards.

'Patacake' (Black, 1989) Creamy orange with deeper hafts and orange beards.

'Peach Eyes' (Blyth, 1987) Pastel peach-pink which blooms early in the season.

'Pink Jubilee' (Palmer, 1992) Clean baby ribbon pink, soft and delicate.

'Pink Prevue' (Jones, 1991) Peach pink with a salmon spot on the falls and pink beards.

'Pipestone' (Lankow, 1985) Soft apricot yellow with a cocoa-pink spot on the falls.

'Priveleged Character' (Black, 1990) Silvery orchid-white ground with a red-violet edge.

'Pumpin' Iron' (Black 1990) Dark red-black with a red-violet rim and blue-violet beards.

'Sass with Class' (Black, 1989)

'Tricks' (Blyth, 1987)

'Split Decision' (Hobbs, 1989)

'Serenity Prayer' (Dyer,1989)

'Raspberry Jam' (Niswonger, 1980)

'Pushy' (Blyth, 1986)

'Star Search' (Willott, 1985)

'Pure Allure' (Ritchie, 1987) Pure white is a colour not often found in dwarfs but this is a nice one.

'Pushy' (Blyth, 1986) Tan standards infused violet, brown falls and blue beards.

'Quark' (Blyth, 1986) Chartreuse standards and ruby-red falls edged chartreuse. Blue beards light up this most attractive iris.

'Rain Dance' (Jones, 1978) Older but still lovely bluebird blue self.

'Raspberry Jam' (Niswonger, 1980) This rich raspberry-pink has been a personal favourite for many years. Great colour.

'Razoo' (Blyth, 1993) Violet standards, white falls with a violet edge, tangerine beards.

'Riplette' (Ritchie, 1990) Ruffled mid-blue with a blue and white beard.

'Ripple Chip' (Aitken, 1988) Mid-blue bitone with frosty white beards.

'Rockabye' (Blyth, 1993) Gorgeous iris with rosy-tan standards and edge to falls surrounding a deeper spot. Lavender beards and sweet fragrance.

'Romanita' (Blyth, 1993) Early flowering greenish apricot with a lavender flush on the falls. Lavender beards.

'Rosy Lulu' (Warburton 1984) Rich magenta rose to rosy violet.

'Sass With Class' (Black, 1989) Light yellow with red-maroon marking on the falls. This is a showy iris and a personal favourite.

'Scat' (Blyth, 1992) Tan standards infused violet and deeper brown falls.

'Scion' (Blyth, 1994) Apricot bitone with a small white area around white beards. Lovely colour gem.

'Serenity Prayer' (Dyer, 1989) This is a choice iris of soft colouring with creamy white standards flushed yellow and pearly cream falls flushed yellow. It is all lit up with dark blue beards. Top award winner and a personal favourite.

'Sheer Class' (Miller, 1988) Beautiful blue-pink with a deeper spot on the falls and coral beards.

'Show Me Yellow' (Anderson, 1990) Rich, intense golden-yellow with velvet texture.

'Shy Violet' (Jones, 1989) Lightly ruffled lilac with amethyst beards.

'Slap Bang' (Niswonger, 1990) Yellow standards, maroon-red falls with a yellow rim and orange beards. Very colourful.

'Slave Girl' (Blyth, 1994) Light pink standards flushed rose and edged gold. White falls with a pink edge and lavender dots.

'Small Flash' (Black, 1983) Chrome-yellow standards and rosy red-purple falls edged yellow.

'Small Ritual' (Hager, 1988) Silky red and cherry-red bitone with pale blue beards. This is a lovely colour combination.

'Smoky Imp' (Blyth, 1990) Smoky pink with a violet overlay on the falls and red beards.

'Smoky Pieces' (Blyth, 1991) Early flowering smoky slate-lavender with a lavender flash and tangerine beards.

'Spanish Empire' (Palmer, 1990) Yellow standards and white falls give a nice reverse colour combination.

'Split Decision' (Hobbs, 1989) White standards and violet-blue falls with a white halo.

'Star Dancer' (Jones, 1988) Mid-blue with darker blue beards.

'Star Search' (Willott, 1985) Light yellow blend with a light blue beard.

'Stardate' (Black, 1987) Well formed clear mid-blue.

'Starlight Waltz' (Helsley 1982) This is a nice combination of yellow and white.

'Straw Hat' (Lankow, 1985) Ruffled lemon with a green-gold spot.

'Sun Doll' (Jones, 1986) Bright sunny yellow which has rebloomed for us.

'Swagman' (Heidi Blyth, 1990) Yellow with a ruby-red thumbprint and cream beards.

'Syllable' (Innerst, 1986) Creamy white standards and golden-yellow falls with orange beards.

'Taja' (Blyth, 1990) White with violet stitching and violet beards. Lovely iris similar to 'Nimble Toes' except for the beard.

'Talk' (Blyth, 1994) Beige-rose with rich burgundy haft spots and tangerine beards.

'Tangerine Tangent' (Black, 1990) Vibrant red-purple with a darker fall spot and orange beards.

'Tender Tears' (Black, 1988) Yellow with pale violet plicata markings.

'Thundercat' (Blyth, 1994) Dark burgundy with a darker area around tangerine beards.

'Tiger Beau' (Paul Blyth, 1983) Old gold with a ruby spot on the falls.

'Toy Clown' (Gatty, 1991) Yellow with a maroon-red rim. Reblooms for a bonus.

'Tramp' (Blyth, 1994) Rich burgundy, red-brown, darker around mustard yellow beards.

'Transcribe' (Black, 1990) Ruffled white with a broad grape-purple border.

'Tricks' (Blyth, 1987) Pink standards, cream falls edged pink, tangerine beards.

'Village Flirt' (Blyth, 1994) Melon-peach with lavender-blue beards.

'Violet Lass' (Jones, 1985) As the name says, violet!

'Voyage' (Blyth, 1993) Early flowering pink on white plicata.

'Wanderer' (Blyth, 1991) Cream-beige standards, coffee falls, lavender beards.

'Well Suited' (Black, 1990) Purple and black bitone with a lighter edge to the falls and white beards. Exciting colour combination.

'Wild Silk' (Blyth, 1994) Apricot flushed lavender standards, darker falls with a rose-brown area around lavender beards. Sweetly perfumed.

'Wind Rose' (Blyth, 1989) Vigorous and pretty pink bitone with light pink standards, darker pink falls and tangerine beards.

'Wine Light' (Blyth, 1989) Burgundy-red with a darker fall spot and violet beards. This lovely iris is a personal favourite.

'Wizard of Id' (Dyer, 1981) Antique gold, flushed purple with near-black beards.

'Zounds' (Blyth, 1984) Very lovely blue-lilac standards with tan falls blended olive and blue beards. Beautiful iris and a real favourite.

In the garden

Of all the iris in cultivation it is the dwarf bearded iris which fit best into the traditional early spring garden flourish of bulbs and annuals, with the added advantage of a semi-permanent position in the garden. Although these iris multiply quickly they can be left in the ground for at least three years before requiring division and can therefore form a permanent basis for an early spring display. For this reason alone they are worthy additions to any garden with suitably cold winters and as the plants are completely frost hardy and even the flowers are moderately frost resistant their value cannot be overstated.

Many irisarians become collectors rather than gardeners, and once injected with the 'iris virus', proceed to grow their iris in mass plantings away from other plants. This seems a pity to me as I can appreciate the use of iris in massed collections but also feel that the use of iris in conjunction with other plants can produce startling visual effects.

Dwarf bearded iris are wonderful plants for the front of perennial border planting where their attractive foliage is a joy in itself. Cultivars can be selected for virtually any colour scheme and combinations of blending and contrasting hues can be used with only the imagination of the gardener/landscaper as a limitation. Because of their relative uniformity of height they are ideal for extended displays.

There is an increasing trend towards colour themes in garden design and I am often asked to assist customers with their plans. I feel grossly inadequate when invited to plan other people's colour schemes and have an overriding view that colours and patterns should be chosen by garden owners to suit their own tastes, not the tastes, no matter how well informed, of garden and landscape design architects. I have heard people speak with utter dismay of the terrible clash of using pink and yellow together, yet others feel this is a pleasing combination. I can well remember the old theme of 'blue and green should never be seen without a colour in between' yet for those prepared to be brave blue, green and purple combined indoors can produce a startling and pleasing effect. Likewise in the garden! Colours and combinations of colours are yours to use to your heart's content if you use dwarf bearded iris in the spring garden and I can only advise people to let their heads go and be as adventurous as they please.

Dwarf bearded iris are wonderful plants for rockeries — quick growing and able to fill a space without becoming invasive as so many perennial plants do. Again colours and patterns for all tastes are available and it is possible to change one's theme from year to year.

Remember that dwarf bearded iris do require sun, do require lime in the soil to get the pH to approximately 7.0–7.2 and then use suitable companion plants to produce the visual effect that satisfies.

Suitable perennial rockery plants as companion plants for dwarf bearded iris will depend on your climate and, of course, on availability. Care must be taken to avoid the iris being overrun by vigorous ground covers or trailers and care must also be taken to ensure that they are grown only with plants of moderate height. Other than these precautions, the gardener will find the dwarf bearded iris easy, rewarding and very accommodating plants.

INTERMEDIATE BEARDED IRIS

The intermediate bearded iris flower on spikes between 40 and 70 cm in height. They are therefore intermediate in height between the dwarf bearded (which reach up to 40 cm) and the tall bearded (which exceed 70 cm). This delightful class of iris has been bred by intercrossing the dwarf bearded and tall bearded and as well as being intermediate for height these iris are

'Crackles' (Blyth, 1990)

'Eye Magic' (Donnell, 1987)

'Hot Spice' (Aitken, 1989)

'Romp' (Blyth, 1988)

'Blue Calico' (Palmer, 1986)

'O'Cool' (Blyth, 1988)

intermediate for bloom period, flowering, in general, after the dwarf bearded and before the tall bearded. It should be noted that many of the *Iris germanica* group from which the modern tall bearded iris have been derived are in fact of intermediate bearded iris proportion in bloom size and spike height.

The establishment of the intermediate bearded iris class was a natural and reasonably easy process of intercrossing dwarf and tall beardeds and fertility presented no problem. The problem of the early bloom of the dwarfs and the much later bloom of the talls was easily overcome by the 'holding over' of pollen stored in refrigerators or the interchange of pollen between gardeners in different climatic regions having dwarf and tall beardeds in bloom simultaneously. There the easy process ended! Intercrossing the 44 chromosome IBs is extremely difficult as they are, in general, sterile among themselves and only limited success has been obtained by crossing the IBs back to the SDBs or TBs. Some success has been achieved with the crossing IB x IB, IB x SDB, IB x TB, but insufficient for any real line breeding compaign.

In recent years Barry Blyth has had amazing success with his unusual IB 'Zing Me' (1990), a gorgeous iris in itself with its creamy lemon standards, creamy white falls with a lemon edge and brown crescents and bushy brown beards, but an even more amazing parent. 'Zing Me' will cross readily with dwarf bearded or tall bearded iris and in 1995 Barry released four new iris from 'Zing Me' parentage. Crossed (as pod parent) with two different siblings of the tall bearded iris 'Imprimis', Barry has released 'Ingenious,' a 55 cm tall border bearded iris of light rosy-violet with a dark ruby-red blot or spot on the falls and 'Soul Sound', a 50 cm tall BB lilac and lavender bitone with a light honey-brown spot on the falls.

Crossed (as pod parent) with the dwarf bearded 'Chanted', 'Zing Me' produced the 35 cm tall SDB 'Celsius' in lemon-gold with a red-brown signal spot and navy-blue beards. Crossed (as pod parent) with the dwarf bearded 'Taja', 'Zing Me' produced the 30 cm tall SDB 'Late for School' for Heidi Blyth. This iris has light violet-blue standards with rosy-burgundy falls surrounded by light violet.

There is little doubt that these hybridising breakthroughs will bring even greater diversity to the tall and border bearded classes but the sterility problem of the IBs remains. Even with this hybridising impasse there has been much development in this class and a wonderful array of hybrids is available to gardeners.

Cultivation

Intermediate bearded iris require the same cultural practice as the dwarf bearded. They need full sun, alkaline soil and good drainage. They are somewhat less demanding than the dwarf bearded in that they need less winter cold to facilitate good bloom and so they are suitable for a much wider climatic area. As their spikes are, in general, well branched and they carry considerably more buds than the dwarf bearded, the intermediate beardeds have an extended bloom season which overlaps that of both the dwarf bearded and tall bearded iris. The colour range is exciting, the uniformity of height is appealing, the extended bloom season is a bonus. These iris form a most satisfying group for the home gardener.

Recommended cultivars

'Affinity' (Blyth, 1989) 63 cm. Vigorous iris with lavender-blue standards, darker blue falls and brown hafts.

'All Right' (Hager, 1988) 53 cm. Tangerine with a deep orange beard.

'Apollo's Touch' (Nichols, 1991) 46 cm Nicely coloured with white standards and yellow falls.

'April Fog' (Nichols, 1990) 50 cm. Blue standards, paler blue falls. This is a pretty iris, most attractive in a clump.

'Art Gallery' (Jones, 1984) 56 cm. Very attractive with white standards, a rose-red spot on the falls and a sweet fragrance.

'Ask Alma' (Lankow, 1987) 53 cm. Beautiful coral-orange with white beards tipped orange.

'Aurean' (Blyth, 1988) 45 cm. Clear golden yellow self.

'Avanelle' (Jones, 1977) 45 cm. An older iris but it still sets the standard for a white median iris. It is vigorous and floriferous.

'Az Ap' (Ensminger, 1980) 60 cm. Classic mid-blue intermediate. Vigorous grower.

'Basso' (Ensminger, 1990) 58 cm. Purple self.

'Becalmed' (Blyth, 1993) 60 cm. Soft pastel apricot with slightly darker falls. Beards are tangerine and white.

'Bedtime Story' (Ritchie, 1982) 54 cm. Light amethyst-violet standards with a darker midrib. Falls are violet shaded lighter at edges. Beards are amethyst.

'Black Watch' (Rosenfels, 1982) 50 cm. Jet black iris of good form and growth.

'Blue Calico' (Palmer, 1986) 46 cm. White ground edged in flax blue.

'Blue Eyed Blonde' (Ensminger, 1989) 65 cm. Ruffled yellow with blue beards. This iris grows very well and is prolific in bloom.

'Bluebird in Flight' (Niswonger, 1986) 60 cm. White with blue on the falls and red beards.

'Brighten Up' (Hager, 1990) 65 cm. Bright, deep orange with tangerine beards.

'Broadway Baby' (Gatty, 1990) 60 cm. Bronze-tan standards and ivory falls banded ox-blood red.

'Bubbly Blue' (Aitken, 1986) 43 cm. Ruffled blue of very good quality.

'Bunnicula' (Innerst, 1991) 64 cm. White standards and soft yellow falls.

'Bush Gossip' (Blyth, 1994) 55 cm. Mushroom pink flushed lavender standards, darker pink falls, bronze beards and musk fragrance.

'California Style' (Jones, 1990) 55 cm. White standards flushed orange; orange falls with a white edge and tangerine beards. This is a colour gem.

'Calling Card' (Messick, 1991) 51 cm. Blue-white standards, green-cream falls and blue beards. Subdued but nice.

'Catalumya' (Blyth, 1992) 60 cm. Gold with a brown overlay on the falls and dark chocolate-brown beards.

'Chagrin' (Harder, 1992) 58 cm Yellow standards and blended brown falls with yellow beards.

'Crackles' (Blyth, 1990) 50 cm. Pure white stitched violet and red beards. Light perfume adds to its charm and it is a great personal favourite.

'Daiquiri' (Blyth, 1988) 65 cm. Apricot with a golden glow in the falls and self beards. This iris has a special iridescence that sets it apart. Excellent.

'Dark Blizzard' (Warburton, 1984) 50 cm. Very attractive white with a violet edge.

'Dark Waters' (Aitken, 1992) 66 cm. Ruffled dark violet with light violet beards tipped mustard.

'Doll' (Keppel, 1987) 56 cm. Rosy beige standards, apricot-cream falls with rosy-mauve hafts and edge, white beards tipped orange.

'Drum Song' (Blyth, 1993) 63 cm. White standards, lemon falls, lavender beards.

'Erect' (Black, 1989) 65 cm. Ruffled yellow with brown horns. Unique 'space-age' intermediate.

'Eye Magic' (Donnell, 1987) 45 cm. Brilliant gold with a red thumbprint and orange-yellow beards. Prolific bloom and vigorous growth make this a personal favourite.

'Fiddle Faddle' (Hager, 1989) 58 cm. Light yellow speckled and washed dark plum-maroon.

'Flirtatious' (Willott, 1992) 53 cm. Ruffled pink with orange beards.

'Flivver' (Innerst, 1987) 45 cm. Light ivory yellow with a rosy fall margin; white and orange beards.

'Foreign Devil' (Blyth, 1994) 55 cm. Smoky beige-pink with deeper hafts and a lavender line down the falls and beards which are lavender and tangerine.

'French Silk' (Robinson, 1984) 55 cm. Fragrant light blue flowers. Very distinctive purple based foliage.

'Friday Harbor' (Lankow, 1989) 56 cm. Light blue standards, blue-white falls and white beards tipped yellow.

'From the Heart' (Gaddie, 1985) 58 cm. White with a blue inner glow in the heart.

'Halfpenny Green' (Blyth, 1994) 63 cm. A difficult blend to describe as it is peachy lemon-apricot with greenish hafts and tangerine beards.

'Harlow Gold' (Black, 1982) 55 cm. High quality rich golden-yellow with excellent plant habits.

'Helga's Hat' (Nichols, 1990) 66 cm. Pure white with yellow beards and white horns. 'Space age' intermediate of quality.

'Hellcat' (Aitken, 1983) 40 cm. Ruffled neglecta with blue standards and purple falls. This is like a scaled-down 'Mystique'.

'He's a Pirate' (Blyth, 1994) 63 cm. Burgundy-wine standards, cherry-black falls, lavender overlaid bronze beards and sweet fragrance.

'Higgledy Piggledy' (Innerst, 1990) 50 cm. Pure white with an ice-blue fall wash.

'Hissy Fit' (Innerst, 1989) 60 cm. Brown with a black fall spot, bronze beards and sweet fragrance. This has rebloomed for us.

'Honey Glazed' (Niswonger, 1983) 60 cm. Cream standards and amber falls.

'Hot Fudge' (Hager, 1983) 58 cm. Light caramel-brown with a dark brown overlay.

'Hot Wheels' (Black, 1990) 55 cm. Orchid-tan standards, white falls banded red-purple. Very colourful.

'Hubbub' (Ensminger, 1989) 51 cm. White with violet stripes and splashes and yellow beards tipped orange.

'Hug a Bunch' (Shoop, 1988) 46 cm. Bright pink with an apricot glow and pink beards.

'Impulse' (Blyth, 1984) 50 cm. Rich golden yellow.

'Indian Idyll' (Blyth, 1993) 60 cm. Red-tan standards, burgundy falls with a deeper edge, mustard-yellow beards.

'Midas Plush' (Blyth, 1990)

'Red Zinger' (Black, 1985)

'Logo' (Keppel, 1986)

'Silent Strings' (Dyer, 1985)

'Strum' (Blyth, 1987)

'Tyrolienne' (Blyth, 1989)

'Triplet' (Keppel, 1988)

'Lacy' (Gatty, 1986)

'John' (Ensminger, 1990) 65 cm. Rosy-bronze standards, rich bronze-gold falls and orange beards.

'June Rose' (Blodgett, 1989) 57 cm. Peach pink and lavender pink bitone with white veins and coral beards.

'Kadaicha' (Blyth, 1990) 50 cm. Tan standards, rosy-violet falls and darker hafts.

'Kensei' (Blyth, 1989) 60 cm. Sky-blue standards, rosy-violet falls, red-brown on the top of the falls and hafts.

'Kermit' (Ensminger, 1990) 53 cm. Green-tan with a large lavender-blue area on the falls and violet beards.

'Lacy' (Gatty, 1986) 50 cm. Light primrose-yellow with a crinkled edge.

'Lady Day' (Lankow, 1990) 60 cm. Warm white with yellow hafts and white beards tipped yellow.

'Let's Elope' (Blyth, 1993) 60 cm. Vibrant coral to rose pink standards with violet midribs. Similar falls with a tan overlay and violet flush beneath red beards.

'Like a Charm' (Byers, 1989) 56 cm. Light yellow and white with blue-violet horns.

'Lilac Hill' (Blyth, 1993) 55 cm. Mulberry standards and plicata edging on white falls. White beards, tangerine in the throat and sweet perfume.

'Longing' (Blyth, 1994) 63 cm. Salmon to tan apricot with a slight violet flush, tangerine and lavender beards.

'Mara' (Blyth, 1993) 60 cm. Pale, pale pink with a white area around soft-pink beards.

'Maui Gold' (Aitken, 1992) 64 cm. Vigorous pure gold self with light-orange beards.

'Maui Moonlight' (Aitken, 1987) 58 cm. Soft lemon-yellow with very vigorous plant habits.

'Megglethrop' (Innerst, 1991) 48 cm. Beautiful light blue with a large deep-blue spot on the falls.

'Memo' (Gatty, 1991) 50 cm. Bright lemon-yellow with a large white fall patch.

'Merry Life' (Blyth, 1990) 50 cm. Slower growing but beautiful iris with rose pink standards and white falls edged burgundy. Red beards.

'Midas Plush' (Blyth, 1990) 55 cm. Brilliant golden yellow self of outstanding quality in every respect. This is a personal favourite.

'Moonfly' (Blyth, 1989) 60 cm. Smoky violet with a red-brown overlay at the hafts and deep-purple beards.

'Mulberry Temple' (Blyth, 1993) 55 cm. Bright mulberry-purple with a white area around the tangerine tipped lavender beards.

'Nectar' (Keppel, 1990) 50 cm. Ruffled apricot-yellow and tan plicata with red beards.

'New Kid' (Shoop, 1987) 46 cm. Very bright yellow with red beards.

'Night Shift' (Aitken, 1986) 60 cm. Smooth deep violet colour with ruffled blooms.

'O'Cool' (Blyth, 1988) 50 cm. Lovely white with lavender crescents on the falls. This iris is vigorous and contrasts well with the darker colours.

'Obligato' (Stahly, 1988) 60 cm. Orange sherbet self with a coral flush and tangerine beard tipped white.

'Only Foolin' (Blyth, 89) 60 cm. Rich brassy gold with darker falls and dark brassy beards. This iris is very vigorous.

'Oolay' (Blyth, 1993) 63 cm. Apricot-infused lilac standards, creamy white falls edged apricot and tangerine beards tipped white.

'Orange Petals' (Niswonger, 1991) 64 cm. Bold orange colour with pink undertones and red beards.

'Pacer' (Aitken, 1989) 50 cm. White stitched dark blue with blue beards.

'Patches on Parade' (Aitken, 1988) 56 cm. Mid violet-blue with a brown spot around white-tipped yellow beards.

'Philanderer' (Blyth, 1990) 55 cm. Tan standards infused red and ruby falls with gold beards.

'Piece of Cake' (Hager, 1989) 56 cm. Pink with some orchid on the falls and faint plicata marks around white-tipped tangerine beards.

'Posh' (Blyth, 1987) 50 cm. Apricot-orange standards with darker falls and an iridescent glow. Vigorous.

'Pun' (Keppel, 1991) 48 cm. Rosy-brown standards, lemon falls with rosy margin and hafts.

'Quivver' (Blyth, 1994) 60 cm. Pink flushed lavender standards, paler falls with lavender-tipped tangerine beards.

'Raindance Kid' (Aitken, 1990) 64 cm. Mid-blue self.

'Rebel Yell' (Blyth, 1990) 63 cm. Antique gold with electric-purple beards.

'Red Zinger' (Black, 1985) 66 cm. Smooth burgundy-red of quality.

'Revved Up' (Innerst, 1985) 58 cm. Gold base with red plicata dots.

'Romp' (Blyth, 1988) 45 cm. Creamy apricot standards, darker falls and tangerine beards. Vigorous.

'Shooting Sparks' (Black, 1989) 70 cm. White ground with blue-purple edging and spicy fragrance.

'Shugar' (Blyth, 1990) 50 cm. Salmon pink with a lighter area around tangerine beards.

'Silent Strings' (Dyer, 1978) 41 cm. One of the oldest medians we still grow and one of the best. Beautiful sky-blue award winner.

'Space Psalms' (Nichols, 1990) 45 cm. White with grey-purple plicata edging.

'Spring Dancer' (Shoop, 1984) 40 cm. White with a tangerine beard.

'Strawberry Love' (Blyth, 1985) 50 cm. Vivid rose pink with red beards makes a great colour display in a clump. Very popular and a favourite.

'Strum' (Blyth, 1987) 50 cm. Creamy white standards and lemon falls with a green overlay. Vigorous and prolific.

'Sunny Dawn' (Jones, 1989) 55 cm. Bright lemon-yellow with an orange wash on the falls and bright red beards.

'Sunshine Boy' (Foster, 1986) 63 cm. Lemon standards, white falls marked yellow and orange beards.

'Talk Magic' (Blyth, 1992) 60 cm. Smoky pink standards, darker falls and electric-blue beards.

'Tchin Tchin' (Gatty, 1988) 55 cm. Peach-pink standards, lighter pink falls, orange beards.

'Theda Clark' (Nichols, 1988) 45 cm. Ruffled deep violet with orange and violet beards.

'Tipsy Maid' (Blyth, 1988) 45 cm. Blue-grey with an olive overlay. It sounds dull but isn't.

'Triplet' (Keppel, 1988) 58 cm. Rose-pink standards, yellow falls with rose-mauve shading and yellow-orange beards.

'Trivia' (Keppel, 1990) 58 cm. Coffee-tan with a heavy burgundy fall wash and tangerine beards.

'Tyrolienne' (Blyth, 1989) 65 cm. Lemon-buff standards, darker falls with a brown overlay and lavender beards.

'Vasqua' (Blyth, 1989) 63 cm. Blue-lavender with a rosy-lavender overlay giving a shot silk effect. Rosy-lavender hafts.

'White Chapeau' (Blodgett, 1989) 45 cm. White standards, yellow falls.

'Wide Blue Eyes' (Gaddie, 1990) 55 cm. Pure white with a wide mid-blue wash on the falls. Creamy white beards, tangerine in the throat.

'Zing Me' (Blyth, 1990) 50 cm. Creamy lemon standards slightly open. Creamy white falls with a lemon edge and large brown crescent and deep-brown, bushy beards. Flaring falls. This is the fertile intermediate bearded discussed earlier.

In the garden

A new era in gardening with an ever-aging population moving to smaller gardens and into units with only small patios has broadened interest in the intermediate bearded iris, and deservedly so. Wherever dwarf bearded iris can be grown there is an opportunity to extend the planting both outward and upward with some intermediates. Wherever tall bearded iris can be grown there is an opportunity to grow these scaled-down versions. For many gardeners the intermediate bearded iris are just right and I admit to being a great fan of their most rewarding garden attributes. Not only do they fill the gap between dwarf and tall in size and stature, but they bridge the gap in bloom period as well.

A massed display of intermediate bearded iris is a spectacular sight, but they are wonderful accents for spot planting and delightful companion plants. Perhaps they are a little tall for many rockery gardens, but here again I can see them as being useful. They are also delightful for lining or edging paths. They are ideal plants for positions where dwarf bearded iris would possibly be lost in the display, yet tall bearded would not be quite appropriate because of size or bloom timing.

Intermediate bearded iris can be grown successfully in pots or containers and their growth habits make them the most appealing of the bearded iris for container cultivation. Add to this the huge colour range and we have a very desirable perennial for most situations.

As these iris flower at the height of the spring bulb display they are invaluable as companion plants for bulbs and spring annuals. Their versatility as regards climate is an added bonus. The intermediate bearded irises, as a class, are personal favourites which have all the advantages of the dwarf bearded and the added advantage of branched spikes and an extended bloom period. They do not have the large, heavily ruffled blooms of the modern tall bearded iris but there is a daintiness about them which is most appealing.

Beautiful pictures can be painted by massing intermediate bearded iris in ribbons or blocks of colour and this is so much more attractive than planting them in rows as so many collectors do. In 1992 I was able to visit the Floriade in Holland and at that time spent a magical day at Keukenhoff Gardens in Lisse, between Amsterdam and The Hague. There I experienced the imaginative use of tulips and other spring bulbs in great masses of colour. While enjoying the spectacle I lamented that I have not been able to see iris used in a similar fashion in a private or public garden. The closest that I have come to this kind of spectacle was to experience

'Tipsy Maid' (Blyth, 1988)

'Zing Me' (Blyth, 1990)

'Strawberry Love' (Blyth, 1985)

'Affinity' (Blyth, 1989)

'Joseph's Coat' (Katkamier, 1930)

'Bumble Bee Deelite' (Norrick, 1986)

'Frosted Velvet' (Fisher, 1988)

the magnificent display gardens at Schreiner's Iris Gardens and Cooley's Gardens in Oregon, USA. Here the emphasis was naturally on the tall bearded iris in which Schreiner's and Cooley's specialise. One of my very few unfulfilled dreams is to establish and maintain a large iris display garden where the planting is done my way. I suppose it is dreams that maintain our enthusiasm and keep us going.

There is a place for one or more clumps of intermediate bearded iris in nearly all gardens, unless they are tropical or completely shaded. Their use, once again, whether as accents, massed planting or as ribbons of colour is only restricted by the gardener's imagination.

MINIATURE TALL BEARDED IRIS

The miniature tall bearded iris (not to be confused with the dwarf or intermediate bearded) form a restricted class that is neither well known nor generally planted. These iris have well branched spikes similar to the tall bearded iris but on stems reaching 40–70 cm in height with flower size strictly in proportion to the height of spike. They are very attractive iris in their own right and can look stunning in large clumps. They have cultural requirements similar to the intermediate bearded iris and are very suitable accent plants when used towards the front of the perennial border. They are very easy, undemanding iris.

Perhaps their greatest disadvantage is that they seem to fit rather awkwardly in the general scheme of the iris world. They are diploid in origin and have petite flowers similar to the IBs but they flower later, more in tune with the TBs and so are out of place in a mass planting of IBs. Their size and general appearance do not lend naturally to placing them in front of TBs, with which they bloom simultaneously. It is the border bearded iris which fill that role so adequately.

Miniature tall bearded iris are very suitable for gardens with limited space where their small rhizomes and heavy blooming habits make them a most economical choice. They are also a floral artist's dream flower and their value for use in floral arrangements probably exceeds their garden value.

It was a great joy to see many of these beauties in full bloom in large established clumps when I visited the USA. My own experience in growing them has been somewhat limited — mainly because of the difficulty I have experienced in obtaining virus-free stock — but those that I have grown have proven themselves excellent garden plants. A list of recommendations then is somewhat shortened as a result of personal experience, but extended as a result of observations in other gardens.

Recommended cultivars

'Bumblebee Deelite' (Norrick, 1986) 46 cm. Yellow standards, maroon falls edged yellow, and orange beards. This is superb in a clump.

'Cherry' (Dunderman, 1989) 58 cm. Violet standards and white stitched violet falls with brown beards.

'Disco Jewel' (Guild, 1977) 64 cm. A blend of copper, henna, orchid and brown.

'Frosted Velvet' (Fisher, 1988) 56 cm. White standards, purple falls edged white.

'Ozark Dream' (Fisher, 1992) 56 cm. Violet standards, purple falls and cream beards. This was beautiful as seen in Oregon.

'Ozark Jewel' (Fisher, 1992) 48 cm. White edged yellow standards, lemon-yellow falls and orange beards.

'Pardner' (Fisher, 1993) 51 cm. Honey-gold standards, red falls with a honey-gold rim. As seen in Oregon this is as nice as any miniature tall bearded. It was stunning in a large massed clump.

'Quiet Place' (Varner, 1989) 51 cm. Mid-blue with a white beard and sweet fragrance.

'Rosemary's Dream' (Dunderman, 1982) 50 cm. Cream base with a rose-pink edging.

'Striped Pants' (Fisher, 1989) 50 cm. Light yellow with brown veins on the falls and orange beards.

The use of miniature tall bearded iris in the garden and landscape is similar to that of intermediate bearded iris.

BORDER BEARDED IRIS

Border bearded iris are lower-growing versions of tall bearded iris with spikes reaching up to 70 cm in height. They are from the same line of breeding as tall bearded iris and flower simultaneously with these. Because they are really short-talls they should be given the same cultural treatment as tall bearded iris. Probably the two main difficulties with this class of iris is the maintaining of proportion and balance in flower size as against spike height and the very likely happening of the iris growing out of class. Very large flowers on short, stumpy spikes look out of place no matter how beautiful the blooms and it often happens that in good growing conditions the flowers produced are larger than normal, but the spikes and plant are not. This is a decided fault. Some border bearded iris, like some naughty children, have a habit of 'growing up'. While this is desirable with the naughty children it is not desirable with the border bearded iris which can become an embarrassment to the hybridiser who has named and registered them only to find them grow out of class and perform as shorter growing tall bearded iris, reaching heights over 70 cm in other gardens.

This is obviously as a result of cultural practices. My own 'Elsedina' has proven a problem child but a very lovely problem child. As grown in Sydney, 'Elsedina' conforms rigidly to the BB class but when planted at Hillview it will occasionally grow over the 70 cm mark. Plants sent to Keith Keppel in the USA all grew over the 70 cm mark and it must have really liked his garden — it probably should have, as it was bred from Keppel lines. When distributed elsewhere it remained within class. The hybridiser is in a real dilemma with these borderline cases. If the iris is classified as a border bearded, some growers find it exceeds the limits; if it is classified as a tall bearded, some growers find it does not reach that height. There is no easy answer. Joe Ghio had a similar problem with his appropriately named 'Borderline'. Although registered as a BB this iris always exceeded the height limits when grown in my own garden. Joe was smart and chose a most appropriate name. Hybridisers are always searching for appropriate names for their new releases — here then is a selection list for those with doubtful short-talls or border beardeds: 'Almost', 'Just Over', 'Nearly There', 'Spot On' (be careful that it has a spot pattern), 'Wee Bit Under', 'Shortie', 'Big Boy' (or 'Big Girl'), 'Unders or Overs', 'Growing Up', 'Down to Size', 'On the Line'. The mind boggles!

Border bearded iris have, as a class, one great drawback. They are, mainly, rather poor growers which increase slowly. Two of Barry Blyth's irises that come to mind are 'Ambling' and 'Curacao'. I can remember first seeing 'Ambling' in tones of orchid-blue and champagne-pink and feeling that it was the nicest iris in this class but I could never get it to multiply. I think it was well named as Barry had the same problems and now neither of us grow this beauty. 'Curacao' is a much better grower but by no stretch of the imagination could it be described as a good grower or fast increaser. This iris is pink-buff and plum-violet edged lilac. I only wish it would perform better, but we both still grow and list it. By contrast there are some border bearded iris which are near perfect performers, but it is always advisable to check their growth habits before purchase. Some of the really great performers are 'Pink Bubbles', 'Whoop 'em Up' and the Australian-raised 'On Wings' hybridised by Beryl James. The growth and increase of these iris would out-perform most TBs. The very name 'Border Bearded' gives you the main use for this class of iris. They are excellent for planting in the front of a perennial border or as a front border for a tall bearded iris planting. As they flower after the main flourish of spring bulbs their use in conjunction with bulbs is somewhat limited.

Recommended cultivars

'Am I Blue' (Denney, 1977) 51 cm. Pale blue with a navy-blue infusion in the standards and navy-blue beards.

'Apricot Frosty' (Niswonger, 1992) 63 cm. White standards with apricot falls and beards.

'Baby Bengal' (Sutton, 1990) 60 cm. Yellow with maroon-red lines and washing in the falls.

'Bimini' (Brown, 1985) 60 cm. Pale blue with mauve hafts.

'Birdbath' (Byers, 1989) 45 cm. Ruffled blue-white with blue beards tipped yellow and having spoons.

'Blackbeard' (Weiler, 1989) 64 cm. Steel-blue with black-violet beards.

'Blackberry Brandy' (Blyth, 1986) 60 cm. Orchid-lilac standards, velvet-purple falls and tangerine beards.

'Blue Bubbles' (Hammer, 1990) 69 cm. Ruffled violet-blue self.

'Blue Glory' (Mohr, 1983) 61 cm. Ruffled blue with a white beard. Very vigorous and prolific but it can grow much taller than its registered height. Great iris and a personal favourite.

'Border Bandit' (Black, 1989) 70 cm. Golden-tan standards, fuchsia-rose falls, tan margins and hafts, yellow beards.

'Boy O Boy' (Ghio, 1986) 65 cm. Warm white with a yellow halo and red beard.

'Brown Lasso' (Buckles-Niswonger, 1975) 60 cm. This is a classic border bearded iris and the only one to win the American Dykes Medal at the time of writing. It is a violet and tan-brown bicolour of impeccable growth habits.

'Calico Cat' (Lankow, 1989) 50 cm. Yellow standards, lavender falls with a yellow edge and rosy hafts.

'Catnap' (Tompkins, 1987) 60 cm. Rose-pink standards, darker falls, red-orange beards.

'Chapter' (Innerst, 1989) 65 cm. Bronze standards, silver-lavender falls edged lavender.

'Classic Treasure' (Burger, 1983) 60 cm. Ruffled white with a blue rim on the falls. This is a very beautiful flower, but is of moderate growth and vigour.

'Copper Glaze' (Hamblin, 1986) 60 cm. Ruffled and laced buff gold with cinnamon hafts and beards.

'Crafty Lady' (Black, 1991) 63 cm. Light apricot-pink with a fuchsia fall overlay.

'Curacao' (Blyth, 1990) 65 cm. Pink standards, plum falls edged lilac and tangerine beards. Colourful and beautifully formed but slow to increase.

'On Wings' (James, 1994)

'Faux Pas' (Keppel, 1990)

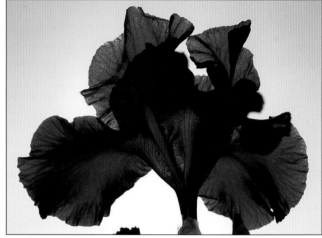

'Red Rooster' (Durrance, 1990)

'Orinoco Flow' (Bartlett, 1993)

'Pink Bubbles' (Hager, 1979)

'Curacao' (Blyth, 1990)

'Whoop 'em Up' (Brady, 1975)

'Calico Cat' (Lankow, 1989)

'Blue Glory' (Mohr, 1983)

'Batik' (Ensminger, 1986)

'Elsedina' (Grosvenor, 1986) 65 cm. White ground with rich purple edging. Prolific and vigorous but can grow taller than its registered height.

'Faux Pas' (Keppel, 1990) 63 cm. Dusky peach with a rosy-orchid wash on the falls and apricot beards. Beautiful form and colour.

'Honky Tonk' (Meck, 1984) 60 cm. Copper and red-brown bitone.

'Inner Circle' (Ghio, 1976) 61 cm. Light blue with a deeper spot on the falls. Lovely form and beautiful, well branched spikes make this a personal favourite.

'Lenora Pearl' (Nichols, 1990) 68 cm. Ruffled salmon-pink with a hot-orange beard. This iris reblooms and is a personal favourite.

'Maid of Orange' (Aitken, 1989) 64 cm. Creamy smooth orange with bright orange beards.

'Marmalade Skies' (Niswonger, 1978) 65 cm. Apricot-pink bitone with excellent growth habits.

'Maui Magic' (Aitken, 1991) 66 cm. Sweetly fragrant dark purple self.

'Mostest' (Durrance, 1990) 60 cm. Bright, ruffled gold.

'Nautical Flag' (Black, 1989) 65 cm. Ruffled, laced and flared lavender-violet with lemon beards.

'On Wings' (Beryl James, 1994) 60 cm. Outstanding Australian iris which won the border bearded class at the Premio Firenze in Florence in 1996. It is a frilly, ruffled light-pink over white with tangerine beards.

'Orinoco Flow' (Bartlett, 1993) 63 cm. White ground plicata with dark blue edging and navy blue beards. This iris won the English Dykes Medal in 1994 for Cy Bartlett and, as seen in Florence in 1992 when it won the border bearded class, it is the best border bearded iris available. I think it was the best iris of any type that I saw in Europe and cannot recommend it highly enough.

'Peccadillo' (Keppel, 1983) 66 cm. Peachy cream with a violet edge on the falls and violet hafts.

'Pink Bubbles' (Hager, 1979) 60 cm. Lovely pink border of good growth and excellent plant habits. This is a long-time favourite.

'Rhinemaidens' (Magee, 1990) 60 cm. White with a gold reverse, gold ring around the falls and gold beards. The falls recurve slightly.

'Rinky Dink' (Keppel, 1993) 63 cm. Peach ground with the falls washed purple and red beards. This iris is colourful and a good grower.

'Ruby Wilson' (Denney, 1989) 60 cm. Rich deep maroon with a cherry-red infusion.

'Shenanigan' (Keppel, 1985) 63 cm. Salmon-pink with a purple plicata wash on the falls. This iris grows well.

'Soft Spoken' (Dyer, 1980) 51 cm. Lilac with white in the throat, white beards tipped coral and beautiful spikes. Slow grower.

'Starlighter' (Nichols, 1987) 66 cm. Purple standards and grape falls with a white centre and white beards tipped orange. The ruffled blooms have a sweet fragrance.

'Summer Promise' (Rhodes, 1991) 66 cm. Yellow standards with a white rim, white falls with a yellow rim and yellow beards.

'Tres' (Dunn, 1992) 46 cm. White standards with slight violet plicata markings, white falls with darker violet plicata markings.

'Whoop 'em Up' (Brady, 1975) 60 cm. Startling yellow with a red overlay on the falls. This is a classic border bearded iris of great vigour and quick increase. It carries a multitude of well budded spikes and is a personal favourite.

'Zinc Pink' (Ensminger, 1986) 58 cm. Ruffled and lacy bright rosy-pink, which is much like its pod parent, 'Pink Bubbles'.

'Zinger' (Stevens, 1983) 66 cm. Ruffled and laced violet with a cinnamon edge.

TALL BEARDED IRIS

The iris flower and flowering spike

THE FLOWER

Plants of the genus iris are perennials, typified by having floral parts in sets of three. Those characteristics of the individual iris bloom considered desirable have evolved over time. This is not uncommon with plants which are being hybridised and there are many, many thousands, probably many millions of iris seedlings being raised and evaluated each year. Each hybridiser will have specific goals, but major aims have been and continue to be the development of the individual bloom in form, substance and colour pattern.

The basic structure of a bearded iris flower is shown in Figure 5.

Flower form is determined by the balance between the standards and the falls and the general shape of these floral parts. It is undesirable to have either the standards or the falls unnecessarily large in comparison with the other. It is generally accepted that the standards should be closed or touching and held erect yet nicely curved at the top. For many years, hybridisers have worked

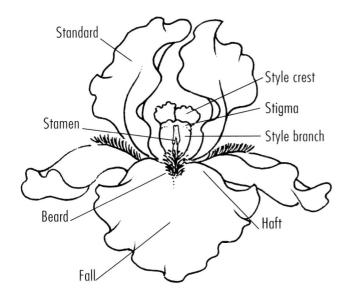

Standard

Style crest

Stigma

Stamen

Style branch

Beard

Haft

Fall

Figure 5. Tall bearded iris flower

hard to 'close up' the standards so that they touch or overlap at the top. In recent years there has been a tendency for some hybridisers to develop iris with stiff, upright, heavily ruffled standards that are open or even outwardly pointing at the top. Fashions change and there is no doubt that some cultivars with 'open standards' have gained acceptance. It is left to the individual to determine what they do and don't like and you should only grow things that you find attractive. A personal view, and probably the majority view, is that the beautiful curved lines of the typical iris standards are lost if we move away from the touching or overlapping 'closed standard' form and I am very traditional in my preference.

Modern hybridisers have developed falls that flare or semi-flare, are wide at the haft and are held firmly in position. There has been a conscious aim to eliminate contrasting haft marks and colour patterns. Flaring falls are, in general, attractive but in some cases this has been overdone to present flowers with horizontal falls — attractive to look down upon but lost for balance when viewed from the side and even more so when viewed from a distance. Width at the haft has helped considerably in presenting a well balanced flower and is a very desirable attribute. In recent times, flowers with very wide hafted falls have been further developed to have a dished effect in the centre of the hafts near the beards and I find this a most attractive addition to the form of the iris. Much has been written and much more said about the contentious issue of striations of a different colour around the hafts of the falls. In general, flowers with heavy striations at the haft have been described as 'rough' or 'hafty' and do not meet with approval. Hybridisers have for many years 'worked' these

striations out of the bearded iris to present a flower with greater purity of colour. Most, if not all, of the bearded species and early hybrids had heavy haft striations. In the 1980s and 1990s some of the most innovative hybridisers have 'worked' fancy colour patterns and striations back into the falls of bearded iris, often with very pleasing results. I can remember being mildly chastised by an American friend that Australian hybridisers were breeding hafts (rough) back into iris after the Americans had bred them out. The point was taken but it was an inaccurate statement. Many of the heavily striated 'older' iris lacked a pleasing colour effect as there was an undoubted clash in the colours and patterns. Not so with some of the beautiful iris such as Barry Blyth's 1995 introduction 'Lipstick Lies' in pure white with red beards and purple lines stitched at the hafts, or Paul Black's 1993 introduction 'Goldkist', in pure white with gold beards, gold hafts and purple veining at the hafts. Then there is Joe Ghio's sensational 'Liaison' (1986) with pink standards, purple falls with a pink edge and starburst pattern at the hafts and around the beards and his even more startling 'Notorious' (1991) in much the same pattern but with even more striated hafts. I have an open mind on haft striations. The four iris previously mentioned are all personal favourites, but there are many 'hafty' iris that I do not find attractive. Much depends on the colour combination and application and my only advice is to evaluate for yourself. One of the most pleasing of all iris colour patterns is the plicata pattern where one or more colours is stitched or edged on to a base colour and, for popularity with the general public, the plicata pattern ranks second to the pure self coloured pattern in terms of iris grown.

Colour, in itself, is a personal choice but the colour should be clear and bright. Bicolours and plicatas should have clarity and precision, either in contrast or blending of the colour patterns.

Ruffling and fluting can enhance the appearance of the flower while lacing of the petal edges can be another attraction. In modern iris there is a trend towards ruffling and I find ruffled iris to be most attractive. It is always an attribute that I look for in my own hybridising but there is much to be said for the simplicity of the plain 'tailored' form of smooth, unruffled petal edges.

The one great attribute that has been bred into modern iris and which sets them way ahead of older varieties is heavy petal substance. The general thickening and firming of petal substance has enhanced the flower, enabling it to stand up to difficult weather conditions and enabling it to last well in the garden or when cut. Most modern tall bearded iris will last three days under normal weather conditions and heavy petal substance enables them to mature slowly and die gracefully. The improvement in petal substance has been dramatic in recent years and is *the* factor which sets the modern tall bearded iris far ahead of those from the past.

'Before the Storm' (Innerst, 1989)

'Bertwistle' (Innerst, 1990)

'Bogota' (Ghio, 1990)

'Break the Ice' (Grosvenor, 1996)

'Boogie Woogie' (Nichols, 1993)

'Blowtorch' (Byers, 1986)

'Abstract Art' (Keppel, 1990)

'Ballet Folklorico' (Williamson, 1987)

'Azure Angel' (Grosvenor, 1994)

'Autumn Circus' (Hager, 1990)

THE FLOWERING SPIKE

The use of bearded iris in the landscape will be determined to a large extent by the flowering spike. The choice of background and foreground planting, whether it be with other iris or companion plants, should be influenced by the height of the flowering spike which normally fits within the range of 70–100 cm. Just as there are desirable traits in the floral parts there are desirable traits in the flowering spike.

The spike should be **strong,** able to support the flowers in all but the worst of conditions and sufficiently rigid to ensure that it will not be blown over by the wind. A quality iris should not need staking in a normal garden situation. The actual stem should be thick but not too thick so as to appear gross.

The spike should be **in proportion** to the foliage. It should always be tall enough for the flowers to be observed above the foliage. The branches that make up the spike should be evenly spaced down the spike. It is undesirable to have flowers bunched at the top and equally undesirable to have very low branches so that flowers are hidden in the foliage.

The spikes should be **well branched** with each branch able to display the blooms gracefully and uncluttered. Multiple flowering buds in each socket are desirable to ensure a long flowering period. There should be two or three branches on each spike and a minimum of six blooms. Some iris are equally satisfactory garden subjects if they carry fewer buds to the spike, but multiple spikes to the clump, although these iris will have a shorter but more spectacular bloom period.

The Dykes Medal winning pink iris 'Vanity' (Hager, 1975) is a typical example of an iris low on buds but high on bloom. This iris will often only have four buds to a spike but will, at times, send up three or more spikes from a single rhizome. The best garden specimens will usually carry eight to ten buds to a spike with two or three buds in each socket. Spikes which carry an excess of buds often produce diminutive flowers towards the end of the flowering sequence and even though some iris will produce 12 or more buds to the spike, the last three or four flowers are often very small. The most heavily laden spike that I have grown was one of Alan Johnson's blue on white plicata 'Rococo Valley', which regularly produces 15 flowering buds to the spike and on one occasion had a spike with 21 blooms. Even the last of these blooms in sequence was of reasonable size.

The **concurrence** of open flowers on the various branches of the spike is also important. A flower from each branch may open simultaneously, giving three· or four open flowers on one spike and making a great splash of colour and giving an ideal spike for exhibition. Alternatively, the flowers may open intermittently, thus giving a longer period of bloom in the garden. Occasionally spikes will have branches which rebranch, giving a multiple bud position. Two iris that have done

this for me are 'Solano' (Luihn, 1974), a rich golden yellow, and 'Song of Erin' (Roach, 1971) a greenish white, both of which produced individual spikes with seven flowers open simultaneously. My own 'Jim Frazier' (Grosvenor, 1998) has had spikes with six flowers open simultaneously, as has 'Megan Elizabeth' (Brown, 1991) in the Hillview garden. When 'Megan Elizabeth' becomes well established it could be an outstanding iris for Australian gardens.

Flower presentation on the spike is also very important, particularly as iris are grown for different use. The best garden effect is obtained from well-spaced, well-branched spikes carrying eight to ten buds with flowers displayed well out from the spike but not so far out as to interfere with adjoining spikes. When branches are carried in candelabra style, widely spaced, the iris are usually excellent show specimens but they can be quite messy in the garden with flowers from different spikes overlapping or intertwining. Tightly branched iris with blooms close to the stem often have a cluttered effect in the garden and flowers may not open properly at times, but these iris are very good for cut flowers as they bunch and tie quite well.

The ideal show spike will have three (sometimes four) perfectly spaced, evenly sized and proportioned blooms open simultaneously and displayed to perfection with back-up buds and clean healthy foliage. What is good on the show bench is not necessarily good in the garden and vice versa, but it is my experience that the best garden irises usually make the best show iris.

In spring with the temperatures, both maximum and minimum, increasing regularly in a normal season it can amaze how quickly the flowering spikes emerge from the foliage. A guide, although not foolproof, for telling if a plant is to flower is a noticeable curving of the central leaves in the fan of the foliage. The presence of a spike can be confirmed by gently feeling the base of the fan. In the early stages of development the spike can be brittle and care should be taken to avoid breaking the spikes, particularly when weeding. It is, therefore, advisable to have your iris clumps weed free before the flowering season. The time taken from the emergence of the spike to the start of bloom varies considerably, but can be as short as one to two weeks. Weather conditions have a considerable effect on how quickly an iris will flower from the time of the emergence of the spike.

Culture

Tall bearded iris can be ranked as being among the easiest of plants to grow. They are undemanding and most forgiving of the worst of gardeners. Much has been written and much more has been said over many many years about the cultivation of bearded iris and no matter what I write here there will be those with a story to tell to contradict mine. We all rejoice in being different and there is always the joy of one-upmanship

— of doing something different and proving the experts wrong or, if not wrong, at least not as knowledgeable as they profess to be. It is probably because of these individuals that we have the pool of knowledge available today and all that I wish to do is to make what I know of that pool available for anyone to obtain from it what they want. I must confess to being one of those individuals, particularly in younger days, and it is only after many years of experience than I have found that there is no right and wrong as far as bearded iris culture is concerned as long as certain basic rules are observed. Bearded iris are also individuals and each will perform differently under conditions and culture supplied even to the extent of performing differently from year to year under the same conditions. But the first question to be answered is: 'What are these basic rules to be observed?'.

Bearded iris require a suitable climate and:
◆ adequate sunlight;
◆ good drainage;
◆ prepared soil (that is neutral to slightly alkaline);
◆ correct planting;
◆ aftercare;
◆ dividing and replanting.

Adequate sunlight

Bearded iris are sun lovers and the best results will be obtained by planting in full sun. Where optimum conditions cannot be supplied there is no doubt that bearded iris can be grown and grown very well in semi-shaded positions. They will grow and flower well in positions where only an average half day of sun can be provided if other conditions are to their liking so they can be grown where light is filtered by trees or blocked by buildings as long as sufficient sun is provided to ripen the rhizomes for bloom in successive years. Exactly where the cut-off is for sufficient or insufficient sunlight, I cannot say. A few guidelines are that more sunlight throughout the day is required in cooler climates with short summers, or where iris are grown in heavy soils and in high-rainfall climates, particularly if the rain is experienced in the growing season. It is also worth noting that some iris by their very nature tend to overbloom, leaving little increase for subsequent years and these 'individuals' will perform better over a long period by the provision of semi-shade to restrict bloom.

GOOD DRAINAGE

Bearded iris will not succeed in waterlogged or poorly drained soil so it is imperative to provide a well drained growing medium. Just how this is done is dependent on the conditions and the effort that the gardener is prepared to make. I have grown bearded iris in light sandy soil and in very heavy soil and am firmly convinced that most success can be obtained by growing bearded iris in raised beds. If these conditions cannot be provided then the iris gardener should give thought to the use of agricultural pipe to ensure that water will be allowed to run off. To grow bearded iris successfully you must ensure that the soil is drained and how you do it is up to you, with particular attention to your own climatic conditions.

SOIL PREPARATION

Bearded iris love to be grown in 'virgin' soil, and will grow particularly well (for the first two or three seasons) in just about any soil that has not previously been used, even if no particular attention is given to soil preparation. The best soil for bearded iris is a medium loam, slightly alkaline and, of course, well drained. You are fortunate indeed if these conditions are provided naturally but, if they are not, every effort should be made to improve the soil.

Bearded iris enjoy growing in a soil with pH 7.0 to 7.2. Many iris will perform quite well in slightly acid soils and I have grown iris successfully in soils with pH as low as 6.0 but that is not to say it is a good thing. Most Australian soils are acid, and they can be made more alkaline by the addition of lime or dolomite to the soil. Dolomite is preferred as it provides both calcium and magnesium salts. It is a good idea to purchase a pH meter and use it to obtain readings and thereby achieve gradual adjustment of the soil pH. These meters are inexpensive and often combine the facility to measure water content as well. Add lime or dolomite to the soil at the rate of approximately a handful to the square metre. Check the pH of the soil before and after adding the lime and you will have a ready guide to the amount needed for the desired result. Above all, do not be frightened by the 'numbers game' and do not attempt to be too scientific. Iris are very forgiving plants and most tolerant of our inexpert mathematics. Remember also that iris are individuals and performance in different soils will differ from iris to iris. Personal experience is that some bearded iris actually prefer a slightly acid soil — a good example is the famous pink Dykes Medal winner 'Vanity', which has always performed better for me in slightly acid soil. There are others with the same trait.

If, on the other hand, your soil is too alkaline the pH can be reduced by the addition of agricultural sulphur. This is done by using the same procedure as stated above. Bearded iris are heavy feeders and the growing medium should be as fertile as possible. Preparation of the soil will depend on its natural condition. As stated earlier, great iris can be produced in both sandy and heavy soils but the culture is different.

With a **light, sandy soil** the aim is to build up the soil with compost or manure. Work as much humus into the soil as possible in a period of up to a month before planting and to a depth of 20–30 cm.

'Black Tie Affair' (Schreiner, 1993)

'Blue Staccato' (Gibson, 1977)

'Breakers' (Schreiner, 1986)

'Charmed Circle' (Keppel, 1969)

'Cajun Rhythm' (Schreiner, 1996)

'Cascade Springs' (Schreiner, 1994)

'Beverly Sills' (Hager, 1979)

'Alpine Journey' (Blyth, 1984)

'Affaire' (Blyth, 1990)

'And Royal' (Blyth, 1990)

Remember, however, that compost or manure should always be worked into the ground, never used as a mulch or as an afterthought once planting has been completed.

In **heavy soil,** the aim is to break down the soil and make it more friable. The soil should be worked by hoeing and tilling to a nice crumbly tilth. The addition of sand in whatever quantity is available and subsequent tilling can only be beneficial. Well-rotted animal manure or compost can be added and carefully tilled or can be used as a sublayer over which the tilled soil is spread to a thickness of 10–15 cm. If manure or compost is worked into the planting medium, take care to perform this task about four weeks prior to planting so that there is little or no chance of 'hot' compost coming in contact with the rhizomes.

PLANTING

If you want to have a few laughs about horticultural matters I suggest that you become a nurseryman and deal with the general public. Most customers are reasonably knowledgeable, well informed and keen to learn. They love their plants and want to do everything possible to ensure that they succeed and they are, in general, a pleasure to meet, but there are always a few . . . and I have had some wonderful stories told to me of the intricacies of iris planting. I have 'learned' over the years that the toe of the rhizome must be planted pointing to the north, to the south, to the east and to the west. I have 'learned' that iris should only be planted within two days of a full moon; that the fans of iris should be planted so that the setting sun hits only the least amount of foliage — I guess this is the same as having the toe facing north or south, but I am not sure which. I have heard all kinds of stories on how much foliage should be left on and how much cut off a newly dug plant and I have heard wonderful stories, even from experienced growers, on the benefits or otherwise of root growth on newly dug plants. There are other stories, too many to mention, but, as previously stated, iris are wonderfully forgiving plants and, if I have 'done it wrong' over the years, they certainly have forgiven me.

The most frequently asked questions are; 'why do you cut back the foliage and roots when lifting and dividing?'; followed by 'do you need to cut back the foliage of established clumps after flowering?'

When the rhizome is lifted and replanted, it needs to re-establish root growth. Until this new root growth is established there will be an excess of leaf surface from which transpiration occurs. This is undesirable, and a suitable balance needs to be maintained between the foliage to be supported, and what nutrients and water the rhizome can supply to support it. Foliage is usually cut back by about half for this purpose. There is the added advantage that the trimmed foliage presents less resistance to wind, and the plant is less likely to be blown over while root growth is being established. The amount of cutting back is not critical. Some customers demand as much foliage as possible. My personal view is that the foliage is best cut back hard, to about one-third of its original size. There is no hard and fast rule — very much like rose pruning. I like to cut back to about one-third of the original foliage to give the plants every opportunity to make good root growth with minimal disturbance. Once root growth is obtained (and this usually takes two to three weeks) the foliage will grow vigorously. Root trimming is only to keep balance above and below and ensure ease of planting, a firm position of the rhizome in the ground and the opportunity for the plant to re-establish quickly.

Sometimes when plants are lifted shortly after bloom the young rhizomes have not developed their root systems and can look quite bald. This is not a disadvantage as far as quality of plant is concerned, and the only practical problem facing the plant and the grower is the need to ensure that the rhizome is firmly positioned in the ground when planted. Iris growers should be aware that as soon as a plant is lifted for replanting the great proportion of the old roots will die as new roots develop. If given a choice of a plant with an extensive root system or one lacking roots I would choose the former, but only for the reason of having a firm basis for anchoring the plant. In reality, I feel that the plant bereft of roots will re-establish just as quickly as one with an extensive root system. There is no doubt that a rhizome without roots just does not look as healthy as one with an extensive root system, but it is really only a matter of appearance.

Now, the age-old question as to whether to trim the foliage after flowering on established clumps which are to be left in the ground. There is no cultural reason to perform what is, for many, a ritual. The plants are feeding through the foliage and if it is attractive leave it alone. Of course, any dead foliage or unsightly dying foliage is best removed from the outside of the fan, but this is only cosmetic or as a prevention against disease. The ritual cutting is not necessary. Does it do any harm to cut back the foliage after flowering? Probably no great harm is done, but certainly no good!

Why are newly lifted rhizomes cut back in an inverted 'V' pattern? I don't know except that everyone else seems to have done it for as long as I can remember. Once again the only logic I can see in this ritual is that it presents a smaller, more streamlined outline to eliminate or at least decrease the effect of wind disturbance. Anyhow, it looks good.

Before discussing when to plant, I feel that it is desirable, if not necessary, to explain a little about the growing cycle of the bearded iris. Tall bearded iris flower in mid spring and bloom is completed in the last month of spring. After the flowering period the iris plant goes into a period of active growth followed by semi-dormancy in mid to late summer. A rhizome, once it has flowered, will not flower again and all its energy is put into developing increase, that is new rhizomes that will flower in the following season. These increases, which

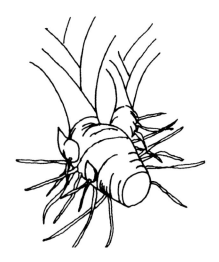

Figure 6. Rhizome and increase

first appear usually in late summer, are the normal vegetative means of propagating iris and they develop from the original rhizome, as illustrated in Diagram 6.

The characteristics of the baby plants will be identical to those of the parent. In the two months following bloom the young rhizomes that have not bloomed grow very vigorously, store food for the following spring, and develop the bloom stalk buds for next season. At the end of this period the rhizome is mature and becomes semi-dormant until late summer when a further period of rapid growth is experienced. The best time to plant rhizomes or divide established clumps is probably during mid- to late-summer dormancy. It can be difficult to know exactly when the switch from active growth to semi dormancy occurs and, in any case, it is not critical.

In brief, planting or dividing can be accomplished any time that is convenient from immediately after bloom in late spring until late autumn. There are advantages and disadvantages in early and late planting, but much will depend on the grower's individual climatic conditions.

Early planting has the decided advantage of having the rhizomes established before the heat of summer, but the disadvantages of rhizomes being relatively immature and the possible interruption of the active growth period. It is important for growers with cold winters to have their planting done as early as possible to ensure bloom for the following season.

Late planting is good in milder areas as rhizomes are mature and the heat of summer is avoided. Sufficient time must be allowed for the plants to establish their new root system before winter dormancy.

Midsummer planting is near perfect for the growth cycle of the rhizome, but has the disadvantage of the plant having to contend with the summer heat and possible transpiration. Rhizomes planted in mid summer benefit from some shading until established (usually two to three weeks).

Bearded iris can be moved successfully at any time of the year, but lifting and replanting at other than the best times may result in lack of bloom or poor quality bloom in the following season. This is particularly true with late autumn, winter or early spring planting. Late planting will usually result in smaller flowers and shorter bloom spikes. My preferred planting time is immediately after bloom in late spring or the first month of summer. My next preference is very early autumn.

Bearded iris are easy to plant and most enthusiasts are aware that the rhizomes should be planted at ground level and not buried as is the case with bulbs. In fact, this seems to have sunk in even with the most novice of gardeners and many are quite keen to display their knowledge at other people's expense. I have quite often

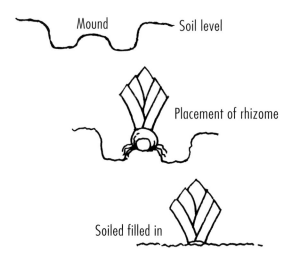

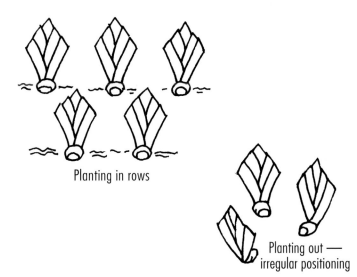

Figure 7. Planting out and positioning

'Caption' (Ghio, 1986)

'Conch Call' (Gaulter, 1978)

'Going My Way' (Gibson, 1972)

'Cheerful One' (Hamner, 1989)

'Coming Up Roses' (Gatty, 1992)

'Cloud Ballet' (Fort, 1990)

'Cregrina' (Foster, 1995)

'Darkside' (Schreiner, 1985)

'Delta Blues' (Schreiner, 1994)

'Dusky Challenger' (Schreiner, 1986)

'Douce France' (Anfosso, 1988)

'Edith Wolford' (Hager, 1986)

heard visitors to the nursery explain in detail to their friends how poorly our rhizomes have been planted because you cannot see the rhizome high and dry. In fact, the planting depth is not as critical as our pedantic friends state and there is a reasonable range of satisfactory planting depths. Ideally, the rhizome should be planted so that you can just see the top of the rhizome. In light soils the rhizome can be covered by up to 2 cm or more of soil, but the overall issue is one of drainage. Care should be taken to ensure that the rhizome is not too high so that it sits out of the ground with roots partially exposed as they reach into the soil.

The mechanics of planting an iris are similar to those for planting a rose. Dig a hole large enough to accommodate two or three plants and then make a mound of soil to about 2 cm below soil level. Place the rhizome on the mound and spread the roots so as to anchor the plant. Incorporate a slow-release (eight to nine month) fertiliser at planting time and fill the hole. This should ensure that the rhizome is at or about soil level. Care should be taken to ensure that the rhizome is horizontal and the fan vertical. The toe of the rhizome needs to be in the ground. Failure to do so can result in dry rot.

Great success in promoting growth and reducing the incidence of rhizome rot has been achieved by incorporating a slow-release fertiliser of the eight to nine month type at the rate of a tablespoon to each rhizome in the soil at planting time. Choose a fertiliser with an N:P:K composition close to 6:10:6, and if necessary err on the side of reducing nitrogen (N). Fertilisers of this type work on the principle of osmosis, releasing small amounts of nutrient with watering over the full growing period right up to bloom.

Ensure that there are no air pockets, particularly under the rhizome, and water in well to settle the soil. Water two or three times a week until the plant has established its new roots and is making active leaf growth. Do not be concerned when little action is seen for the first two or three weeks as all the action is beneath the ground. Once the new roots are formed the new growth is seen to develop as a central green leaf appears. Outer leaves gradually die off and the plant develops its new green foliage from the centre out. With good site selection, correct ground preparation, including attention to drainage and correct planting, the majority of the tasks have been completed and iris really are easy-care plants. Each rhizome correctly planted and given care should produce one flowering spike with from six to ten or more blooms and sufficient increase to be grown on for future years.

AFTERCARE

Much more harm is done to bearded iris by over-fertilising and over-caring for them than by neglect. It has been said many times that bearded iris thrive on neglect and while I cannot completely endorse this statement, I do subscribe to observing good clean gardening practices and otherwise leaving them alone. Once planted, the iris will develop quickly with the growth of lush green foliage. Being a typical perennial the outer foliage of bearded iris will die off as new growth emanates from the centre. This foliage should be removed and this is easily accomplished by pulling the leaf in a direction away from the fan and towards the toe. Clean cultivation will minimise disease problems and helps to control the problem of snails and slugs which use the declining foliage as a refuge. Clean cultivation requires weed control and this can be achieved in a variety of ways. Hand weeding is effective but time-consuming and often at the expense of damage to the plants as well as the weeds. In particular, one needs to take care not to damage surface roots when weeding around iris plants. The use of chemical control, either pre-emergent or post-emergent, is also effective. Pre-emergent sprays act by forming a film or cover through which the weeds cannot germinate. The chemical trifluran is the active agent in such commercial sprays marketed as 'Treflan' and 'Surflan' in Australia. There are reports that growers have experienced poor bloom following the use of these sprays, but this has not been my experience and I feel that there were probably other factors that affected bloom for the growers in question. There is no doubt that weed inhibitors are effective within their parameters — they control most annual grasses and many perennial grasses and some broad-leaf weeds. They certainly do not control clovers. In conjunction with other control measures they can be effective in large iris plantings but are of limited value in small plantings. Post-emergent sprays fall into two categories — the systemic type such as 'Roundup' or 'Zero', with the active constituent glycophosphate, and the knockdown sprays such as 'Tryquat', with the active constituents paraquat dichloride and diquat dibromide monohydrate.

The glycophosphate-type sprays are effective but have been known to get into the soil and have an adverse effect on future performance. They need to be applied with great care in 'zero wind conditions'. Even the slightest mist can have an adverse effect on valuable plants. They also take about two weeks to have the desired effect. Knockdown sprays have the advantage of immediate effect but can be quite dangerous if handled without due care and protection. These sprays should only be used by gardeners suitably attired in protective clothing and in ideal conditions with no wind at all. For most effective use, sprays should be used when there is no rain predicted and irrigation should be withdrawn until the spray has had a chance to be effective. In all cases, the manufacturers' instructions should be followed in detail.

Control of water is the key to most facets of gardening and successful growing of bearded iris is dependent on watering and water control. The importance of good drainage has already been emphasised and cannot be stressed enough. Provided drainage is good, I am confident that bearded iris will not only tolerate but will flourish with more water than they have generally been allocated, particularly in the summer months.

It has generally been accepted that iris require a lot of water in the growing period coming up to bloom and I subscribe to this view. However, too much water at bloom time can induce rhizome rot, particularly if accompanied by warm, humid conditions. In general, water is withdrawn after bloom but I feel that bearded iris can be maintained as attractive foliage plants through summer if adequate water and good drainage are provided. Summer watering twice a week with a good soaking maintains attractive foliage and ensures good growth for the following season. Continue solid watering through autumn and then cut down and withdraw watering as winter dormancy approaches. Bearded iris need little water in the winter months.

The next question is how to water and I suppose that any form of watering is better than none. For many years I used overhead watering with mixed success, but in recent years I have switched almost exclusively to drip irrigation with a dramatic improvement in iris performance. No longer is there a concern about keeping up an adequate water supply without damaging precious blooms and control of water supply is easy as long as spring storms do not wreak havoc. There has also been a dramatic improvement in disease control. Water applied overhead has a tendency to splash fungus spores on to the foliage with the consequent leaf spot and rust problems, but plants grown with drip irrigation are far less susceptible to fungus diseases and are much more attractive garden subjects. Hand watering has the same effect as overhead watering in that it will splash fungus spores on to the foliage. It has the advantage of not causing damage to blooms but can be tedious, particularly with large plantings. Water is essential. Control is important. Overhead watering with a sprinkling system is good. Hand watering is better. Drip irrigation is the most effective and best.

Fertiliser is an important factor in all gardening. As I have said to many customers and interested growers 'we all need food and water to survive. How would you survive if you did not eat and drink?' The drinking doesn't seem to present a problem — most gardeners water their plants — but it never ceases to amaze me that people who will spend many dollars on expensive and valued plants are reluctant to spend the time and money to ensure that they are adequately fed.

I have, in the past, felt that bearded iris cannot be over-fed. Now, I am convinced that the opposite is the case and that bearded iris that are over-fed or unwisely fed will not only suffer as a result, but may even die. In most cases the use of slow-release fertilisers is safe and adequate. It is a very effective way to give the iris a good start in life. Bearded iris love superphosphate and this can be added to the soil before planting and at specific times on established plantings. These times are in late winter when new growth is starting or about to start, immediately before bloom and immediately after bloom. Iris do not like to be 'forced'; any forcing of leaf growth can be harmful and nitrogen should be kept under control. Care must be taken with animal manure because of its high nitrogen content. This will encourage leaf growth at the expense of flowers and is a source of 'soft rot' problems. In remaking iris beds where iris have been grown previously and the soil is obviously depleted, the use of compost and manure is distinctly advantageous but care should be taken that this operation is repeated once only in three to four years. For those who wish to lift and divide their iris earlier, my advice is leave well enough alone and do not add too much manure to your soil.

PESTS

The final step in aftercare is the attention to pests and diseases. In the Southern Hemisphere, gardeners are fortunate that many of the pests which can wreak havoc in Northern Hemisphere gardens just do not exist. The rigid quarantine laws of Australia and New Zealand have ensured that we do not have to contend with the iris borer, which can be a problem in the eastern and mid-western states of the USA. The iris borer is the larva of a native American moth and the young larva will attack iris foliage commencing at the tips and working down. Damage is observed as pin holes with the leaves and notches eaten from the edge of foliage. Cannibalistic by nature, the larvae eat one another as well as the iris foliage until only one reaches the rhizome, tunnels in and proceeds to eat out the fleshy material, reducing the rhizome to a shell. In clumps with smaller rhizomes the one grub may travel from rhizome to rhizome decimating the clump. In the final stages of decline the whole fan may collapse or be easily pulled from the rhizome. Control is best effected by interrupting the moth's life cycle and destroying the eggs before they develop into larvae. Clean cultivation, which includes the removal (and burning) of spent foliage and accumulated weed growth in spring and autumn, is a major help and then spraying in accordance with local and state regulations to kill off any eggs will give the best protection.

There are numerous types of thrips which can be of nuisance value in spring when the flowers are formed. They are a menace in hot, dry conditions but the most commonly encountered, gladiolus thrip, does little damage to the flowers. It can strip the pollen, making hybridising difficult. Control is not easy and, as most of the more effective insecticides cause a streaking effect on the flowers, the cure is often worse than the complaint. Control is aided by keeping the plants well watered and a

'Classic Look' (Schreiner, 1992)

'Daredevil' (Keppel, 1988)

'Dance Man' (Blyth, 1989)

'Esmeralda' (Ghio, 1988)

'Excite Me' (Grosvenor, 1996)

'Elegant Impressions' (Schreiner, 1993)

'Divine Duchess' (Blyth, 1990)

'Dazzling Gold' (Anderson, 1981)

philosophical approach, accepting the bad seasons with the good. It is interesting to note that with iris, just as with roses, the thrips prefer the lighter coloured to the darker cultivars.

Aphids can be a problem in most gardens and are even more troublesome as they are responsible for the transmission of virus diseases. Aphids can be washed off buds or foliage with a spray of water from the hose. Pyrethrum-based sprays are effective contact controllers as is the more powerful malathion. There are other systemic sprays of value and once again it is a question of seeking assistance from your local supplier or government agency. Snails and slugs love to establish homes in thick clumps of tall bearded iris which afford them a safe refuge. They can cause a great deal of damage both to foliage and precious bloom spikes, but are relatively easy to control if the gardener is persistent. Search and destroy methods, either in the evening or early in the morning, when these pests are active, are effective. Chemical pesticides are quite effective but care must be taken, if chemicals are used, to ensure that domestic pets are not poisoned. Green Defender powder and pellets are less attractive to pets than the blue pellets of Baysol, but there is an antidote for the Baysol pellets available. We have found, commercially, that the use of Mesurol spray is most effective.

Grubs, caterpillars, moths, butterflies and birds all can create problems with precious ripening seed pods. The best defence against these unwanted pests is the physical protection of the seed pods by covering with a protective material square which allows warmth and light in but is a barrier to pests. We have successfully used a thin material used to cover crops. This is marketed in Australia as 'Evolution Cloth'. Old stockings are equally useful.

In certain areas under certain conditions grass-hoppers can be a major problem. In my first season at Hillview in the central west of NSW, a grasshopper plague all but wiped out a large planting of over 5000 seedlings. In some cases whole rows of seedlings were destroyed while in others there were just the odd few plants left. As I had gardened in city areas all my life this was a rude introduction to country farming and the growing of stock plants and seedlings in large quantities. It is interesting to note that out of a cross of over 100 seedlings of 'Esmeralda' x 'Samurai Silk', only two plants survived. One was a most unimpressive, one could even say ugly, iris which was quickly disposed of on maiden bloom while the other was eventually named 'Hills District', a bitoned orange iris with a darker band on the falls. This iris won me an Award of Merit and the Gordon Loveridge Hybridisers Medallion as outstanding trial garden iris of its year.

Grasshoppers, in plague proportion, will severely damage the foliage of established plants, but they just ate the seedlings to the ground and as resilient plants attempted to grow again they were once again eaten to the ground. The 'S' series of seedlings was nearly doomed from the start and it is amazing the number of named irises which eventuated from these crosses. It took a little while to learn, but eventually I found that for good protection, newly planted seedlings need to be covered and here again 'Evolution Cloth' was used.

Another typically Australian pest is the sulphur-crested cockatoo. These beautiful white birds with the yellow crests can be a real menace as they are vandals when it comes to iris. They will descend in flocks of a few up to hundreds and will destroy rhizomes by chewing them to pieces, and are particularly attracted to and destructive of newly planted rhizomes. The cockatoos do not eat the rhizomes, merely tear them apart. We have large flocks of black cockatoos and the smaller pink and grey galahs regularly visit the Hillview property but, to my knowledge, they do not inflict any damage. Our most vulnerable time is late winter, early spring and the only protection is to cover the planting with 'Evolution Cloth', which the cockatoos will not attack. It is unfortunate that these beautiful birds can be such a problem. They also fancy young seedlings and several of the 'V' series of crosses were victims of their 'war games'.

Southern Hemisphere gardeners do not have to contend with the iris borer, but there is another 'nasty' that is an ongoing problem. This is the larva of the Christmas beetle. For many years I considered this pest as harmless to iris, but recent experiences have changed that opinion. An infestation in the particularly wet spring and early summer of 1993 and subsequent observations have confirmed that this is a widespread problem pest, that damp conditions are very much to its liking and that the larva will do considerable damage to iris. It commences its tour of destruction by eating the roots and then proceeds to bore into the underside of rhizomes, seeking further nutrients. Damage can be considerable but not as devastating as that caused by the iris borer. Rhizomes do recover after attack but are not a pretty sight, with roots eaten and the underside of the rhizome pock marked and the sides of the rhizome also eaten. I have found that drenching the soil with Lorsban has had a productive effect and that spraying the perimeter of a large iris planting with Lorsban late in spring will also present a barrier which grasshoppers are not inclined to cross. 'Two birds with the one stone', one could say — and our thanks to our NSW Department of Agriculture for this valuable information. It emphasises my point, that if you have a local problem the best place to seek advice is your local Department of Agriculture. You may have specific problems, but it is there that you can obtain accumulated general knowledge and, very often, a solution to your problem. I am quite sure that there are many other localised pest problems that irisarians have encountered. Most are of a transient or minor concern and it is only with personal experience and the assistance of others who have experience that these problems can be overcome.

DISEASES

Fortunately the diseases of bearded iris are not numerous and, in general, not fatal. Diseases can be categorised as viral, fungal or bacterial, while others are of unknown source.

VIRAL DISEASES

It seems that bearded iris are just about universally infected with a mosaic virus of some form or other and particular cultivars and particular species show a great difference in reaction to the viruses. There are four known viruses that attack bearded iris — bearded mosaic virus, cucumber mosaic virus, broad-bean wilt virus and tobacco ringspot virus. The bearded mosaic virus is most common and is probably present in most bearded iris. Many, if not most, bearded iris are tolerant and show no visible effect from this virus. They are, to all intents and purposes, virus free. Some iris will show mottling and streaking of foliage with alternate lighter and darker areas while severe cases can result in deformed flowers or flowers with streaks or blotches of other than the normal colour. Foliage symptoms are most obvious in colder weather and once a plant is infected there is no cure. Badly infected plants should be lifted and burned, as virus diseases can be spread by aphids. Symptoms show up more readily on the smaller growing dwarf and intermediate bearded iris than on the larger tall bearded iris. Arilbred iris are particularly susceptible to mosaic virus. The other three virus diseases have been found in bearded iris but are very uncommon. Rigid quarantine laws have ensured that virus diseases are kept to a minimum in Australia and New Zealand, but I have found virus-infected plants in both countries. An interesting experience that I had in 1995 was to receive some foliage of spuria iris in the mail from New Zealand. The sender had tried unsuccessfully to have the problem diagnosed and, in desperation, had sent it to me. The foliage was badly infected with mosaic virus and the lady in question was advised to destroy the plant, but the important question of the inability of rules and regulations to be policed was raised. Certainly no harm was done as the foliage was destroyed. If, however, the virus had not already been in this country, it could have been quite innocently spread. The best regulation of all is self-regulation and most gardeners do not want to propagate disease-ridden stock and will take steps to keep their plantings clean. In 1992 I travelled extensively through the United Kingdom and Europe. There did not seem to be any harsh or rigid quarantine regulations and yet I did not see any sign of mosaic virus in all my travels. I was particularly impressed with the health and cleanliness of the iris plantings seen in the United Kingdom and equally impressed with those in Italy. A further visit in 1995 confirmed my observations. In 1994 I travelled extensively in the USA and saw iris grown in several states. I did not see any evidence of mosaic virus in any planting. Again I have no doubt that mosaic virus is entrenched both in Europe and in the USA but iris growers have kept their plantings clean.

FUNGAL DISEASES

There are four main fungal diseases that can attack bearded iris. Known commonly as crown rot, botrytis, leaf spot and rust, these diseases can make plants most unattractive and a preventative spraying program with a fungicide such as mancozeb (or its commercial counterparts) is recommended to minimise these problems.

Crown rot (*Sclerotium rolfsii*) is observed in warm, wet weather as a yellowing of the leaf tips, rotting at the base of the foliage and possible rotting of the rhizome. It is most common in semi-tropical climates in the warmer, more humid weather and is a limiting factor in how far south iris can be grown successfully in the USA and how far north they can be grown in coastal Australia or northern New Zealand. Badly infected plants can be lifted, cleaned, treated with a suitable fungicide and replanted.

Botrytis (*Sclerotinia convoluta*) is observed as a black mould over the rhizome and roots, particularly in cool wet weather in early spring. Foliage remains dry and brown and does not grow, while the rhizomes experience a dry rot. This disease is more common in cooler areas and, while no cure is known, a preventative fungicide spraying program can only be beneficial.

Leaf spot (*Didymellina macrospora*) is the most common fungal disease and is observed as small circular spots which darken to yellow and brown and often enlarge. Severe infection can see the whole leaf become brown and unsightly and the leaf will usually die back from the tip. Although this disease is not fatal it is most unsightly, and much easier to prevent than to cure. The fungus spores live in the soil or on dead or previously infected leaves and the fungus becomes a problem in wet weather, particularly if it is humid as well. Overhead watering will also aggravate the problem as spores are splashed up onto the foliage. The disease is more or less universal and may attack at any time. Clean cultivation, the removal of spent foliage and debris from around the plant and a preventative spraying program with mancozeb give the best protection. If the disease is noticed, all the infected foliage should be cut back and burned and a preventative spraying of the foliage and surrounding soil administered to prevent further infection.

Rust (*Puccinia iridis, Puccinia sessilis*) is observed as rusty red-brown markings which may cover the entire leaf. It is common in times of high humidity and rain and can be encouraged by overhead watering. It has the same unsightly effect as leaf spot and all infected foliage should be removed and burned if it is observed. A preventative spraying with mancozeb gives good protection.

'First Movement' (Grosvenor, 1993)

'Cher' (Nelson, 1991)

'Flights of Fancy' (Keppel, 1993)

'Glenhaven' (Grosvenor, 1998)

'English Charm' (Blyth, 1989)

'First Interstate' (Schreiner, 1991)

'Jolt' (Weiler, 1988)

'Liaison' (Ghio, 1986)

BACTERIAL DISEASES

Leaf blight *(Xanthomonas tardicrescens)* is easily confused with leaf spot, but is even more unsightly with larger, darker and more irregular spots. It is not a common disease and is best controlled by clean cultivation and the removal and burning of any infected foliage should it be observed.

Soft rot — bacterial soft rot *(Erwinia carotovora)* is, by far, the worst disease affecting bearded iris. While normally not fatal it can, under certain circumstances, wipe out a whole iris clump. Soft rot starts where the fan leaf meets the rhizome and can be accompanied by yellowing of foliage and the death of the leaf fans. In advanced stages the rhizome becomes a spongy mass which gives off a foul odour.

Soft rot, which is quite common, is prevalent in wet and humid weather in spring, summer and autumn. Some cultivars are prone to the disease while others are never affected. The most often affected iris are the vigorous, sappy growers, so prevention is helped by keeping the nitrogen supply low.

In my experience, soft rot is brought on in the spring just before bloom and again in the summer months as a result of an oversupply of water after plants have been kept dry. One cannot control natural rainfall and there is little doubt that areas with heavy summer rainfall are less productive as iris growing areas than those with long, dry summers where the water supply can be controlled. Recent experiences suggest that bearded iris are not only more tolerant of far more summer watering than has been previously thought but, in fact, thrive on continuous summer watering. Consistent watering throughout the growing season has helped keep soft rot to a minimum in all but the worst affected cultivars. I am convinced that iris will perform far better in areas with long dry summers if they are grown in raised beds with drip irrigation and consistent (every second or third day) watering. As long as the water is allowed to run off the iris relish this additional water supply and remain virtually disease free. In more temperate, humid climates where there is the likelihood of heavy summer downpours the iris seem to benefit from being grown more dry. As already stated, one can only advise from personal experience and the experience of others and it is for gardeners to study the climates in which they live and, from their own experience, develop the best gardening habits.

Cure of soft rot is difficult and there are many suggestions as to chemical treatment of infected rhizomes. Once soft rot is noticed, the infected plant should be scraped dry and left to further dry out in the sun. Even more drastic care can be taken by lifting the plant, scraping dry and then replanting after it has dried out. This is usually unnecessary. There are reports of growers limiting the effects of soft rot by treating infected plants with Condy's crystals, household bleach, sulphur or gypsum. While, no doubt, these growers have succeeded in arresting the problem by using these agents I am not convinced that they would have achieved anything less by merely removing the spongy part and keeping the rhizome dry. However, once again, it is a case of finding out and doing what works for you.

Plants infected with soft rot are most often growing vigorously when the disease is noticed. Even though the parent rhizome and its flowering spike can be lost there is usually sufficient increase to ensure the continuing propagation of the cultivar.

OTHER DISEASES

Pineappling is a mystery disease peculiar to the bearded iris. The rhizome becomes enlarged, the foliage stunted and pleated and flowering stems are either non-existent or very short and malformed. The rhizome often does not make increase and there is no known cure, nor, in fact, is there a known cause. As the problem is more prevalent in warmer, more humid climates, it is my opinion that it is a result of the iris not acclimatising. This opinion is supported by the fact that clumps can improve from one year to the next, but rarely deteriorate and that, at times, only one of several newly planted rhizomes is affected. The disease is usually noted in iris planted for the first time and coming from a colder climate to a warmer climate. In the last five years, I have experienced no problem with pineappling when planting iris in the colder Hillview climate and this lends support to my argument. However, it should be noted that in the last five years I have had no complaints from customers regarding pineappling and as the iris are being dug at Hillview and despatched to mostly warmer climates this does nothing to support my argument. Pineappling is not common and is best treated by removing the affected rhizome and replanting with new stock. Any reputable nurseryman will replace, free of charge, newly purchased stock so affected.

SCORCH

Scorch is an uncommon disease which is more prevalent in warmer areas. Leaves brown off from the tips and start to die off and roots also tend to die off. It can attack only one or a few rhizomes in a large planting and there is no known cure or preventative action that can be taken.

I have tried to describe the pests and diseases of bearded iris so that irisarians can enjoy their precious plants, take preventative action to ensure success and recognise, and if possible treat problems when they arise. Do not allow this discussion to contaminate any positive thinking because I stress again that iris are easy growing, hardy, resilient and forgiving plants with very few growing problems from either pests or diseases. They are less prone to disease and far more resilient than most plants. Normal care and maintenance will just about ensure trouble free iris growing.

Established clump ready for dividing

Lifting a clump

Dividing up an old clump

Divided plant ready to send out

Figure 8. Lifting and dividing

DIVIDING AND REPLANTING

The two major issues with dividing and replanting are 'when' and 'how'. Perhaps 'why' does become an issue in so far as the main purpose for dividing and replanting is that iris do become crowded after being grown in the same spot for some time, with a corresponding deterioration in flower quantity and quality and a corresponding deterioration in rhizome quality. Perhaps 'where' does become an issue in so far as it is not desirable to replant newly divided iris in their original position unless the soil has been improved and replenished. Many gardeners, limited by space, do have to replant in original positions. In that case the soil should be dug over and liberally fertilised with

'Feature Attraction' (Schreiner, 1994)

'Fancy Brass' (Schreiner, 1987)

'Marriage Vows' (Ghio, 1987)

'Hello Darkness' (Schreiner, 1992)

'Goldkist' (Black, 1993)

'Lullaby of Spring' (Schreiner, 1987)   'Instant Pleasure' (Gibson, 1985)   'Jelly Roll' (Gaulter, 1983)

'Lady Friend' (Ghio, 1981)

'God's Handiwork' (Ghio, 1990)

'Goddess' (Keppel, 1981)   'Gold Country' (Ghio, 1987)

superphosphate. The addition of compost or manure to be spread below the planting area can be beneficial if the dividing process is not performed too often. If compost or manure is used, ensure that there is an 8–10 cm cover of unmanured soil into which the rhizomes are set.

When to lift and divide covers two issues — how many years after the original planting and at what time of the year. Commercial growers like to divide and replant every year or every second year. This is primarily to ensure quality rhizomes to be sent to customers each season. The two biggest iris nurseries in the USA, in fact the two biggest in the world, have different policies. Schreiner's like to lift and divide each alternate year while Cooley's like to lift and divide annually. In Australia, the two biggest iris nurseries in the Southern Hemisphere also have different policies. Barry Blyth at Tempo Two grows his iris in light sandy soil and likes to divide annually and we at Rainbow Ridge, growing iris in much heavier soil, try to divide in alternate years.

For the home gardener, lifting and dividing can be a chore and most can obtain very good results by leaving iris undisturbed for a period of four years. As a general rule, a clump of bearded iris will reach its peak after three years. Extremely quick increasers and very vigorous growers can reach a peak after only two years while slower growers will obviously take longer. Some iris resent being moved and will not perform well in the first year after dividing or planting while others produce excellent results in their first year from newly planted rhizomes. Much of the pleasure in growing iris is getting to know your cultivars and coaxing the best results from them. Two TB irises — the garnet-red 'Lady Friend' and the white 'Wedding Vow' — produce their best show spikes on first-year-planted rhizomes. Both these iris are bred by Joe Ghio and he lifts and divides his iris every year. Is this coincidence?

Perhaps even more coincidental is that most of the Schreiner irises produce their best spikes on second or third year established clumps. For those who wish to show their iris it is a sound policy to get to know those that are good show irises and like to be replanted annually. Then a rhizome or two or more can be taken from the larger clump and reset each year for the sole purpose of obtaining show-quality spikes. When showing iris I observed this policy each year with 'Wedding Vow' and over a period of years won many grand champion awards with this iris.

How often do you lift and divide your iris clumps? From what I have experienced the home gardener can do this in anything from every two years to every five years. I do not advocate yearly lifting and I feel that five years is the very outside limit to leave iris undivided. Again I suggest that you, the gardener, develop your own policy from the experience that you gather. If you leave it too long the plants will 'tell' you by producing poorer quality blooms, but it is best to be one step ahead and not have to be 'told'. When growing iris

purely for the pleasure of it and with no commercial interest, I always liked to have at least two clumps of the 'better' iris going simultaneously. If space permits and you are an avid grower and shower of iris, I can thoroughly recommend this practice.

Having decided how many years you will leave your iris in the ground, the next important decision is at what time of the year should you lift and divide. Once again the answer is to find out what suits you best and, more importantly, what suits the iris best. The benefits and drawbacks of early, mid and late season planting have already been discussed, and I suggest that a similar pattern should be worked out for lifting and dividing. If your iris collection becomes large (as they tend to do) and time becomes a major consideration, I feel that planting should take precedence over lifting and dividing. This is particularly so if you get into the pattern of having two or more clumps going, as the timing for the clump to be lifted and divided becomes less critical. After all, we know that iris are hardy, easily grown, forgiving and resilient plants and dividing can be done at any time.

WHY LIFT?

If an iris fails in a particular part of the garden there is every possibility that moving it to another place in the garden will produce the desired results. This is a good enough reason to move an iris provided it has been given every chance to perform. There are many examples of iris which do spectacularly well in some gardens while performing dismally in other gardens in the same area. Fortunately, there are those universally great iris which perform well everywhere and these are the cultivars recommended for the beginner or the enthusiast who has room for only a few plants.

The most usual complaint heard from gardeners about their iris is 'they flowered well last year but they didn't flower this year'. This is often a result of the gardener's lack of knowledge of the growth cycle. Although there is no fixed rule, digging and replanting are essential parts of iris growing. Rhizomes must be grown to size before producing any spikes, let alone quality flowers on quality spikes, and rhizomes left in the ground to deteriorate in impoverished soil will not perform. Lifting, dividing and replanting is part of the rejuvenation process.

Because of the habit of growth of bearded iris, the best plants are to be found on the edge of the clump so when dividing select only the best and strongest rhizomes for replanting and discard the rest. Remember that once a bearded iris rhizome has flowered it puts its energy into the side shoots for the following year's bloom and will never flower again. There is no problem in the first or second year after planting, but in future years the clump extends radially with an increasingly large 'dead' centre. After three or more years there is little of value in the centre of a clump and any increases that are growing are inhibited by the spent rhizomes.

Having selected the best rhizomes trim back the foliage, leaving about 20 cm of growth, and then trim back the roots (if any are present) leaving up to 8 cm. Newly purchased plants will be prepared this way for you by the nursery. Your plants are now ready for planting and this procedure has already been discussed.

Remember that there are some cultivars which resent being moved, and these will often not flower in the first year after division. Nearly always these produce a large clump and spectacular bloom in the second year. Remember also that this problem can be overcome by taking one or more plants from the outside of the clump each year to ensure both continuous and quality bloom and satisfactory increase.

PLANTING FOR EFFECTIVE DISPLAY

Dwarf bearded iris should not be planted any closer than 15 cm apart and median iris no closer than 20 cm apart. Tall bearded iris are best planted 30–50 cm apart, but these are all guidelines. Much depends on how quick a display, how effective a display and how soon one is prepared to lift and divide as to how close plants should be set out.

Some gardeners want great masses of the same colour and for them rhizomes should be planted in bulk. This can be costly but very effective. Others want as great a range of colours and patterns as possible and so are happy to settle for one each of as many cultivars as possible. Care then needs to be taken to ensure that a pleasing garden effect is created. Some wish to coordinate colour groupings of three to five rhizomes of a variety of colours or patterns while others are so intoxicated by the beauty of the iris blooms that they care not how and where they are planted as long as they are fitted in or in many cases 'squeezed in'. It really doesn't matter which category you fall into as long as you can find the garden space to accommodate your plants and obtain sufficient money to finance what can become a very expensive hobby, fascination or obsession. Many enthusiasts do become collectors and iris are given their own particular garden or spot in the garden where each cultivar is grown and appreciated for its own beauty, without any consideration for its neighbours near or far. Again I must emphasise that gardening is for pleasure so you should do what you like. None of us should be above listening to and accepting advice, but ultimately it is your garden or your collection.

Recommended cultivars

With over 1500 new iris being registered each year and with tall bearded iris being in the majority of iris registered, it is easy to see what a daunting task it is to give recommendations. I have no doubt that, for a variety of reasons, many quality iris never reach the level of popularity that they deserve. I also have no doubt that many highly praised and well publicised iris do not live up to expectations. No grower, no matter how enthusiastic, can grow them all and, even if you could, you would find performance would fluctuate from year to year. However, to defend my position, I do try to grow a very wide range of iris from a variety of sources and I am only recommending cultivars that have proven themselves over a range of climates and a period of time, or those that show exceptional promise. I have tried to keep them in colour classes but with the ever-increasing diversity of patterns this has proven almost impossible. For those wishing to grow a few iris or starting a collection, this should then be of some help. For the experienced growers it will be merely a testing ground against their own observations and experiences.

WHITE

White has always been a very popular colour and there is a huge selection from which to choose, despite the fact that white iris have been overlooked by most hybridisers in the last 10 years and many of the newer releases are byproducts of other breeding campaigns. There are many subtle variations in 'white' with the availability of cool whites, warm whites, milky whites, creamy whites, and blue whites. Beard colours also have a major effect on the final appearance of the flowers and beards of white, shades of blue, shades of yellow, orange and tangerine through to red and bitoned and bicoloured beards all add to the great diversity.

Many irisarians are happy to have just one white iris and I am often asked to name the best available. It is difficult to explain that the best white iris early in the season could be well finished bloom by the time the best late flowering white iris comes into bloom and that several others will have reached perfection in the meantime.

'Skating Party' (Gaulter, 1983) has been my favourite white iris for many years. It is a pure white with a white beard, heavily ruffled and of very attractive form. The very strong spikes carry eight to ten blooms which open nicely in sequence for an extended period, making this iris ideal in the garden and on the show bench. Health and vigour are both excellent and 'Skating Party' will produce a large clump in two years from a single rhizome. It moves easily and establishes quickly and I have found it admirable in a variety of climates. The tall spikes, reaching 90–100 cm, are in bloom mid to late season and are able to withstand all but the worst weather. I have observed 'Skating Party' over many years and it never performs badly, even in less than perfect seasons. Its breeding is ('Portrait of Larrie' x 'Carriage Trade') x a sibling.

'Leda's Lover' (Hager, 1980) is a very heavily ruffled creamy white with lemon beards. The form is distinctive and most appealing to those who like ruffled blooms. Spikes reach 95–100 cm in height,

'He Man' (Blyth, 1988)

'Indian Caper' (Brown, 1989)

'Hilltop View' (Gaulter, 1990)

'Lord Olivier' (Grosvenor, 1993)

'Hot Streak' (Ghio, 1988)

'Liqueur Creme' (Blyth, 1989)

'High Roller' (Grosvenor, 1998)

'Honkytonk Blues' (Schreiner, 1988)

are held well in all weather and produce about eight blooms in good sequence. The iris is healthy, vigorous and a quick increaser to give a nice clump in two years from planting. If divided every third year, 'Ledas Lover' is an excellent performer. Its breeding is 'Geometrics' sibling x 'Ice Sculpture'.

'Wedding Vow' (Ghio, 1972) has passed the test of time with honours. It is a snowy white with great purity of colour right through to the white beards. The form is broad and ruffled and 'Wedding Vow', although a little long in the falls by modern standards, is still an excellent iris for the garden or the show bench. Spikes reach 95–100 cm and carry six buds which sequence nicely, but will often open three simultaneously to provide perfect show spikes early in the season. In the 1970s and 1980s I was able to exhibit 'Wedding Vow' and win grand champion at the NSW Iris Championship in Sydney on no fewer than six occasions. 'Wedding Vow' is a very clean, healthy grower of excellent vigour and is quick to increase. It is also very fertile, sets pods easily, and is a tough iris in the garden, able to withstand most weather conditions with its thick, strong spikes. Because it is so adaptable to all climates and soil conditions, 'Wedding Vow' is an excellent iris for beginners. Complex breeding is ['Patricia Craig' x ('First Courtship' x 'Nina's Delight' sibling)] x ['Junior Prom' sibling x 'First Courtship')].

'White Lightning' (Gatty, 1974) is another classic and even earlier to bloom than 'Wedding Vow'. It is often one of the first to bloom in the season and for that reason may not be suitable for very cold areas which experience late frosts. Because of its ease of growth, 'White Lightning' is ideal for milder, more humid climates where other bearded iris may fail and for that reason it is recommended as an excellent iris for beginners. This iris is white with an inconspicuous yellow netting at the hafts and very bright cadmium yellow beards that light up the flower. Blooms are ruffled with closed standards and semi-flaring falls which will sometimes recurve slightly. The strong, well branched spikes carry about eight buds which sequence nicely. The spikes hold well and resist wind and rain. 'White Lightning' is an easy parent and when crossed with 'Georgia Girl' gave me the beautiful yellow 'Joan McClemens'. 'White Lightning' is classically bred from 'Launching Pad' x 'New Moon'.

'Fine China' (Gatty, 1986) is a quality crystalline white with a white beard, yellow in the throat. The form is globular and heavily ruffled and it flowers early to mid season. While its registered height is 90 cm, 'Fine China' flowers shorter than that for me and produces masses of flowers on well branched spikes. It is an easy, strong grower and has the bonus of a pronounced sweet fragrance. It is also very tolerant of bad weather as the spikes are strong. Its breeding is 'Social Whirl' x 'Dream Affair'.

'Pemcaw' (Harding, 1994) is an Australian-raised iris of excellent quality, being the winner of an Award of Merit and the ISA Medal. It is a pure white with a white beard, nicely formed and ruffled. It reaches 85–90 cm in height and the six to eight buds come on well branched, sturdy spikes. Its breeding is ('Mary Frances' x 'Crown Sterling') x 'Winter Olympics'.

'America's Cup' (McWhirter, 1988) is a pure white with a white beard. The blooms are nicely formed and produced eight to ten to the spike in mid season on spikes which reach over 100 cm in height. The flowers have a slight, sweet fragrance. Growth is excellent and increase is quick. This iris is no great improvement on its parent, 'Skating Party', but it only has to be as good to be outstanding. Its breeding is 'Skating Party' x 'Winterscape.'

'Break the Ice' (Grosvenor, 1996) has superb form with undulating ruffles and great width and balance which it has inherited from its great parent, 'Silverado'. Spikes reach over 100 cm in height and carry eight or more flowers well displayed and well sequenced to give a long flowering period. Only time will tell if this iris will achieve greatness, but all the indications are that it will be one of the best. It grows well, multiplies quickly and is robust in the garden. Its breeding is 'Silverado' x 'Scandia Delight'.

White iris with tangerine or red beards are plentiful enough, but most that are released are byproducts of pink or other breeding lines. Some make quite reasonable garden plants but are not at a level that would warrant recommendation. The best that I have grown is 'Wish Waltz' (Blyth, 1993), which has been consistently good for me. It is a pure white, well formed with ruffles and lace and tangerine red beards. It is well branched and carries about eight buds in mid to late season. The flowers have a spicy fragrance. Of particular interest is its bicolour parentage, being bred from 'Precious Moments' x 'Town Clown'. It should produce some fascinating seedlings with a wide range of partners.

'Lipstick Lies' (Blyth, 1985) is difficult to classify. It is a pure white, with rich, vibrant red beards and a few purple 'plicata' stitchings at the haft. The flowers are well formed and produced on easy growing plants with about eight buds to the spike. Of particular interest is the parentage, 'Ranee's Palace' x 'Touch of Bronze' neither of which have any plicata heritage. I prefer to think of this as a white with a red beard (and some haft markings) but no matter how you look at it, it is a classy iris well worth growing.

'Goldkist' (Black, 1993) is another of those white iris which aren't white iris and are very difficult to classify. The basic colour is pure white but with golden-yellow hafts around golden-yellow beards. To add to the colour pattern there are purple striations at the haft, much the same as in 'Lipstick Lies'. This presents a most beautiful and striking colour pattern which excited the judges at the 1995 Premio Firenze in Italy, where 'Goldkist' was a major award winner. I have had limited experience in growing this iris but it gives indication of being an adequate grower and as an iris of distinctive colour pattern is well worth trying. It is from complex breeding [('Coffee House' x 'Hombre') x ('Old Flame' x 'Instant Charm')] x ['Porcelain Ballet' x ('Tequila Sunrise' sibling x 'Entourage')].

BLUE

Blue is a colour much prized in the floral kingdom but lacking in so many families. One of the great joys of iris growing is the availability of flowers in so many shades of blue. Iris are available in the palest of blue shades, close to white, right through to rich dark navy blue and those blue-violet tones which present difficulty in classification. In recent years the paler blues have been over worked by hybridisers to such an extent that any iris in this colouration needs to be spectacular to merit attention — a problem amplified by the superb quality of iris in this class. I must confess to having a particular affection for blue iris so my list is possibly longer than is necessary.

LIGHT TO MID BLUE

'Silverado' (Schreiner, 1987) is my favourite of all the iris that I grow. I fell in love with a catalogue photo before I first saw this iris. Very often the reality does not match the expectation, but this is one case where it not only matched but surpassed all my expectations. 'Silverado' is a pale silvery-blue to blue-white of exquisite form. Near perfect balance between standards and falls is complemented by precise ruffling and matching beards. The flowers are large but not gross, and they come eight to the stem on thick heavy spikes which stand tall (about 100 cm) in all weather conditions. The branching is excellent and the flowers are produced in good sequence from mid season. Plant habits are exemplary with good foliage, good growth and rot-free rhizomes. 'Silverado' is an outstanding garden iris but an equally outstanding show iris. I can remember judging at the Oklahoma City Iris Show in 1994 where a spike of 'Silverado', exhibited by Perry Dyer, was Queen of the Show. I have walked along a row of 'Silverado' at our Hillview property and observed over 100 spikes, all of perfect or near perfect show quality. Its fame as a garden iris and a show bench iris is matched by its quality as a breeding iris where, both as pod and pollen parent, it has proven its worth by producing seedlings of excellence. 'Silverado' is

bred from ('Starina' x 'Navy Strut') x 'Carriage Trade' and this emphasises the value of 'Carriage Trade' as a parent, because it has also produced the outstanding white 'Skating Party'. Of even more interest is that both 'Starina' and 'Navy Strut', while nicely formed, were never good garden iris. After all the superlatives, what more can you ask? Well, for iris growers, just one more thing — an iris of the quality of 'Silverado' in each of the other colour categories.

'Portrait of Larrie' (Gaulter, 1979) remains a classic sky-blue, despite all the more recent introductions. It is a lightly ruffled mid sky blue with a lighter area on the haft and blue beards tipped white. It is the clarity of colour which most impresses with this iris and this, coupled with exemplary garden habits, produces an iris to be highly treasured. Strong spikes reaching 90 cm in height carry an average eight buds on well displayed branches. Health, vigour and good increase are hallmarks of this iris, which is bred from 'Sapphire Hills' x 'Mill Race'.

'Rapture in Blue' (Schreiner, 1990) is a personal favourite and one of the best of the more recent iris. It is a heavily ruffled light blue with a white beard and as an individual flower, a most attractive iris. Spikes reach 90 cm in height in mid season, but are variable for quality and bud count. In a clump there can be some spikes of show quality while others may be short in stature and low on bud count, but as a garden iris it presents a most appealing spectacle. 'Rapture in Blue' is an average to good grower and despite its shortcomings is well worth growing. It is bred from 'Sailor's Dance', 'Sapphire Hills', 'Tide's In' and seedlings.

'Altruist' (Schreiner, 1987) is a very subtle blue with some white that practically makes it bicoloured. The standards are flax blue with a white midrib and the falls flax blue with a chalky white centre and white beards. Blooms are ruffled, fluted and exquisitely formed. Spikes are of show quality with eight or more buds in sequence from early to mid season. Growth can be a little sparse and vigour and increase are average. I would doubt the performance of this iris in mild climates, but the lovely flowers are a real enticement. Breeding involves 'Victoria Falls', 'Tide's In' and a seedling.

'Victoria Falls' (Schreiner, 1977) is a fascinating iris which won the American Dykes Medal in 1984. It is light blue in colour with a white area in the falls around the white beards. Form is variable with some flowers appearing loose and floppy but it is usually well formed, tightly held, well substanced and ruffled. It blooms early and then throughout the season with one of the longest bloom periods of any iris. It will then regularly rebloom in the autumn and winter and invariably, on rebloom, the quality is

'Leda's Lover' (Hager, 1980)

'Latin Lark' (Blyth, 1988)

'Opportunity' (Keppel, 1990)

'Point Made' (Innerst, 1988)

Above: 'Jesse's Song' (Williamson, 1983)

'Portrait of Larrie' (Gaulter, 1979)

'Lillypilly Wine' (Blyth, 1987)

outstanding with beautifully ruffled blooms. Spikes are also variable but always high in bud count, from ten to 15 on a spike. Reblooming spikes are usually better than those produced in the main season. The main variation in the spikes comes in their strength — at times they will fall over in windy weather while at other times they stand firm and erect. At its best, 'Victoria Falls' is an outstanding iris, at its worst it is still as good or better than most iris in the garden. Growth habits are vigorous and increase is good, which befits an iris as abundant in flower production as this is. One of its great attributes is its versatility in that it will grow well in all climates. In fact, in milder climates it can be even more productive than in cooler climates. 'Victoria Falls' produces excellent show spikes and has proven a great parent for many excellent iris in blue shades. It is bred from a Schreiner seedling x 'Violet Favor'.

'Tinted Crystal' (Hager, 1988)—I have hesitated about this iris — whether to include it as a white or a blue, or not at all. The standards are white, tinted blue and more intense at the base, while the falls are white tinted blue and more intense at the hafts and throat. Beards are pale yellow and the overall garden effect is one of pale blue. It is a gorgeous iris of exquisite form and is a garden spectacle on perfectly branched and multibudded spikes, eight to nine flowers to a spike, but it has proven a slow grower for me. Plant growth is vigorous but it is slow to increase and, as it often reblooms in late autumn and winter, it is difficult to multiply. I have obtained some beautiful seedlings from this iris and can recommend it to those with good growing conditions and a little patience. It flowers from mid to late season and is bred from ('Scenario' x 'Pleasure Dome') x 'Ron'.

'Quintessence' (Hamner, 1990) is a lovely light to mid blue with a self beard and sweet fragrance. The blooms are nicely ruffled and very nicely formed and are produced from early to late in the season on spikes which are firm, well held and carry ten or more buds. I have found this iris to be a good grower, quick increaser and to have excellent garden habits. Despite numerous attempts I have not been able to set a pod on it but its pollen is fertile and it produces good seedlings. It is from interesting breeding — 'Bubbling Over' x 'Classic Profile'. 'Bubbling Over', its pod parent, is a beautiful iris but very inclined to rhizome rot, but I have had no problems with disease in 'Quintessence'.

'Just Magic' (Blyth, 1990) has icy blue standards and slightly paler falls close enough in colour to the standards to call this a blue self with a white beard. The form is ruffled and nicely balanced and the spikes, carrying seven or eight buds, appear early in the season and are produced over a long period.

Branching is very good and the plant habits are excellent. It is healthy, vigorous and a quick increaser. Breeding is 'Perfect Couple' x 'Pledge Allegiance'.

'Divine Duchess' (Blyth, 1990)—I can remember standing with Barry Blyth and John Taylor in Barry's seedling patch at Tempo Two Nursery when we first evaluated this iris as a seedling. My only comment was that I wished that I had not seen 'Silverado' before I saw 'Divine Duchess' because it spoiled a memorable experience. This iris is the same silvery blue colour as 'Silverado', but it has a white beard. It has beautiful form and is produced on show spikes up to 100 cm in height. Bloom is mid to late season and it is a strong, vigorous grower. It has proven a top award winner in Australia on the show bench and in garden trials, but it was born a few years too late. It is difficult to explain but, while 'Divine Duchess' is an outstanding iris, I like 'Silverado' just that little bit more. Breeding is 'Leda's Lover' x 'Morning Shadows'.

'Full Tide' (Brown, 1972) has been around for a long time but is still a very worthy iris. When first released, it was way ahead of its time and I still feel that it is one of the best iris not to have won a Dykes Medal. The blooms are large, wisteria blue in colour and are fluted and ruffled, with pale blue beards. Flowers are produced on excellent spikes, with ten to 12 buds. The spikes are strong, erect and are produced from early right through mid season. Health and vigour are good, increase is excellent and this iris has passed the test of time. It will often rebloom in late autumn to winter and is bred from 'Babbling Brook' x [('Lipstick' x 'Country Cuzzin') x 'Bright Cloud'].

MID-DARK BLUE

The next difficulty is where to draw the line between pale-mid blue and mid-dark blue. I am trying to sit on the fence by recommending an iris of my own hybridising as the lightest in colour of the mid-dark blue range.

'New Tune' (Grosvenor, 1996) has proven a delightful surprise as it is from a cross used only as a stepping stone to later goals. When it appeared it was too good to overlook and it has now been highly praised by Australian judges and seems destined for a bright future. It is a very wide and nicely ruffled mid-blue self with yellow beards tipped white. Light veining in the falls adds to its appeal. Blooms are produced from mid to late season on show spikes with wide candelabra branching holding up to ten blooms, perfectly placed and nicely sequenced. It is a sure winner on the show bench as well as for garden display. Health, vigour, increase and sturdiness are all excellent and this iris should be grown proudly for many years. It is bred from

'Silverado' x 'Skyblaze' and as 'Skyblaze' carries the tangerine-red beard factor and 'Silverado' does not, 'New Tune' does not exhibit red beards but now carries the factor to produce them in the next and subsequent generations. I am looking for a blue with a red beard and the form and growth habits of 'Silverado' and now feel that this can be achieved.

'Breakers' (Schreiner, 1986) is one of the great iris and has been an all-time favourite. It is a rich clear mid-blue self with a blue beard tipped yellow in the throat. The blooms are fluted, heavily ruffled and of impeccable form with beautiful balance between the standards and the falls. Flowering period is mid season right through to late, with spikes carrying eight to ten well spaced blooms in good sequence. The spikes are very strong, to 95 cm in height and will withstand bad weather. 'Breakers' is an excellent iris in the garden and on the show bench. It has also proven a good parent. I have observed 'Breakers' over several seasons and it always performs well, even in mild climates. I can confidently recommend this iris as the best garden performer in the true mid-blue colour range as it is so reliable, so healthy and so quick to increase. Its breeding is 'Victoria Falls' x ('Shipshape' x 'Sailor's Dance').

'Honky Tonk Blues' (Schreiner, 1988) has quickly become one of the established great iris, culminating in winning the American Dykes Medal. It is a distinctive iris with its hyacinth blue colour, grey-white streaking and edging on the falls and hyacinth-blue beard. The form is wide, ruffled and very attractive. With its healthy, purple-based foliage and unique flowers this is an iris that will not be mistaken for any other. 'Honky Tonk Blues' flowers mid season over an extended period and has tall, upright, strong spikes which reach 95 cm. I have nothing but praise for this outstanding iris which is of complex breeding, from 'Admiral Blue', 'Sailor's Dance', 'Neptune's Pool', a 'Royal Regency' sibling and Schreiner seedlings. Already 'Honky Tonk Blues' is proving a parent of quality.

'Riverboat Blues' (Schreiner, 1991) is another distinctive iris from the best breeding line in the iris world. It is a ruffled medium blue with a white beard and unusual fluted and undulating ruffled form. It is amazing how Schreiner's can continue to develop blue iris each of outstanding quality and each so distinctive. The tall spikes, to 100 cm, carry about eight buds. Breeding involves 'Memphis Blues', 'St Louis Blues' and Schreiner seedlings.

'Yaquina Blue' (Schreiner, 1992) has already established itself as an iris of quality and is recognised as one of the best Schreiner blues. The blooms are very ruffled mid-blue with yellow beards tipped white. Spikes are tall, well held and upright, reaching 95 cm in height. In my limited experience of growing this iris it has shown very desirable garden habits, as is evidenced further by it being judged the best blue iris at the 1995 Premio Firenze in Italy. Breeding is complex and involves 'Sailor's Dance', 'Sapphire Hills', 'Neptune's Pool', a 'Royal Regency' sibling and Schreiner seedlings.

'Scented Nutmeg' (Maryott, 1982) is worth growing for its outstanding nutmeg perfume alone but, as a flower, it is also most attractive with its deep lavender-blue colouration and ruffled form. Spikes carry six to seven blooms and are well held, reaching 90 cm in height, from mid season on. All its garden habits are good and increase is satisfactory. 'Scented Nutmeg' is bred from 'Full Tide' x 'President Farnsworth'.

'Navy Waves' (Black, 1984) is a true navy blue, a colour not found very often. It has blue beards tipped yellow and a slight sweet fragrance. Flowers are produced from mid season on strong spikes carrying seven flowers in good sequence. The iris is healthy and of average growth and vigour. It is worth growing for the rich colour and is bred from 'Waltzing Widow' x 'Navy Strut'.

'High Waters' (Blyth, 1989) is in that difficult-to-describe colour range between rich mid-blue and blue-violet. Flower form is attractive, ruffled and flared and it carries light blue beards. Blooms are provided over a long flowering period from early to mid season on 95 cm tall, well branched and strong spikes. Each spike will carry nine or ten blooms in good sequence. Health, vigour and increase are all excellent to make this an outstanding garden iris. Breeding is 'Perfect Couple' x 'Pledge Allegiance'.

'Blenheim Royal' (Schreiner, 1990) is another iris in rich mid to dark blue with a cream beard. Flowers are very well formed and of attractive balance between standards and falls. This iris has that extra something that sets it apart from others and, as seen at Schreiner's Gardens in Oregon in 1994, is an outstanding garden iris. This was verified by a similar performance at Hillview in 1995 where the tall, strong spikes carrying eight or more buds were in bloom from mid season for an extended period. All garden habits of 'Blenheim Royal' are excellent and it increases quickly. It is from complex breeding involving 'Sailor's Dance', 'Navy Strut', 'Full Tide', 'Master Touch', a 'Miriam Steel' sibling and Schreiner seedlings.

I hesitate to recommend any iris that I have not grown and flowered, but 'Rippling River' (Schreiner, 1995) cannot go without mention. As seen in Oregon it is the epitome of excellence for form and brings the 'Silverado' quality into the dark blues. I have imported this iris and while it has not yet bloomed for me it is growing quite well. 'Rippling River' is a very heavily

'Magharee' (Blyth, 1986)

'Many Thanks' (Gaulter, 1990)

'Exotic Dancer' (Mohr, 1987)

'Memphis Blues' (Schreiner, 1987)

'Mulled Wine' (Keppel, 1982)

'Northwest Pride' (Schreiner, 1993)

'Overjoyed' (Gatty, 1994)

'Mind Reader' (Keppel, 1994)

'Mystic Waters' (Mohr, 1983)

'Mountain Majesty' (Ghio, 1995)

'Notorious' (Ghio, 1991)

ruffled and perfectly formed navy blue self with blue beards. It has beautiful balance between standards and falls. I cannot report on height of spike and bud count, but its registered height is 91 cm. 'Rippling River' comes from breeding lines involving 'Land o' Lakes', 'Sailor's Dance', 'Pacific Panorama', 'Parisian Blue', 'Sapphire Hills', 'Neptune's Pool', 'Royal Regency', 'Jean Hoffmeister' and Schreiner seedlings and it will become a classic if it performs well in a variety of climates.

VIOLET-PURPLE

Violet-purple presents further difficulty in colour delineation and that which was a very backward class for quality iris just a few years back can now boast an array of outstanding iris.

'Dusky Challenger' (Schreiner, 1986) has set the standard for dark purple iris since its release. It is a heavily ruffled silky rich purple self with deep violet-black beards and the form is quite pleasing although the falls are a little long to have perfect balance with the beautiful closed standards. The flowers are huge and the overall effect is one of rich dark blue-purple with very little 'red' influence. Spikes are large, ramrod stiff and very strong to carry the huge flowers, eight or more to a spike, with ease. I have never seen this iris exhibit problems in bad weather. Bloom period is mid to late season and is extended over a long period. 'Dusky Challenger' will regularly open three perfectly spaced blooms simultaneously and is an outstanding show iris for those late shows. I have found 'Dusky Challenger' to be an above-average increaser, healthy and vigorous and, while I have heard reports that it is a doubtful performer in mild climates, this has not been my experience. To see 'Dusky Challenger' in Oregon was quite an experience, but none to match that of one spring morning at Hillview when I walked down to the fields in the crisp morning air to find a long row of 'Dusky Challenger' with over 100 spikes each having opened two or three huge flowers overnight. In many memorable iris experiences this probably ranks as my most exciting. Words cannot describe the scene on that magical day. 'Dusky Challenger' is from unknown parentage as seed became mixed and unlabelled but it is probably a seedling from 'Titan's Glory'. There is no great evidence of 'Dusky Challenger' being a quality parent but from a cross with 'Silverado' I was able to obtain quality seedlings which did not exhibit the rather elongated falls which 'Dusky Challenger' passes on to its progeny. 'Dusky Challenger' was awarded the American Dykes Medal in 1992 and has been top of the AIS popularity poll for a number of years.

'Titan's Glory' (Schreiner, 1981) is a rich purple self including the beard and is the winner of the American Dykes Medal in 1988. Flowers are large, ruffled and carried on excellent spikes with eight or more blooms in good sequence. Growth is strong but 'Titan's Glory' has never been a quick increaser. It is nevertheless an outstanding performer both in the garden and on the show bench where it has the advantage of flowering earlier than 'Dusky Challenger'. 'Titan's Glory' is bred from 'Navy Strut' x a Schreiner seedling involving 'Rococo', 'Prince Indigo' and more Schreiner seedlings.

'Temptone' (Grosvenor, 1994) What do you get when you cross two of Schreiner's Dykes Medal winners, 'Silverado' and 'Dusky Challenger'? The answer is the satisfaction of winning the Australian Dykes Medal in 1995 with one of the seedlings from the cross. 'Temptone' has been a hybridiser's dream as it is a rich dark purple from the red-purple side of the spectrum with delightful form, more compact and rounded than 'Dusky Challenger', but not quite of the quality of 'Silverado'. The flowers are very large and well ruffled with self beards. The spikes appear from mid season and are of outstanding quality. Flowers are held at five blooming points and this iris opens three or four large blooms, well spaced and displayed simultaneously with the greatest ease. These spikes reach 95 cm, are strong and hold well to make 'Temptone' an excellent garden and show iris. It really combines the attributes of its two great parents. Plant habits are excellent and increase is quick.

'Larry Gaulter' (Brown, 1988) carries a great name and is a worthy iris in rich dark violet colouring with beards tipped silvery white. The flowers are nicely formed, ruffled and well displayed eight to a stem on spikes that reach 90 cm in mid season. Growth, health and vigour are good and increase is quick. This iris is bred from 'Titan's Glory' x ('Night Hawk' x 'Grandmaster' sibling) and it has given me some very nice seedlings.

'Star Master' (Dunn, 1987) is a ruffled royal purple self with dark violet beards tipped yellow. Form is good and so are the quality spikes with seven to eight buds in midseason. Growth habits excellent. Bred from 'Blue Maxx' x 'Hilow' This is yet another quality dark purple.

'Indigo Princess' (Schreiner, 1992) is an iris that I fell in love with at first sight. It is a different shade of indigo violet and is an iris of distinction with yellow beards tipped blue. Blooms are ruffled and held on quality spikes, 100 cm in height, that appear mid to late season. Everything about this iris is quality, both for the garden and on the show bench where it opens three or four flowers simultaneously with ease. I predict that 'Indigo Princess' will be grown proudly for many years. It is bred from 'Breakers', 'St Louis Blues' and Schreiner seedlings.

'Holy Night' (Mohr, 1983) is a lightly ruffled and velvety deep violet-purple, very dark with deep purple beards. It has the distinction of being an early bloomer and an easy grower even in the mildest of climates where many of the darker ones do not perform well. The quality, strong spikes reach 90 cm and will hold up in all weather. They carry seven or eight blooms to the spike over a long flowering period and 'Holy Night' is a healthy, vigorous iris which increases well. It is bred from 'Dusky Dancer' x 'Royal Ballet' and my only hybridising efforts with it produced nothing of consequence.

'Mountain Majesty' (Ghio, 1995) is a deep purple self with a black sheen and violet beards that I first saw in Oregon in 1994. The heavily ruffled blooms are of near perfect form and while I have imported this iris and am growing it well, so far, I am unable to report on growth habits. It could be a great iris. Breeding is 'Peace and Harmony' x 'Darkside'.

BLACK

Black is very popular and there is no doubt that black iris are startling in the garden, particularly when used in conjunction with the lighter colours such as white, pale blue and yellow. Many of the black iris available have been of doubtful quality and, to me, of novelty value only until a recent set of developments in this difficult class.

'Hello Darkness' (Schreiner, 1992) has surpassed all previous iris in this colour class and cannot be recommended too highly. The colour is purple black, very dark with black beards. The form is lightly ruffled and the overall presentation is excellent. What sets 'Hello Darkness' apart is its willingness to grow and increase and its early bloom. Spikes are 95 cm tall, well branched and carry six or seven buds. They hold well in all weather. This iris created a sensation in Florence in 1995 and was particularly beautiful in Schreiner's gardens in Oregon in 1994. If popularity is a test of merit this iris will be an all-time great. It is bred from a Schreiner seedling, 'Titan's Glory' and 'Midnight Dancer'.

'Before the Storm' (Innerst, 1989) is another popular iris, even darker than 'Hello Darkness'. It is jet black with black beards tipped bronze and a slight fragrance. While 'Before the Storm' is the blackest iris available, it is only of average form with slight ruffling and a tendency for the falls to turn upwards at the edge but it does produce a startling effect in the garden. Spikes are produced mid to late season with six or seven buds that are well displayed. Growth is moderately vigorous and increase has been satisfactory. It breeding is 'Superstition' x 'Raven's Roost'.

'Witches Sabbath' (Maryott, 1986) has the distinct advantage of early bloom and, as it carries eight or more buds, it blooms well into mid season. Colour is very dark purple-black with strongly contrasting mustard-bronze beards. The form is ruffled but the blooms are only average in size and can, at times, be loose with open standards. It is nevertheless a stunning garden iris and, because of its excellent spikes, a very good show iris. I have won Grand Champion exhibit at the Sydney Show of the NSW Region of the ISA with 'Witches Sabbath'. Breeding is 'Waltzing Widow' x [('Prophecy' x 'Gypsy Belle') x 'Intuition'] and I know that Keith Keppel is using it in an attempt to obtain a black iris with a red beard.

'Night Ruler' (Schreiner, 1990) is probably not dark enough to be called black — it is really a very dark inky-purple with a black sheen and self beards. What sets it apart is the nice ruffling of the well formed blooms. Spikes are strong, reach 100 cm in height and carry seven to eight blooms while health, vigour and growth are good and increase is reasonable. This iris blooms mid season and has an complex pedigree involving 'Matinata', 'Navy Strut', 'Miriam Steel', 'Ermine Robe' and Schreiner seedlings involving 'Black Onyx', 'Tabu', 'Black Banner', 'Black Castle', 'Night Spot' and 'Prince Indigo'. It is a classic result of black x white breeding to put ruffles on black iris.

'Blackout' (Luihn, 1986) is a very popular silky black-violet with falls a shade darker than the standards and dark blue-black beards. The blooms are large, lightly ruffled but variable for form — at times being a little loose while most often being very acceptable. It has a slight sweet fragrance. Tall spikes reach 100 cm and carry six to seven buds. They are of moderate strength. 'Blackout' is a reasonable grower and is bred from 'By Night' x 'Navy Chant'.

ORCHID-LAVENDER

This is a difficult colour class to define, but it has been dominated by the releases of Larry Gaulter in the early 1970s through to 1980. Three in particular have become classics in their own right and I propose to discuss them together. They are 'Mary Frances' (Gaulter, 1973), 'Rondetta' (Gaulter, 1974) and 'Orchidarium' (Gaulter, 1980) all from the same line of breeding, all of outstanding quality and all in the blue-orchid-lavender tones. Sufficient to say that you cannot go wrong with any of these iris.

'Mary Frances' came first with its beautiful form and outstanding growth. It has a white beard touched yellow — 'Rondetta' has a tangerine beard and 'Orchidarium', a direct descendent of 'Mary Frances', a white beard and more fluted and ruffled form. They all bloom about mid season on spikes carrying seven or eight buds and reaching 90 cm in height. They are all excellent garden irises and, as garden irises, have not been surpassed, even though more recent releases will have wider, more ruffled form.

'Mandolin' (Ghio, 1977)

'Let's Dance' (Nelson, 1986)

'Pink Swan' (Gibson, 1984)

'Mystique' (Ghio, 1975)

'Paradise' (Gatty, 1980)

'Spring Image' (Hager, 1988) is a laced and fluted icy orchid self with a white beard. Flowers are wide and nicely formed and the somewhat shorter spikes, reaching 80 cm, display the flowers well. Garden habits and growth are quite good and this iris increases well. It is bred from 'Pleasure Dome' x 'Monaco'.

'Peace and Harmony' (Ghio, 1991) is a lavender-violet and difficult to classify. The wide, ruffled and well formed blooms have white beards and are borne on tall spikes reaching over 100 cm. As grown at Hillview, the spikes are strong and hold up well but I was disappointed to see the spikes virtually horizontal in what was perfect weather in Oregon. I find it hard to believe that this is typical and there was possibly some misadventure. This iris is potentially one of excellence and it is bred from 'Inaugural Ball' sibling x 'Silverado'.

BURGUNDY

Burgundy is a most attractive colour in iris, but there have been very few iris of quality available in this colour.

'Burgundy Bubbles' (Maryott, 1986) is a smooth rich burgundy with a self beard. The blooms are well ruffled and nicely formed. Spikes reach 90 cm, are strong and carry six or seven nicely positioned blooms from mid season. Growth, health and vigour are fine and increase is quick. This iris has a complex pedigree involving 'Seeing Red', 'Maroon Bells', 'Malaysia', 'San Jose', 'Commentary', 'Claudia Rene', 'Ponderosa', 'New Moon', 'Homecoming Queen' and a 'Louise Watts' sibling.

'Almaden' (Maryott, 1990) is a lightly ruffled dark maroon red with a self beard with a slight sweet fragrance. The blooms are attractive and carried on strong spikes which reach 90 cm and flower from mid season. There are usually seven blooms per spike. Growth, health and vigour are good and increase is very quick. Parentage is unknown but it is likely that 'Almaden' is from the same line of breeding as 'Burgundy Bubbles'.

RED

Red in the sense that we think of it as pillar box or fire engine red is a colour that is not, as yet, found in iris. There are quite a lot of iris which are loosely described as red but it is a class which, in general, has lacked vigour, been difficult to increase and carry over and particularly difficult to grow in milder climates.

'Lady Friend' (Ghio, 1981) approaches red from the dark pink side, being a garnet-rose or garnet-red in colour and quite distinctive with its self coloured beards. The flowers are large and of reasonable form. They are carried on excellent, strong spikes with about seven well spaced flowers that bloom early and then continue through the season. Spikes will reach 95 cm in height and are able to hold up well in all weather. 'Lady Friend' is a superb garden iris in every way. It is healthy, vigorous and quick to increase. It seems unperturbed by soil or climatic conditions and is an outstanding performer in mild climates. It also re-establishes very quickly and will perform very well on a first-year planting. It is an iris that seems never to fail even when treated quite harshly. 'Lady Friend' is from interesting breeding, 'Indian Territory' x 'Countryman' and although I know of others who have been able to achieve nice seedlings from it, I have been unable to obtain much of quality. When it was first released it was thought that 'Lady Friend' would open the door to a range of reds from the pink side, but this has not happened. 'Lady Friend' is an excellent show iris and has been champion at the NSW Region of the ISA show in Sydney.

'Mulled Wine' (Keppel, 1982) is described as raspberry-burgundy with apricot-beige undertones and terracotta beards. This iris is much the same colour as 'Lady Friend', slightly lighter, with a slight musk fragrance. I have never really liked the form when viewed close up but have difficulty in saying why. There is a looseness about it that defies description. However, the iris has been popular and flowers late in the season on 90 cm spikes which carry six to seven buds. It is healthy and above average for increase. 'Mulled Wine' is from complex breeding involving 'Amigo's Guitar', 'Rippling Waters', 'Gypsy Lullaby', 'Marquesan Skies', 'Babbling Brook', 'Salmon River', 'Maraschino' and a Jones seedling. 'Mulled Wine' has also failed to unlock the box of red-toned iris we await so eagerly.

'Warrior King' (Schreiner, 1984) has proven the best performer from a long line of Schreiner reds from what I will call the red-brown side. It is a velvety rich dark red with a self beard. The flower form is attractive and lightly ruffled while it carries about eight buds on well branched spikes reaching 85 cm from mid season. This iris is of reasonable vigour and healthy and increase is adequate to good. It is bred from Schreiner seedlings, 'Spartan', 'Vitafire' and 'War Lord'.

CERISE-MULBERRY-CLARET

Shades of pink to red that enjoy great popularity but don't fit easily into any category have not been common, but there are now some very classy iris available and these can be readily recommended.

'Aplomb' (Ghio, 1992) is a sensational iris and the best derivative from 'Lady Friend'. It is a mulberry-plum colour with deeper hafts and burnt-brick-red beards. The flower is very well formed with perfect balance between the standards and falls and a metallic sheen which really lights up the ruffled blooms. Branching is good and the strong spikes, which reach over 100 cm, carry the seven to eight blooms with ease from mid to late season. Plant habits are excellent and increase is quick. Breeding is [('Act of Love' x 'Lady Friend') x 'Caption'] x 'Stratagem'.

'Mulberry Punch' (Schreiner, 1992) is a richly coloured cerise-purple with claret overtones and blue-purple beards. Flower form is ruffled and flared and the most impressive blooms come on 95 cm spikes in mid to late season. These sturdy spikes are well able to carry the 12 to 14 blooms typical of this iris. Growth is adequate and so is increase, but this iris is very hard dormant (disappearing completely beneath the ground) from autumn so presents little of value as a garden specimen for half of the season. Its parentage is unknown, and it is a doubtful performer in mild climates.

'Loyalist' (Schreiner, 1986) is a rich claret-wine self with a cerise-claret beard. Flowers are well formed, ruffled and have an iridescent glow. This iris blooms from early to late on strong 90 cm spikes with six to seven blooms. It grows well and has average increase. Breeding involves 'Master Touch', 'Rondo' and a Schreiner seedling.

'Lady Marilyn' (Grosvenor, 1993) has proven too popular and was obviously released too early as I had insufficient stock to meet the demand and it was oversold. Fortunately it is a very good grower and will consequently be available again. Colour is a dark rose to cerise-red self with red beards. Flowers are of average form and lightly ruffled but have great carrying power in the garden. Strong spikes carry up to 12 buds and reach up to 100 cm in height early in the season. Health, growth and vigour are good and increase is excellent. Breeding is 'Mollie Savell' x 'Lady Friend'. It is the one good seedling that I have been able to grow from 'Lady Friend'.

BROWN

Brown is a colour that is not usually found in flowers but is quite common in iris. While lacking the popularity of some of the other colours, brown iris have a solid band of admirers, possibly because of the novelty. Colours range from tan through to rich dark brown but many iris in these colours have been difficult to grow and have had poor quality, 'skimpy' foliage, making them less than desirable as year-round garden subjects. Progress in their development has been slow as seed from brown lines has been notoriously difficult to germinate.

'Tobacco Land' (Powell, 1987) is in conflict with most that is written above in that it is very vigorous, has rich, lush foliage and is quick to increase. This is an excellent garden iris in dark tobacco brown with a darker patch below orange beards. Flowers are lightly ruffled and come early to mid season on 90 cm spikes, seven to a stem over a lengthy flowering period. This iris is bred from 'Financier' x 'Hash Marks'.

'Rancho Grande' (Ghio, 1988) has proven the best of the Ghio browns. This is slightly bitoned brown with mocha-brown standards and honey-mocha falls with honey beards. The form is full and ruffled with nice balance between the standards and the falls. Flowers are produced from early to mid season on 90 cm spikes with six or seven buds per spike. The flowers are well held and the spikes are strong. Foliage is quite good, and vigour, health and increase are above average. 'Rancho Grande' has an interesting pedigree from all yellow breeding lines [('Financier' x 'Temple Gold') x 'Speculator'] x 'Speculator'.

'Cafe Society' (Ghio, 1985) is a golden tan self with a tan beard. Flowers are nicely formed and gently ruffled. I find the colour very attractive. Spikes are good, carrying up to eight flowers to a height of 100 cm from early midseason to late. The foliage is 'skimpy' and does not present a good garden effect throughout the year, but it is adequate. Health is good and so is increase. 'Cafe Society' is bred from 'Toastmaster' sibling x 'Praline'.

'Praline' (Ghio, 1983) has always been a favourite flower of mine. The standards are a dark tan while the falls are a lighter creamy tan with tan beards. The nicely formed and gently ruffled flowers have an attractive glow to them. This iris flowers very early on 90 cm spikes which carry six or seven well spaced flowers. Spikes are of show quality and this iris has been Grand Champion at the NSW Region of the ISA show in Sydney. Foliage is fair, growth is fair and increase is good. Breeding is from 'Preface' x 'Norwegian Wood'.

'San Jose' (Ghio, 1976) is a doubtful starter in this class because of the violet wash over the tan falls which accompany the tan standards and tan beards. It is a most attractive colour combination and these well formed and gently ruffled blooms have stood the test of time. Spikes from early through to late reach 100 cm in height and carry six to seven buds. This iris grows well, increases well and has attractive foliage. It is bred from [('Ponderosa' x 'New Moon') x ('Tawny Mink' x 'New Moon')] x [('Ponderosa' x 'Travel On') x 'Peace Offering'].

'Rustler' (Keppel, 1988) is another doubtful starter in this class as it is really a bitone. The standards are antique golden-amber to rose-brown with the darker falls a

'Queen of Angels' (Schreiner, 1995)

'Quintessence' (Hamner, 1990)

'Proud Tradition' (Schreiner, 1990)

'Purple Pepper' (Nearpass, 1986)

'Polished Amber' (Gibson, 1984)

'Queen in Calico' (Gibson, 1980)

'Regal Affair' (Shoop, 1989)

'Perfect Couple' (Ghio, 1984)

'Radiant Energy' (Maryott, 1986)

'Rapture in Blue'
(Schreiner, 1990)

henna-brown paling to golden amber at the edge and gold beards tipped orange. The blooms are well formed and nicely ruffled and, no matter where it is classified, this is a beautiful iris and a personal favourite. Spikes appear mid season and carry seven or eight buds in good sequence. The spikes reach 95 cm in height and are strong and weather resistant. Garden habits are really top quality with growth, health and vigour to match the flower quality. Breeding is interesting, being 'Laredo' x 'Dazzling Gold' so it will breed plicatas. I have used 'Rustler' as a parent and obtained some gorgeous seedlings of quality.

'Copatonic' (Blyth, 1994) is a gorgeous flower in shades of brown but is really a bitone. The standards are russet brown, falls are plush ruby-brown edged the same colour as the standards and the beards bright mustard-yellow. Blooms are heavily ruffled and beautifully balanced. Spikes are obtained early to mid season, reach 85 cm in height and carry seven or eight buds. The growth and vigour are adequate as is the increase. 'Copatonic' is bred from 'Swain' x 'Rustler'.

ORANGE

Orange-coloured iris have only recently reached a high level and this has been accompanied by a great increase in popularity. I can remember despairing of ever being able to market orange-toned iris but, with the superb quality from the Ghio line now available, they are much in demand. Orange is a bright colour in the garden and will blend nicely with yellow and brown while being a most attractive contrast for blue and purple tones.

'Bogota' (Ghio, 1990) has set a standard of excellence with very early flowering blooms of deep orange with red undertones and tangerine beards. Flowers are ruffled, of most attractive form and have the heavy substance so much lacking in earlier varieties. They are carried on superbly branched show spikes with eight or more buds, regularly opening three well spaced flowers at a time. These spikes are strong and withstand all weather conditions. Growth, health and vigour are excellent and 'Bogota' is a very good increaser. It is from complex breeding involving 'Creme de Creme', 'Financier', 'Ballet in Orange', 'Coffee House', 'Cafe Society', 'Guadalajara' and a 'Cinnamon' sibling.

'Santiago' (Ghio, 1989) dominates the late-flowering scene in orange iris just as 'Bogota' is outstanding in the early season. This iris is even darker than 'Bogota', a real red-orange with tangerine beards and is equally as well formed with even heavier ruffling. It matches 'Bogota' for performance in all other facets and is bred from a 'Stratagem' sibling x 'Guadalajara'.

'Hills District' (Grosvenor, 1995) will fill the bill for an orange-toned iris that flowers mid season. It is an interesting iris with orange standards, slightly lighter falls darkening at the edge to form a rim and red beards, but the overall effect is orange. The nicely ruffled blooms are of excellent form and are carried on well branched show spikes reaching 100 cm in height. There are usually eight or more buds to a spike and the spikes are very strong, enabling them to withstand all weather. Health, growth and vigour are all good as is increase. 'Hills District' has enjoyed great popularity in Australia because of its unique colour pattern and ease of culture. Its breeding is 'Samurai Silk' x 'Esmeralda'.

'Caracas' (Ghio, 1991) is from the same breeding as 'Bogota' but flowers a little later and continues through the season. It is also an iris of quality and performs very much in the same manner as 'Bogota'.

'Good Show' (Hager, 1988) is a heavily ruffled bright orange with a pink flush in the standards and deep tangerine beards. The flower form is good and while it is registered as reaching 88 cm in height, it grows shorter than that for me. Spikes are well branched with seven to eight buds in mid season. This iris grows and increases well. It is from complicated breeding involving 'Cinderella's Coach', 'Hayride', 'Norah', 'Thisbe', 'Glittering Amber', 'Picture Perfect', 'Fresno Calypso' and a Hager seedling.

'Fireside Glow' (Schreiner, 1988) has been grown by default as I originally overlooked it but obtained it as an extra. It is a lightly ruffled orange with an orange beard and great intensity of colour which makes it a beacon in the garden. The form is only average but it certainly compensates for that with a magnificent display of colour on excellent spikes which reach 90 cm with ease, are strong and well able to support the eight buds which occur early to mid season. 'Fireside Glow' is an excellent garden iris which increases quickly and it comes from interesting breeding, featuring 'Henry Shaw', 'Tufted Cloud', 'Son of Star', 'Dream Time' sibling and seedlings.

YELLOW

Yellow is such a vibrant colour in the garden and yellow is a very dominant colour in iris breeding, so it is not surprising that there are many yellow tall bearded iris available. What is surprising is how few are of excellent quality and so deserving of recommendation. I feel that this is primarily because most of the leading hybridisers have not pursued yellow lines in their breeding programs and so many of the more recent releases have been byproducts of other lines.

'Opportunity' (Keppel, 1990) is the outstanding yellow iris available. It is a rich dandelion-yellow and slightly bitoned as the falls are a little brighter and darker in colour. Beards are cadmium yellow and the blooms have a strong, sweet fragrance and lovely ruffled form. Spikes are huge, reaching 105–110 cm, but they are strong and well able to support the eight to ten buds which appear early to mid season. Growth, health and vigour are all good and increase is above average. This iris is bred from 'Orangerie' x 'Praline'.

'Bahloo' (Rita Caldwell, 1986) is an Australian-raised iris of great quality and was placed second at the Premio Firenze in Italy in 1987. The colour is a pure sulphur-yellow with a self beard deepening to orange in the throat. Flowers are ruffled and of attractive form. Flowering spikes are excellent and carry up to ten buds for a long flowering season from early right through to late. The spikes are strong enough to support the blooms in all weather conditions and they reach 90 cm in height. This iris is healthy, vigorous, a good grower, quick increaser and very consistent. It is one of the best garden irises available and has an interesting pedigree, involving plicata and bicolour lines. Its pedigree involves 'Caramba', 'Lilac Champagne', 'Sunset Snows', 'Campus Flirt', 'Barcelona', 'Outer Limits', 'Spanish Gift' and 'Solano'.

'Catalyst' (Keppel, 1980) is an excellent iris in bright clear yellow with yellow-orange beards. Blooms are ruffled and well formed. This iris is registered to reach 88 cm but it usually grows shorter for us and its well branched and multibudded spikes with eight to ten buds provide bloom over a long, extended season from early through mid season. Compact growth and a multitude of spikes ensure a colour spectacle in the garden. Catalyst is healthy, vigorous and generous to increase. It is bred from 'Generosity' and Keppel seedlings.

'Gold Country' (Ghio, 1987) has proven itself an outstanding iris in gold tones. It is a complete gold self including the beards and the large flowers are ruffled and well formed. This iris flowers early on tall spikes reaching 100 cm and the bud count is usually six or seven. In one disappointing season this iris carried only one bud in the top socket of many spikes, but this has not been typical of its performance. The spikes are strong and well able to support the large flowers. Growth, health, vigour and increase are all excellent. Its pedigree is ['Veneer' sibling x ('Capitation' x 'Coffee House')] x ('Lady Friend' sibling x 'Speculator').

'Lightning Bug' (Durrance, 1987) is a real favourite in soft luminous yellow. The well formed and nicely ruffled blooms are carried on strong stems with seven or eight buds. Spikes reach 85 cm in height in mid to late season and are both strong and weather resistant. Growth, health, vigour and increase are all good. 'Lightning Bug' is bred from 'Dream Affair' x 'New Moon' and is a worthy addition to any garden.

'Radiant Energy' (Maryott, 1986) has an outstanding flower of impeccable form and ruffling. It is a rich deep yellow colour with a self beard. As an individual flower it is close to the best but the spikes are very variable, sometimes carrying as few as four buds but often with six or seven. It is registered at 95 cm for height but rarely reaches that height for me. All its garden habits are good and it has rebloomed at Hillview in late autumn. 'Radiant Energy' is a good garden iris and its breeding is [('Shining Light' x 'Honey Rae') x ('Gypsy Belle' x 'Victorian Days')] x 'Hindenburg'.

'Dance Man' (Blyth, 1989) has the largest of flowers in the yellow class and they are a rich bright yellow with a lighter area around gold beards. The blooms are wide and nicely ruffled and are carried on strong, husky spikes to 95 cm in mid to late season. 'Dance Man' carries six to seven blooms and the plant is healthy, vigorous and of better than average increase. It is bred from 'Speculator' x 'Orangerie'.

'Black Hills Gold' (Brown, 1986) is slightly bitoned with lemon-yellow standards blushed pink and mimosa-yellow falls blushed tangerine on the shoulders and with a lighter area around tangerine beards. The blooms are ruffled, well formed and the colour effect is very attractive. The well branched spikes reach 95 cm and carry six to seven well spaced blooms from early to mid season. This iris is healthy and of average but not quick increase. It is very beautiful in the garden and is bred from 'Fresno Calypso' x 'Mandolin'.

CREAM

Cream is a colour much in demand but there are few quality tall bearded iris available in this sought-after area. Again it is difficult to classify where creamy white ends and cream begins, and where cream ends and lemon-yellow begins.

'Liqueur Creme' (Blyth, 1989) gives a very cream effect in the garden and is the best in its class. The standards are cream and the falls creamy white with a lemon edge and gold beards. The flowers are large, ruffled and very well formed. 'Liqueur Creme' produces seven to eight flowers on spikes which are strong and robust from mid season and reaching 95 cm or more. Foliage is superb, healthy, clean and vigorous with a purple base. Increase is quick. This iris is a landscape spectacle with great appeal throughout the year. It is particularly attractive at the bud stage and I thoroughly recommend it. Breeding is 'Easter Time' x ('Flare Up' x 'Gold Galore').

'Scented Bubbles' (Byers, 1988)

'Rustler' (Keppel, 1988)

'San Jose' (Ghio, 1976)

'Scented Nutmeg' (Maryott, 1982)

'Royal Honey' (Blyth, 1992)

'Rare Treat' (Schreiner, 1990)

'Rock Star' (Byers, 1991)

'Ruffled Feathers' (Innerst, 1990)

'Precious Moments' (Gatty, 1982) is really a reverse amoena with cream standards and creamy white falls, darker at the hafts with dandelion-yellow beards giving a very cream effect in the garden. Flower form is excellent with the ruffled blooms having great carrying power and appeal. Spikes are very good with excellent branching to display seven or more buds in good sequence from early to mid season and reaching 85 cm in height. 'Precious Moments' is bred from ['Heaven's Best' x ('Winter Olympics' x 'Azure Lace')] x 'Dream Affair'.

PINK

Pink is currently and has been for many years the most popular colour in bearded iris and it is easy to understand why this is so when you observe the large range of quality iris available in the many shades of pink. It seems that most hybridisers cannot resist the temptation to 'dabble in pink' and so we have a huge pool of iris from which to select. Many pink iris have been less than satisfactory garden subjects and many have proven quite difficult to grow, but there are now plenty of pink iris with admirable garden qualities.

'Social Event' (Keppel, 1991) is my pick as the best all round pink iris available. Keith Keppel describes it as buff-peach, Barry Blyth describes it as apricot pink yet for me it is a very clear light to mid pink with some peach overtones and a slightly lighter area beneath the flame-red beard. No matter how it is described it is a most beautiful iris which gives a very pink effect in the garden. The form of the flower is outstanding with beautiful balance between the standards and falls and heavily ruffled and laced petals of excellent substance. In quality of bloom it takes pink iris to new heights. Quality of spike is also excellent with seven to eight blooms mid season on strong 90 cm tall stems and a long bloom period. The spikes are firmly held and weather resistant. To complete the picture we have an iris that is healthy, grows well and increases quickly. Breeding is ('Maraschino' sibling x 'Thelma Rudolph') x 'Satin Siren' sibling.

'Beverly Sills' (Hager, 1979) remains one of the great iris of all time. It is a vibrant coral pink with a tangerine beard and is nicely ruffled and lightly laced. This is one iris which draws people from a distance and has proven to be most popular over many years. Spikes reach 90 cm in mid season and carry six, sometimes seven flowers, well held and well spaced. 'Beverly Sills' will often rebloom in early summer and, for us, is even more attractive on summer rebloom. Growth and health are good and increase is quick to establish nice clumps in two years. I first imported 'Beverly Sills' in 1980 and the rhizome did not grow; a further attempt in 1981 was equally futile but in

1982 the iris 'took off' and I can only think back on the thousands of rhizomes we have produced and the fact that I was on the point of discarding this iris but for the rave reviews it was receiving in the USA. There is no doubt now that those reviews were justified as 'Beverly Sills' is an outstanding garden iris which has won all the major awards including the American Dykes Medal in 1985 and the Italian Premio Firenze in 1981. This iris seems to grow well in all climates even though it does not make large rhizomes. Its breeding is 'Pink Pirouette' x 'Vanity'.

'Pink Belle' (Wood, 1984) is a lavishly ruffled and heavily laced pink with a tangerine pink beard. Form is a little narrow at the hafts but it gives a beautiful effect in the garden where it is a colour standout. Spikes reach 85 cm and carry six to seven buds that are well held and come into bloom early to mid season. The spikes are strong and firmly held and the general growth, vigour and increase are all good. Breeding is complex and involves 'New Frontier', 'Signature', 'Glendale', 'Pink Divinity', 'El Monsour', 'Christmas Time', 'Pink Sleigh' and a Wood seedling.

'Pink Swan' (Gibson, 1984) is a ruffled, fluted and lightly laced light to mid pink with a lighter area around red beards. Although a little long in the falls it is an attractive iris and was particularly beautiful as seen in Oregon in 1994. Spikes reach 90 cm and carry seven to eight buds from mid season. Growth and vigour are average, as is increase. 'Pink Swan' is bred from 'Playgirl' x 'Perfectly Clear'.

'Miss Jeanie' (Hamner, 1986) is a clear mid pink with a white spot on the falls and a red beard. Flowers are ruffled, of acceptable form and the garden display is beautiful. This iris is prolific and the well branched spikes from mid to late season reach 90 cm in height and carry six or seven buds. 'Miss Jeanie' is a thoroughly reliable and consistent iris that performs well in mild climates. It is healthy, vigorous and a good increaser. It is bred from 'Beauty Crown' x ('Party Parfait' x 'Melissa Sue').

'Vanity' (Hager, 1975) is a classic light pink with a darker tangerine pink beard which won the American Dykes Medal in 1982 and has been a long-time favourite. The flowers are well formed and lightly ruffled and the colour is oh so appealing. Spikes are strong and reach 90 cm, but usually carry only four to six large flowers. Compensation for the lack of flowers on each spike is provided by each rhizome often throwing two or three spikes to ensure a most attractive garden display. It is well documented that Ben Hager was reluctant to name and release this classic iris because of its lack of buds on each spike, but whereas it regularly produced only four buds for its hybridiser, I have found it more generous. Vanity is a great iris for beginners as it seems to tolerate acid soil and mild climates far better than other iris. It is easy growing, healthy, vigorous and a good increaser. Vanity is bred from 'Cherub Choir' x 'Pink Taffeta'.

'Presence' (Gatty, 1987) is probably the best all-round performer from a long line of pink iris bred by Joe Gatty. The Gatty pinks are superb flowers but often difficult to grow; this is not the case with 'Presence'. Colour is a mauve-toned light pink with a salmon beard shaded lilac at the tip. The well formed and ruffled flowers have a sweet musk fragrance. Spikes are well branched and carry eight buds from early to mid season. They reach 80 cm in height. Health and vigour are good and increase is satisfactory. 'Presence' is bred from 'Paradise' siblings crossed with 'Simply Pretty'.

'Ribands' (Grosvenor, 1994) is a lovely pink, slightly bitoned and bred from my apricot line. Standards are clear pink, falls have a lighter centre, apricot hafts and red beards. The blooms are ruffled and the overall effect is very pleasing. Spikes are strong, reach nearly 100 cm in height and come in early to mid season. Bud count is six and I only wish this iris carried one extra branch and two more buds. Growth and health are good, increase is above average. Breeding is 'Snow Cream' x 'First Movement'.

APRICOT-PEACH

Apricot-peach and associated colour tonings of pink are very popular in tall bearded iris and deservedly so. There are so many subtleties of colour that are variations, no matter how slight from true pink and each is attractive in its own way.

'Goddess' (Keppel, 1981) is one of the all-time great iris for subtlety and clarity of colour. Words cannot describe the effect that this iris had on me when I first saw it. Alas, it proved difficult to establish and it was several years before I was able to grow it to satisfaction. 'Goddess' is classified as a glaciata, or plicata recessive — a term reserved for iris from plicata breeding but showing no plicata markings. Glaciatas exhibit great clarity of colour. In 'Goddess' this colour is a pinkish cream giving a light peach effect, lighter in the centre of the falls and darker at the hafts which are a golden buff. Beards are pale cream with orange in the throat. Flowers have beautiful form and ruffling. Spikes are strong and carry the flowers well. Bloom is early and bud count is variable, as I have found from six to ten buds per spike but branching is good. As I write this in the second week of winter I have two spikes of 'Goddess' on my desk — one with large flowers six to the spike which has two branches, the other carrying ten flowers on a spike with four branches. Each is beautiful and 'Goddess' is, for me, a regular late autumn to winter rebloomer. Growth

and health are quite good and increase is very satisfactory. 'Goddess' is from very complex plicata breeding involving Keppel seedlings, 'Apricot Blaze', 'Irma Melrose', 'Tea Apron', 'Full Circle', 'Rococo', and 'Osage Buff'.

'First Movement' (Grosvenor, 1993) has been my most successful iris, winning the Australian Dykes Medal in 1992. It is a rich, bright apricot colour with a red beard and has wide form with very ruffled flowers. This iris has perhaps been a little too successful as it quickly won awards, gained early entry into the Dykes Medal Trial Garden and was a winner on first eligibility — even before it was ready for release. Although the super-ruffled form and colour are standouts, the spikes are less than perfect, carrying only six or seven buds with branching that is variable — sometimes quite good and sometimes tight. 'First Movement' flowers early in the season and reaches 90 cm in height. Garden performance is very good with a great display of bloom throughout the season. Health and vigour are excellent and increase is very, very quick. This iris is bred from 'Preface' x 'Words and Music'.

'Words and Music' (Grosvenor, 1984) is a melon-apricot self with a green reverse around the middle of the falls and a red beard. The flowers are nicely ruffled and of very good form. The excellent spikes carrying eight to nine buds are produced mid season and reach 85 cm in height. This iris will often rebloom in the autumn. The branching on 'Words and Music' is excellent and it regularly produces show spikes. I have won grand champion exhibit with it at the NSW Region of the ISA show in Sydney. For all of its excellent performance, 'Words and Music' will probably be most remembered as the parent of 'First Movement', but it is a most worthy iris in its own right. Its breeding is 'Mandolin' x 'Metaphor'.

'Close Your Eyes' (Blyth, 1989) is an iris that deserves more attention than it has received. Colour is a creamy apricot-melon with an apricot beard. Form is wide and ruffled. Very tall spikes reach 110 cm and are quite capable of supporting the large flowers. Branching is variable — I have experienced seasons when this iris is top heavy with only six or seven buds on beautifully branched spikes. Although quality of spike has been variable this iris is very consistent in that it will flower well each season in all types of climates. It is healthy, vigorous and a good increaser. It is a sister seedling to 'Samurai Silk', a darker tone of apricot with all the desirable attributes, and breeding is 'Edna's Wish' x 'Orangerie'.

'Peach Bisque' (Maryott, 1987) is a heavily ruffled, creamy peach self with a tangerine beard. Flower form is very good and this iris has been very

'Sky Hooks' (Osborne, 1980)

'Shine on Wine' (Lesley Blyth, 1987)

'Sneezy' (Keppel, 1996)

'Social Event' (Keppel, 1991)

'Sombrero Way' (Schreiner, 1996)

'Sostenique' (Blyth, 1975) — winner of the Australasian
Dykes Medal

'Shiralee' (Blyth, 1988)

'Spanish Leather' (Schreiner, 1985)

popular. Well branched spikes reach 95–100 cm in height and carry seven to eight blooms from mid season. Growth, health, vigour and increase are good. Breeding involves 'Carved Cameo', 'Songster', 'Entourage', 'Homecoming Queen' and a 'Paris Original' sibling.

'Answered Prayers' (Keppel, 1994) is a new glaciata with 'Goddess' in its pedigree. The heavily ruffled and beautifully formed blooms have light pink standards, pinkish white falls deepening to pink edges, buff hafts and red beards tipped white. As seen in Oregon it was sensational and while I am growing it I have yet to be able to judge its overall performance. It is from very complex breeding involving Keppel seedlings, 'Classmate', 'Goddess', 'Joyride', 'Roundup', 'April Melody', 'Irma Melrose', 'Tea Apron', 'Full Circle', 'Rococo' and a 'Mistress' sibling.

BICOLOURS AND BITONES

Iris are classified as bicolour if the standards are a different colour to that of the falls and are bitoned if the standards and the falls are two shades of the same colour. To complicate (or simplify) the classification, depending on your outlook, those iris with white standards and falls of any other colour are called amoenas while those with blue standards and darker blue or purple falls are called neglectas. A new classification has evolved where the standards are coloured and falls white and these iris are called reverse amoenas. The variegata pattern has yellow standards and falls of a darker colour, red, brown, purple etc. There are so many colour combinations available now, the quality is so very good and each year new colour patterns become available to an eager public. Fancy-coloured iris are very popular and this popularity is increasing. In making recommendations I have found that I have had to prune my list, and there are many others well worth growing.

AMOENA

White standards, coloured falls

'Glistening Icicle' (Maryott, 1982) has white standards and smooth mid-blue falls. The blooms are well formed and heavily ruffled. Spikes are registered as 90 cm but it does not reach that height for me. They carry six to seven blooms from mid season. Growth, health and vigour are good and increase is very satisfactory. This iris is bred from 'Full Tide' x 'President Farnsworth'.

'Sierra Grande' (Schreiner, 1992) is a gorgeous flower with white standards, blue falls and light yellow beards tipped white. The blooms have excellent form and balance and heavy ruffling to set them apart from others. Spikes are tall, reaching 100 cm, carry seven to eight buds and come into flower mid season. Growth

is very strong but increase is only moderate. Breeding is 'Pledge Allegiance' x 'Glistening Icicle'.

'Ride the Wind (Schreiner, 1991) has white standards and blue falls lightening to a white edge. Beards are lemon tipped white. The gently ruffled blooms are well formed and produced in mid season on spikes reaching over 100 cm, but strong and well able to support the nine to ten blooms. Growth, health, vigour and increase are all good. Breeding involves Schreiner seedlings, 'Rococo', 'Margarita' and 'Pledge Allegiance'.

'Conjuration' (Byers, 1989) is not an amoena in the true sense as the white standards have a pale blue-violet edge while the falls are deep amethyst violet with a white central area surrounding white beards tipped tangerine with fuzzy white horns. This 'space age' iris is ruffled, has good form and gives a blue-violet amoena effect in the garden. Spikes reach 90 cm in mid to late season, are strong, well held and support the eight or more buds. Growth, health, vigour and increase are all good, as is the general garden effect of this beauty. Breeding is ('Skyhooks' x 'Condottiere') x 'Alpine Castle'.

'Alpine Journey' (Blyth, 1984) has long set the standard by which all yellow amoenas are judged. The snow-white standards sit atop golden-yellow falls with golden-yellow beards. Flower form is fair with blooms lightly ruffled. Colour clarity and definition are excellent as are the spikes, which are tall (to 100 cm), very well branched and carry ten or more blooms early in the season and extending right through to mid season. Garden habits are exemplary with plants showing excellent health, vigour, growth and increase. This is a great iris both in the garden and on the show bench and it is bred from 'Tranquil Star' x ('Love Chant' x 'Festive Skirt').

'Wings of Gold' (Maryott, 1991) is an outstanding iris with pure white standards with a pale lemon midrib and smooth bright golden-lemon falls adorned with lemon beards tipped white. The ruffled flowers have wide, flaring falls. Spikes reach 100 cm in height, appear mid season, are well branched with eight or more flowers. Growth, health and increase are good. Breeding is 'Alpine Journey' x ('Tranquil Star' x 'Frosted Buttercup').

'Amber Snow' (Blyth, 1987) is a true apricot amoena with pure white standards and rich apricot falls with tangerine beards. Flower form is very attractive and ruffled and flowers are obtained very early in the season on spikes reaching 90 cm, strong and firm. Branching is tight and spikes carry six to seven blooms, but garden effect is stunning. Growth, health and vigour are good while increase is superb with often ten or more increase on each rhizome.

This is an outstanding garden iris bred from 'Alpine Journey' x 'Beach Girl'.

'Aztec Burst' (Blyth, 1993) takes the apricot amoena line to new heights for overall quality. Standards are white, falls are apricot to light orange, beards are apricot-tangerine. The quality, ruffled flowers are nicely displayed on show-quality spikes, very early in the season. Strong spikes reach 100 cm in height and carry eight to nine buds. This iris is one of excellent quality as the growth, health and increase are all superb. It is from complex breeding, involving 'Alpine Journey', 'Beach Girl', 'Tranquil Star', 'Coral Strand', 'Persian Smoke', 'Chimbolam' and 'Chocolate Vanilla'.

'Fondation van Gogh' (Anfosso, 1990) When is a typical Blyth iris not a Blyth iris? Answer, when it is bred in France but from the Blyth line of breeding. This iris has creamy white standards lightly flushed apricot, apricot falls with a creamy border and pink-orange beards. Well branched and multibudded spikes reach 90 cm in height and flower mid season. This iris is healthy, grows well and increases quickly. Breeding is ('Snowline' x 'Snow Peach') x 'Magic Man'.

'Mind's Eye' (Blyth, 1994) has pure white standards, peachy apricot falls edged white and bright red beards. With its ruffled and laced form and wide petals it is a garden standout. It blooms early to mid season with seven to eight buds on variably branched spikes reaching 85 cm in height. Growth, health and increase are good. Breeding involves 'Lover's Lane', 'So Rare', 'Ringo', 'Color Bash' and 'Town Clown'.

NEGLECTA

Blue standards, darker falls

'Mystique' (Ghio, 1975) won the American Dykes Medal for Joe Ghio in 1980 and has long set the standard for neglectas with its beautiful colour contrast and majestic form. Light blue standards have a deep purple flush at the midribs and the wide, deep blue-purple falls are nicely ruffled. The whole flower has a brilliant metallic sheen which sets it apart form all others and gives it a 'mystique' that none can match. Well branched spikes from early to mid season carry seven to eight buds, to 90 cm in height. Growth, health, vigour and increase are all good. 'Mystique' is from involved Ghio line-bred seedlings and has proven one of the great iris parents.

'In Town' (Blyth, 1988) has blue-tinted lavender standards, slightly deeper at the midribs while the falls are velvety blue-purple with a distinct lavender edge and tangerine-red beards. Blooms are nicely ruffled and of average to good form. Bloom is early

to mid season on 95 cm spikes, strong and able to withstand bad weather. These spikes carry eight or more blooms and 'In Town' puts on a lovely display in the garden. Growth, health and vigour are good and increase is quick. Breeding is 'Tomorrow's Child' x 'Magic Man', a cross which also provided Barry with 'Moomba', 'Witch's Wand', 'London Lord' and 'Pass the Wine'.

'Blues Brothers' (Lesley Blyth, 1989) has light blue standards, mid-blue falls and blue-white beards. Form is wide and ruffled with the rounded falls being very flared. Garden effect is very beautiful. Bloom is early through to mid season on well branched spikes reaching 85 cm. Bud count is high with up to ten or more buds. Unfortunately there can be too many buds with a spur producing blooms which often gives a crowded effect at the top of the spike, but this is a minor and easily forgiven fault. 'Blues Brothers' is a personal favourite in the neglecta pattern with excellent garden habits, health and increase. Breeding is 'Song of Norway' x ('Copy Cat' x 'Mystique').

'Revolution' (Anfosso, 1989) is very close to the red, white and blue colour pattern which has an attraction for hybridisers all over the world. Standards are blue-white, falls are blue and beards are tangerine to give a startling effect. Blooms are ruffled, well formed and on strong 90 cm spikes in early to mid season. With eight or more blooms to the spike and excellent growth, health and increase, 'Revolution' makes a beautiful garden iris. It is bred from seedlings involving 'Flamingo Blues', 'Caro Nome', 'Actress' and 'Wedding Vow'.

'Mystic Waters' (Mohr, 1983) is registered as an amoena but for us is a pale neglecta with blue-white standards, blue falls and yellow beards. Form is wide, ruffled and most attractive. Spikes are excellent with eight buds mid season and reaching 85 cm. Garden effect is lovely and it has produced some beautiful seedlings. Breeding is 'Boardwalk' x 'Sea of Galilee'.

'Royal Crusader' (Schreiner, 1985) has huge flowers with icy-blue standards, deep blue falls and white beards tinted light blue. Flowers are ruffled and, at times, somewhat loosely formed but present a garden spectacle. Strong spikes, and they need to be to hold the huge blooms, reach 90 cm in height and flowers, up to seven or eight to a spike, are evident in early and mid season. All garden habits of 'Royal Crusader' are good and it increases quite well. Breeding is [('Blue Chiffon' sibling x 'Music Maker') x 'Study in Black'] x 'Pledge Allegiance'.

'Proud Tradition' (Schreiner, 1990) has the best form of the neglectas available. It is a wide, ruffled and well balanced flower with light blue standards, mid-blue

'Spiced Cider' (Sexton–Black, 1989)

'Skating Party' (Gaulter, 1983)   'Stolen Dream' (Hager, 1990)

'Silverado' (Schreiner, 1987)

'Snowbrook' (Keppel, 1986)

'Sierra Grande' (Schreiner, 1992)

'Speculator' (Ghio, 1983)

falls and blue beards tipped yellow. Excellent spikes carry eight or more blooms in early to mid season and reach 90 cm in height. Health is good, vigour is fair and increase is only average. Breeding involves 'Royal Crusader', 'Navy Strut' and a Schreiner seedling.

'Azure Angel' (Grosvenor, 1994) is a most worthy iris of lovely ruffled form with light blue standards flushed violet at the midribs and dark blue falls rimmed blue, and white beards. It is a distinctive flower on quality spikes with eight to nine buds early to mid season. Spikes reach 90 cm and are strong enough to withstand bad weather. Garden habits are excellent as is increase. Everything about this iris is quality, as you would expect from its predigree 'Silverado' x 'Snowbrook'.

REVERSE AMOENA

Blue or purple standards, white falls

'Perfect Couple' (Ghio, 1984) is well named as it is close to being a perfect garden iris and this is coupled with extensive rebloom in autumn and winter. Standards are mid blue, falls are white with a slight blue cast and beards are pale yellow. Blooms are well formed, lightly ruffled and come on tall 90 cm spikes, very strong and robust to support the seven or eight blooms early in the season. Rebloom is prolific and with flowers equally as good or better than main season bloom. Garden habits are great and increase is quick, as is needed to support such heavy rebloom. Breeding is ['Surf Rider' x ('Sea Venture' x 'Mystique')] x ['Crushed Velvet' x 'Intuition'].

'Olympiad' (Ghio, 1984) is difficult to classify. Standards are pale blue with a very large darker area in the centre to give a mid to dark blue effect. Falls are light blue with a mid-blue wash through the centre and light blue beards. Strong spikes to 100 cm in height come early through to late and carry the six to seven large blooms with ease. Garden habits and increase are both very good and the breeding is 'Bubbling Over' x 'Mary Frances'.

'Incantation' (Ghio, 1987) is probably the best of the Ghio reverse amoenas. Standards are light blue with a deeper flush at the midrib, falls are white and beards are light blue. Flower form is wide, ruffled and particularly attractive while spikes are strong, to 100 cm in height and carry seven or eight buds from early to late season. This iris grows and increases well and is quite healthy. Breeding involves 'Surf Rider', 'Sea Venture', 'Mystique', 'Crushed Velvet' and 'Intuition'.

'Wide Horizon' (Gatty, 1991) has very large flowers with light lavender-blue standards blended paler, white falls and blue-white beards, yellow at the tips.

Flowers are wide, lightly ruffled and carry a slight sweet fragrance. Strong spikes carry six or seven flowers early to late and reach 100 cm in height. Increase is good as is health and growth. Breeding is 'Royal Elegance' sibling x 'Little Much'.

'In Reverse' (Gatty, 1993) has fantastic colour contrast as seen in the Oregon gardens. Standards are rich mid to dark blue, falls are palest blue fading to white, beards are white to blue-white, yellow deep in the throat. Flowers are large, very nicely formed and a colour gem. While I grow this iris I am, as yet, unable to report on its performance but if it grows well in a variety of climates it will be a most popular iris. Breeding is 'Edge of Winter' x 'Swirling Seas'.

VARIEGATAS

Standards in shades of yellow, falls darker in shades of red, brown and purple

'All that Jazz' (Denney, 1982) is a true variegata with bright yellow standards, yellow beards and falls, which although registered as bright red, are red-brown in our garden. Flowers are well formed, lightly ruffled and give a pleasing garden effect. Spikes reach 90 cm and flower mid-season with seven buds nicely spaced. Growth, health and vigour are good and increase is quick. Breeding is 'World News' x 'Gypsy Caravan'.

'Shine on Wine' (Lesley Blyth, 1987) has honey-yellow standards and light red-brown falls with gold beards. Flowers are well formed and nicely ruffled while the 95 cm spikes carry seven to eight buds that bloom early to mid season. This is a quality garden iris with excellent plant habits and good increase. Breeding is 'Broadway' x 'Show Biz'.

'Supreme Sultan' (Schreiner, 1988) has simply huge flowers with great carrying power in the garden. Standards are indian yellow, falls are chrysanthemum crimson and beards are yellow. The enormous flowers are ruffled, slightly laced but appear, at times, to be loosely formed and lacking in substance although holding power is good. The strong spikes reach over 100 cm in height and hold the six to seven flowers with ease from mid to late season. This is a most attractive garden iris, strong, healthy and with average increase. It is bred from 'Gallant Moment' x 'Peking Summer' and is proving a good parent in its own right.

'Syncopation' (Gatty, 1984) has tan-gold standards and aconite violet to brown violet falls with old-gold beards. Flowers are nicely formed and lightly ruffled. Strong spikes, very well branched and reaching 100 cm in height, are registered as flowering mid season but bloom for us is always towards the end of the season. Garden habits and increase are very good. Parentage is 'Velvet Flame' x 'Show Biz'.

OTHER BICOLOURS

'Edith Wolford' (Hager, 1986) created a sensation with its blue and yellow colouration when first released and has retained its popularity, winning the American Dykes Medal in 1993. Standards are clear canary yellow, falls mid blue-violet with blue beards tipped orange and the blooms are ruffled and well formed. Spikes are registered as reaching 102 cm but they rarely exceed 90 cm for me. Bloom is mid season and the well branched spikes carry the eight buds with ease. 'Edith Wolford' has not proven consistent for me, having off seasons when it performs poorly, but in good years (most years) it is superb both as a garden and show iris. Growth, health and vigour are good as is increase. Breeding is 'Merry Madrigal' x 'Freedom Road'.

'Sweet Musette' (Schreiner, 1986) is one of the great irises with its light lavender-pink to flamingo-pink standards, warm rosy-pink falls and tangerine beards. Flowers are beautifully formed, ruffled and lightly laced giving a stunning effect in the garden. Blooms are produced mid to late season on strong spikes reaching 95 cm and carrying the eight buds with ease. This iris is a good, strong, healthy grower with above average increase. The involved breeding features Schreiner seedlings, 'Son of Star', 'Sandberry', 'Rippling Waters' and 'Dream Time'. 'Sweet Musette' is one of the very best garden irises, consistent in every way and a personal favourite.

'English Charm' (Blyth, 1989) has a stunning flower and is a spectacular garden iris. I can well remember the excitement when I saw this iris on maiden bloom and my enthusiasm for it has not waned. Creamy standards are veined lemon and the light but rich apricot falls are banded in cream and carry tangerine beards. Flowers are produced in mid season on 85 cm spikes which are a little tightly branched but carry the seven or eight buds with ease. Growth, health and vigour are good, increase is quick and there is reliable autumn rebloom. 'English Charm' is a great garden iris in most areas, but is not at its best in mild climates. Breeding is ('Love Chant' x 'Festive Skirt') x 'Cameo Wine' and I prefer it to the very popular sibling 'Magharee' (Blyth, 1986) which has white standards flushed pink and rose to orchid-pink falls. 'Magharee' is a very beautiful flower and comes on better spikes than 'English Charm', but its general garden performance, though adequate, is not as good.

'Champagne Elegance' (Niswonger, 1987) is a beautiful iris and my personal favourite from this talented hybridiser. Standards are pale lavender-pink, falls light buff-apricot and beards amber. The nicely formed and ruffled blooms give a delicate effect but they are strong and well substanced. Bloom is mid season on 85 cm spikes which carry the seven to eight buds with ease and a feature of this iris is its consistent and reliable rebloom in autumn. All its garden habits are good and increase is excellent. Breeding is [('Magnetic Isle' x 'Rhythm and Blues') x 'Snowlight'] x ['Coral Strand' x 'Peach Spot'].

'Heather Blush' (Hamner, 1977) has been one of the great garden iris and retains its popularity because of its consistently good performance. Standards are fuchsia-pink flushed violet, falls are amethyst-violet with a blue-violet flush when fresh and the beards are tangerine. Flowers are produced early to mid season on strong 90 cm spikes which support the eight or more buds well. Growth and health are good and increase is quick as befits an iris which is so generous in its autumn rebloom. Breeding is 'Touch of Envy' x ('Touche' x 'Misty Dawn') and this iris is a great garden performer, so satisfying to grow. 'Heather Blush' is a parent of 'Heather Cloud' (Hamner, 1981), an iris in similar but more clear-cut colouring. 'Heather Cloud' is an excellent performer but has lacked the popularity of its illustrious parent.

'Berry Sherbert' (Mohr, 1990) is a seedling from 'Heather Blush' — its breeding is 'Exotic Flare' x 'Heather Blush' — and it continues the colour pattern with blue-pink infused rose-violet standards, rose-violet falls and coral-orange beards. The nicely formed blooms are achieved early to mid season on 90 cm spikes. This is an excellent iris with good garden habits and hybridising potential. I prefer it to 'Berry Blush' (Hamner, 1988) which also continues the line, being bred from 'Persian Berry' x 'Heather Blush' and having pastel pink flowers with a violet influence and red beards. This iris flowers mid season on 85 cm spikes and is a very quick increaser and healthy grower.

'Planned Treasure' (Burger, 1985) has sensational colour with flesh-pink standards and white falls, washed orchid-purple halfway out and a wide orchid-purple band. Beards are tangerine and the well formed blooms are ruffled. Flowers are produced early to late on 85 cm spikes with seven blooms. Growth is not vigorous but increase is good. It is healthy but is a doubtful performer in mild climates. When grown well this is a beautiful iris. Breeding is 'Timely Treasure' x 'Dream Romance'.

'Latin Lark' (Blyth, 1988) presents a colour spectacle and is an iris with great popularity. Standards are buff-pink with a coral-pink influence, falls are light ruby-red edged in the standard colour and carrying tangerine-red beards. Blooms are well formed and ruffled and are carried on 90 cm spikes with six to

'Surf Lady' (Blyth, 1988)

'Supreme Sultan' (Schreiner, 1988)

'Success Story' (Ghio, 1987)

'Sweet Fortune' (Grosvenor, 1998)

'Spin Off' (Maryott, 1987)

'Spring Tidings' (Shoop, 1989)

eight buds from early to mid season. Growth, health and vigour are good, increase is above average. Breeding is ('Capricorn Cooler' x 'Anon') x 'Queen in Calico'.

'Liaison' (Ghio, 1986) is a very popular iris and deservedly so as it has spectacular colour and great garden effect. Standards are pink with peach-pink midribs, falls are deep velvety purple with a pronounced pink band and orange beards. Flowers are well formed, lightly ruffled and produced mid to late season on 90 cm spikes which carry seven buds. Growth, health and vigour are all excellent as is increase. This iris is bred from 'Ringo' x 'Magic Man' and is one of the most colourful garden irises.

'Honeymoon Suite' (Ghio, 1991) has pastel orchid-pink standards and darker orchid-pink falls with tangerine beards. Flower form is beautiful with heavily ruffled flowers of great substance. Spikes reach 90 cm and carry seven to eight flowers from mid to late season. Growth and health are good and increase is quick. This iris is bred from 'Newlywed' x ('Caption' x ['Dream Affair' x ('Artiste' x 'Tupelo Honey')]).

'Affaire' (Blyth, 1993) is a new colour combination with standards a blue-lavender to blue-grey colour, falls a greenish mustard tan and mustard beards. The mustard-tan colour is subdued but bright and the nicely ruffled flowers are well formed and large. Flowers are produced early to mid season on 90 cm spikes which are well branched and carry seven to eight blooms for a very impressive garden display. Breeding involves 'Alpine Journey', 'Beach Girl', 'Tranquil Star', 'Coral Strand', 'Persian Smoke', 'Chimbolam' and 'Behold a Lady'.

'Celebration Song' (Schreiner, 1993) has apricot-pink standards, blue-lavender falls and tangerine beards. The lightly ruffled flowers are produced in abundance from early to late on 95 cm spikes which carry up to ten blooms to present a garden spectacle. On early growing experience I feel this iris could be destined for a great future as it grows well, flowers well and increases quickly. Its breeding is 'Lullaby of Spring' x 'Frances Gaulter' and it won the Premio Firenze in Italy in 1996.

'Royal Honey' (Blyth, 1992) is one of my favourite irises of all time from Barry Blyth. Blooms have such appeal with creamy mango standards edged lemon and golden-mango falls with orange beards and an overall iridescence which is impossible to describe. Sufficient to say that these nicely ruffled flowers present a garden spectacle. Add to this a pronounced sweet fragrance, strong spikes that carry up to eight large flowers with an extended bloom season through early, mid and late season and you have an outstanding plant. Spikes reach 100 cm in height

and plant habits are excellent with health, vigour and increase that are all most satisfying. This iris is bred from 'Tango Bravo' and a seedling that involves 'Alpine Journey', 'Beach Girl', 'Tranquil Star', 'Coral Strand', 'Persian Smoke' and 'Chimbolam'.

'Cheerful One' (Hamner, 1989) is registered as a yellow with a white edge but for us it is a definite bitone or bicolour and one of the best iris we grow. In the bud stage it is the nicest iris I have yet seen and there is no disappointment when it opens. Standards are creamy yellow, darker in the centre to give a white and yellow infused effect. Falls are yellow with a white edge and the beards are also white tipped yellow. Blooms are well formed, ruffled and carried in abundance on spikes which though registered at 80 cm reach 100 cm or more for us. Bloom period is long, from early to mid season and even later. When I look at the registration I wonder if the hybridiser and I are talking about the same iris. This iris is bred from Hamner seedlings and has perfect garden habits and excellent increase. It is one of the really great iris and I cannot recommend it hightly enough.

PLICATA

Plicata is the name given to a pattern with a base colour, edged, dotted or stitched in another colour and the plicata pattern with all its variations is extremely popular. In recent times we have seen hybridisers extend the plicata pattern by having edges in two or more colours, by having differently coloured edges on the standards than on the falls and by having standards of solid colour with no edging and stitched falls. This latter pattern is called bicolour plicata or amoena plicata. With the wealth of gene pool there is little doubt that this pattern will be further extended, bound only by the imagination of the hybridiser. The classic plicata has been one of white ground colour with edging in shades of blue, violet or purple and this has remained the most popular pattern of all.

BLUE-PURPLE PLICATAS

'Rare Treat' (Schreiner, 1987) is top of the plicata popularity poll with its snow white ground, rich cornflower blue stitching on standards and falls and blue beards. The well formed, ruffled flowers have great clarity of colour and great carrying power in the garden. Flowers are obtained early to mid season on 85 cm spikes carrying eight buds with ease. Health, growth and vigour are good and increase is excellent. As a garden specimen it is top class and its breeding is 'Blue Staccato' x ('Quiet Times' x 'Socialite').

'Blue Staccato' (Gibson, 1977) has pure white ground lined, edged and speckled in rich royal blue. Beards are yellow tipped blue and the blooms are ruffled and well formed. Although well branched, the spikes of 'Blue Staccato' seem thin and wiry yet they support the seven to eight blooms easily enough. Spikes reach over 100 cm in height and produce blooms in early to mid season. I have always liked this iris but find the bud placement less than perfect. In spite of these faults it is recommended as a hardy, healthy variety with quick increase. Breeding is 'Indigo Rim' x ('Bold Overture' x 'Opening Night').

'Charmed Circle' (Keppel, 1969) is probably the oldest tall bearded iris I recommend and is not without its faults but what an advancement it was when first produced. Little wonder at Keith Keppel's excitement when he first saw it, as the well formed and ruffled blooms in pure white with a rich blue edge and blue beards have stood the test of time and retain their popularity. Although registered as 80–85 cm, spikes rarely reach that height and this results in a compact iris suitable for the front of any display. 'Charmed Circle' grows well, is healthy and of good increase. It is bred from ('Happy Meeting' x 'Rococo') x ('Full Circle' x 'Rococo'). 'Charmed Circle' has been judged grand champion at the Sydney Show of the ISA, NSW region.

'Going my Way' (Gibson, 1972) is another older iris but still worth its place in the garden. Pure white ground with wide, heavy purple bands and blue-tipped beards set this iris apart. Flower form is good with ruffles and nice balance. Bloom is in mid season on 90 cm spikes carrying seven to eight flowers with ease. Growth, health and vigour are good and increase is well above average. Breeding involves 'Dot and Dash', 'Rococo', 'Stepping Out' and a Gibson seedling.

'Jesse's Song' (Williamson, 1983) is one of the all-time great iris, an American Dykes Medal winner and a garden and show iris without peer. Base colour is white with the standards and falls stitched and dotted methyl-violet. Flower form is very attractive with wide ruffled blooms produced throughout the season from early to late on 90 cm or taller spikes that carry from ten to 12 quality blooms. 'Jesse's Song' is healthy, vigorous, and a very quick increaser to provide a garden spectacle in all climates where its versatility and consistency ensure success. On the show bench 'Jesse's Song' is superb and I have taken grand champion with it at the NSW Region of the ISA show in Sydney in a year when the two best spikes at the show were both of 'Jesse's Song'. Breeding is ('Charmed Circle' x 'Kiss') x ('Smoke Rings' x 'Decolletage') and I cannot recommend or praise this iris highly enough.

'Classic Look' (Schreiner, 1992) is the premier blue-on-white plicata available for quality of flower and all round performance and, in time, will be recognised as a great iris. Ground colour is white, stitching and edging are in mid blue and the beards are yellow tipped blue. Flower quality is superb with wide, ruffled blooms of excellent form carried on spikes which reach 90 cm or more in early and mid season. These spikes carry ten to 12 well spaced and well held blooms to provide a long bloom season. Garden performance is excellent all round, and increase is quick. This iris was a standout as seen in Oregon in 1994, in Italy at the Premio Firenze in 1995 and in the home garden at Hillview. Breeding is from a Schreiner seedling, 'Spinning Wheel' and 'Go Round'.

'Handshake' (Ghio, 1992) is a fancy plicata of great appeal that is already immensely popular. Standards are blue-white with a deeper flush around the midribs while the white falls have a deeper lavender-blue wash and stitching darkening even more around the hafts. Beards are yellow and flowers are beautifully formed and ruffled. They are produced very early in the season on 85 cm spikes which carry the seven to eight buds with ease. Growth, health, vigour and increase are all good. Breeding is 'God's Handiwork' x 'Snowbrook'.

'Zipper Stitch' and 'Talbingo Sky', two new plicatas bred by the author, will be released in 1998. These iris, together with 'Glenhaven', have attracted much attention as seedlings and have been withheld from release to build up sufficient stock for the anticipated demand. Breeding involves 'Daredevil' and 'Snowbrook', both of which have proven themselves outstanding parents with unlimited potential.

'Snowbrook' (Keppel, 1986) has pure white standards and white falls with a bright blue edge intensified at the hafts. Blooms are sweetly fragrant, have white beards, yellow in the throat and are most attractively formed with gorgeous ruffling. Spikes reach 90 cm in early to mid season and carry eight buds in beautifully branched and positioned show spikes. Growth is adequate, health is good and increase is fair. This is a delightful iris and is from complicated breeding involving 'Vaudeville' and a sibling, 'Montage', 'Charmed Circle', 'Charmed Life', 'Gene Wild', 'Majorette' and 'Rococo'.

'Acoma' (Magee, 1990) has a beautiful individual flower but spikes which carry only four or five buds. Standards are pale blue, falls are ivory with light violet plicata edging and some indiscriminate dotting. Beards are henna-brown and the nicely ruffled blooms are very attractive. The spikes, growth and increase are only barely adequate but, if you can forgive its faults, this is a beautiful iris. Breeding involves a Cook seedling, 'Claudia Rene', 'Orchid Brocade', 'After All', 'Moon River' and 'Capricious'.

'Titan's Glory' (Schreiner, 1977)

'Tiger Shark' (Maryott, 1986)

'Twice Thrilling' (Osborne, 1984)

'Sweet Musette' (Schreiner, 1986)

'Talbingo Sky' (Grosvenor, 1998)

'Tennessee Woman'
(Innerst, 1990)

FANCY PLICATAS

'Storyline' (Ghio, 1990) is a quality iris with an apricot base colour sanded and dotted rose pink with a tangerine beard. The flower form is wide and ruffled but what sets it apart is the very strong growth, excellent spikes and quick increase, all of which contribute to make it the best garden subject in this colour class. Bloom period is very early to early on 85 cm spikes which carry seven to eight buds. Breeding involves 'Goddess', 'Rancho Rose', 'Flare Up', 'Osage Buff', 'Vanity', 'Anon' and an 'Indiscreet' sibling.

'Secret Melody' (Schreiner, 1988) has apricot standards and apricot ground falls heavily stitched, raspberry red-purple and tangerine beards. Flowers are ruffled, well formed and are produced mid season on 90 cm spikes with seven flowers. Spikes are well branched and strong, growth is healthy and vigorous and increase is good. Breeding is 'Capricious' x 'Queen in Calico'.

'Cupid's Arrow' (Ghio, 1990) has pink standards and white falls with a strong orchid-purple edge and red beards. Well ruffled and attractively formed blooms come early to mid season on 95–100 cm spikes with seven to eight buds. The well branched spikes hold the flowers nicely and garden habits and increase are good. Breeding is 'Desert Fox' x ['Goddess' x {'Rancho Rose' x [('Flare Up' x 'Osage Buff') x ('Vanity' x 'Anon')]}].

'Power Surge' (Ghio, 1991) is well named, as you plant it and stand back while it takes off with instant growth — a real power surge. Standards are salmon-pink ground, heavily overlaid magenta to give a solid colour effect. Falls are salmon-apricot lined and edged magenta with red beards. Flower form is wide and ruffled and flowers are produced from early to late on very tall spikes, reaching over 100 cm in height. There are seven buds to the spike. Breeding involves 'Beyond', 'Flare Up', 'Osage Buff', 'Rancho Rose', 'Vanity', 'Anon' and siblings to 'Test Pattern' and 'Indiscreet'.

'Raspberry Fudge' (Keppel, 1989) has standards with a yellow ground almost completely covered with a suffusion of raspberry-tan to mauve. Falls are creamy yellow with a small white area near the white based beard tipped orange and a raspberry-purple edge and hafts. Form is rounded and ruffled and bloom is early to mid season on 90 cm spikes carrying seven buds. Health is good, growth and vigour are satisfactory and increase is fair. Breeding is 'Gigolo' x 'Columbia the Gem'.

'Faint Praise' (Keppel, 1992) is a very pale but attractive plicata. Standards are white with a pale lilac all-over suffusion. Falls are white with a pale pink-violet dotting around the hafts, and lilac-pink shading at the edges. Beards are white tipped orange. Blooms carry a pronounced sweet fragrance and are wide and nicely ruffled. Flowering period is early on 85 cm spikes with seven buds. Growth, health and increase are all good. Breeding is very complex and involves 'Pink Froth', 'Roundup', 'Osage Buff', 'Barcelona', 'Marquesan Skies', 'Babbling Brook', 'April Melody', 'Irma Melrose', 'Tea Apron', 'Full Circle', 'Rococo', 'Pink Taffeta', 'Pink Confetti' and seedlings.

'Roman Song' (Blyth, 1993) is a very pretty plicata with pastel-pink standards and white falls stitched rosy lavender with pastel-apricot beards. Flower form is good with ruffled blooms in flower early in the season on 90 cm spikes with seven buds. Growth, health, vigour and increase are good. Breeding is 'Just Delicious' x 'Shiralee'.

'Fancy Woman' (Keppel, 1995) could be the best of the fancy 'luminata' plicatas of Keith's. It has french lilac blended grey and tinted at the edge and base of the standards and falls blended and washed purple to french lilac with a narrow edge and paler veining and a white area around orange beards on a white base. Blooms are ruffled, well formed and produced very early to mid season on 95 cm spikes with eight buds. It is too early to discuss its overall garden performance but it may be more robust than 'Mind Reader' and 'Spirit World', which are others from this line of breeding which is very complex and involves 'Irma Melrose', 'Tea Apron', 'Full Circle', 'Rococo', 'April Melody', 'Joy Ride', 'Roundup', 'Mistress', 'Goddess', siblings to 'Peccadillo', 'Gigolo' and 'Rose Cloud'.

'Burst' (Blyth, 1993) has golden butterscotch standards and similarly coloured falls with a red infusion halfway down giving a burst of colour around the mustard-yellow beards. Blooms are wide, ruffled and appear early to mid season on 90 cm tall, well branched show quality spikes with eight buds. This is an excellent garden iris with robust growth, health and vigour. Increase is quick and it should perform well on the show bench. Breeding is 'Swain' x ('Mountain Melody' x 'Polished Amber').

ARILS AND ARILBREDS

The pure aril irises are characterised by an aril or collar, usually white in colour, on one end of the seed while arilbreds are hybrids obtained by crossing the pure aril species with other bearded irises, either species or hybrids. Most arilbreds have been obtained by crossing arils or part arils with hybrid tall bearded iris and in recent years a class of 'arilmeds' has been established by introducing dwarf bearded iris into breeding campaigns. Of the aril species, the more common belong to the oncocyclus and regelia groups.

Oncocyclus iris

Oncocyclus iris are native to the middle east, reaching north into Russia and south to the Mediterranean, where they grow mainly in arid areas without summer rain. They normally flower early in spring, go dormant during summer, and recommence growth in the autumn. Any summer moisture is likely to cause rhizome rot, although the plants need some moisture in the growing season. They obviously need special care to be grown successfully and, to many people, the work involved does not make their culture worthwhile. In most areas these iris need to be potted and the pot kept in a warm dry position during summer. After active autumn growth they once again require storage in cool dry conditions during winter. They need a sunny growing position and sharp drainage so ground or pot preparation is very important. Over a base of gravel or crushed rock a mixture of garden soil and coarse sand well sweetened with dolomite and well fertilised (preferably with eight to nine month slow release fertiliser) provides the best medium.

Growing oncocyclus iris is, to understate the case, difficult, but experimentation and persistence can be rewarded with spectacular results. The typical oncocyelus flower is borne singly on the spike and often looks disproportionate as the strongly recurved falls appear small by comparison with the large upright standards. The patterns and markings are unique in the iris world and most flowers carry large, spectacular signal patches.

It is probably accurate to say that these iris are only for enthusiasts or collectors who are: prepared to give them their cultural requirements; overloaded with patience and determination; resigned to failure in most of their endeavours; and who take the greatest of pleasure from minor successes. As these are virtues that I have only in minimal quantities I have left the growing of these iris in other, more capable hands.

There is still much debate about the classification of oncocyclus iris. Iris which have been given species status may be hybrids and many that have been listed in the literature are from a very limited location, of doubtful garden value and well nigh impossible to cultivate, even if they could be obtained. However, there are three oncocyclus iris which are worthy of special mention.

I. gatesii came originally from Iraq. It has an attractive and very large flower of green-grey with a network of inconspicuous pale violet veins and mustard beards. The styles are spotted purple and are arched and curved over the falls, which are adorned with a purple signal patch.

Flowers can reach 20 cm in diameter and flowering spikes are up to 60 cm tall.

I. paradoxa is found in Caucasia, Armenia and Iran. It is a dwarf growing iris with very large standards compared to the tiny falls. This iris has a violet base colour with darker veining and dark purple beards.

I. susiana (the Mourning Iris) is the best known and most often grown oncocyclus species. It is also the easiest to cultivate. Originally from Syria, *I. susiana* is the recommended starting point for those who wish to try these arils. Ground colour is cream, veined and dotted and stippled brown-purple with large dark purple signals and brown-black beards. Flowers are large — up to 15 cm — and the falls are typically rounded and recurved. There are several recorded colour forms of *I. susiana*.

Other oncocyclus species of importance are: *I. bismarckiana,* which has a variety of forms; *I. atrofusca,* a variable iris from Palestine; *I. lortetii,* a beautiful but difficult species from Lebanon which has pinkish standards, darker falls and red markings around the brown beard; *I. atropurpurea,* a dark red-purple with a green signal patch surrounded by black, native to Syria; *I. sofarana,* which could be a colour variation of *I. susiana;* and *I. barnumae,* a smaller iris variable in colour which has a yellow form known incorrectly as *I. urmiensis.*

Regelia iris

Regelia iris are native to Russia and Afghanistan and are closely related to oncocyclus iris. They have the same cultural requirements but are somewhat less demanding, although it must be stressed that they are still difficult to grow. The regelia iris do not make winter growth and this accounts for them being of easier cultivation than the winter-growing oncocyclus.

Blooms are smaller and much less intricately patterned than the oncocyclus iris. They also lack the ruffled petal edges.

These iris can be cultivated in warm, sunny positions and they must have perfect drainage to succeed. If grown outdoors, they should be covered in any areas where there is summer rainfall as they require a summer dormant period of at least three months.

I. korolkowii (the Pagoda Iris) is a native of Turkestan and is the most commonly grown regelia. Base colour is grey-cream with veining in various shades of brown. Beards and signal patch are red-brown to red-purple. Flowers are somewhat pointed with upright narrow standards and narrow pendent falls. There are several forms of *I. korolkowii,* some of which may be hybrids.

I. hoogiana comes from central Asia and has light blue to blue-violet flowers, self coloured and iridescent. There are no markings on the flower and the beard is gold. Standards are upright and waved while the falls are smaller than the standards, drooping and while wide at the hafts are pointed at the base. It is the easiest of the regelia iris to grow and, as such, is a

'Syncopation' (Gatty, 1984)

'Light Beam' (Lesley Blyth, 1985)

'Temptone' (Grosvenor, 1994) — winner of the
Australasian Dykes Medal

'Marbre Bleu'
(Cayeux, 1993)

recommended starting point. There are several different colour forms.

I. stolonifera is a native of Bokhara and Turkestan. It is variable in growth and this has led to synonyms *I. leichtlini* and *I. vaga* being used for this iris. These are both probably colour variants of the species. Standards and falls are waved and ruffled and the basic colour is a copper bronze with a blue metallic sheen. Other colour forms are lilac, shades of blue and purple. Beards are blue and this property alone has been of hybridising value in intercrossing the arils as the blue beard has been able to be established on the hybrids.

I. humilis (synonym *I. flavissima*) is of interest as it has the typical aril seed but is otherwise unlike the other regelias. It is found in Hungary, where it was known as *I. flavissima*, and in Siberia, where it was known as *I. arenaria*. Flowers are bright yellow with brown haft veining. This iris is dwarf growing and hybridises readily with the standard dwarf bearded iris.

I. bloudowii is another iris very similar to *I. humilis* but somewhat easier to grow.

Some other regelia iris of lesser interest are the greenish yellow *I. darwasica*, *I. falcifolia*, in yellow with purple spots and veins, and the violet-blue *I. heweri*. There are others which may be true species but are quite possibly variants of the above.

Pseudoregelia iris

Pseudoregelia iris form a small group of species from the Himalayas and central Asia. Their seeds have the typical aril and the species are typically dwarf growing and flower in shades of blue-lavender and violet with deeper-coloured blotches. Cultivation is difficult and they are really plants suitable only for specialists and, as such, have little garden value. Their needs are similar to those already discussed in the oncocyclus and regelia sections, although they do grow naturally in somewhat different conditions to the others.

I. hookeriana is a native of the Himalayas, Tibet and Kashmir at elevations from 3000 to 4000 metres. A dwarf iris, to 30 cm in height, it carries flowers that are relatively large, in shades of white, lilac, violet and purple with the falls heavily dotted in darker coloration. It is rarely found in cultivation.

I. kamaonensis is very similar to *I. hookeriana* and from the same region. Flowers are mallow-pink to lilac with dark purple veins and spots. Both these species are sweetly fragrant.

I. goniocarpa comes from China, Tibet and the Himalayas. It is a variable iris, slimmer flowered than the two previous species, narrower of foliage but with a taller scape, reaching 30 cm or more in height. Flowers are blue-violet to mallow-pink with darker spots and a white beard.

I. potaninii and *I. tigridia* are similar species formerly classified as regelias. *I. potaninii* is yellow in colour and

without fragrance while *I. tigridia* comes in shades of blue, yellow and purple and has a fragrance.

I. sikkimensis is given species status but is quite likely a hybrid between *I. kamaoensis* and *I. hookeriana*. Its flowers are violet with darker spots and a white beard.

Arilbred iris

Arilbred iris are hybrids obtained by intercrossing the aril species or by crossing the aril species with other bearded iris.

Crosses between oncocyclus and regelia iris were made with the obvious intention of retaining the beauty of the former while improving their garden value with the injection of the hardier regelia iris. There is no doubt that this has been achieved to a certain extent, but the offspring are still quite difficult to cultivate. They are demanding of a dry, dormant summer period and still require special attention.

Better results from a cultivation viewpoint were obtained by intercrossing these iris and the pure species oncocyclus and regelias with the bearded iris, usually the tall bearded. This new race of iris, called arilbred or oncobred, had its beginnings in the USA in the early 1920s. Blooms produced are large, rounded and subdued in colouration. They usually have a distinctive signal patch.

Many of the arilbred iris can be grown under normal garden conditions in suitable climates. They still require dry summers and many are not cold tolerant to the extent of the tall bearded iris. In recent years another new class, arilmeds, has been established by intercrossing the arilbred iris, and the original species with the dwarf bearded iris. These iris retain the dwarf to intermediate flower size and habit of growth and are, to a large extent, more cold hardy.

The main difficulty with the development of the arilbred iris is that the greater the injection of bearded iris 'blood' to improve garden performance, the further one gets from the beauty, unique colouration and form of the species, the oncocyclus species in particular.

Arilbred iris flower very early in spring and while their timing is in tune with the main bulb display, their particular cultural needs do not allow them to be used as companion plants in any but the most suitable of climates.

Summer rainfall is the major problem facing growers of arilbred iris and if they are grown in the open garden, good drainage is essential. They enjoy a rich soil which retains warmth and they often fail if winters are cold and wet. Many cultivars are susceptible to virus infection and fungus diseases in all but suitable climates. Enthusiasts in less than perfect climatic conditions grow their arilbreds in pots which can be covered to reduce natural watering and can also provide ideal conditions for the regular fertilising program required. Fertilising little and often will produce good results with the use of an all-purpose rose food desirable in late winter, after flowering in spring, in early summer and again in late summer. These iris all need extra lime or dolomite.

Arilbred iris have been further divided into two separate classes, depending on the amount of pure aril blood in them. Those with less than 50% aril are often referred to as Mohr type arils, so named as William Mohr was a pioneer hybridiser incorporating bearded iris and aril lines. Another pioneer hybridiser of arilbreds was Clarence White who worked the arils with diploid bearded iris to produce many beautiful aril-like hybrids. Many, in fact most, of this line of breeding proved infertile but they have remained as valuable garden plants. White also worked the arils with tetraploid tall beardeds and it is this line of breeding which has given us the basis of the modern fertile tetraploid arilbreds.

It is difficult to recommend arilbred cultivars as my own experience in growing them is limited and there is only slight interest shown by the gardening public in growing them. Enthusiasts will, no doubt, be able to contact specialist growers who will be able to help them both in selection and cultivation. My travels to the United Kingdom, Europe and USA revealed only limited interest in these iris and there were very few to be seen in public or private plantings. This should not stop enthusiasts from finding a reliable source and attempting to grow these exotic beauties. In Australia, Sam Fankhauser from Victoria has grown and hybridised arilbred iris for many years and he has some attractive hybrids, while Barry Blyth and his son Tim have dabbled in arilmeds in developing dwarf and median lines.

Recommended cultivars

ARILBREDS

'Ben David' (Fankhauser, 1989) 70 cm. Light lavender standards, lightly veined deeper lavender. Falls are buff, blended and washed lavender. Small brown signals below striking brown beards.

'Cool Oasis' (Hager, 1981) 80 cm. Standards are light lavender-violet; falls are mauve-purple. Small black signals below dark brown beards.

'Heart Stealer' (Peterson, 1976) 65 cm. Pink self with faint lavender overlay. Deep brown beards.

'Mehetabel' (Rich, 1984) 76 cm. Standards are dark purple; falls are red-black. Black-purple beards. Globular form.

'Sandy Dandy' (Danielson, 1983) 60 cm. Tan touched gold with a maroon signal. Dull gold beards tipped brown.

'Trophy' (Linse, 1958) 90 cm. An oncobred. Lobelia-blue self. Deeper blue beards.

ARILMEDS

'Naomi of Mara' (Fankhauser, 1989) 45 cm. Red-violet with brown beards.

'Nightlight' (Rich, 1975) 23 cm. Dark purple with near-white area on falls. Beards flax blue, orange in throat.

'Orb' (T. Blyth, 1988) 55 cm. Lilac with some deeper veining. Rosy-violet area around bluish bronze beards.

'Xillia' (T. Blyth, 1988) 55 cm. Standards are opalescent grey; falls are similar with a more pronounced chartreuse overlay. Gold beards.

'Wings of Gold' (Maryott, 1991)

'Winning Smile' (Ghio, 1992)

'Xanthippes Halo' (Niswonger, 1992)

'Victoria Falls' (Schreiner, 1977)

'Khyber Pass' (Kidd, 1983)

'Humohr' (Hager, 1981)

'Turkish Tangent' (Hager, 1984)

CHAPTER 2

BEARDLESS IRIS – APOGON IRIS

Most iris are grown from rhizomes and we can further divide the rhizomatous iris into subdivisions of (a) pogon iris — those with beards, (b) crested iris — those with crests, and (c) apogon iris — which carry neither beards nor crests, hence beardless iris. Nearly all beardless iris have some distinguishing feature, in place of the beard. This usually takes the form of a signal, a central stripe or blotch on the falls.

Within the beardless iris there exists great diversity in terms of size, height, form, growth and culture. There are iris which require cold, cool, warm and hot climates. There are iris which require dry and others wet conditions. There are iris which require acid soil and others which require alkaline soil. There are those which make magnificent specimens to over two metres in height while others are the daintiest of plants, primarily suitable for rock gardens and the like. There are those iris which demand full sun for good growth while others relish a shaded or semi-shaded position. Indeed there is a beardless iris of some type suitable for any position in any garden.

Emphasis will be on suitable garden plants with particular emphasis on those species and hybrids readily available in the trade. Mention will be made of those iris of particular significance or interest even if they are not readily available. With thousands of new cultivars being named each year, it is not possible to make reference to them all.

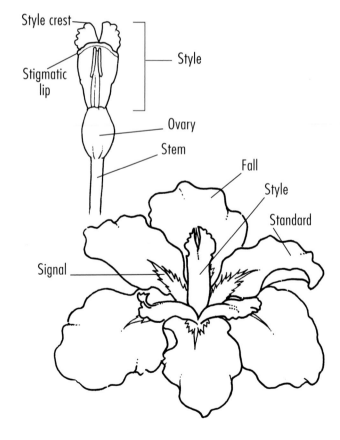

Figure 9. Louisiana iris flower. A typical beardless iris

The beardless iris that the average gardener and most ardent collectors are likely to grow fall into the following divisions — Siberian iris, Californian iris, Spuria iris, Louisiana iris and Japanese iris.

SIBERIAN IRIS

Siberian iris fall readily into two distinct groups, those with 28 chromosomes (2n=28) and those with 40 chromosomes (2n=40). The 28 chromosome group consists of two species, *I. sibirica* and *I. sanguinea* and hybrids derived from these species. It is this group that has been generally known and grown as Siberian iris. The iris in this group have become popular because they are tough, hardy perennials which are relatively easy to grow, with an ever increasing colour range. The 40 chromosome group is made up of eight species and hybrids derived from them. This group has been relatively neglected until recently.

28-chromosome species

I. sibirica is found in a wide, natural habitat through Europe and Asia where it naturalises in damp meadows. Plantings have been found throughout Germany, Czechoslovakia, Russia, Siberia, the Balkan States and into Asia Minor.

This iris is heavily dormant in winter and the thin, graceful, grassy foliage appears in early spring. It is a rich green in colour, erect and slightly arched at the tips. The flowers are held above the foliage on spikes that are variable in height but average 90–100 cm in good conditions. Flowers are blue-violet in colour, 8–10 cm across and there are up to five flowers to the spike. Bloom is in late spring.

Culture is reasonably easy if the climatic conditions are satisfactory. They prefer a generally cool climate but relish cold winters and damp but not wet soil. Soil should be slightly acidic. Planting is best done in late autumn but early spring planting is desirable in areas with very cold winters.

I. sanguinea is a native of Siberia, China, Korea and Japan. It is very similar to *I. sibirica,* but the spike is shorter and not as tall as the foliage, which is inclined to arch over. It carries no branches and only two flowers which are larger than those of *I. sibirica* and usually darker in colour, being dark blue-violet with some veining, although a white form also exists. *I. sanguinea* blooms earlier in the season than *I. sibirica,* but culture and growth are similar.

28-chromosome hybrids

I. sibirica and *I. sanguinea* will readily intercross. An excellent, and ever-increasing, range of named hybrids derived from these species is available to the gardening public through specialised nurseries. It is these hybrids that have become commonly known as 'Siberian Iris' and I wish to treat them in some detail as they have great garden appeal due to their flowering habits and vigorous growth.

One of the major achievements of the great amount of serious hybridising which has been done mainly in the United States, but also in the United Kingdom, Europe and to a lesser extent in Australia and New Zealand, is the very wide colour range that is now available. Flowers now come in white, cream, shades of yellow, all shades of violet and purple, those tending towards red and true bitones and bicolours. Much work is still to be done to make the pinks 'pinker', the reds 'redder' and the yellows 'yellower,' but the initial work has been done. Work has continued over the last 30 years on a new race of induced tetraploids and there are now exciting tetraploid hybrids on the market. As with most plants the tetraploids have larger flowers with better substance and improved foliage, and the doubling of the chromosomes has given the hybridisers the opportunity to develop a greater colour range. From the mid 1980s quite a few tetraploids have become available and now in the mid-1990s there are distinct breeding campaigns with both the diploid and tetraploid strains being worked on in the United States and Germany. Also of significance are the hybridising efforts from England, Australia and New Zealand, where the 1994 Australasian Dykes Medal was awarded to a Siberian iris 'Emma Ripeka', hybridised by Frances Love of Carterton, New Zealand.

With the increased work being done on hybridising Siberian iris has come improved quality in size, form, texture and substance of the blooms and greater diversity in plant habits. There are true miniature flowers of 7 cm or less diameter on miniaturised plants with spikes that range in height from 15 to 45 cm and hybrids with blooms over 13 cm in diameter on spikes over 120 cm in height. Size of flower and height of spike are dependent more on climate than on cultural practices and I have seen quite a few somewhat neglected Siberian iris thrive in the colder areas of Australia. The difference in the quality of bloom between Siberian iris seen in Oregon and those seen in California is amazing. These iris demand a cold winter for optimum performance but are somewhat forgiving, as many will bloom in more temperate climates but with flower size and height of spike greatly reduced. Personal experience is that Siberian iris will grow well and produce flowers in Dural, NSW, but the same iris are absolutely spectacular in the colder climate of our farm at Hillview, near Orange in central NSW. There are some notable exceptions. The older cultivars 'Caesar's Brother' and 'Marilyn Holmes' perform very well in the milder Dural climate.

The form of Siberian iris has changed in recent years with the development of hybrids with rounded, ruffled

'Creme Chantilly' (McEwen, 1981)

'Shaker's Prayer' (Warner, 1990)

'Frosty Rim' (Bush, 1979)

'Lady Vanessa' (Hollingworth, 1985)

petals and falls which flare horizontally. There is a place for these 'state of the art' beauties, but also a place for the traditionally formed iris. Increased substance has given the flowers a stiffness and starchiness not recognised in the species. Many of the newer hybrids lack the apparent fragility of the traditional varieties and hence, for some, lack the charm. I find the whole group attractive and one of the most attractive of all iris in the garden. Individually, they do not have a long bloom season but they do have the added bonus of the most attractive of foliage in the growing season.

Most Siberian iris will carry from three to five flowers on a spike, giving each spike a bloom period of seven to ten days in good weather. A continuity of spikes and the planting of early, mid-season and late bloomers will give an average bloom season of about a month. Recently developed reblooming Siberian iris have a habit of giving their rebloom only two to three weeks after the initial flourish and so, with a carefully chosen collection, the bloom season can be extended to some eight weeks. Siberian iris bloom with and towards the end of the tall bearded iris in the latter half of spring. There is occasional spot bloom in summer and this can extend into early autumn.

Culture of Siberian iris can only be described as easy. If they have any fault it is that, once established, they do resent being moved but to many gardeners this is not a fault. Newly planted Siberian iris will often take a season to re-establish and so they are plants for the patient gardener. Bloom in the first season after planting or replanting can not be guaranteed and even if the iris do bloom it will not be to their full potential. Bloom in the second season will be much better and will be further improved again in the third and subsequent seasons.

Opinions on planting or dividing clumps differ, with recommendations varying from immediately after the completion of bloom to early spring and most times in between. In the main planting of Siberian iris at Hillview, where we have cold winters with some frost but little snow and a hot, dry summer, I have found that autumn is the best time for planting or replanting.

The small, thin rhizomes should be planted 3 cm below the surface in soil that really does not need any special preparation. These iris will do well in soils with a pH range from 5 to 8, but seem to perform best in slightly acid to neutral soil with pH between 6 and 7. Planting is done by digging a hole to double the planting depth, making a central mound, placing the rhizomes on this mound and then spreading the roots over the mound.

Once the hole is filled, the newly planted rhizomes should be well watered in and then kept moist, but not sodden, until the new roots are established. In moving or planting Siberian iris, care needs to be exercised to ensure that the roots never dry out. Similar damage can be done by overwatering before the new white roots establish. As in most things, common sense and moderation are key words. Once established, Siberian iris are quite drought tolerant but they do thrive on being grown in a moist soil. A sunny, open position is desirable but I have grown Siberian iris very well in a semi-shaded position. Siberian iris are not bog or water plants so drainage is important. They should be planted in a situation where they will remain for several years as they form a mat of roots and are not easy to remove once established. They combine well with other perennials and annuals and look particularly fine when grown with Russell lupins as companion plants. They respond well to an organic mulch and seem to be indifferent to the type of mulch selected. I would strongly recommend mulching in areas where summers are hot and dry. There is the double advantage of maintaining the moist quality of the soil and keeping weeds to a minimum. Two warnings: if growing Siberian iris with Russell lupins remember that the Russell lupins resent the use of animal manures in the soil or as a mulch; be very careful with weed infestations of annual or perennial grasses with Siberian iris as the grass will intertwine with the thickly matted rhizomes and roots of an established clump, making it essential to lift and wash and possibly divide the iris with the resulting setback to its growth.

When dividing and replanting Siberian iris, I find it desirable to leave divisions reasonably large with several of the small rhizome intact. Replanting larger divisions seems to give the plants a much better start. Siberian iris are very easily raised from seed, which sets freely with natural pollination. If planting chance seedlings be aware that they will not be true to the parent although 'look alikes' are common. If setting out to develop new cultivars it is essential to take precautions to ensure that your desired cross is the one made. This can be done by covering the pod parent before and after pollination. Seed germinates readily and if natural pods are not removed before splitting there is every likelihood that 'rogue plants' will develop in your planting. Pods ripen in mid summer and should be harvested when they start to brown. Sowing of seed is a question of trial and error until an optimum time for your climate is obtained. In milder climates good results can be obtained by delaying sowing until mid autumn. Germination is quick and efficient and seedlings are often well under way before winter. If planted out in the following spring, bloom can be obtained in one year from planting.

Siberian iris are virtually untroubled by diseases and if the common pests of snails and slugs and those other nuisances such as wildlife native to your area are kept under control, an excellent display of bloom can be expected in late spring from established plants.

Recommended 28-chromosome cultivars

Giving recommendations is always chancy, as tastes will differ. Because of the somewhat limited colour range, Siberian iris are easier to list and recommend.

'Alter Ego' (Hager, 1982) grows to 85 cm and has stylish pale blue flowers, dark blue under the styles, cream signals and pencil lines radiating out on to the falls.

'Ann Dasch' (Varner, 1978) grows to 95 cm and exhibits a distinctive two-tone effect with its light blue-purple blooms edged darker blue-purple.

'Anniversary' (Brummitt, 1968) is a top award winner originally released in 1968. This wide, rounded white iris with a few yellow lines at the hafts has stood the test of time. It grows to 76 cm.

'Ausable River' (Cassebeer, 1969) is another older iris being first released in 1969. It is a lobelia blue bitone, heavily substanced and very reliable even in milder climates. It grows to 80 cm.

'Bellissima' (Warburton, 1986) is a gorgeous, ruffled white self with green signal lines and fringed style arms. Growing to 90 cm in height, this iris is a real favourite.

'Bernard Mclaughlin' (McEwen, 1985) is a special iris. Beautiful, rounded and lightly ruffled form and lovely creamy buds opening white present a spectacle in full bloom. Height is 85 cm.

'Butter and Sugar' (McEwen, 1977) is a top award winner in the USA and when first released was quite sensational as it is a true amoena with white standards and yellow falls. It grows to 70 cm and is a landscape delight.

'Caesar's Brother' (Morgan, pre–1930) is an old and reliable cultivar which reaches over 1 m in height. The dark blue-purple flowers in abundance can be obtained even in milder climates. This is a classic for colour, growth and vigour although the form is now somewhat dated.

'Contrast in Styles' (Hollingworth, 1989) is well named. The basic colour is wine red with beautiful light blue styles and a blue halo around a white signal blaze. This beautiful iris grows to 85 cm.

'Coolabah' (Blyth, 1988) has the distinction of being our first Siberian iris to bloom each season and it is often in bloom with the late tall bearded iris. It is a lovely wine-rose colour with a green-brown throat and a white signal patch. The form is wide and ruffled and it grows to 80 cm.

'Coronation Anthem' (Hollingworth, 1990) is another favourite. The ruffled blooms are mid blue with darker shadings, light blue styles and a creamy white signal. It grows to 90 cm.

'Creme Chantilly' (McEwen, 1981) has very rounded, full petals in white with a cream influence. The blooms are lightly ruffled and spikes reach 85 cm in height.

'Dancing Nanou' (Miller, 1983) is a favourite. It has large light blue-violet flowers of excellent form and wide blue-green foliage. Spikes reach 90 cm in height.

'Dear Diane' (McEwen, 1979) was a favourite when seen in Oregon. Beautiful, wide and ruffled flowers are blue-violet with a hairline lighter rim. It grows to 90 cm.

'Devil's Dream' (Schafer/Sacks 1990) is a late-blooming beauty in rich dark wine red with a purple blaze on the velvety falls and lighter styles. The ruffled blooms are carried on 90 cm spikes.

'Ego' (McGarvery, 1967) is an attractive light to mid blue which grows to 80 cm. It is very attractive in a clump.

'Emma Ripeka' (Love, 1996) is a blue bitone with paler blue style arms. This iris achieved distinction in 1994 by being the first New Zealand bred iris to win the Dykes Medal. It is an easy grower which reaches 85 cm in height.

'Frosted Cranberry' (Miller, 1991) has unusual colouring of rose pink with a frosty sheen, a dark wine area around the hafts and near white styles. It grows to 85 cm.

'Frosty Rim' (Bush, 1979) is a favourite in dark blue with a silver edge. Blooms are ruffled and spikes reach 90 cm. This iris is very beautiful in a clump.

'Green Eyed Queen' (Varner, 1991) has a real 'knock your eyes out' flower as seen in Oregon in 1994. Rounded and lightly ruffled flowers are lavender violet with a dark red-violet area in the falls reaching down as a spray pattern. Laced styles and a two-spot signal in green cream which looks like a pair of eyes set this iris apart. I was unable to determine its true height or habit of growth as it was a young planting with only a few flowers on short spikes. This is one to look for in the future.

'Halcyon Seas' (McCord, 1972) has dark blue standards and darker falls. This is an easy grower even in milder climates and, as such, is recommended. It was released in the USA in 1972 and winner of the Morgan Award — top award for Siberian iris — in 1975.

'Harpswell Happiness' (McEwen, 1983) is one of the new breed of tetraploid Siberian iris. The ruffled blooms are creamy white and the spikes reaching 90 cm are well branched.

'Harpswell Haze' (McEwen, 1977) is a smoky mauve-blue with white signals. This tetraploid Siberian iris has unusual colour and reaches 85 cm.

'I'm Just Blue' (Blyth, 1989) is well named. The large, rounded blooms in royal blue come late in the season. This is an easy growing iris to 75 cm.

'Lights of Paris' (Rich, 1967)

'Orville Fay' (McEwen, 1970)　　　　　　　'Over in Gloryland' (Hollingworth, 1993)

'Roaring Jelly' (Schafer/Sacks, 1992)

'White Swirl' (Cassebeer, 1957)

'Indy' (Hollingworth, 1985) flowers early in the season and is very colourful. Flowers are red-violet with blue shadings and veins and lighter coloured styles. It grows to 80 cm.

'Jaybird' (Hager, 1982) is a very attractive mid-blue with standards slightly lighter than the falls. It grows to 90 cm but is a rather slow grower and less vigorous than others.

'Jewelled Crown' (Hollingworth, 1985) is a shorter growing (65 cm) tetraploid iris of quality. The very ruffled deep wine-red flowers have large white and gold sunburst signals and blue-violet styles, giving a tricolour effect. It is one of the most spectacular Siberian iris and a personal favourite.

'Lady Vanessa' (Hollingworth, 1986) is another standout. The standards and styles are light wine-red while the falls are medium red-violet with a white signal. It reaches 90 cm and makes a beautiful clump.

'Lake Keuka' (Borglum, 1991) is a lovely blue-violet of rounded, ruffled form with lighter blue styles. It grows to 85 cm and is magnificent in a clump.

'Liberty Hills' (Miller, 1989) is a mid blue-violet, darker in the signal area and with lighter styles. It grows to 80 cm.

'Lights of Paris' (Rich, 1967) is a heavy-blooming white with golden yellow hafts giving quite a yellow effect in a clump. This iris blooms late and reaches 1 m in height.

'Lime Heart' (Brummitt, 1970) is a well-substanced white with lime green hafts. This late-flowering iris, first released in England in 1970, is very attractive in a clump, reaching 90 cm in height.

'Mabel Coday' (Helsley, 1985) is a nicely formed blue-violet with a white signal patch. Spikes are 85 cm tall.

'Marilyn Holmes' (McEwen, 1972) is a rich blue-violet with small gold signals. It is another older Siberian, first released in 1972, that is quite good even in milder climates. It grows to 70 cm.

'Marshmallow Frosting' (McEwen, 1984) is another lovely white with just a touch of yellow around the hafts. It grows to 85 cm.

'Music Royal' (Blyth, 1990) is a very large flower in pure royal blue. This is an easy-to-grow iris reaching 75 cm in height. It is hard to beat for purity of colour.

'On and On' (McEwen, 1977) has violet flowers with a white fall blaze, violet styles and midribs. It flowers early, reaches 95 cm in height and often reblooms immediately after its initial bloom, hence the name.

'Orville Fay' (McEwen, 1970) has nice mid-blue flowers with textured veining. It is a tetraploid first released in the USA in 1970 and winner of the top award in 1976. It grows to 90 cm.

'Over in Gloryland' (Hollingworth, 1993) is a stunning iris in blue-purple with a large sunburst white signal. Flowers are rounded and ruffled and the quality is excellent. It reaches 90 cm in height.

'Pas de Deux' (Hollingworth, 1988) is a personal favourite with white standards and styles and light yellow falls. Flowers are rounded and lightly ruffled. Spikes reach 85 cm.

'Percheron' (Warburton, 1982) is a distinctive iris with large flowers veined and dappled blue-violet on a blue ground. It grows to 85 cm.

'Pink Haze' (McGarvey, 1980) is a mauve pink self with a hazy overlay. Falls are slightly darker than the standards. It grows to 95 cm.

'Pink Sparkle' (Hager, 1985) has white standards tinged pink and darker pink falls. It is a lovely colour and an easy grower, reaching 90 cm in height.

'Rare Jewel' (Varner, 1978) is in tones of lilac and wine with blue style arms and white signals. It grows to 63 cm.

'Regency Buck' (McEwen, 1985) has perfectly rounded and gently ruffled flowers of royal blue purple with a white dotted spray pattern as a signal patch. Spikes reach 85 cm.

'Rikugi-Sakura' (Shidara/Hager, 1988) is unusual in that it has no standards and six falls. Flowers are a lilac-mauve pink with ochre-yellow hafts extending into white spray signals. The flower is open and narrow. It is a most attractive novelty. Spikes reach 80 cm.

'Roaring Jelly' (Schafer/Sacks, 1992) is a gorgeous bitone with lavender-mauve standards and blue-violet falls. Blooms are ruffled and spikes reach 75 cm. Lovely.

'Rose Quest' (Hager, 1983) has rose orchid colour on compact blooms with better form than many in this colour range. Spikes reach 1 m in height.

'Ruffled Velvet' (McEwen, 1973) is a velvet dark-violet and purple bitone with white signals and feathered style arms. Although first released in the USA in 1973, this iris remains one of the outstanding cultivars available. A personal favourite, this iris reaches 95 cm in height.

'Sailor's Fancy' (Schafer/Sacks, 1991) has light blue standards over darker sky-blue falls and light blue-violet styles. It grows to 90 cm and is a lovely iris.

'Savoir Faire' (DuBose, 1974) is a deep, glowing velvety royal purple with small yellow signals. It grows to 90 cm.

'Shaker's Prayer' (Warner, 1990) is a novelty. It has violet standards and red-violet styles. The falls are white on the upper half with lilac veins and brown hafts and blue-violet on the lower half with the darker veins running the full length of the falls. It grows to 90 cm.

'Shirley Pope' (McEwen, 1979) is a strong blue-purple bitone with a white spray signal. This is a stunning iris in a clump and a personal favourite. It reaches 90 cm in height.

'Shirley's Choice' (McEwen, 1987) is one of the nicest of all white Siberian iris with gently ruffled flowers on 80 cm spikes. There is a touch of yellow at the hafts to light up the flower. It is beautiful in a clump.

'Silver Edge' (McEwen, 1974) is another of the McEwen tetraploids. It is a lovely mid blue with a distinctive silver edge around the petal edges and gold signals. It is a top award winner in the USA and reaches 70 cm in height.

'Star Glitter' (Hager, 1985) has white standards and lemon-yellow falls. Buds are quite yellow and the landscape effect is stunning. Spikes reach 90 cm.

'Strawberry Fair' (Hollingworth, 1992) is really a knockout! The form of Siberian iris is brought into a new dimension with these heavily ruffled and beautifully rounded blooms. Flowers are a red-violet colour with lacy blue-toned styles and a bicolour signal of ochre yellow brown and white. I stood and gazed in wonder at this iris at the 1994 Iris Convention in Oregon, USA, and eventually voted for it as the outstanding iris for the prestigious Franklin Cook Cup — for best iris bred out of region. I couldn't believe that I had done this as there were so many magnificent iris to be seen and so many of these were my beloved tall bearded iris. I guess I wasn't the only one to be impressed as 'Strawberry Fair' won the cup from over 2000 entrants. This iris stood tall at 90 cm in Oregon but I have not, as yet, grown it. I believe that it will revolutionise the hybridising of Siberian iris.

'Sultan's Ruby' (Hollingworth, 1988) is a deep red-violet with lighter styles, feathered midribs and edges. Colour of flowers and texture of petals are superb. It grows to 90 cm.

'Super Ego' (McGarvey, 1966) has large flowers with pale blue standards and darker blue falls with lighter edges and a dark blue halo around the signals. It grows to 75 cm.

'Swank' (Hager, 1969) is a shorter-growing Siberian iris at 70 cm. Standards and falls are mid blue with the standards slightly lighter in colour.

'Temper Tantrum' (McGarvey, 1986) is a ruffled deep red-purple that grows well. It reaches 95 cm in height.

'Vi Luihn' (DuBose, 1974) is a sister seedling to 'Savoir Faire' and, while in the same colour range, is much better branched. It is a rich cobalt blue and grows to 85 cm. This is an outstanding iris, first released in the USA in 1974, but still a very worthwhile addition to the garden

'Vicky Ann' (Warburton, 1989) was one of the nicest blue Siberian iris seen in Oregon. It is a mid sky blue with slightly lighter styles and slightly darker blue-violet hafts. It grows to 80 cm and is a delight in the landscape.

'White Swirl' (Cassebeer, 1957) is a snow-white with lemon-yellow in the centre of the flower. It grows to 85 cm and is a long-time favourite.

'White Triangles' (Warburton, 1987) is a well named flaring white self with great purity of colour. It grows to 85 cm.

40-chromosome Siberian iris — Sino-Siberians

SUBSERIES CHRYSOGRAPHES

There are eight species recognised in the subseries Chrysographes, of which three are doubtful in their classification.

I. bulleyana is quite possibly a hybrid tracing back to *I. forrestii* and *I. chrysographes*.

I. dykesii has unknown origins. Dykes, after whom it was named, had it flower in his garden and suspected it was a species. It was named, as such, after his death. It is evidently similar to, but an enlarged and improved, *I. chrysographes*.

I. phragmitetorum is unknown in cultivation. It was collected once in the Yunnan province of China. Reports suggest a resemblance to *I. sanguinea* (2n=28) and to *I. clarkei* (2n=40). It is doubtful as to whether it is a true species.

In terms of the development of garden plants, the other five species are far more significant in the production of the Sino-Siberian iris available for cultivation.

I. chrysographes is also known as the gold pattern iris, and gold net iris, referring to the golden yellow patterning on its falls. It is a native of China, Burma and Tibet. Foliage is strappy, grey green in colour and reaches the same height as the flowering spikes which can vary from 30 to 75 cm and carry two flowers. These flowers are rich dark purple with a variable amount of gold netting on the falls.

'Coolabah' (Blyth, 1988)

'Pas de Deux' (Hollingworth, 1988)   'Pink Haze' (McGarvey, 1980)

'Jewelled Crown' (Hollingworth, 1985)

'Pink Sparkle' (Hager, 1985)

'Strawberry Fair' (Hollingworth, 1992)

There is a considerable amount of colour variation in the species, which includes a red-purple form known as 'rubella' and a spectacular black form known as 'nigra'. The typical *I. chrysographes* has erect standards and wide pendent falls. Bloom period is very late spring to early summer.

I. clarkei is a native of Nepal, Tibet, India and Burma. It is distinctive in that, unlike others in the Sino-Siberian species, it has solid stems. It has quite wide glossy foliage and branched spikes which reach 60 cm in height. There is considerable colour variation in blues and violets with distinctive white signals on the falls. Bloom is in early summer. This iris requires acid soil, kept moist but not wet, and full sun for best results.

I. delavayi is a native of China and has the tallest spikes and widest foliage of the Sino-Siberians. It will grow up to 150 cm in height with its somewhat drooping, dark green foliage up to 4 cm wide. The spike is well branched, carrying up to six or seven blooms of unusual form. Narrow standards are nearly horizontal and the spoon-shaped falls hang vertical. Colour is dark violet with white veining and signal patch. This iris will tolerate quite wet conditions and is suitable for a bog garden. Best conditions are a sunny position with slightly acid soil for optimum performance. Bloom is in early to mid summer.

I. wilsonii is a native of China and is distinctive in both flower shape and colour. The broad, dull blue-green foliage is as tall as the 70–80 cm spikes, but hangs at the ends. The unbranched spikes carry two flowers that are wider than they are tall. The standards are pale primrose yellow, held almost horizontally, while the deep yellow falls droop gently. These falls are veined and netted brown. Bloom period is late spring to early summer.

I. forrestii, the other yellow Sino-Siberian, is a native of China. It can be distinguished from *I. wilsonii* by its closed upright standards and narrow oval falls which lack the intensity of veining. Foliage is narrower and the overall plant is smaller than *I. wilsonii*. It is less vigorous and more demanding than the other Sino-Siberians, with which it will intercross easily.

There are known crosses involving all the Sino-Siberian species and these have formed the basis of hybridising campaigns resulting in some lovely garden cultivars. Much of this work has been done by Thomas Tamberg from Germany and Lorena Reid from the USA who both have some excellent named hybrids. The Sino-Siberians are more demanding than the 28-chromosome Siberians but, if given the right climate and correct cultivation, they will thrive.

Essentially these iris require the same culture as the Siberian iris. They need an acid soil, preferably around pH 6, they need moisture in the soil, particularly until well established and they need humus in the soil so mulching is desirable. Peat moss dug into the soil helps to lower pH and retain moisture so is very beneficial. They like winter cold and can accept summer heat as long as the soil is well watered.

This is not to say that growing the Sino-Siberians is easy. They are native to areas of high altitude and tropical latitude, conditions which nearly all gardeners interested in growing iris will not be able to duplicate. Perfect climatic conditions would involve cool summers, mild winters, abundant rainfall and high humidity. As they obviously do not like extremes the challenge to the gardener is to provide conditions as close as possible to optimum. While they flourish naturally in full sun it is desirable to provide some shade in areas with hot, dry summers while avoiding the obvious pitfall of planting too close to established trees.

Propagation by division is best done in autumn and larger divisions will give the plants a better opportunity to establish. When lifting, dividing and planting care must be taken to ensure that plants never dry out. Plants sent through the mail should always be sent damp. Probably the best way is to pack in wet peat moss with the roots wrapped in paper, tissue or plastic. Sweating does not appear to be a problem if these iris are sent in plastic wrapping. They invariably arrive fresh without any sign of rot.

Propagation by seed is also very easy but seedlings obtained from hybrids will not be true to the pod parent. All the more fun! Seed collected and sown in late summer, early autumn will germinate easily in a seed raising mix and bloom can be expected in many cases in two seasons. As the species and hybrids intercross very easily the gardener needs to be careful to collect seed to avoid having unwanted 'rogue' plantings in their iris. There is great variation in growth, form and colour from intercrossing the Sino-Siberians and some fascinating patterns have been developed.

Iris chrysographes has been used extensively in Sino-Siberian hybridising and crosses outside the subseries have been made, particularly with the Californian iris. There are known hybrids involving *I. forrestii, I. hartwegii, I. tenax, I. delavayi* and *I. wilsonii*.

Hybrids of *I. delavayi* x *I. wilsonii* and of *I. forrestii* with the others in the series and also the Californian iris are documented.

While the 28-chromosome Siberians intercross among themselves and the 40-chromosome Sino-Siberians all intercross among themselves there are few documented crosses between the 28 chromosome and 40-chromosome groups. Most successful crosses between the two groups have produced sterile offspring, the very noteworthy exception being the fertile 'Foretell', an iris produced by William McGarvey from the 40-chromosome *I. forrestii* and the 28-chromosome 'Super Ego'.

In performing planned crosses, care must be taken to ensure that you obtain the desired cross. Because Siberian iris are so easily pollinated naturally, it is best to use unopened flowers both for pod and pollen parents. To force the unopened pod parent is relatively easy as long as a fat bud, ready to open, is selected. The flower can be covered and the anthers removed by forcibly opening the flower. When the flower is ready and the cross is made it should be immediately covered again. We use a fine mesh cloth (Evolution Cloth), sold as a crop cover, cut into large squares and tied into the spike with plastic ties. A similar method is used in all our hybridising of Louisiana iris. In a similar manner, pollen is only used from selected unopen flowers which are forcibly opened and the anthers removed with tweezers. Pollen from unopened flowers is usually viable, but care must be taken to make any crosses only after the pod parent flower would have opened naturally. Experimentation will give hybridisers their own favourite techniques but by adhering to the above principles a technique to obtain near perfect success of pods set is guaranteed.

RECOMMENDED CULTIVARS

Development of modern Siberian iris in the 40-chromosome series has been slow but in recent years some excellent new named hybrids have become available in Germany and the USA.

'Berliner Riesen' (Tamberg, 1978) is a cross between *I. delavayi* and *I. clarkei*. This iris has near horizontal violet standards and similar coloured falls with a white signal surrounded by a darker purple area. The falls hang vertically and this iris is quite attractive in the garden with spikes reaching over a metre in height.

'Anticipation Orange' (Reid, 1994) is an exciting new colour bringing golden orange into the Siberian iris. Standards are pale orange with a dark gold midrib, styles are dark gold with pale orange edges and falls are pale orange with a large dark gold signal shading paler to blend in with the orange. This iris will grow to 75 cm.

'Beautiful Forty' (Tamberg, 1993) will grow to 90 cm. The standards are light violet and the falls are pale yellow with a violet sunburst pattern. Signals are gold stitched violet. This iris has been an excellent parent for new colour patterns.

'Blue Forty' (McEwen, 1971) grows to 75 cm and is pale blue in colour with darker veins and stipples.

'Boop Eyes' (Reid, 1995) is bred from a 'Beautiful Forty' seedling crossed by 'Butterfly Mode'. The standards and styles are mid lavender and the falls are mid lavender with large navy blue, bordered white signals and black lines in the throat. It grows to 90 cm.

'Butterfly Mode' (Reid, 1991) has violet blue standards and darker violet blue styles. The falls are violet blue with a white signal with black lines and a dark violet-blue edge. It grows over 100 cm in height.

'Camouflage' (Witt, 1966) grows to 90 cm and has a white ground colour, veined and dotted in blue.

'Cascade Creme' (Reid, 1991) has white standards and styles. The semi-flaring falls are white with a pale creamy-yellow centre. It grows over 100 cm in height.

'Dimity Butterfly' (Reid, 1993) has white standards with a blue-lavender midrib and tips, white styles feathered with blue-lavender lines and broad white falls with a light blue-lavender line pattern. The large butterfly-type signal is dark navy blue violet with yellow rays. This is a spectacular flower on spikes which grow to 120 cm.

'Dotted Line' (Reid, 1992) created a sensation at the 1994 American Iris Society Convention in Oregon. I was fortunate enough to see it at the convention and then viewed it later in the season in the hybridiser's home garden in Springfield, Oregon, where it was even more impressive. The standards are violet blue with darker vertical stitching and a crinkled white edge. Styles are violet blue. The wide, broad falls are vertically stitched violet blue on white. There is a large white signal with a blue-black edge and centre lines. No description can do this iris justice — it is a beauty beyond compare. 'Dotted Line' will grow to 90 cm and has produced some absolutely beautiful seedlings for Lorena Reid.

'Enbee Deeaych' (Reid, 1989) is very tall growing, reaching 150 cm or more. It is a hybrid of *I. delavayi* and has a broad, deep rich-purple flower with a black eye spot signal and a white centre line edged in diamond dusting.

'Foretell' (McGarvey, 1970) is particularly interesting because it is a cross between the 40-chromosome *I. forrestii* and 28-chromosome 'White Swirl' seedling. This older hybrid has pale blue standards and styles and yellow falls stitched with blue lines. It will grow to 80 cm.

'Idson' (Reid, 1985) is a deep purple self darkening to black around the white and yellow signal stitched black purple. This vigorous iris grows to 45 cm.

'Lightly Touched' (Peyrard/Hansen, 1992) is a cross between *I. clarkei* and an *I. delavayi* seedling. The standards are milky white, styles are palest of yellow and the falls are milky white to ivory with violet veins. It grows to 90 cm.

'Mauve Mood' (McEwen, 1971) has mauve flowers with a dark purple to black signal stitched mauve. It grows to 85 cm.

'McKenzie Violet' (Reid, 1995) is a seedling from 'Dotted Line' with mid-violet standards and light violet styles with a pale midrib. The broad falls are mid violet with a near black signal marked with a white centre line. This iris will grow to 90 cm.

Reid seedling 90-S-11

Reid seedling 92-S-90

Reid seedling 90-S-1

Reid seedling 90-S-10

Reid seedling 90-S-22

Reid seedling S86-11-19

I. bulleyana

'Dotted Line' (Reid, 1992)

'Butterfly Mode' (Reid, 1991)

I. chrysographes

I. clarkei

'Puget Polka' (Mize/Ruggles)

'Prairie Warbler' (McEwen, 1981) has pale yellow standards and styles and falls of yellow-green with brown signal markings. It grows over 100 cm in height.

'Purple Princess' (McEwen, 1975) is an *I. chrysographes* hybrid with red-violet standards and dark purple velvet falls. It grows to 65 cm.

'Rainbow Island' (Reid, 1973) has mid-violet standards mottled darker and dark-purple styles. The flaring falls are pale gold with navy veins. It grows to 60 cm.

'Tigger' (Reid, 1973) is shorter growing, reaching only 35 cm in height. Standards are pale purple, styles are bright maroon-purple with a jagged gold border and falls are bright gold with line veining of purple.

'Varied Bunting' (McEwen, 1984) has standards and styles in pink-lilac with a plum midline. Falls are slightly lighter in colour with a plum area and short yellow line signal. It grows to 115 cm.

Many of the new hybrid Sino-Siberians are of near unbelievable colour and pattern and the hybridising groundwork has been done to give a wonderful foundation for anyone wishing to work in this area. They are not easy plants to establish and grow but are breathtaking in their beauty. They are highly recommended to anyone who can provide their basic climatic and cultural requirements.

CALIFORNIAN IRIS

The Californian iris, often referred to as Pacific coast iris, are natives of the western coast of the USA. These delightful small iris consist of some 11 species, of which four have made a significant contribution to the wealth of hybrids that has been developed. They are, in general, evergreen and form small, compact plants which send up flowering spikes from early to mid spring. While they are found in the foothills of higher ranges, they are not alpine plants. A preferred climate is one of high winter and early spring rain followed by long dry summers. They tolerate cold in the winter and relish heat in the summer.

Californian iris are very tolerant of soil condition as long as they are given good drainage. They seem to perform best in a neutral to slightly acid soil which is well mulched. While full sun is satisfactory in all but the hottest climates, most of these iris will grow best in a semi-shaded position.

Propagation by division is difficult and many losses are experienced in transplanting. Care must be taken to replant only young divisions and only when the new white roots are forming in late autumn, early winter. To move plants over any distance the divisions taken

should be large with many young shoots and these divisions need to be transported damp by wrapping in tissue paper or sphagnum moss. The resentment that all Californian iris have for moving makes the division and propagation of named cultivars a frustrating and often disastrous venture.

Although it is relatively unrewarding to attempt to divide and replant these iris, they can be easily raised from seed. The species will come true to parent from seed but flowers of great diversity in form and colour can be obtained by intercrossing the hybrids. Plants set seed readily, both naturally and when crossed by hand. Seed should be collected in summer when the pod hardens and browns and before it splits. If this seed is planted in autumn most of it will germinate in winter and spring. Seeds can be planted in seed raising mix in pots or directly in the ground where they will flower in the year following planting.

Superb quality hybrids have been raised from the breeding program started in Australia by Dan Hargraves. His work was continued by Chas Blyth and Barry Blyth in Victoria and by Helen Grosvenor in New South Wales while seed sent to the USA was used as a basis for part of the breeding program of Joe Ghio from California, who has continued to produce outstanding named cultivars in the 1980s and 1990s. On a visit to the USA in 1994 I was able to see outstanding Californian iris hybrids in California, Oklahoma, Texas, Oregon and Washington State. They were grown in a great diversity of climates and garden situations, giving further credence to my feeling that these are outstanding garden iris, much to be prized in the landscape.

Equally rewarding were the large and beautifully grown clumps of these iris seen growing in England, Italy and Switzerland on a European visit in 1992.

The Californian iris have a chromosome count 2n=40, the same as the Sino-Siberian iris and interspecific crosses have been made. I was able to see quite a lot of these in Oregon, particularly in the garden of hybridiser Lorena Reid. These Cal-Sibs, as they are called, are worthy garden subjects but none that I saw equalled the Californian hybrids for beauty.

Species

I. bracteata occurs naturally in Southern Oregon. It has wide, stiff sparse foliage, coming from long slender rhizomes. It is dormant in winter with fresh foliage appearing in early spring. Flowering spikes are 25–35 cm tall and have sheathing leaves (bracts) at short intervals up the stem. Flowers are large and yellow in colour with some forms flushed and veined in shades of red, brown and maroon. They are carried one or two to an unbranched spike. This species is not particularly vigorous.

I. chrysophylla also comes from Oregon and has evergreen, narrow light blue-green foliage. The unbranched flowering spikes are up to 20–25 cm tall and carry two rather fragile, narrow cream to white flowers veined darker yellow. It has no great value as a cultivated garden plant.

I. douglasiana occurs in an extended narrow coastal strip from Northern California to Southern Oregon. It is the most adaptable and robust of the Californian species and is widely grown. It is hardy, sun tolerant, vigorous and floriferous. *I. douglasiana* is not particular about soil conditions and forms a solid circular mass of evergreen foliage under normal growing conditions. This foliage is coarse, variable shades of green in colour and deep red at the base. Flowering spikes are 30–50 cm tall and well branched. They can carry up to nine blooms which vary considerably both in size and colour. Even within the colour range there is a delightful variation in patterning. Flowers can be mauve, lavender, violet, cream, pastel apricot shades and veining and patterning is mostly in darker tones. These are beautiful flowers on very attractive plants that make excellent garden subjects. *I. douglasiana* is easy to grow but prefers a soil rich in humus and well drained. It does not like lime or the use of animal manure. While it is sun tolerant, best results are obtained in a semi-shaded position.

I. fernaldii is a native of California and has narrow, compact grey-green evergreen foliage often richly coloured red at the base. Flowering spikes are 25–35 cm in height, unbranched and carry two creamy yellow flowers which are often veined. It hybridises readily and naturally with the other species, but is insignificant as a garden plant.

I. hartwegii is a dwarf species from the Sierra Nevada foothills in California. The sparse foliage is narrow, light green in colour and dormant in winter. The unbranched spikes are slender, reach 20 cm in height and carry two cream or lavender blooms with some veining. This species requires full sun, is a shy bloomer and of little significance as a garden plant.

I. innominata, the iris with 'no-name', is a native of Oregon and California and a most appealing iris. It is a hardy plant, sun tolerant and frost tolerant and is found naturally in rich, well drained acid soil. This iris requires a fair amount of moisture in spring but likes to dry out in summer. Although sun tolerant, it is best grown in semi-shade.

Foliage is evergreen, narrow, green in colour with a lighter underside and compact. Many unbranched spikes from an established clump will produce one or two flowers. These spikes grow to a height of 40 cm and carry flowers in shades of yellow, mauve, lavender, purple, delicate cream, pink and apricot. Many flowers are veined and netted in red, brown, maroon or purple.

This is an excellent iris for the garden as the abundance of bloom spikes compensates for the lack of bloom on each spike. The colour range and patterning is extensive and bloom season can be extended for up to two months or more by having a variety of clumps.

Propagation by division can be difficult and must be done at the specific time of the year when the white roots form, but raising plants from seed is relatively easy and is the recommended way to start a collection or to increase stock.

I. macrosiphon is a native of California, variable and widespread. The long, narrow leaves are blue-green to dark green in colour, often white at the base and evergreen. Spikes are short and carry one or two flowers in a wide array of colours and patterns similar to *I. innominata.* However, its habit of growth, flower form and difficulty of culture all make it a less attractive garden plant than *I. innominata.*

I. munzii is a native of California and comes from partially shaded areas with moist soil conditions. The natural climate is mild and this iris is tender in cold and frosty areas. The evergreen foliage is wide, grey-green and grows to about 50 cm. Flowering spikes reach 70 cm, are unbranched and carry up to four blooms. Colour ranges through shades of blue and purple, often with attractive veining and often quite ruffled. Despite being frost tender this is a prized garden plant for its colour.

I. purdyi is a native of northern California and as it occurs in redwood country is known as the redwood iris. The evergreen foliage is grey green in colour and flowering spikes up to 40 cm in height are unbranched and carry two blooms. These blooms are light yellow, veined and stippled in red-purple to brown-purple and carrying a lavender wash. This is an attractive iris which hybridises readily, but has not been used much in gardens.

I. tenax is found naturally in Oregon and Washington state. This iris is the original species brought into cultivation, but it is inferior to *I. douglasiana* and *I. innominata* as a garden plant. It is an easily grown, adaptable plant, hardy and sun tolerant. Foliage, which dies down in winter, can reach 50 cm in height and is narrow. The base of the green foliage is often spotted mauve-pink. Flowering spikes are unbranched, grow to about 30 cm and carry single blooms in a wide colour range of yellow, mauve, blue, lavender and purple.

I. tenuissima is a native of northern California and has narrow, grey-green, evergreen foliage with a red base. It grows to about 40 cm in height with spikes variable in height carrying two narrow, recurved blooms. These blooms are cream with red or brown veining. This iris is of little value as a garden subject.

Recommended cultivars

Most of the Californian iris hybrids available have been developed by intercrossing the four species, *I. douglasiana, I. innominata, I. tenax* and *I. munzii* and a spectacular array of hybrids, far surpassing the species, has been developed. *I. douglasiana* offers branching and bud count, vigour and hardiness. *I. innominata* offers a

'Dotted Line' seedling

'Camouflage' (Witt, 1966)

CALIFORNIAN IRIS

Californian iris seedling

Californian iris seedling

Californian iris seedling

Californian iris seedling

Californian iris seedling

Californian iris seedling

Californian iris seedling

Californian iris seedling

wide colour range and patterning with the bonus of good garden habits and long bloom period. *I. tenax* combines many of the above attributes while *I. munzii* with its blue tones and ruffled form extends the colour range and puts ruffle on the blooms. What a wonderful gene pool with which hybridisers can work and this, coupled with the ease with which seed is set, has ensured some outstanding garden plants.

As with most of the species, these hybrids are best grown either in a woodland setting with semi-shade or in full sun in milder climates. The soil should be well drained, neutral to slightly acid and enhanced with humus. They require an adequate supply of moisture in winter and spring, but are best suited to areas with a long, dry summer. They demand good drainage and will not tolerate 'wet feet'. They resent the use of lime or animal manure. Pests and diseases are normally not a problem.

The difficulty of dividing and replanting has already been discussed in the species and it is no less difficult with the hybrids. This makes the naming and marketing of selected clones a frustrating business. I have learned to love and enjoy these marvellous iris in the garden but have long stopped trying to market them, particularly through the mail where losses are high, no matter how careful and how professional the nurseryman is. As these iris will grow quite well in pots there is a market for plants grown from vegetative increase taken at the right time or grown from seed sown directly into pots, but I feel that their best means of distribution is by seed taken from selected high-quality parents. Of course, these seedlings do not come true to the parent (or parents), but what a wonderful array of colours, forms and patterns can be obtained. Specific hybridising programs have developed flowers of exceptional width, roundness and size. These are enhanced with extravagant ruffling and intricate patterning. I have the greatest admiration for these wonderful hybrids while cherishing many of the more simple forms. There is great diversity in acceptable flower form for these iris and it is purely personal preference which determines one's favourite. As garden perennials the Californian iris are outstanding and rank very close to being my favourite garden plant.

After all this, a list of recommended cultivars would be somewhat hypocritical, but for those interested there are sources of named hybrids and these can be tracked down. Seed is usually quite commonly available.

Californian iris can be used extensively in different garden situations. I have seen massed plantings in large garden beds and long rows along paths and driveways, each of which gave spectacular displays over a long bloom period. As feature or spot plantings among other perennials or annuals, they shine like beacons. Another great use is as underplanting for standardised plants in circular or square beds of their own. Love of the same conditions make azaleas excellent companion plants. A particularly nice feature is a standardised azalea underplanted with Californian iris.

Californian iris also look good with various species of primula — a personal favourite of mine being *Primula obconica,* where recent hybrids have overcome its major problem of causing skin irritation. For me, the best use of Californian iris is in a rock garden where they will find as many companion plants as the imagination allows.

Because these iris grow so well in pots, they can be grown to large potted specimens or used as companion plants in pots of various sizes with other perennials or annuals. Once you have grown these most rewarding plants they will be a favourite for many, many years of enjoyable gardening.

In conclusion, I would like to expand a little on the breeding program of Joe Ghio, from Santa Cruz in California. Joe Ghio is one of the world leaders in hybridising tall bearded iris and from the time he started to work with the Californian iris he has taken these fascinating plants to new heights. Not everyone wants their flowers rounded, frilly, ruffled and in new and fascinating colours and the simplicity of form of the Californian iris species is a great attraction in itself. If, however, you do want the latest colour patterns, if you want beautiful rounded form and ruffled edges then a selection of 'Ghio' Californian iris is for you. While avoiding a recommended list, I feel that even the most fastidious irisarians would find Californian iris in colours and patterns to suit their tastes from the Ghio collection.

Plants are available in all the warm colours — yellow, orange, gold, russet and red. On the cool side, there are white, shades of blue, violet and purple through to black. There are also pink, apricot, mauve, peach, orchid and heliotrope. With their veining and signal patches, many of the Californian iris are bicolours and bitones, with tricolours also available. Blending and contrasting styles add to the beauty. Most of these hybrids grow from 25 cm to 40 cm in height and, as already stated, are magnificent rockery subjects.

CAL-SIBS

All the Californian iris species and the Sino-Siberian iris have a chromosome count ($2n=40$) and so were ready made for experimental hybridising. Probably the most significant early intercrossing of the species resulted in 'Margot Holmes', which won the British Dykes Medal in 1927. This iris is a cross between *I. douglasiana* and *I. chrysographes.*

Crosses between the Californian iris species and the 28-chromosome Siberian iris have been successfully accomplished, but are far more difficult. All the offspring of these crosses are sterile.

In the last 40 years work has continued somewhat spasmodically, with a few stalwarts making limited progress. Leaders in the field have come from the USA,

England and Germany. In recent times Jean Witt and Lorena Reid in the USA and Thomas Tamberg in Germany have all worked on the Californian-Siberian crosses as well as the Siberian iris and Californian iris.

When visiting Oregon in 1994 I was able to see some lovely Cal-Sibs in the garden of Lorena Reid. Of particular interest were two of her 1993 releases, 'Pacific Smoothie' and 'Party Paleface'.

'Pacific Smoothie' grows to 90 cm and has one or two branches carrying up to seven flowers. The standards are violet, deeper in the centre, paler at the edges while the falls are dark violet with large, unmarked black-purple signals.

'Party Paleface' grows to 90 cm and has one or two branches carrying up to seven flowers. The standards are pale blue veined darker while the falls are red-violet with a paler near-white edge and reverse. The blooms are gently ruffled and of attractive form.

The culture of the Cal-Sibs is similar to that of their parents and does not warrant repeating here, except to state that they require less summer watering than Siberians and more summer watering than Californians, as would be expected.

The main advantage these iris have as garden plants is that they increase the range of satisfactory climates where their parents often do not do well. Many Californian gardeners are not able to grow Siberian iris well because of lack of winter cold and this would be true of gardeners in milder European climates as well as the more coastal regions of southern Australia and the more northerly parts of New Zealand. Likewise the Californian iris are often not hardy in cold climates. Cal-Sibs will often fill the gap for frustrated enthusiasts.

As garden subjects I find them less attractive than the better Siberians and less attractive than the better Californians, both of which thrive in our climate and soil conditions at Hillview in central western New South Wales.

The sterility of these hybrids gives no opportunity for hybridisers to develop extended breeding lines. Progress is essentially slow, but with a new wave of quality Siberian and Californian iris now available there is every possibility of the development of new and exciting cultivars in the late 1990s and into the 21st century.

LOUISIANA IRIS

The Louisiana iris, native to the USA, consist of five species found in a very limited region of that country embracing Texas, Florida and Louisiana. These form the series Hexagona of the Apogon (beardless) iris. Of the five species, there is some argument as to the legitimacy of one. I. hexagona and I. giganticaerulea are very similar, differing primarily in size and vigour and natural location. The larger and more vigorous I. giganticaerulea has been found only in South Louisiana while I. hexagona is found in Florida, Georgia and the Carolinas. According to the distinguished irisarian Joseph Mertzweiller, they may be two separate species but if further study shows them to be one and the same, I. hexagona will have priority as the correct name as this name was first used.

I. hexagona has sword-like, yellow-green foliage 60–90 cm high and 2.5 cm wide. Spikes carrying up to five blooms at four positions reach 90 cm in height. The blooms are up to 12 cm in diameter in shades of blue, violet, purple and occasionally white. The large rhizomes can reach 30 cm in length.

I. giganticaerulea has sword-like green foliage which grows to 90 cm high and 2.5 cm wide. The very tall spikes can reach 160 cm in height, but are often shorter. They are unbranched and carry up to five blooms in four positions. These blooms are up to 15 cm in diameter in shades of blue, purple and white. There is wide variation in size of bloom, height of spike and colour. This could be a result of natural hybridisation. Both bloom in mid spring.

I. brevicaulis, also known as I. foliosa, is found predominantly in south Louisiana, but does occur in other states. It has flowers that resemble I. giganticaerulea in shape and colour but there the similarity ends. While I. giganticaerulea is the giant of the Hexagonae, I. brevicaulis is the dwarf. Foliage barely reaches 50 cm, usually shorter, and bloom spikes grow only to 25–35 cm in height. These spikes are short and thick and double budded at up to four positions on zig-zag stems. The blooms start low down on the spikes and most are found among the foliage. These blooms are in shades of blue and violet and rarely white. They are up to 11 cm in diameter. I. brevicaulis is hardy and quite tolerant of low temperatures. It blooms in late spring.

Just as there is controversy over the status of I. hexagona and I. giganticaerulea, there was early controversy over the status of I. fulva and I. nelsonii. This latter controversy has been resolved with each being given species status.

I. fulva occurs primarily in south Louisiana although it has been found in other states. Foliage can reach 50–60 cm with flowering spikes up to 90 cm. These spikes are erect, carrying up to five buds, double socketed at the terminal and single blooms at the other flowering positions. This iris is found in full sun to partial shade, often in flooded areas in rich fertile acid soil. It is distinguished by having the blooms closest to red in the whole iris family, flowers being in various shades of red with rust and copper tones through to yellow. As distinct from the previously mentioned species the flowers are, in general, somewhat drooping. I. fulva flowers in mid spring.

I. nelsonii has been found only in a very limited area south of Abbeville in Louisiana. In many ways the

Californian iris seedling

Californian iris seedling

Californian iris seedling

Californian iris seedling

Californian iris seedling

Californian iris seedling

Californian iris seedling

blooms are similar to *I. fulva,* although more vibrant in colour with a range through red to red-violet, purple, brown and russet tones. Foliage reaches 75 cm with flowering spikes from 80–105 cm in height. Blooms reach 12 cm in diameter and are often found double socketed at up to four flowering positions on the branched stems. These iris were only discovered in 1938, by W.B. MacMillan, and their unique location led to them being called the Abbeville reds. Much discussion has taken place as to their closeness in flower colour and form to *I. fulva.* Morphological characteristics closer to *I. giganticaerulea* have led to the suggestion that *I. nelsonii* is a species established over many years as a natural hybrid of *I. fulva* and *I. giganticaerulea.*

Irrespective of its status or its origin, *I. nelsonii* has been the dominant species used by hybridisers to develop these magnificent iris to the level available as we near the end of the 20th century. Studies of the characteristics of the five species readily show the possibilities of obtaining superbly variable hybrids as we have short and tall growing species, branched and unbranched spikes, straight and zig-zag stems, small and large flowers, flared and drooping form, wide and narrow petals, large and small rhizomes, and above all a 'natural' colour variation unknown in any of the other series of iris. In the brief history of the hybridising of Louisiana iris, these plants have been developed at an astonishing rate. The range and quality of the diploid cultivars available today surpasses that of all other iris except the bearded iris. The chemical conversion to tetraploids and the early hybridising with tetraploids by pioneers such as Joe Mertzweiller leaves one in awe of what is yet to come from these wonderful irises.

In recent times the myths surrounding the cultivation of Louisiana iris have largely been exploded. Gardeners worldwide are finding: that they can be grown in a 'normal' garden without having to be in standing water; that they are more alkaline tolerant than at first thought; and that they are far more cold tolerant and frost hardy than first thought. Hybridisers have already overcome major criticisms of these iris — that they produce too much foliage with too few flowering spikes and that the rhizomes are too large and wander all over the place with each rhizome over 30 cm long. Many modern hybrids are very compact garden plants that are a mass of bloom in a controlled space and improvements will continue to be made.

The first description of Louisiana iris was given in 1788. No doubt they had been observed before that date, so the word discovery can be misleading. There is evidence of the wild iris being collected and transplanted into gardens in the early 1900s but it was in the late 1920s to early 1930s that John K. Small, Curator of the New York Botanical Gardens, 'discovered' the Louisiana iris species and did much to publicise their existence, thus bringing them to the attention of the world. The first Louisiana Iris Society was established in spring 1941, when a small group of iris collectors formed the Mary Swords DeBaillon Iris Society in Louisiana. In the comparatively short period since that first meeting the progress in the establishing of the Louisiana iris as a most valuable garden plant has been astonishing. Through the efforts and dedication of members of the Society for Louisiana Iris, interest in these iris has spread through America, Europe, Asia, Africa and Australasia.

Early involvement by hybridisers resulted in the crossing of *I. fulva* x *I. brevicaulis* by W.R. Dykes, who obtained 'Fulvala' from this cross in 1910. From the same parentage, E.B. Williamson was able to produce 'Dorothea K. Williamson', which was registered in 1918. This iris was one of the first that we were to grow in Australia and although it did not feature in any hybridising programs, it is interesting to note that even in this country we were virtually in on the ground floor of Louisiana iris hybridising. One cannot overestimate the value of the input of early collectors and hybridisers and one of the most prominent in the history of Louisiana iris is Marie Caillet of Little Elin in Texas. Marie has not been a hybridiser, but as a spokesperson for Louisiana iris there has been none better. In over 50 years of involvement since that meeting in 1941, when she was a charter member, Marie has dedicated herself to the promotion of her beloved Louisiana iris. Her efforts have been primarily to publicise and distribute the iris and she has been most successful in doing this. It was a great privilege for me to visit her garden and be her guest during a visit to the USA in 1994.

Advancement in the development of Louisiana iris was slow in the early stages but a solid platform of collecting and growing had been established from which an increasing number of new hybrids became available in the 1950s. Early hybridisers Claude Davis, Sidney Conger, Marvin Granger and Frank Chowning did much to advance the Louisiana iris, but it was in the 1950s and early 1960s that the efforts of two major contributors came to the fore.

Charles W. Arny Jnr, of Lafayette, Louisiana has had the greatest impact of any hybridiser in the development of the modern Louisiana iris. In a hybridising career spanning some 40 years, Charles Arny introduced well over 100 named cultivars and produced a gene pool which has influenced all hybridisers who have followed him. Several of his iris have become classics. 'Charlies Michelle' introduced ruffled petal edges to the Louisiana iris and although it was never a great garden iris, often being a reluctant bloomer, 'Charlies Michelle' has contributed very heavily to the modern rounded, ruffled form so much in vogue. I can remember a spike of 'Charlies Michelle' that Bob Raabe exhibited at the NSW Region Show of the Iris Society of Australia and with which he won grand champion exhibit. This was the first time, to my knowledge, that a Louisiana iris had been grand champion exhibit at an Australian show and it was a very worthy champion among some well grown and exhibited tall bearded iris. Perhaps the greatest claim to fame of 'Charlies Michelle' is being the parent of the wonderful 'Clara Goula', a heavily ruffled white iris that has been the foundation for nearly all Louisiana iris hybridising of quality to have followed. 'Clara Goula' is a much better garden performer than 'Charlies Michelle', being more vigorous, more healthy and a more reliable bloomer, but it has lacked the superb growth and blooming capacity of many of its offspring. Both these iris will be remembered more for their breeding potential than any other single attribute. It was in the early 1970s that I first corresponded with Charles Arny and it was at this time that John Taylor, my wife Helen's brother, had first become interested in hybridising Louisiana iris. Charles, very generously, sent us a plant of 'Clara Goula' as a pre-release gift with an order for Louisiana iris. In our correspondence, Charles stressed the need to seek individuality in one's seedlings and he particularly stressed that he felt that 'Clara Goula' had remarkable potential. Strangely, he did not pursue his own advice to the ultimate and while he did use the 'Charlies Michelle'-'Clara Goula' line in later years, it was John Taylor who explored the line to the fullest extent and he, working on the Arny lines, has brought the Louisiana iris to the rounded, extravagantly ruffled flower that is in evidence as we near the end of the 20th century. Other Arny irises that have been profound in their influence are: 'Clyde Redmond', a most strikingly coloured brilliant blue — small flowered but nicely formed on well branched spikes; the very heavily ruffled 'Charjoy's Mike'; the soft tan to brown 'Valera', which brought new colours to the Louisiana iris; and 'Easter Tide' in blue-lavender and yellow, one of the first of the bicolours.

Joseph K. Mertzweiller of Baton Rouge in Louisiana began working on the chemical inducement of tetraploid Louisiana iris in the 1960s and in 1973 registered 'Professor Ike' and 'Professor Claude', the first two stable tetraploid hybrids. Both of these iris proved fertile and excellent garden plants with colour, form, vigour and very healthy luxuriant foliage. A new era in the development of Louisiana iris had commenced. Both 'Professor Ike' and 'Professor Claude' are violet selfs with little to differentiate between them. I always preferred 'Professor Ike' as it seemed the better grower. Easy to multiply, 'Professor Ike' will regularly grow to 120 cm or more in height. It carries about six buds and is a very rewarding garden and show iris. Progress was very slow and it wasn't until 1980 that Joe Mertzweiller released 'Professor Paul', another induced tetraploid in a pale lavender-blue colouration. 'Professor Paul' had widened the colour range available for hybridisers, but nothing was bred from it in over ten years. Ken Durio of Opelousas, Louisiana has taken up the challenge of hybridising tetraploid Louisiana iris and in the period 1980 to 1983 introduced nine hybrids from intercrossing or selfing the two initial professors. As would be expected, most of these were variations on the violet coloration but 'Sauterne', obtained by selfing 'Professor Claude', is a pale yellow hybrid released in 1981 and 'Welcome Change', a lilac and yellow bicolour from the same cross was released in 1983.

Joe Mertzweiller further expanded the tetraploid colour range with the release of 'Professor Jim', a dark red bred from 'Chimera' x 'Professor Ike' in 1986 and 'Professor Fritchie', a yellow with a blue cast in 1993 and the similarly coloured 'Professor Barbara', released in 1992. On my 1994 visit to Marie Caillet's garden I saw a white seedling claimed to be a tetraploid. There was some disagreement about its naming, parentage and hybridiser and I hesitate to mention it but a white tetraploid Louisiana iris . . . we could be off and racing (or at least crawling).

Already acclaimed for his contribution to the Louisiana iris as a scientist, a hybridiser, an author and an innovator, Joe Mertzweiller has given the world a start into the hybridising of tetraploids and it could well be that, in time, he will be recognised as the most influential of all in the development of the Louisiana iris. The task now is for someone to take up the challenge, convert some of the extremely beautiful diploids available and go forward with the tetraploids.

In the USA there has been significant development of diploid Louisiana iris and leading hybridisers Dorman Haymon, Mary Dunn, Neil Bertinot and Richard Goula continue to produce advances while in Europe, the French hybridisers have produced some lovely iris, but it is in Australia that John Taylor has produced many of the exciting hybrids of the 1990s. Starting with the Arny irises in the 1970s, John Taylor has done for the Louisiana iris what Joe Ghio has done for the Californian iris. He has increased the colour range, developed new colour patterns, with rims, edges and reverses and increased the bud count and strength of spike. All of these would be outstanding achievements in themselves, but added to that he has developed the flower form to the highest level, producing hybrids with rounded and very ruffled petals and substance that rivals leather. Again I must stress that not everyone wants these attributes and there are those gardeners who wish to retain simplicity of form and pattern. Here we have one of the most desirable features of the Louisiana iris — the wide acceptance of flower forms and spike heights. We do not have a standard 'acceptable' form and this diversity is one of the major attributes of these beautiful flowers.

Other major contributors to the development of Louisiana iris in Australia have been Bob Raabe, Janet Hutchinson, Craig Carroll and Heather Pryor, all of whom have developed quality award-winning irises. Bob Raabe was the first major hybridiser in the

'In Stitches' (Reid, 1987)

'Ann Chowning' (Chowning, 1973)

'Bushfire Moon' (Pryor, 1996)

I. fulva

'Coorabel' (Raabe, 1988)

'Emigré' (Dunn, 1990)

'Desert Jewel' (Taylor, 1987)

'Dural Bluebird' (Taylor, 1994)

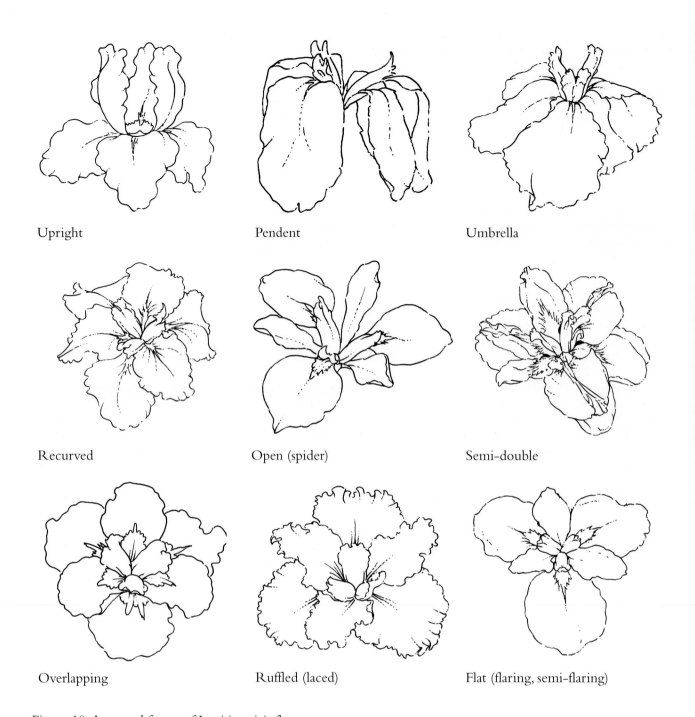

Upright   Pendent   Umbrella

Recurved   Open (spider)   Semi-double

Overlapping   Ruffled (laced)   Flat (flaring, semi-flaring)

Figure 10. Accepted forms of Louisiana iris flowers

country and he did much to popularise these iris in the early 1970s. Major achievements in his hybridising campaign were 'La Perouse', a stunning royal blue iris bred by selfing 'Clyde Redmond', 'Magistral', a red-purple tetraploid obtained by selfing 'Professor Ike' and 'Sinfonietta', a tall, healthy, beautifully rich blue which is his most acclaimed iris.

With limited garden space and resources at her disposal, Janet Hutchinson has produced some special Louisiana iris. Her major achievements have been the soft yellow award of merit winner 'Soft Laughter' and the pink bitone 'Popsie', winner of the 1993 Sydney Louisiana Iris Spectacular. One of her most attractive flowers is 'Our Mr Bailey', a lovely blue but a poor grower, while 'Honey Star', a soft honey bitoned iris has proven very popular.

Heather Pryor has delved extensively into the Taylor gene pool and in a short hybridising career has already produced some most attractive seedlings. Much more will be heard of from this talented hybridiser whose first irises were released in Australia in 1996. Already she has won major awards with 'Charlotte's Tutu' (Pryor, 1996) a ruffled cerise, 'Frosted Moonbeam' (Pryor, 1997) a ruffled soft cream and 'La Stupenda' (Pryor, 1996) a delicate blend while 'Crushed Ice' (Pryor, 1997) is a beautiful wide and ruffled white, bred from the classic 'Dural White Butterfly'. 'Crushed Ice' has the potential to match its illustrious parent.

There is little doubt that the most interest in Louisiana iris outside the USA is from Australia, and these iris have become very popular in this country. With talented hybridisers on both sides of the Pacific Ocean working on these irises, their future seems assured.

Cultivation

The cultivation of Louisiana iris in areas outside their natural habitat is far easier than has generally been thought in the early years of their distribution into gardens. From personal experience and all the recorded literature it is obvious that successful cultivation of Louisiana iris depends primarily on two major factors — an adequate supply of quality water and the combined effect of acidity and fertility to ensure a quality growing medium.

These iris are rather adaptable to situation, giving good results in full sun or part shade. They certainly do require about half a day of sunlight, but seem to do equally well in positions that have full sun for part of the day and shade for the other part and those that provide filtered sunlight throughout the day. From this it is clear that they can be grown in semi-sheltered positions near housing or in woodland type situations where they are grown under the canopy of trees allowing a fair amount of sunlight penetration. They do perform to their best in a warm sunny situation and this is their best growing position if it can be provided. In climates which provide very hot summers, Louisiana iris are at their best if provided some protection.

Ground preparation is essential to achieve satisfactory results. Louisiana iris like a rich, heavy soil, so large quantities of compost or well rotted animal manure can be incorporated in the soil and then well worked to ensure there are no patches of solid compost or manure. Many growers achieve spectacular results by providing an acid bed, which consists of an area dug out to spade depth, lined with plastic sheets and then the soil heavily dosed with sulphur before being replaced. This will provide the acid soil and moisture retention in the soil so important in the cultivation of Louisiana iris.

These iris grow actively in spring and autumn. I have found a certain degree of summer dormancy unless plants are kept actively growing by heavy summer watering. As they require so much water in the growing seasons, Louisiana iris can be grown in the ground, in standing water or in pots placed in ponds. They are gross feeders and can be heavily composted and fed with well rotted animal manures. Recent experience leads me to believe that the small amounts of alkalinity provided by some animal manures is of little, if any, concern. Care should be taken with potted iris to ensure that the soil mix or potting mix used is rich and fertile and that nutrient is replenished regularly.

Talking of pot cultivation of Louisiana iris reminds me of the fascinating story of the experience of a good friend and colleague of mine, who, in one of her roles as a columnist for a leading Sydney newspaper, used our Louisiana iris as a special promotion. This promotion went particularly well with several thousand iris distributed and a host of very satisfied customers. The quality of plants was good, the information given out was good and the promotion was good. There was one solitary complaint! A lady telephoned my friend some months later to complain that, while the iris had not died, they had not grown particularly well and only one out of five had flowered. Much questioning about position/conditions etc. finally revealed that the iris had been used in a large fish pond and when all other attempts to track down the problem failed my friend suggested that it could possibly have been the potting medium used or the manner of planting which resulted in the limited success. A brief pause — do we call it a pregnant silence? — and then the answer. 'Oh, I didn't put them in pots or anything like that. You said they could be grown in water, so I just threw them into the pond'. The humour in the story probably surpasses the fact that we learned how tough and adaptable these iris are but we also learned how careful you have to be in being explicit and thorough in dealing with people with little or no experience in handling plants. From that day on I have always been careful to enlarge on 'these iris can be grown in water' to ensure the full message gets across.

Provision of food for Louisiana iris is essential and so a fertilising program is necessary. As already stated, they are gross feeders and I have not heard of these iris being killed by over fertilising, although I am sure that it could be done. In the ground, we have often covered Louisiana iris with 5–8 cm of well-rotted manure (duck) and they have responded magnificently. Enough is enough and I feel that 8 cm is as far as I would like to go! This application was on well-established, strongly growing plants.

A similar application to newly planted rhizomes before they had established root growth would possibly prove fatal. Likewise, we have established that Louisiana iris love water but too much at the wrong time can present great problems. When planting or replanting new rhizomes, we must be careful to give the plant the opportunity to establish new roots before supplying too much water. When a rhizome is lifted it is normal for all the old roots to die and new roots to develop. At this stage the rhizomes can be kept damp, but care must be taken to avoid rhizome rot which can occur if the rhizome is overwatered without having an adequate root system. Iris being established in pots for future growing in water should be given three to four weeks during which the new roots are established and then the pot can be placed in water. But then again you can be lucky

'C'est La Mote' (Dunn, 1989)

'Crushed Ice' (Pryor, 1997)

'Charlotte's Tutu' (Pryor, 1996)

'Dancing Again' (Taylor, 1997)

'C'est Si Bon' (Taylor, 1984)

'Berenice' (Anfosso, 1988)

— at least one person has been able to just throw them in the water and they have not only survived, one even flowered.

At planting time we recommend the use of a teaspoon of eight to nine month slow-release fertiliser for Louisiana iris. Timing of follow-up fertilising is probably not as critical as we may think, but can involve chemical or natural fertiliser to ensure continued growth. Heavy fertilising as plants grow vigorously in early spring has traditionally been frowned upon because of the likelihood of producing vegetative growth at the expense of flowers. My experience is that the flowering spikes have been formed in the rhizome well before this time and that heavy spring fertilising is beneficial rather than detrimental. For great bloom, the main requirement in spring is adequate water.

Louisiana iris respond to azalea/camellia packeted fertiliser, to slow release fertiliser, to cotton seed meal, to most if not all animal manure so the answer for you is to experiment and come up with your own favourite schedule. I do particularly recommend summer mulching to protect the rhizomes from heat and to retain moisture. Winter mulching is an added safeguard against frost and extreme cold. Suitable media are bark, leaves or acid compost as well as manures; all give protection to the rhizomes which are inclined to rise toward the surface. For this reason they are best planted from 3–5 cm below the surface.

In suitable growing conditions many Louisiana iris cultivars are rampant growers and very quick increasers, therefore needing to be divided and replanted after three years in the ground. Dividing and replanting is best done in autumn, although there is an argument for dividing Louisiana iris immediately after they have flowered in late spring. Vegetative increase varies with cultivars but, on average, one can expect from two to six increases in a growing year. The most increase we have experienced in one year was 18 plants from one rhizome of 'Clyde Redmond'. This was amazing in itself, but all the more so because 'Clyde Redmond' is certainly not our quickest grower normally. Some Louisiana iris can, in perfect growing conditions, be invasive so care should be taken to plant them sufficiently far apart to give them room to move and to keep them apart. We recommend 60 cm should be allowed between rhizomes when planting.

PESTS AND DISEASES

The aftercare of Louisiana iris consists mainly of controlling pests and diseases. Fortunately these iris are not subject to many disease problems although they can be devastated by rust and leaf spot. Treatment is with any suitable fungicide. Mancozeb seems to be the most effective and is available under a variety of marketing names. It should be applied quickly and at weekly intervals if either of the problems arise. This will prevent the spread of the disease, but will not cure infected foliage which should be cut back to clean healthy leaves and the diseased parts burned.

Prevention is regarded as far more acceptable then cure and there are several theories as to the best methods of preventing these most serious diseases. My own theory is that weather conditions and soil conditions have the most effect on leaf spot and since the weather is beyond our control the best approach is clean cultivation, provision of the best possible growing conditions, a regular preventative spraying program and vigilance. If leaf spot does occur — and it will on certain cultivars in humid weather or when cool nights are followed by warm days — then removal of the infected leaves and treatment of the others is advisable. For optimum cultivation, water control is our greatest chore. The provision of adequate water in spring will all but eliminate disease problems except in very susceptible cultivars and probably these should not be grown. Not only is the provision of water important, but so also is its manner of application and its quality. Overhead watering is much less desirable than the provision of water at ground level, either by growing the iris in a wet or boggy position or by the use of drip irrigation. Above all, the water quality must be good. If all other conditions are excellent and your water supply is highly alkaline or saline then you will have problems in growing Louisiana iris to perfection.

It is well known that certain cultivars are more susceptible to leaf spot than others and I would strongly recommend that only those with a certain inbuilt resistance to disease should be grown. It is indeed unfortunate that the time of greatest vulnerability to leaf spot seems to correspond with bloom and the period immediately preceding bloom. It gives little joy to see the clump at bloom time decimated by unhealthy foliage. For this reason I would rate quite a few popular Louisiana iris very low as garden subjects and I see no future for any Louisiana iris unless it has an inbuilt resistance to disease.

If, as I suggest, climatic condition is a cause of leaf spot, the very climates in which these iris do so well are the types of climate to promote disease, then hybridisers will have to place health very high on their priority list before plants are named and introduced. One final point on fungal diseases — I have not seen any Louisiana grown in favourable conditions with adequate water suffer severely from fungal diseases. Even the least healthy seem to get by with minor infection if the growing conditions are good so I would endorse the Louisiana iris as a healthy, disease free, valuable garden plant under 'normal' circumstances.

Rhizome soft rot does not normally affect Louisiana iris. I have seen newly planted rhizomes affected when they are given too much water before root growth commences, but even this is not usual. I have never seen this problem in an established clump.

If you can keep your Louisiana iris free of attack by snails and slugs you have virtually solved the pest problem. There can be minor irritations for hybridisers when native bees or wasps strip valuable pollen, but for the average gardener wishing to delight in spring flowers on healthy, clean-foliaged plants, there are only the ubiquitous snails and slugs with which to contend. No doubt all gardeners have their own approach to this problem and it is pointless to go into detail as this topic is discussed under bearded iris. One point worth making though is that the most brilliant of displays of Louisiana iris can be devastated by snails and slugs unless they are eradicated prior to bloom. If left too late these pests will climb the flowering spikes, hide under and among the blooms and cause havoc. We have found the best control to be an early spring spray with a Mesurol powder mixed into a spray and liberally spread on to the foliage. It will run down the foliage and give very good protection. Mesurol, purchased as a powder and used as a spray is expensive but very effective. A possible follow-up as spikes appear ensures nearly complete control.

LANDSCAPING WITH LOUISIANA IRIS

A major factor in the greatly increased popularity of Louisiana iris is their diversity both in colour and form. Equally important has been the extension of the height range available so that there are plants available with flowering spikes from 35 cm to nearly 200 cm in height. These factors coupled with the definite progress made in recent years to make the Louisiana iris a more compact garden plant with more bloom per unit of foliage have made the Louisiana iris a most desirable landscape plant. For sheer diversity, the Louisiana iris has very few, if any peers, but it is also a most adaptable plant being quite comfortable in a 'normal' garden situation either solitary or in a perennial border or as an accent plant; being quite comfortable in a bog garden; being quite comfortable grown in standing water around lakes, dams or natural wet areas and being quite comfortable as a potted plant used in or out of water. Add to these attributes the ability of this iris to perform well in full sun, part shade or dappled sunlight and its ability to cope with tropical, temperate and moderately cold climates and you have one very adaptable plant. Can I add just one other major attribute and that is the magnificence of Louisiana iris as cut flowers for floral arrangement or massed cut flower effect to ensure that these plants are seen as having something to offer everyone with an interest in gardening or horticulture. While having the deepest admiration for the sculptured form and beauty of the bearded iris and their many uses in the garden and the landscape, I feel that they are greatly surpassed by the Louisiana iris as cut flowers for display or arrangement.

The typical Louisiana spike will emerge from the foliage and remain some three weeks before the blooms open. This is in sharp contrast with the bearded iris which race quickly into bloom once the flowering spike has emerged. The modern Louisiana iris spike is well branched but this branching is variable from cultivar to cultivar and from season to season and even from one garden to another. Thus branching and bud count will depend on cultivar, growing conditions, culture and climate. Most Louisiana iris cultivars carry a minimum of two branches plus a terminal with double buds in the top socket and a minimum of five flowers which will open sequentially, often with two or more flowers open simultaneously. Each bloom will last two to three days, again depending on the cultivar and the weather conditions. In general, the heavily substanced cultivars will last longer than those with poor substance. It is not unusual for the leathery 'Margaret Lee' to last four days in cool weather while the poorly substanced 'La Perouse' will only live one day in hot conditions. Each spike should provide bloom from six to ten days, again depending on cultivars and conditions. I have seen a spike of the superb yellow Louisiana iris 'Koorawatha' with 15 buds, all of which reached flowering size and full development, giving a three-week display from this outstanding heavily substanced iris. This is, of course, the exception, but many modern hybrids are multi-budded and heavily substanced with spikes carrying from eight to ten or more buds for an extended bloom period.

In evaluating the worth of any iris but, in this case, the Louisiana iris, we should place importance on the general garden value of the plant, the spike and its bud count and positioning and timing of buds to come into bloom, but it is the flowers themselves for which we grow the plant and in flower shape, colour and pattern the Louisiana iris again exhibits great diversity. There are many accepted forms and while modern trends are towards rounded, ruffled and heavily substanced blooms there is much to say for the great array of choices open to Louisiana iris enthusiasts. Bloom form may be flat, pendent, umbrella-shaped, recurved, open, overlapping, semi-double, double, ruffled, rounded and even 'tall bearded' form with upright standards.

Because the Louisiana iris is a flat flower, there have been two ways of describing the floral segments — either as standards and falls (as in the bearded iris) or as sepals and petals. Although I have always used the latter terminology in the past I intend to refer to the floral parts as standards and falls in this publication. I have reservations about this terminology because, with most Louisiana iris, the standards do not stand upright as they do with bearded iris and the falls do not fall as they do with bearded iris. However the use of standards and falls will keep continuity of usage for all the iris in this publication and will also bring me in line with the terminology used by Joe Mertzweiller in *The Louisiana Iris*. The standards are the narrower parts while the falls are the wider parts adorned by signals and overlaid by the styles. Again, we need to be careful not to confuse, as many modern hybrids have the standards widened and

'Glowlight' (Taylor, 1986)

'Exclusive Label' (Taylor, 1997)

'Better Watch Out'
(Taylor, 1997)

'La Stupenda' (Pryor, 1996)

the petals rounded to such an extent that all the floral parts appear similar. This is particularly the case when we have the 'star effect' centre where all the floral parts are adorned by signals. The one major distinguishing feature in all iris is that the styles are associated with and overlay the floral parts called falls. The knowledge of standards, falls, signals and styles and the meaning of each is essential in understanding the descriptions of Louisiana iris because of the great diversity in all these facets in describing form, pattern and colour.

These descriptions refer to the positioning of the floral parts relative to the horizontal and vertical.

Flat — an iris is described as flat or flaring if the falls spread outwards on opening to a horizontal or near horizontal position. The standards may also lie flat or can be at varying positions from horizontal to vertical. Vertical standards throughout the flower's life would have it described as upright. Blooms are said to be semi-flaring if there is a slight angle of downward arching of the falls from the horizontal.

Pendent — form is described as pendent if the falls hang vertically or nearly so. The positioning of the standards is variable but usually they will hang at the same angle as the standards. If the flower is full with all floral parts touching or overlapping and both standards and falls 'hang' at the same angle the flower is said to be umbrella shaped.

Recurved — form is described as recurved if the falls are held so that the lower part is rolled back at an angle greater than the vertical in much the same manner as the aril and arilbred bearded iris.

These descriptions refer to the width and positioning of the floral parts relative to one another.

Open — form is described as open if the floral parts are narrow and there are obvious gaps between standards and falls.

Overlapping — form is described as overlapping if the floral parts are wide and there are no gaps between standards and falls. This has led to the terminology 'full' flowers meaning no gaps between segments.

These descriptions refer to the type and number of floral parts.

Single — the 'normal' bloom with a set of three standards and three falls.

Semi-double — form is described as semi-double if it carries more than six floral parts or has extra petaloids. The typical semi double 'Cartwheel' form has six falls and extra petaloids.

Double — form is described as double if it has floral parts of nine or 12 or even more, often including extra petaloids.

Some cultivars are unstable, having both single and double flowers from the same planting and, at times, even on the same spike.

Very much the 'in-thing' in the late 1990s is to have Louisiana iris that are rounded and ruffled. Much of the pioneering work for these modern beauties has been done by John C. Taylor from Australia.

Rounded — form is exemplified in flowers having floral parts, both standards and falls, circular in shape and positioned so that the whole flower has a circular outline.

Ruffled — form is exemplified in flowers having floral parts with crimping and undulation to break up the outline of the petal edges.

As well as diversification for form there exists great diversification in the colour and pattern of Louisiana iris. The colour range of Louisiana iris is extensive with various shades of white, yellow from pale cream through to rich gold, blue in every shade and purple and violet shades right through to black. There are Louisiana iris in various shades of tan, brown, chocolate and red. There are Louisiana iris in shades of lilac, mauve and orchid through to pink. Great advancement in recent years has seen the development of true pink and we are well on the way to a true orange. There are green-toned whites and green-toned yellows.

As well as diversification for form and colour there is much diversification in the patterning of Louisiana iris with great variation coming out in the Taylor bloodlines in particular. There are now Louisiana iris available that are true bicolours and even tricolours. Different coloured reverses to the floral parts have become common and there are many iris showing rims on the edges, spray patterns and plicata type patterns with one colour edged or overlaid with another. As distinct from bearded iris, the style arms of Louisiana iris are very visible and form an important part of the colour patterns observed. Style arms vary considerably in colour from blending with to sharply contrasting with the colours of standards and falls. Some style arms are themselves bicoloured or bitoned and there are even styles with laced edges and some which sit tight like a pom pom in the centre of the flower ('Real Treasure'). The style arms also vary in size both in length and width.

A further major variable in patterning is the wide diversification of signals in Louisiana iris. The signals are usually on the falls and similarly positioned to the beards on bearded iris. However, recent developments have seen many iris with signals on all floral parts, giving a six-pointed star effect. This outstanding attribute is particularly attractive and has been developed to the fullest in the Taylor irises where we have coined the term 'star centre'. Signal patches have usually been in shades of yellow, but a feature of the Taylor releases and their progeny has been the diversification in colour with quite green signals now being available, some palest cream near to white and others in true bicolours with combination of yellow and green with pale creams, golds and oranges often with dark brown and burgundy to purple lines. Some signals are now into bicolour patterns. This has been accompanied by spray patterns where the signals or areas around the signals in different colours to the falls, spray out onto the falls, giving great contrast. Not only are the colours and patterns of the signals diverse, but so also is their actual size. This ranges from being practically non-existent line signals to being very large and boldly patterned. The combination of brilliant colours of the floral parts, colour and patterning of signals and the adornment of obvious styles makes the Louisiana iris the most vibrant and colourful of all of the genus. Louisiana iris are truly colour spectacles in themselves.

Recommended cultivars

The iris scene changes very quickly and nowhere is this more in evidence than in Louisiana iris. The development of these iris in the early 1990s surpassed development and improvement of all other iris with the possible exception of the Californian iris. What Joe Ghio has done for the Californian iris in the USA, John Taylor has done for the Louisiana iris in Australia. In both fields there have been other hybridisers making great contributions, but the Taylor iris reign supreme in the world of Louisiana iris. With such dramatic improvement going on we can but evaluate the best available at the time of writing and I propose to do this by colour.

WHITE

White Louisiana iris had been of rather poor quality by comparison with other colours until the release of 'Clara Goula' by Charles Arny in 1975. This iris is well formed, ruffled and reasonably vigorous, producing creamy white flowers on showy spikes that are tall and well branched. The foliage is quite healthy. 'Clara Goula' has proven itself a wonderful parent. It was allocated the Mary Swords Debaillon Award in the USA in 1982 and when the Awards System was changed in 1986 it was awarded the Mary Swords Debaillon Medal in 1987.

From his first batch of seedlings from 'Clara Goula', John Taylor named and released the magnificent cold-white 'Helen Naish'. A late bloomer, 'Helen Naish' is an outstanding, ruffled white with green veins and a slightly green influence in the petals. Like its parent, it is a healthy iris and reasonably vigorous. 'Helen Naish' was released in 1983 and proved a sensation in Australia, surpassing its parent both as a garden plant and as a breeding iris. It went on to win numerous awards in trial gardens, culminating in being awarded the first Australasian Dykes Medal in 1985. This was the first time a Louisiana iris had been awarded a Dykes Medal anywhere in the world.

Surpassing both these iris as a garden plant is the startling beauty 'Dural White Butterfly', released by John Taylor in 1990. This is an all-time great garden iris producing masses of pure white flowers with greenish toned styles and signals on quality spikes which come from a compact clump. Bred from the 'Clara Goula', 'Helen Naish' line, 'Dural White Butterfly' has become the most highly awarded iris ever bred in Australia. It has won an Award of Merit and the Gordon Loveridge Medallion as outstanding iris in the NSW Region Trial Gardens. It then went on to win the ISA Medal as outstanding beardless iris in 1992, the Dykes Medal in 1993 and the Sydney Louisiana Iris Spectacular in 1994. In 1994 it was voted in second place on the Society for Louisiana Iris popularity poll in the USA, an outstanding feat because of its limited distribution in that country so early after its release, and in 1996 was voted number one in the same poll. It is, by far, the most popular Louisiana iris grown in Australia at the time of writing. As with many great iris, there is a story attached to this one. Bred from 'Screen Gem', a pink Louisiana from Charles Arny, and the great 'Helen Naish', this iris was only kept by John because it was carrying the pink blood lines from 'Screen Gem', a lovely iris, good for colour but a slow, difficult grower and low on bud count. In two consecutive years he was going to dispose of it as he had not been able to breed any pink iris from it and he felt that it did not have any great advancement in form. Twice he was persuaded to give it 'one more year' and each year it performed better and better as a garden plant so eventually he entered it in trial gardens, named and released it. Many gardeners have been made happy as a result. No iris has given me the satisfaction provided by 'Dural White Butterfly'. Now the pink hybrids are arriving from this line and, with persistence, 'Dural White Butterfly is proving a great parent for both pink and white Louisiana iris.

Some other white iris of quality are the older 'Ashley Michelle' (Mertzweiller 1986) and the more recent and heavily ruffled 'Dural Dreamtime' (Taylor, 1993) and 'First Favourite' (Taylor, 1993). Probably the nicest individual flower is on 'Obvious Heir' (Taylor, 1992), a rounded and heavily ruffled milk white with green veins and signals. This is another child of 'Helen Naish', but unfortunately we have found it to lack stability, sometimes showing only four or five floral parts, and to our knowledge this lack of stability has only been noticed in the home garden. It is a very good garden iris, of medium height and with strong stems.

'White Umbrella' (Taylor, 1991) is a very large, umbrella-shaped iris of good quality, excellent growth and exemplary garden habits. It has green-gold veins giving a warm effect and has wide overlapping petals.

Apart from 'Clara Goula', probably the best white Louisiana iris to come from the USA is the Arny-bred 'Acadian Miss', a smaller flower but heavily ruffled and nicely rounded. It was bred from two Arny classics, 'Clara Goula' and that great blue 'Clyde Redmond', and was released in 1980. Two newer whites from the USA are 'Good Doctor' (Mertzweiller, 1993) and 'Cotton Plantation' (Dunn, 1994) while the older 'Marie Dolores' (Haymon, 1988) is pure white with pom pom styles.

'Jack Attack' (Taylor, 1994)

'Jazz Ballet' (Taylor, 1989)

'Honey Star' (Hutchinson, 1993)

'Honored Guest' (Taylor, 1992)

'High Rank' (Dunn, 1991)

'Heather Pryor' (Taylor, 1994)

'Koorawatha' (Taylor, 1987)

'John's Lucifer' (Taylor, 1987)

'Dural White Butterfly' (Taylor, 1990)

YELLOW (INCLUDING CREAM, GOLD)

The most famous early yellow hybrid is 'G.W. Holleyman' (Holleyman, 1960), a large yellow which traces back to *I. fulva*.

Yellow is a dominant colour in iris and the development of Louisiana iris has reached a peak in this colour range and once again it is the Taylor irises which dominate the scene. Starting with 'Dural Charm' in 1983, John Taylor has produced a procession of superb quality yellow Louisiana iris, each with its own particular attraction. Bred from Arny seedlings, 'Dural Charm' received the ultimate award with its Dykes Medal in 1987. This early flowering multibudded and well branched iris is a rich canary yellow of beautiful rounded form. It is a vigorous grower on a healthy plant, its one fault being a tendency to sprout an extra branch at times, giving a crowded and bunched effect to the flowers. While this can be a failing it is nevertheless a superb garden plant.

John crossed 'Dural Charm' into the 'Clara Goula' line and obtained the optimum result when 'Koorawatha' turned up in the seedling patch. Until 'Dural Charm' was released, yellow Louisiana iris were renowned for having rather poor stems and for fading badly, being anything but colour-fast. 'Koorawatha' retained its parent's colour-fast attribute, produced strong upright spikes and had the added bonus of multibudded stems with up to 15 of the most heavily ruffled rich yellow flowers yet seen on a spike. So heavy was the ruffling that it was feared that blooms would have difficulty in opening. This was not to be and not only did they open, but they opened in classic display with three and four well spaced blooms regularly opening on show spikes, making this a near perfect show iris. John Taylor released 'Koorawatha' in 1987 and I will never forget its sensational year in 1988. This was a convention year in Sydney and visitors from all over the world attended the event. At the NSW Region show renowned German irisarian Thomas Tamberg was one of the judges and I will not forget his amazement and near disbelief as he evaluated a spike of 'Koorawatha' carrying 15 buds and five open flowers displayed symmetrically on a spike. He asked me if this was how the iris came always and I was quick to tell him that while it was always excellent it did not always produce 15 buds and five open flowers. 'Koorawatha', bred and exhibited by John Taylor, was unanimously judged Grand Champion Exhibit in the show (equivalent to Queen of the Show in the USA) and went on to win John his third Dykes Medal for Louisiana iris when evaluated in the trial gardens. After the death of Charles Arny in 1993 the Society for Louisiana Iris initiated a Charles W. Arny Junior Award for the iris judged first on the popularity poll in the USA. In 1994 'Koorawatha' won that prestigious award.

In the 1990s John Taylor has released several outstanding Louisiana iris in the yellow shades.

'Alluvial Gold' (Taylor, 1992) is a clear mid-yellow with darker ribs. It is ruffled, well formed and both healthy and vigorous.

'Apollo's Song' (Taylor, 1991) is a tall, unfading mid-yellow with ramrod stiff spikes and beautiful well spaced blooms on show stems. Very healthy!

'Classical Note' (Taylor, 1991) is a lighter yellow with a gold influence, deeper yellow veins and styles. Flowers are fluted and ruffled and the plants are healthy and vigorous.

'Lydia's Love' (Taylor, 1991) is a soft cream and it is special because it is the first Louisiana iris to bloom in the season at Rainbow Ridge.

'Spanish Ballet' (Taylor, 1993) is a shorter growing cream iris with heavily ruffled and pleated, perfectly rounded flowers. The blooms are smaller and in proportion to the shorter spike which is well branched and multibudded.

'Rachel's Request' (Taylor, 1994) is taller and a paler cream, near white. This superb iris is very round, very heavily ruffled and of the highest quality.

'Pamela Hart' (Taylor, 1994) was named for a good friend and irisarian. For flower form and colour it takes yellow Louisiana iris to new heights of beauty and grace. It is a bright mid-yellow, very round, ruffled and serrated, giving a lacy effect. It also carries green-yellow signals on all petals. 'Pamela Hart' is healthy and vigorous — an all-round great garden iris.

Other yellow Louisiana iris well worth growing are the older 'Lucille Holley' (Arny, 1979), the best yellow Louisiana iris of its day and to be found in the background of most of the Taylor yellows, and 'Monument' (Mary Dunn, 1978) a bright cream of quality. Also of interest are 'President Hedley' (Mertzweiller, 1979), a heavily colour-saturated yellow which has great carrying power in the garden and the unusual 'Uptight' (Arny, 1970), a light yellow which opens with upright standards as in a tall bearded iris and semi-flaring falls.

From Australia there are John Taylor's 'Green Elf' (1986), a smaller yellow with a green influence and 'Noble Planet', a ruffled and serrated cream, and Janet Hutchinson's 'Soft Laughter' (1987), a warm cream with gold veins and signals. The more recent 'Sorbet' (Dunn, 1992) is an unusual glowing lemon cream and lime green beauty which will be very popular while 'Girl Crazy' (Dunn, 1993) is a shorter-growing ruffled yellow. In 1992 Joe Mertzweiller released the first yellow tetraploid Louisiana iris with 'Professor Barbara'. This is a heavily textured mid-yellow of quality. I was particularly impressed with this iris as seen in the USA and feel sure it will be a winner when established in

Australia. Another new yellow, 'Rokki Rockwell' (Haymon, 1992), is a vibrantly coloured mid-yellow with some gold.

Heather Pryor has some very nice yellow seedlings and in 1996 released the ruffled and serrated lemon bitone 'Acacia Rhumba' and the richly coloured dark orange-yellow 'Bushfire Moon', while John Taylor has the luscious primrose-yellow 'Icarus' and the superbly ruffled light yellow 'Successful Bid' scheduled for 1997 release.

BLUE

Blue is a favourite colour in irises and there are many quality blue Louisiana iris available. Charles Arny's 'Clyde Redmond' (1971) has been the outstanding blue Louisiana iris, both as a garden plant and a producer of outstanding progeny. A third generation seedling from *I. giganticaerulea,* 'Clyde Redmond' is a smallish flowered rich cornflower blue on well branched, well budded spikes to medium height. It is a particularly vigorous iris and is also particularly healthy. This iris increases quickly and one plant gave us our best increase ever with 15 increases in one season. By selfing 'Clyde Redmond', Bob Raabe produced the startling vibrantly coloured 'La Perouse', an even richer blue than its parent and the first Australian-raised iris to receive international acclaim. Also very vigorous, 'La Perouse' had one major failing, being low on substance so that individual blooms rarely lasted two days. I can remember seeing it for the first time in the hybridiser's Sydney home and I was absolutely captivated by its beauty.

The other great blue iris from Charles Arny was the 1967 release 'Eolian', a beautiful sky blue of colour clarity that has still not been equalled. 'Eolian' is vigorous, healthy and a superb garden iris. It is a second generation seedling from *I. giganticaerulea.* Both 'Clyde Redmond' (1974) and 'Eolian' (1967) are winners of the Mary Swords Debaillon Award.

While Charles Arny released 'Bit o' Blue', a seedling of 'Clyde Redmond' in 1975, he did little work on this colour in latter years, with the vigorous 'Geisha Eyes' (Arny 1987) being his most noted contribution. 'Geisha Eyes' is a large rich blue with light yellow signals on all floral parts, giving the 'star centre' effect.

Henry Rowlan released 'Francois' in 1985. This short-growing, rather spidery rich deep blue is very attractive in the garden. 'Exquisite Lady' (Owen, 1987) has had much acceptance in the USA and in Australia. It is a mid sky-blue with a silver rim, nicely formed and reasonably vigorous. 'Bluebonnet Sue' (Chenoweth 1986) is another sky blue which has nice flowers and good garden habits while Dorman Haymon's 'Wake Up Susie' (1988) is a very vigorous light blue with a lavender overlay which has proven to be a quality iris. 'Sea Knight' (Henry Morgan, 1989) is a short-growing, brilliant cobalt blue.

Two excellent blue Louisiana iris to come from Bob Raabe in Australia in recent years are 'Byron Bay' (1986) and 'Sinfonietta' (1987). 'Byron Bay' is a tall, vigorous gentian blue of quality while 'Sinfonietta' is one of my two favourite blue Louisiana iris. This tall, healthy and vigorous iris carries intensely rich mid-blue flowers of nice rounded form. Stems are strong and this iris is a garden spectacle. My other personal favourite is Mary Dunn's 'C'est La Mote' (1989), a shorter-growing, compact clumping iris in the richest of mid-blue with yellow signals. This iris produces many, many blooms in a small area and is gorgeous when in full bloom. It is very vigorous and very healthy but has one failing in that it is tightly branched. This failing is easily overlooked when it is seen in bloom. Mary Dunn has made the blue and purple Louisiana iris her trademark and she has several other outstanding blue Lousiana iris on offer. 'Gulf Shores' is an older cultivar still valuable because it is short growing, very blue and suitable for the front of the garden.

'Emigré' (Dunn, 1990) is particularly beautiful, ruffled, serrated and texture veined blue with a slight violet infusion. The blooms are large and nicely rounded. It grows tall and is spectacular in the garden.

'Over There' (Dunn, 1992) is a mid-blue with a white area beneath blue styles. It is another quality iris. 'Rapport' (Dunn, 1991) is a tall-growing mid-blue with a chartreuse centre and signals.

The Taylor blue iris are also very impressive and quite distinctive. Superb among them is 'Sea Lord' (Taylor, 1991), a brilliant royal blue on erect, strong spikes with the healthiest of lush foliage. Flowers are rounded, ruffled and of the highest quality but this iris has two faults: it flowers very late in the season when most of the other Louisiana iris are finished and it therefore is not part of the general scene and often has to cope with hotter weather; and it is a very slow increaser. If only we could get one like it without these faults.

'Dural Bluebird' (Taylor, 1994) has medium-sized, rounded and ruffled flowers of mid to dark blue with a slight violet influence. Plants are vigorous, spikes are tall and it is multibudded and healthy. 'Malibu Magic' (Taylor, 1991) is a distinctive blue iris, slightly bitoned with feathering on all the floral parts. It is quality in every respect and has proven very popular. 'Sea Consul' (Taylor, 1991) is a sky blue with a white centre and rim on the petals. It is also a high quality iris. Also good among the Taylor blues are 'Poseidon's Pool' (Taylor, 1990) a tall mid-blue, 'Quiet Harbour' (Taylor, 1992), a lightly ruffled soft sky blue and the older 'Cammeray' (Taylor, 1987), a ruffled mid-blue. John's 'Freedom Ride', scheduled for 1996 release, is a gorgeous, ruffled mid-blue with a violet influence, white styles tipped blue-violet, green-yellow signals on all floral parts giving a star centre effect and a lighter rim and reverse. It is a very distinctive iris.

'Far and Away' (Dunn, 1992)

'Flight of Fantasy' (Taylor, 1989)

'Never Say'
(Taylor, 1994)

'Lucy Payens' (Taylor, 1993)

'Surprise Offer' (Taylor, 1995)

'Sea Lord' (Taylor, 1991)

'Successful Bid' (Taylor, 1997)

'Purple Pallas' (Taylor, 1992)

'Professor Neil' (Mertzweiller, 1992)

The only blue-toned tetraploid available is 'Professor Paul' (Mertzweiller, 1980), a pale blue-lavender bred from 'Chimeras'. It is tall, healthy and vigorous but low on buds. 'Professor Paul' is a beautiful iris in the landscape.

PURPLE

Purple is a very dominant colour in Louisiana iris and with shades of violet, purple, red-purple and the very dark ones through to black there is a multitude of iris available in these shades.

Two classic irises in these tones are 'Black Widow' (W.B. MacMillan, 1968) and 'Marie Caillet' (Sidney Conger, 1963). 'Black Widow' has become a classic and is beautifully named for its very dark, near black, open, spidery blooms. It is not particularly vigorous but has garden value for its colour and form. 'Marie Caillet' by contrast is a very vigorous, easily grown violet purple. It is tall, well branched and healthy and is well worth a position in the garden. Purple is not a colour that the late Charles Arny worked with to any great extent. He did release the well formed 'Charles Arny III', named for his son, but this iris lacks vigour and is not of good garden value. 'Charjoys Mike' is another Arny iris, shorter and ruffled in light purple bitone, while 'Mighty Rich' is a lustrous rich red-purple of excellent form and shorter growth. Perhaps his best in these shades is the bitoned light rosy-violet 'Charlies Tress', a vigorous and prolific grower with nicely formed flowers. Richard Goula released 'Joel Fletcher' in 1979 and this attractive lavender-purple bitone has retained popularity. It is a vigorous and healthy grower. 'Brookvale Nocturne' (Myrtle Murray, 1982) is an Australian-raised iris of quality. It is an attractive blue-violet on well branched and multibudded spikes. Foliage is very healthy and attractive and growth and increase are excellent. 'Hurricane Party' (Haymon, 1986) is an excellent iris. It is vigorous and healthy and produces many ruffled red-violet flowers on perfect show spikes. 'Jeri' (Neil Bertinot, 1985) has dark grape-purple flowers in abundance and is a most vigorous grower. This iris won the Charles W. Arny Award and Debaillon Medal double in the USA in 1995.

'Grace Duhon' (Dorman Haymon, 1988) is an outstanding dark purple to black iris with a velvet sheen, ruffled flowers and contrasting bright-yellow signals. It is one of the best available in this colour range. 'Empress Josephine' (Haymon, 1990) is a satin-textured very dark purple, nearly black with large yellow signals. As seen in the USA, this could be *the* outstanding near-black Louisiana iris. 'Full Eclipse' (Ben Hager, 1978) is another true black worth growing.

The other outstanding diploid Louisiana iris in these colours have been developed by Mary Dunn in the USA and John Taylor in Australia. Both these hybridisers have made outstanding contributions with many cultivars to their names. ''Bout Midnight' (Dunn, 1989) is very dark purple, nearly black, with virtually no signal. Although a mediocre grower this iris has been very well received for its spectacular dark blooms. 'Louisiana Derby' (Dunn, 1987) is a flat-formed wine-violet, 'Louie' (Dunn, 1988) is a rounded dark blue-violet with a velvet sheen. 'Satchmo' (Dunn, 1987) is a rich dark purple, on tall spikes with well-spaced blooms. 'Wine Country' (Dunn, 1988) is a ruffled burgundy-purple of exquisite form. The blooms are inclined to hug the stem. 'Concours Elegance' (Dunn, 1989) is a glowing metallic magenta plum purple all waved and ruffled. These are all good irises, but in the 1990s the quality has improved dramatically. 'Extraordinaire' (Dunn, 1992) is a beautiful iris with large blue-purple flowers serrated and ruffled. It has a star centre with signals on all floral parts. 'Far and Away' (Dunn, 1992) is a more red-purple flower with flowers serrated and ruffled. It also carries a star centre. 'High Pitch' (Dunn, 1992) is a sultry dark red-purple with a velvet sheen. Form is full and the plant is vigorous.

Some newer ones as seen in the USA are even further improvements, but at the time of writing they are only getting established in Australia. We can look forward to 'Even Handed' (Dunn, 1994), a large, smooth, milky violet with overlapping form. 'Inner Beauty' (Dunn, 1991), a vivid violet with deeper veining and lime green styles. 'Rich and Famous' (Dunn, 1993), a smooth metallic red-purple. 'Sure Bet' (Dunn, 1994), a velvet red-purple, very dark near black in the centre of the falls and 'Star Power' (Dunn, 1993), a crepe-textured royal purple with pleated ruffles. This iris is very vigorous and is already well received in the USA. In 1995 Mary Dunn released 'Boy Crazy', a cup-shaped blue-purple with darker veining. It is lightly ruffled and has a metallic sheen. Also released were 'Chez Michelle', a slate-purple umbrella-formed iris with ruffles. 'True Reward', a rosy violet with a cream halo and ruffled flowers and 'Whistling Dixie', a luminous red-violet with a black sheen. It is fluted and ruffled.

The Australian purples are no less impressive and equally diverse. 'C'est Si Bon' (Taylor, 1984) is a huge purple with a white edge and spray pattern reminiscent of the plicata pattern in tall bearded iris. This iris is vigorous and multibudded but the flowers are somewhat soft for substance. 'Barossa' (Taylor, 1988) is an iridescent, ruffled grey-purple that has proven popular. You either love it or hate it! 'Lina' (Taylor, 1989) is another love-hate iris. It is a heavily ruffled smoky, greyed violet with rounded flowers. This one I do love. 'Good Vibes' (Taylor, 1991) is a huge rich purple with the six-petal star effect in yellow. It is round, flat, ruffled form and a good strong grower. 'Glittering Prize' (Taylor, 1992) is a strangely coloured dark purple bitone with velvet texture, while 'Honoured Guest' (Taylor, 1992) is a round, ruffled clear purple with a lighter edge and reverse. 'John's Lucifer' (Taylor, 1987) is a large-flowered dark red-purple with ruffles. It is vigorous and healthy and a particularly beautiful iris. 'Midnight Drama' (Taylor, 1991) is ripple-ruffled and slightly bitoned purple with a lighter rim and reverse. The medium-sized blooms have cream styles and rounded form.

'Rich Tradition' (Taylor, 1991) is a mid-purple with a mauve reverse and edge. It carries the star centre and is heavily ruffled. 'Tahitian Night' (Taylor, 1994) is in much the same colour pattern as 'Rich Tradition', but it is more waved and ruffled and blooms later in the season. 'Jazz Ballet' (Taylor, 1989) is an outstanding iris. Flowers are large spectrum-violet with a silver rim and reverse. They are heavily ruffled and have a pronounced star centre with yellow-green signals on all floral parts. The strong stems carry many buds on show spikes. This iris makes big rhizomes but they form compact clumps. It is late to bloom and, while strong and vigorous, only a moderate increaser. When first evaluated in the trial gardens in Australia, 'Jazz Ballet' created a sensation and it has won all the top awards, culminating in the Dykes Medal in 1990. It is bred from the Arny iris 'Secret Spell', a renowned difficult iris to grow but nevertheless a beautiful flower, crossed with the Dykes Medal winning 'Helen Naish'. Its sister seedling, 'Limited Edition' (Taylor, 1989) is equally beautiful in paler lavender-violet but is a poor grower. Another beautiful Taylor iris is 'Purple Pallas' (1992) which is a serrated, purple bitone with a lighter edge. This is a high-quality iris. 'Paul Payens' (Taylor, 1993) has attractive, slightly recurved purple bitoned flowers with a lighter edge and reverse and marbled and feathered standards. Flowers are ruffled.

'Jack Attack' (Taylor, 1994) is a tall, well branched and budded purple bitone with very large, ruffled blooms. Three newer Taylor cultivars complete the scene and they are each distinctive and magnificent. 'Silencio' (Taylor, 1995) is a great personal favourite and a favourite of all who see it. The wonderfully rounded and ruffled flowers are blue-violet with a lighter rim and reverse on all floral parts and a yellow star centre. This tall-growing iris carries a multitude of flowers well positioned on excellent straight spikes. Growth, health and vigour are all excellent. 'Stella Pelissot' (Taylor, 1994) is another great favourite as is the lady after whom it is named. Standards are light purple with darker feathering, falls are purple with yellow signals. The ruffled blooms have great clarity of colour and come on outstanding, tall show spikes with many perfectly placed blooms. This iris is vigorous, healthy and a real champion. 'Real Treasure' (Taylor, 1994) was on everyone's 'want list' before its release in 1994 and it subsequently sold out in its first year and has had to be withdrawn from sale. This fascinating iris had the garden name 'Purple Star' because of its purple colour and the fact that it took the star centre pattern to new heights of perfection. The perfectly rounded and ruffled floral parts have a lighter reverse and narrow rim. They are lit up by yellow signals on all floral parts with green line signals superimposed and

widening to form a very green centre. The signals are further adorned by dark burgundy-red purple lines running parallel to the green line. As if this is not enough, the styles are light mauve-pink on cream and they often tuft in the centre of the flower to give a pom pom effect. This iris is vigorous, well branched, multibudded and healthy. It could become one of the all-time great Louisiana iris.

THE PURPLE TETRAPLOID SCENE

The first two tetraploid Louisiana iris to be released were in the purple tones. 'Professor Ike' and 'Professor Claude' were both released by Joe Mertzweiller in 1973. They were the result of years of patient work in converting diploids by the use of colchicine and intercrossing chimeras. Both these iris are strong, vigorous growers with very healthy broad foliage. There is little difference in flower form, but 'Professor Ike' has proven the better iris both in the garden and on the show bench. It is quite tall and has large, well formed and rounded flowers in violet-purple at four bud positions.

No further additions to the tetraploid Louisiana irises were made until 1980 when Joe Mertzweiller released 'Professor Sigmund' a dark red-violet obtained by using the pollen from 'Professor Ike' on a Chimera. In the same year, Ken Durio released the red-violet 'Bayou Rouge' and the dark purple 'King Kong', both from the cross 'Professor Claude' x 'Professor Ike'. He followed these with several others from the same cross — 'Bowie' (1981) in violet, 'Bozo' (1981) in red-violet, 'Decoy' (1981) in red-violet, 'Ragin' Cajun' (1981) in dark violet-purple, and 'Wine Cooler' (1983) in dark violet-purple.

Meanwhile, Bob Raabe in Australia selfed 'Professor Ike' to produce the red-purple tetraploid 'Magistral' and this was followed by possibly the best tetraploid to date — 'Coorabell' (Raabe, 1988), a velvety-textured rich purple with a yellow signal. This iris grows well, has lovely, healthy foliage and a quality flower.

Joe Mertzweiller's latest contributions in this colour range have been 'Professor Ellis' (1986), a ruffled blue-purple of excellent quality and 'Professor Sigmund' (1988), a rich velvety-purple.

I look forward to seeing and growing 'Charlie Arny' (Richard Goula, 1993), a rich velvety-purple named and released by Richard Goula to honour his friend and neighbour. From photos this is a beautiful iris.

PINK

The pink coloration so popular in tall bearded iris has not been easy to develop in Louisiana iris and while many iris have been described as pink, it was not until the very recent development of the Taylor pinks that we have observed truly pink Louisiana iris. There is little record of earlier pink hybrids and it was not until 'Screen Gem' (Arny, 1983) was released that we had what could really be called a pink Louisiana iris.

'Real Treasure' (Taylor, 1994)

'Josephine Shanks' (Taylor, 1993)

'Going South' (Taylor, 1994)

'Imperial Magician' (Taylor, 1991)

'Stella Pelissot' (Taylor, 1994)

'King's Dream' (Taylor, 1997)

'Screen Gem' has nicely formed mid-pink flowers of heavy substance. It does not carry more than five or six flowers on somewhat short spikes, but the spikes are strong and erect. Plant growth and vigour are only moderate, but 'Screen Gem' gave John Taylor a start on his pink line. Many of the earlier pinks tended to be darker, tending to magenta and often somewhat dull.

'Dazzling Star' (Taylor, 1988) is one such iris. This subdued, dull magenta pink is quite unstable for colour pattern, often being edged, blotched and blended in cream. It is, however, very round and very heavily ruffled and comes on strong spikes with well-spaced multibudded branches, is quite vigorous and healthy and has the added advantage of showing the star pattern. 'Dazzling Star' has proven a great parent and when crossed with 'Helen Naish' produced a wonderful array of seedlings, among them the classics 'Margaret Lee', 'Dancing Vogue', 'Obvious Heir' as well as the sometimes doubles 'Surprise Offer' and 'Gate Crasher'. 'Dazzling Star' has also proven an excellent parent when crossed with other cultivars and is one of the most productive iris in the Taylor breeding program.

'Dancing Vogue' (Taylor, 1994) is the best pink Louisiana iris available. It is a clear, rich mid-pink with lighter reverse and a narrow lighter rim. It is the clarity of colour which sets it apart from all other pinks, but it is also nicely ruffled and rounded. Growth, health and vigour are all very good. This iris is an Award of Merit and Loveridge Medallion winner. It is destined for greatness.

'Josephine Shanks' (Taylor, 1993) is the other outstanding pink Louisiana iris. From a different line of breeding to 'Dancing Vogue', this iris has lovely fluted and ruffled flowers in mid-pink with a porcelain finish, a lighter edge and reverse and a yellow star centre. It is a quality garden iris with all the desirable garden features and has rebloomed for us in autumn. In three successive seasons John has intercrossed 'Dancing Vogue' and 'Josephine Shanks' in an effort to combine his lines and further develop the pink lines. Each time he has been frustrated in failing to obtain pods or failing to germinate seed. I am sure it will all happen eventually. There is no doubt that by combining these lines and by incorporating the 'Dural White Butterfly' line (as 'Dural White Butterfly' is bred from 'Screen Gem') that a full range of high-quality pinks will be obtained. John has also worked the 'Dancing Vogue' line through its sister seedling 'Margaret Lee' into the 'Watch Out' line and has two remarkable iris for 1997 release in 'Better Watch Out' and 'Dancing Again'. These iris are distinctly different, but beauties in their own right. 'Better Watch Out' is a shorter-growing pink bitone with brilliant contrast between the standards and falls, while 'Dancing Again' is a taller, more refined iris of exquisite form in a slightly mauve pink. They are eagerly awaited.

'Watch Out' (Taylor 1988) is a magenta pink with a rich yellow rim. It is a near-perfect show iris with strong multibudded spikes carrying blooms which often open four simultaneously with perfect placement. 'Watch Out' is strong, vigorous and healthy. 'Tranquil Spirit' (Taylor, 1988) is a soft marshmallow pink with a mauve influence. The flower is beautiful but the substance is weak and blooms will barely last two days. Growth, health and vigour are good. 'Time Keeper' (Taylor, 1991) is a violet-pink with a white rim and yellow star centre. 'Trend Setter' (Taylor, 1988) is a ruffled, rose-pink bitone with feathering on the standards. 'Patient Reward' (Taylor, 1987) is a ruffled and vigorous mid to dark pink.

'Natural Wonder' (Taylor, 1991) is a huge-flowered dark, dusky pink with darker veining and a yellow star centre. Floral parts are wide, overlapping and fluted. Plant habits are very good. 'All Agaze' (Taylor, 1990) is a definite bitone. The standards are light pink, the falls (and styles) are salmon pink and slightly recurved. Flowers are lightly ruffled and serrated. 'Art World' (Taylor, 1988) is a waved and fluted mauve-pink bitone of nice rounded form. It is a particularly pretty flower, a healthy plant and a rampant grower. 'Currency' (Taylor, 1994) is subdued but colourful with medium-sized flowers of creamy buff pink veined and flushed darker pink. The standards are lighter than the falls, which are adorned with yellow signals surrounding a green line. This plant is vigorous, healthy and prolific. Two older iris from John Taylor in the pink bitone colouration that are still worthy additions to the garden are 'Edith Fear' (1983) and 'Commandment' (1983).

While the development of pink Louisiana iris has been dominated in recent years by John Taylor, there have been some nice approaches to pink from hybridisers in the USA. 'Lavender Ruffles' (Richard Goula, 1979) has long been the nicest flower in its colour class of lavender pink. It is well named for its nicely ruffled flowers. It has always been a finicky iris that has lacked vigour in our climate. Two iris named for Kitty Dyer from Blanchard in Oklahoma, USA have attracted attention and each is in pink tones. 'Kitty D.' (Dorman Haymon, 1990) is in lilac-orchid tones and 'Oklahoma Kitty' (Marvin Granger, 1992) is a lavender-pink bitone. Both these iris are vigorous, healthy growers.

'Maries Choice' (Haymon, 1988) is another lavender-toned pink, but the nicest of the American near pinks is 'Kay Nelson' (Granger, 1986), a large wide and ruffled lavender pink. 'Aunt Shirley' (Mertzweiller, 1992) is a vigorous coral-rose bitone. Two smaller-flowered pinks from Henry Rowlan are very attractive. 'Pink Poetry' (Rowland, 1988) is a dainty soft pink while 'Twirling Ballerina' (Rowlan, 1986) is a small, ruffled pearl shell pink with a yellow star signal. It is short growing and distinctive. 'Berenice' from Anfosso in France was released in 1988. It is an orange-pink with a large yellow signal. The blooms are ruffled, of beautiful form and colour and come on tall, well branched spikes. It is a very lovely iris. 'Bubblegum Ballerina' (Haymon,

1990) is a nice lavender pink bitone with deeper veins and white spray pattern. It is tall, healthy and vigorous.

'Fait Accompli' (Mary Dunn, 1990) is in rosy pink tones with green styles, while 'Makebelieve World' (Dunn, 1993) is a cool orchid-pink bitone with green styles, and 'Raison d'Etre' (Dunn, 1990) is in rosy grape tones, perhaps more purple than pink. Another Australian-raised iris that hovers between pink and pale purple shades is 'Gerry Marstellar' (Bob Raabe, 1988). This is an attractive iris in a light to mid pinkish purple or purplish pink depending on how one sees it. Flowers are large and plants are vigorous. The only tetraploid Louisiana iris in pink shades is 'Professor Marta Marie' (Joe Mertzweiller, 1992) a medium rosy orchid pink with green styles. Perhaps mention should be made here of 'Charlies Michelle' (Arny, 1969) not a true pink but best described as an amaranth-rose bitone. Although a rather difficult iris to grow, it is worthy of special mention as the first really ruffled Louisiana iris and as the parent of 'Clara Goula'. When grown well, this iris produces beautiful show spikes.

BROWN AND TAN

Brown and tan-coloured Louisiana iris were developed by Charles Arny to a high standard of non-fading, good garden plants. These colours have traditionally been less popular with gardeners than with flower arrangers, to whom their subtle and often drab colours have extensive appeal. The brown-toned Louisiana iris have always been more popular than their bearded counterparts. Early hybrids were 'Amber Goddess' (Arny, 1963), an amber bitone, 'Bayou Comus' (Arny, 1970), a lovely small-flowered tan, 'Charlies Karen' (Arny, 1972), a beige-toned bitoned flower, and 'Dean Lee' (Arny, 1971), a compact small-flowered russet copper. 'Valera' (Arny, 1980) reached new heights in this colour range with multibudded spikes, and good growth all combined with large, rounded dark-tan to mid-brown flowers. This was a milestone in breeding. The other great achievement in these colours is 'Gladiator's Gift' (Taylor, 1991), a rich chocolate brown with heavy undulating ruffles to set it apart from all others. Medium-sized blooms are heavily substanced and rounded. They are carried on excellent spikes on a healthy, vigorous plant. 'Fine Warrior' (Taylor, 1991) is a more ruffled and better-foliaged plant than 'Valera', with flowers in much the same colour.

'Heavenly Glow' (Henry Morgan, 1989) has flowers in a burnt henna-copper shade. It has green styles and signals. 'Honey Star' (Janet Hutchinson, 1993) possibly belongs in this class, although it is multicoloured but the honey-tan colour predominates. This is a very vigorous iris of excellent health and great garden value. It is a honey-cream and apricot-buff bitone with some wine veining, very soft and appealing.

'Praline Festival' (Haymon, 1992) is a caramel-tan of good form, excellent growth and vigour. 'Little Nutkin' (Heather Pryor, 1996) is a shorter-growing, heavily ruffled tan-brown with a yellow star centre and raised, crest-like signals. It is unique.

RED

With the influence of *I. fulva,* the closest to red of all the iris species, it is not surprising that the red colouration is more noticeable in Louisiana iris hybrids than in any other types of iris. Although there is not a true pillar-box red, there are quite a few Louisiana iris available in shades ranging from orange-reds and rose-reds through to the very dark currant, wine, raspberry and burgundy reds.

The great hybridising achievement in this colour is 'Ann Chowning' (Frank Chowning, 1973), a large and slightly recurved dark currant-red self with a large, dominating yellow signal. This iris is clean, healthy and of reasonable vigour, producing quality flowers on medium to tall spikes. When in full bloom it is a garden spectacle. This iris won the Mary Swords Debaillon Award in 1980 and was the first winner of the Debaillon Medal when the award was raised to medal status in 1986. It was also the first recipient of the Charles Arny Jnr Award for the most popular iris in the Society for Louisiana Iris popularity poll when this award was introduced in 1993. It has become the most popular Louisiana of all. Although quite effective when used as a parent, 'Ann Chowning' has not produced the advances one would have expected in red breeding and its large yellow signal has been very dominant when it is used as a parent. It would seem that further advances in red are going to come from other lines.

'Frank Chowning' (Henry Rowlan, 1987) is a shorter-growing, more compact red with a burnished look making it a duller colour and less attractive than 'Ann Chowning', although it is not without appeal. 'Red Echo' (Rowlan, 1984) is a small terracotta red which is very vigorous. Shorter growth gives it some appeal. Charles Arny did little work on reds, but his 'Top Notch' (1980) is well named. The medium-sized flowers are bitoned in rich rose-red and dark ruby-red. This iris is a prolific grower and increaser, very healthy and one of the best reds available. Richard Goula has released two new reds worthy of recognition. 'Miss Verret' (Goula, 1993) is a nicely rounded rose-red, 'Creole Raspberry' (Goula, 1993) is a bitone with rosy standards and dark red falls and styles which cover the short signals. This iris is ruffled and rounded.

Richard Morgan has continued with the breeding line of the late Frank Chowning and has several red Louisiana iris to his credit. 'Bold Pretender' (1984) is a bright red bitone with large yellow signals. It is healthy and vigorous. 'Parade Music' (1986) is a short-growing bright ox-blood red with yellow signals. 'Tomato Bisque' (1989) is another short iris in tomato red, while 'Cherry Cup' (1989) is a short, compact bright cherry red. More recently, he has released 'Tanako' (1993) a rich full red with a bright orange-yellow signal.

Albopurpurea monstrosa

Laevigata seedling

'Royal Cartwheel', 'Regal', 'Alba'

Albopurpurea colchesterensis

John Taylor's 'Wine and Dine' (1990) is a very deep wine-red, tailored in form, large and imposing with large yellow signals while Neil Bertinot's 'Bellevue Medicine Man' (1984) is an unusual brick-red colour. It is not particularly vigorous. Two red Louisiana iris from that great hybridiser of so many different types of iris, Ben Hager, are worth mentioning. 'Cajun Country' (1986) is a flat, maroon to scarlet red with inconspicuous yellow line signals. It has only moderate vigour, while 'Cajun Cookery' (Hager, 1990) is a flat, rich scarlet with an inconspicuous signal and a velvet sheen to the petals.

My favourite red iris of all those available is 'Pièce de Résistance' (Mary Dunn, 1988), which is a vivid neon orange-red, quite distinctive from all those mentioned above. It is rounded in form and always attractive in the garden or as a cut flower. Of moderate vigour, this iris is healthy and a colour gem.

Two new burgundy-toned iris from John Taylor are very exciting — 'Exclusive Label' (1997) and 'Kings Dream' (1997) are both great advancements in this colour range.

Two red tetraploid Louisiana iris are both excellent cultivars. 'Professor Jim' (Mertzweiller, 1987) is a rich mid-red with bright yellow signals. It is well formed, medium tall and healthy. 'Professor Neil' (Mertzweiller, 1992) is a rich wine-red, bright and beautiful with brilliant sunburst signals. This iris is also healthy and vigorous.

FANCY TONES AND PATTERNS

With all the modern developments in hybridising Louisiana iris we have seen many new and fancy colours and patterns emerging. There are true bicolours, even tricolours and many with fancy rims, edges and reverses. Great attention has been paid to the development of contrasting styles and the emergence of fascinating signal patches and spray patterns. Several new cultivars have marbled petals while true plicata-type patterning can now be observed. The fancy colour patterns in the earlier days were developed by Charles Arny and Joe Mertzweiller. 'Easter Tide' (Arny, 1979) is a soft bicolour with lavender standards and yellow falls. Flowers are nicely formed but I have never found this iris to be a good garden subject. It is cold tender and not a good increaser. Foliage is not particularly disease resistant. 'Evelyn Boon' (Arny, 1977) has brighter blue standards and soft off-white to cream falls with a blue influence. It is a better garden iris than 'Easter Tide' but is inclined to fade. 'Dizzy Lizzy' (Arny, 1979) has near-white standards with some maroon veining and maroon falls. It is a vigorous, healthy iris and a good garden subject. 'Colorific' (Mertzweiller, 1978) has white standards and lavender-rose falls. It is an excellent garden plant, vigorous and healthy and very free flowering.

'Just Helene' (Mertzweiller, 1990) is an improved 'Easter Tide' in every way. It is richer in colour, a much better grower and far more healthy, but is in the same colour pattern of lavender blue and yellow. 'Glowlight' (Taylor, 1986) carried on the tradition of 'Colorific' with near-white standards and deep blue-violet falls. It is tall, vigorous and healthy and a good garden iris. It has one slight failing — soft substance with individual flowers lasting only two days.

'Our Parris' (Craig Carroll, 1990) is an interesting iris from Australia and very difficult to describe. The standards are creamy white with buff-apricot infusion while the falls are a buff-apricot blend somewhat darker than the standards but still soft in colour. The flower form is open and airy but the substance is quite good. Plants are vigorous and healthy and increase is rapid. This is a good garden iris.

'Bob Ward' (Morgan, 1982) is also an interesting iris in that it approaches a pink amoena. The very pale standards are nearly white while the darker falls open a soft violet-pink and gracefully fade to soft pink. Of average growth and vigour, this iris is always pretty in the garden.

'Top Start' (Taylor, 1991) is a true neglecta with light blue standards and blue-violet falls, a darker midrib and yellow signals. The medium-sized flowers are rounded and very heavily ruffled. Plants are healthy but growth and increase are only moderate. 'Flight of Fantasy' (Taylor, 1989) is an exciting iris in white and blue-violet. The white standards are often marbled and veined blue-violet while this same pattern is much more heavily applied on the falls. Blooms are large, well formed and heavily substanced. Growth is vigorous and increase is quick on these healthy plants. 'Guessing Game' (Taylor, 1995) is an improvement on 'Flight of Fantasy'. The blooms are pale blue-mauve, irregularly dotted and veined darker blue-violet. It has green line signals surrounded by a cream signal patch. Flowers are rounded and ruffled and the plant is healthy and vigorous. 'Heather Pryor' (Taylor, 1994) is a beautiful soft tricolour pastel. The cream ground is veined and flushed pink, more heavily marked towards the edge of the falls and then carrying a very pale pink to white rim. Styles and signals are green and the standards are variable. The form is rounded and ruffled, the spikes are tall and multibudded and the plant is very healthy and vigorous.

With the release of 'Margaret Lee' in 1992, John Taylor took the fancy patterns to new heights for flower form and colour. This iris could be described as a pink bitone with pink standards and magenta falls, but seasonal and climatic conditions will see colour variation. The standards can be marbled at times and flowers will often vary in the same garden. In all its variation it is a most splendid flower, large, very heavily ruffled and exciting. It is a darker, more luxuriant and more impressive 'Charlie's Michelle', a better grower than that cultivar but nevertheless on the slow side. Show spikes with multiple buds are outstanding and the plant is healthy. While 'Margaret Lee' is an excellent garden iris it is as a parent that it has reached great heights, producing many cultivars in a multitude of colour patterns. 'Margaret Lee' has certainly opened the hybridisers' Pandora's Box. Another great bicolour from John Taylor is 'Lucy Payens' (1993) a very tall, very vigorous and very early true variegata. 'Lucy Payens' has creamy apricot-yellow standards and purplish red falls giving a very definite yellow and red effect from a distance. Flowers are rounded and ruffled and carried on quality show spikes. Growth and increase are quick, but in recent seasons I have noticed a tendency to succumb to fungal spots on the leaves just as it is coming into flower. Even more spectacular and destined to become an all-time favourite is 'Never Say' (Taylor, 1994) a hybrid from two great iris ('Lucy Payens' x 'Margaret Lee'). 'Never Say' is a more refined 'Lucy Payens' with creamy standards, often flushed pink and dark magenta-pink to red falls with a lighter rim, yellow signal and distinctive green line. The flowers are very round and ruffled and this iris is vigorous and healthy.

'Marble Cake' (Taylor, 1994) is another 'Margaret Lee' child and is spectacular. Standards are cream, lined, splashed and marbled in pinkish purple and purple. Falls are solid purple with a lighter reverse and yellow signals. Blooms are rounded and ruffled. Spikes are tall, well budded and well branched. Growth is healthy and vigorous. 'Stop the Nation' (Taylor, 1995) is yet another 'Margaret Lee' seedling, this time crossed with its sister seedling 'Dancing Vogue'. This iris has smallish white standards and white falls heavily overlaid mauve to violet pink, giving a solid effect at the edges which are rimmed in pale mauve pink and lightening towards the centre. The leather-substanced flowers flare flat and horizontal. Health is good and vigour is average. 'Shy Royal' (Taylor, 1995) has pale pink veined deeper pink standards and darker toned pink falls with a light edge and reverse. The falls are adorned by green line signals surrounded by yellow and cream styles tipped pink. Flowers are fluted and ruffled. Plants are healthy and vigorous.

'Watch for It' (Taylor, 1996) has soft violet-pink standards with a darker central stripe and both falls and styles are dark violet-pink, giving a pink and purple bicolour effect. Falls have a lighter rim and reverse and carry yellow signals. This iris blooms prolifically and gives a great garden effect as it has all the best garden attributes. 'Desert Jewel' (Taylor, 1987) is a beautifully named multicoloured iris. The basic colour is a desert sand gold with brown and mauve highlights, creamy standards and green signals. It shines like a jewel on a soft background and is one of John's most significant colour breaks as it opens the way to an outstanding array of seedlings to come on to the market in years to come. Thin rhizomes form healthy, vigorous plants and well branched and multibudded spikes. 'Dural Fantasy' (Taylor, 1995) is a real fantasy for colour with white standards flushed and irregularly marked mauve-pink and lavender-pink falls carrying green styles tipped mauve and white. The

medium-sized flowers are ruffled and slightly recurved. It is healthy, vigorous and a lovely garden iris.

Some very exciting Louisiana iris in fancy colour patterns continue to emerge from the USA, but none more attractive than Joe Mertzweiller's 1993 release 'Cajun Sunrise'. As seen in the USA in 1994, this iris is right at the top of recent releases. It is difficult to describe but here is an attempt. Basically it is a red and golden yellow iris with brick-red base colour all heavily veined and rimmed in amber gold with a brilliant golden-yellow ray pattern emanating from the top of the falls and covering them in gold. I have only just started to grow this iris and it seems healthy and vigorous.

'Coup d'Etat' (Dunn, 1990) is a fascinating iris in blended copper tones of orange, bronze and tan. Standards are lighter than the falls which are adorned with green styles. This is attractive. 'High Rank' (Dunn, 1991) has a gold base infused and edged in henna red. It is another iris which had great appeal when seen in the USA. 'Southerner' (Joe Ghio, 1981) is an older iris and a parent of 'High Rank'. It is a true bicolour in ochre gold and rusty red, darker at the edges. The falls carry a large yellow signal overlay covering much of the flower. It is a good grower, vigorous and healthy. 'Swamp Flame' (Mertzweiller, 1987) is a large flower in copper-orange tones intricately veined and netted in red and bronze. The falls carry large yellow signals. 'Festivals Acadian' (Haymon, 1990) is another knockout for colour pattern. The flower is basically a red-violet with a dark network of veining covering most of the flower and a yellow halo on all floral parts. It is healthy and vigorous. 'Danielle' (Marvin Granger, 1991) is a compact iris with pure light-pink standards and darker rose-pink falls with a light pink rim. Perhaps it should be in with the pinks but it is a beautiful iris wherever it is classified.

It is difficult to describe where we go from here, but John Taylor and Heather Pryor each have beautiful fancy-toned iris from 'Desert Jewel' ready for release and there are so many other fancy colours becoming available. 'La Stupenda' (Heather Pryor, 1996) is a fancy bitoned 'Desert Jewel' seedling, darker in colour than its parent and carrying a very green centre. It is very beautiful with large, slightly reflexed blooms. 'Popsie' (Janet Hutchinson, 1996) is the winner of the 1993 Sydney Louisiana Iris Spectacular. It has white standards veined light wine purple with a dark centre line and edge. Falls are light wine purple with a white edge and rich gold signal on a white background. It is an excellent grower, vigorous and healthy and produces a multitude of flowers.

'Prix d'Amour' (Taylor, 1997) is one of the nicest individual Louisiana iris blooms that I have seen. Flowers are ruffled and laced with a distinct bitone effect and a fascinating veined pattern of rose pink over light pink. It carries a narrow rim of light pink and a green line signal surrounded by yellow. The plants are healthy, but increase has only been moderate. 'Magic Style' (Taylor, 1997) is another fancy colour pattern with pale pink-violet

I. pseudacorus

I. pseudacorus (tetraploid form)

'Roy Davidson' (Hager, 1987)

'Disappointer' (Tamberg)

'Gerald Darby' (Darby, 1967)

I. pseudacorus 'Linda West' (Hutchinson, 1991)

'Royal Cartwheel' (Reid, 1981)

standards suffused violet and purple falls edged lighter, green line signals edged yellow and cream styles. Flowers are fluted and ruffled. Plant habits are good. 'Dark Lover' (Taylor, 1998) is a startling bicolour in purple with bright yellow rims and reverse, green line signals surrounded by a yellow patch and yellow styles brushed violet. So far growth has been moderate.

LAEVIGATA (IRIS) AND OTHER WATER IRIS

I. laevigata is a native of eastern Asia. It is found naturally in Japan, but also in China and Korea. Akira Horinaka in his book *Iris Laevigata,* reports seven different species or strains of *I. laevigata.* These are quite possibly different strains of the single species which is a very hardy, water-loving plant. This iris grows to 80 cm with smooth green foliage, dormant in winter. Height and growth are very dependent on the water content of the soil in which the iris is grown. Blooms are carried up to three to a spike, which is unbranched and will vary considerably in height depending upon water availability. In standing water and in rich soil spikes will reach up to 150 cm. Under good cultivation some branching of the spikes is often noticed and blooms may reach up to 15 cm in diameter. These iris require a rich, acid soil and perform best in full sunlight.

There is a variegated-leaf form but it is slow and difficult to grow. It is, however, a very beautiful plant when growing happily.

Horinaka lists many named cultivars, but very few of these have found their way into western home gardens. Some that are available follow.

'Alba' is white with lilac tracings on the styles and falls. This iris is a strong grower and is floriferous. It makes a most attractive pond specimen.

'Regal' is rosy magenta in colour with small, upright standards and flaring falls.

'Semperflorens' has a deep blue-violet colour with small upright standards and pendant falls.

Albopurpurea colchesterensis has double flat flowers with all petals similar in a rich deep blue with a narrow white edge on all petals. This is one of the most beautiful of all iris and a well-established clump or pot in a pond is a breathtaking sight. The iris is not overly vigorous but well worth any effort made to grow it.

Albopurpurea monstrosa is similar to *A. colchesterensis* but it is taller, comes in a lighter shade of blue and has a less regular area and broader white edge on all petals. While very attractive in its own right, this iris does not have the impact of the startling *A. colchesterensis.*

There are some named hybrids available for the gardening public. Probably the best known is 'Royal Cartwheel', released by Lorena Reid of Springfied, Oregon in 1981. This iris is a rich navy-blue to blue-purple with a deep white slash down the centre of each fall. This iris is double with six falls, quite vigorous and an excellent iris specimen. I can remember exhibiting a large pot of 'Royal Cartwheel' with a dozen or more spikes at an iris display and this iris attracted more attention than any of the illustrious tall bearded iris which formed most of the exhibition. Another release from Lorena Reid is 'Midnight Wine' (1992), a single deep maroon with narrow upright standards and broad, darker falls each with a white signal slash.

'Jester's Motley' is a very interesting laevigata released in 1996 by Janet Hutchinson from Sydney, Australia. This iris has mid-purple flowers, irregularly blotched, striped and marbled in fuchsia pink. It has a white signal and small pale yellow centre line.

When I visited Lorena Reid in 1994 she had, as yet unnamed, some beautiful laevigata seedlings in white and pink and others in shades of purple. No doubt these and others will come onto the market in years to come. 'Snowdrift' is another white quite similar to 'Alba' and often confused with it. 'Snowdrift' is more double in form and is a most attractive iris.

I. pseudacorus is known as the English water iris or English water flag, but it occurs naturally through most of Europe and parts of Asia and Africa. I have also seen it naturalised in parts of the USA, Australia and New Zealand, so it is now virtually worldwide in its distribution.

Although essentially a water or swamp plant, *I. pseudacorus* will grow well under normal garden cultivation and it is tolerant of dry conditions. As with all water iris, growth will be determined by the growing conditions, particularly with respect to the availability of water. Under suitable conditions *I. pseudacorus* will have foliage to 200 cm in height. This foliage is dark green, swordlike and broad, to 3–4 cm. Flowering spikes carry a multitude of yellow blooms with a dark brown to black central pattern. These flowers reach up to 10 cm in diameter under good conditions and, although fleeting, are a most attractive sight in full bloom. Bloom is continuous for several weeks as the multibranched spikes carry double and triple flowers in each socket. This iris is ideal for poorly drained or naturally wet positions. It is spectacular when grown in ponds or lakes, but care must be taken as it can become invasive. It is well documented that this iris can and will break through or overrun plastic pots, and the huge rhizomes can then really take over an area.

I. pseudacorus sets seed very easily from insect pollination and the seed germinates readily. If the seed is left on the spikes it will be spread and one can have *I. pseudacorus* throughout the garden in a short time. The actual spent spikes with the seed pods can be quite attractive for use in floral arrangements. Under control, *I. pseudacorus* is a most attractive plant for the garden, pond or lake and for ease of culture it surpasses all other iris.

There is an attractive variegated-leaf form of *I. pseudacorus* with green and gold leaves in spring. These leaves turn all green in summer. I have noticed that the variegation differs both in colour and pattern from season to season and position to position. The yellow colouring in the foliage will vary from cream to rich gold. The variegated form is much less vigorous than the green-foliaged form. Quite a few different forms and hybrids of *I. pseudacorus* are available. All are smaller and less vigorous than the species and most are attractive garden or pond plants in their own right.

I. pseudacorus bastardii is a natural form found in Great Britain. It has pale sulphur-yellow flowers.

I. pseudacorus superba, also known as 'Golden Queen', is a more richly coloured clear yellow form without the dark markings so typical of the species.

I. pseudacorus ecru is a pale yellow to ivory colour with a black circular signal.

I. pseudacorus 'Ivory' has pale, almost-white flowers with silver-grey veins.

I. pseudacorus 'Primrose' has pale lemon-yellow flowers.

I. pseudacorus 'Floraplena' has rich golden-yellow flowers very double and, to me, quite unattractive although I am sure there are those who would see value in it as a garden plant.

I. pseudacorus 'Linda West' is a collected form released by Lorena Reid in 1991. It is an ivory-white with a yellow signal and grey lines. It is well branched and multibudded. This is an attractive, though subtle, form. There are also strains known as 'Dwarf' and 'Tall' for obvious reasons. 'Holden Clough' has uncertain parentage but is seemingly an *I. pseudacorus* hybrid. The, tall well-branched spikes carry gold flowers heavily marked in brown-purple. The broad leaves are similar to *I. pseudacorus*, as are the flowers which are somewhat narrow.

'Roy Davidson' (Hager, 1987) is a seedling of 'Holden Clough'. The largish flowers are about 8 cm in diameter, bright yellow with dark brown crescent signals. The blooms are well substanced and last three days in normal weather. A succession of bloom ensures a long blooming period. This iris is semi-dormant in our mild climate, very vigorous and altogether a most desirable garden or pond plant that is highly recommended.

There are tetraploid forms of *I. pseudacorus* achieved by treating the seeds with colchicine. These have been available in the UK and Europe for some years. No doubt they have also been available in the USA and in the Southern Hemisphere as well, although I have not come in contact with them.

Janet Hutchinson has a beautiful *I. pseudacorus* which is a clear yellow with little or no markings. The flowers are 10 cm or more in diameter, well substanced and come in profusion on well branched spikes. Each bloom lasts three days and I feel sure that this beautiful iris, to be named 'Come in Spinner' and released by Rainbow Ridge Nursery in 1998, is of tetraploid origin.

I. versicolor is a true water iris native to the north-east and mid-west of the USA. This hardy iris requires the same culture as *I. pseudacorus* and, while not as vigorous as that iris, it will also grow quite well under normal garden conditions. It requires acid soil and a plentiful supply of water in summer.

I. versicolor has broad, heavily ribbed green foliage to 80 cm and produces spikes to that height in normal garden conditions. Growth and spikes are higher in wet conditions. The branched spikes carry numerous flowers in two or more to each socket and 3 cm in diameter. Bloom is normally in very late spring to early summer and it is dormant in winter. *I. versicolor* is, most likely, a natural tetraploid hybrid from *I. virginica* and *I. setosa* parentage. There is a wide variety of colour forms available and as a bonus, *I. versicolor* is particularly fertile among its own colour variants and also with other species. Crosses have been successfully made between *I. versicolor* and *I. laevigata*, *I. virginica*, *I. pseudacorus*, *I. fulva*, *I. brevicaulis* and *I. setosa*.

There is lots of colour variation in *I. versicolor*, but blue-violet to blue-purple is the most common colour. Standards are narrow and falls are rounded with darker veins on the base colour and a green-gold signal. Seedlings are available in white, various shades of blue and purple, maroon, violet and shades of pink. There are also several named varieties available in the trade and these are all attractive garden plants. Best known are 'Kermesina', a deep bright red-purple with a white signal, and 'Claret Cup', a dark red-violet with white and yellow signals. Some others are:

'Cat Mousam' (Warburton, 1985) is a mid violet-blue with tan and brown signals. 'Little Rhyme' (Schafer/Sachs, 1990) has white standards, yellow in the centre and white falls with green hafts and yellow signals veined green. 'Mint Fresh' (Warburton, 1983) is white with magenta lines. 'Mysterious Monique' (Knoepnadel, 1986) has violet standards, and dark violet, near black falls and a white signal. *I. rosea is* a soft rose-pink with white signals. 'Vernal' (Sindt, 1983) is a clear orchid-pink. 'Version' (Sindt, 1986) is a bright pink. 'Whodunit' (Warburton, 1986) has a white ground heavily veined mid violet. Wildwine' (Sindt, 1983) is wine red.

I. virginica is another USA native, found mainly in coastal areas in the east and south of the country. This iris resembles *I. versicolor* but is more demanding in its culture and far less cold tolerant. *I. virginica* requires wet, acid soil to flourish and is not as rewarding a garden subject as *I. versicolor*. Its foliage is rich, dark green and heavily ribbed. It can vary considerably in height, up to 90 cm and this factor is mainly dependent on position and cultivation. Spikes will reach 100 cm in height, are usually unbranched or carry one branch with up to four blooms.

I. versicolor 'Claret Cup' (Hillson)

I. versicolor 'Kermesina'

I. versicolor 'Mint Fresh' (Warburton, 1983)

I. setosa 'Nassauensis'

'Rose Queen' (S.J.I., 1991)

'Confetti Shower' (Payne, 1950)

'Azure Perfection' (Hazzard, 1965)

I. virginica is a more slender plant than *I. versicolor* with larger, longer standards. Colour range is predominantly in blue-violet to blue-purple shades, but seedlings are available in white, shades of pink, orchid, maroon and lilac. Hybrids of *I. virginica* x *I. versicolor* are available and *I. virginica* crosses with *I. laevigata, I. ensata, I. pseudacorus* have been made.

There are three named varieties:

'Dottie's Double' (Warrell, 1983) has six violet falls with yellow signal and is a form of *I. virginica* var 'Shrevei'. The well-known 'Gerald Darby' (Coe/Darby, 1967), a late-flowering (summer bloom) dark violet with dark spikes reaching 100 cm in height, is probably an *I. versicolor* x *I. virginica* hybrid, and the lesser known 'Mountain Brook' (Kennedy, 1984) is of similar parentage but in deep blue-lavender colour.

Akira Horinaka reports on crosses being made in the 1960s between *I. versicolor* and *I. laevigata* which produced bright, deep red flowers similar in form to *I. versicolor*. Subsequent crosses have produced flowers in bright red and deep lavender. I have not been able to see or grow these iris, most of which are reported as sterile, although it is further reported that some varieties have set seed. Horinaka reports that these are beautiful flowers on vigorous plants which should make good garden specimens.

I. setosa is a cold-climate plant native to Canada, Alaska, Siberia, China and reportedly the most cold hardy of all iris. It requires acid soil, rich in humus, and sun. Although moisture-loving, this iris can be grown in the garden but it does require a lot of water in spring when the ground in its natural habitat would be thawing out. The foliage is green with a red base, prominently ribbed and forms thick clusters reaching 80 cm in height and 2.5 cm in width. Flowering spikes are branched and the flowers are unique in that the standards are reduced to tissue ribs while the falls are up to 7 cm long, hence their classification in the Tripetalae. Typical colouring is violet veining on a paler ground. There is a white form, 'Alba', which is lavender in the bud opening to beautiful white flowers on spikes reaching 45 cm.

There are some named cultivars. 'Arctic Goldheart' (Reid, 1994) has lemon buds opening cream with a round gold signal. 'Arctic Rebloomer' (Lankow, 1992) is blue violet. 'Kosho En' (Davidson, 1984) is pure white with foliage dark at the base. 'Arctic Lavender' (Reid, 1995) is light lavender with deeper lavender veins and a small yellow signal bordered white and veined deeper yellow.

There are hybrids between the Siberian iris (Sino-Siberian 40-chromosome type) and *I. setosa*. These are all hardy, vigorous garden plants. 'Berlin Chrytosa' (Tamberg, 1993) is light blue-violet with darker blue-violet signals. 'Mauve Snowtop' (Reid, 1994) is mauve-pink and flaring with tiny lavender-white standards. 'Royal Dolly' (Reid, 1995) is dark maroon with gold signals edged white and lined dark violet. The tiny standards are lavender. 'Stilles

Wasser' (Stillwater) (Berlin, 1979) is a light sky blue. These all bloom in late spring and early summer.

I. tridentata is native to the south-east USA and although hardy, it is less so than *I. setosa*, the other member of the Tripetalae. This iris has flowering spikes, usually with only one bloom, to 35 cm and shorter than the dark green, somewhat dull foliage edged darker in red brown. The rounded 4 cm blooms are blue-purple, veined darker and with an off-white signal. It blooms in late spring through early summer.

I. ensata, also known as *I. kaempferi*, 'Higo Iris', 'Marhigo Iris' and 'Japanese Iris', is arguably part of the Laevigatae. Although recognised as part of the Laevigatae, *I. ensata* is worthy of a section on its own. The species is somewhat nondescript, with stiff, upright, ribbed foliage in a dull shade of green to a height of 120 cm. The branched spikes flower in among the foliage to a height of 140 cm. Flowers are small and variable for colour from white through shades of blue to purple.

I. ensata is found naturally in Japan, China, Tibet, Mongolia, Afghanistan, Siberia and Caucasia. It makes a densely rooted mass but remains compact. It dies down completely in winter but foliage begins to shoot in late winter, early spring. This iris differs from *I. laevigata, I. pseudacorus, I. versicolor* in that it is not a true water or bog plant. It prefers rich soil, well drained in winter, but flooded in spring and summer.

JAPANESE IRIS

The Japanese iris as we know them are hybrids derived from *I. ensata*. These are magnificent flowers, the beloved Hanashobu of the Japanese, and they bloom in very late spring through early summer to bring the main iris season to a spectacular conclusion. Flowers are often huge, but not coarse, buds are exquisite and the partly opened flower has a beauty of its own. At every stage these flowers have a beauty unequalled in the floral kingdom.

While somewhat limited in colour range to white, shades of pink, shades of blue, violet, purple and beet red, there is an unusually large range of patterns and forms. As well as self colours, Japanese iris can be veined, marbled, speckled, rimmed, edged or dusted with blending or contrasting colours on the base colour, thus providing many true bicolours and tricolours. As most Japanese iris have a yellow signal patch, some varieties do become colour spectacles but there is no yellow Japanese iris available. New breakthroughs in colour or pattern are very difficult to achieve, but each hybrid from a cross will give some distinctive characteristic to set it apart from all others within the overall framework.

While yellow and the associated oranges, tangerines and pure pink do not form part of the Japanese iris spectrum, there is a move in that direction through crosses with the yellow *I. pseudacorus*.

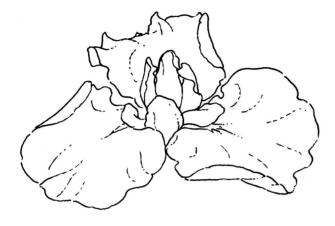

Single

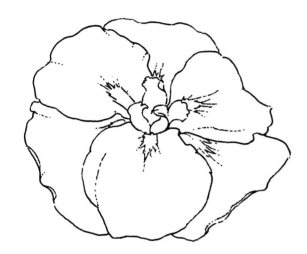

Double

Multi-petalled

Figure 11. Forms of Japanese iris

Probably best known of these is 'Kimboshi' (Ukei, 1971) which has yellow flowers with three falls — much larger than *I. pseudacorus* but smaller than the typical Japanese iris hybrid. The form is similar to a single Japanese iris with the signal area of *I. pseudacorus*. This iris has yellowish foliage and while it will grow under good cultural conditions, it is not vigorous. There is little doubt that, in time, particularly if sufficient hybridisers interest themselves in the project, a fertile hybrid between *I. ensata* and a yellow species will be obtained and a whole new colour spectrum will be opened up for these magnificent flowers but, at this stage, development is in its infancy.

Classification and development of Japanese iris

The Hanashobu have been cultivated in Japan for over 500 years with literary references dating back to the twelfth century. Nineteenth century cultivation of these iris in Japan centred on three areas, and this has led to a classification of three strains of Japanese iris.

EDO JAPANESE IRIS

Named Edo for the ancient name for Tokyo, this strain of iris was grown and developed in and around that city from the late 1860s. These iris were field grown for massed display and showed great variation in size, colour and form. Development was both through planned crossing and natural hybridisation.

ISE JAPANESE IRIS

The Ise strain of Japanese iris come from the Ise-Matsuzaka district of central Honshu. Developed around the same time as the Edo strain, these iris were primarily developed for pot culture whereby they were grown outdoors but were able to be brought inside when blooms were ready to open. Ise Japanese iris are typically single in form with three downward hanging 'falls' and three smaller 'standards' held at right angles to the falls. Most of the strain is somewhat poorly substanced, but are in exquisite pastel colours, with some of the pinks in the Ise strain being of gorgeous colouration.

HIGO JAPANESE IRIS

The Higo strain of Japanese iris was developed in Higo, an old province in Kyushu. These iris were originally developed for pot culture from existing Edo strains. Under the direction of a feudal Lord, Hosokawa, a vigorous and intensive breeding campaign was established with a number of groups working in direct competition to produce new cultivars. Many new iris were developed, primarily to be brought inside at flowering time and displayed on a scarlet cloth in front of a gold screen. This led to a restricted colour range of white and rich self

'Asato Biraki' (Hirao, 1969)

'Butterflies in Flight' (Aitken, 1991)

'Centre of Attention' (Rich, 1986)

'Dazzling Debutante' (Payne, 1964)

'Springtime Snow' (Reid, 1983)

'Rose Adagio' (Payne, 1969)

colours being preferred, with an emphasis on the production of an unbranched spike with one large, spectacular bloom.

It was not until 1914 that the Higo strain became generally available, and plants were exported to Europe and the USA. From that time there has been widespread development of the Japanese iris in other countries while, in Japan, hybridisers have continued to develop these beautiful iris with Shuichi Hirao, until his recent death, being the leading hybridiser. Hirao worked with all three strains, and by intercrossing widened the horizons and made the group differences less sharp.

'MARHIGO' JAPANESE IRIS

Walter and Louise Marx from Oregon, USA imported a collection of Higo irises from Japan in the 1930s and began a highly successful hybridising campaign, which resulted in many of the best Japanese iris hybrids available. As these iris were from the Higo strain, they became known as the Marhigo iris. When Walter Marx died in 1978, his iris were well distributed and have since been used as a solid foundation for Japanese iris breeding in the USA.

Also in the 1930s, W. Arlie Payne, from Indiana USA, imported a collection of Edo irises and line bred them over a period of some 40 years. Meticulous selection and meticulous recording by Payne has given the USA a second leading hybridiser and the combined efforts of Payne and Marx have resulted in a wonderful pool of varieties from which modern hybridisers in the west have been able to work.

While it is usual to classify Japanese iris according to their physical attributes, it is important that the above historical development be recognised so that we can more fully understand the form of modern hybrids, many of which are now a complex mixture of the Edo, Ise and Higo strains. We need also to recognise the more recent development of induced tetraploid Japanese iris, by both Hirao in Japan and Currier McEwen in the USA. As a result of the work done by Currier McEwen, the first tetraploid Japanese iris 'Raspberry Rimmed' was released in 1979. Although development has been slow, known tetraploid Japanese iris have been produced in recent years in Japan, Germany and the USA, and possibly elsewhere. This has been achieved by treating plants with colchicine.

In his book, *The Japanese Iris,* Currier McEwen states: 'When a plant is treated with colchicine there are four possible results: (1) it may be killed outright (2) it may be unaffected and remain diploid (3) it may be completely converted to the tetraploid state (4) it may be only partially converted — a chimera.'

In practice the treated plant is rarely fully converted; most of those that survive are unaffected or chimeras. Depending on the degree of conversion, crossing two chimeras may result in diploid or tetraploid seedlings. A chimera may, in time, revert to the diploid state but once the second generation of tetraploidy is reached the plant is completely stabilised and can no longer revert.

Tetraploid Japanese iris do not differ significantly from diploid forms in many characteristics. Colour is much the same but can be intensified. Leaves and spikes are often larger and stronger. Blooms are more heavily substanced and often larger while ruffling is often increased.

Classification by form

As with all iris, the Japanese iris have six floral parts in sets of three. Although the terms can be misleading, I will refer to these floral parts as standards, the upper and, at times, upright petals and falls for the lower petals which can hang in pendent fashion to be virtually vertical or may flare horizontally. Usually, the falls are held at an angle somewhere in between these two extremes.

Classification according to form allows the Japanese iris to be divided into three types — single, double and multipetalled.

I. ensata has single form with three small standards, three pendent larger falls, three styles and three stamens. This is the basic form so much admired by the Japanese, and is often referred to as three petalled, although this is strictly incorrect.

Double Japanese iris have much larger standards, of size equal to the falls so we have a flower in which all the petals have a similar appearance. These iris are referred to as six petalled and this gives the flower a circular or disc-like form. Each bloom has three styles and three stamens.

Multipetalled or peony form Japanese iris vary considerably in appearance but are characterised by having extra petals or petaloids giving a much fuller effect to the flower. Floral parts may be in sets of nine or twelve neatly arranged, may be very informal or may be the customary six with extra tufts of petaloids. Very often in the multipetalled cultivars, the styles and stamens are confused and not easy to find.

Although essentially a more flat flower than the bearded iris, which have the standards reaching upwards and the falls reaching downward, the Japanese iris has much variation in the way the standards are held relative to the falls. The modern trend is to hybridise for full, flat, rounded form with the blooms giving an unbroken circular effect. There is also a trend towards ruffled and flaring floral parts. While very attractive in their own right, these hybrids should not be grown to the exclusion of the more simple, smooth-petalled (tailored) iris with upright or horizontal standards and somewhat pendent falls. There is a place in the garden for the various forms and patterns. One obvious advantage of the heavily substanced, more ruffled, modern forms is that the flowers will last longer, both in the garden and when cut. This is a decided advantage as the Japanese iris bloom in early summer and hot days can play havoc with poorly substanced blooms.

The Japanese iris flower varies considerably in size with smaller 'miniature' cultivars having flower diameter of 8–10 cm while the largest cultivars will have blooms reaching 25 cm or more in diameter. Flowering spikes will vary in height to 100 cm under normal conditions, but under excellent conditions I have grown these iris to 30 cm in diameter and nearly 200 cm in height. Each bloom will last up to three days under good weather conditions and, depending on climate, flowers can be expected for about four weeks on average. A major project for hybridisers is to extend the bloom period and to extend the 'shelf-life' of individual blooms. Lorena Reid from Oregon, USA has been working on producing earlier blooming cultivars and her Springtime series of Japanese iris contains very worthy additions for the garden. Although Japanese iris normally bloom about four weeks after tall bearded iris, Lorena has these wonderful blooms coming on immediately after bearded iris bloom.

Cultivation

Japanese iris are very demanding in their cultural requirements and, primarily for this reason, have not gained their deserved popularity. For those prepared to put in that extra little bit of effort, the rewards are great and there has been a steady increase in interest in recent years.

Japanese iris demand acid soil — a pH of 5.5 to 6.0 is desirable — and they will not tolerate lime in any form. Eleanor Westmeyer in *The World of Irises* relates the fascinating story of a German horticulturist who planted out 10 000 Japanese iris seedlings in heavily limed soil and then intercrossed the 10 surviving plants in the hope of developing a strain tolerant of alkaline soil. He died before completing his work.

Water is the other major requirement of these iris and while it must be stressed that they are not water plants and do not have to be grown in or near water, they require copious supplies of water in the growing season, from spring through to autumn. If the home gardener controls the soil conditions and water supply, spectacular results will be achieved.

These iris are best grown in a rich, well-prepared soil containing plenty of humus. This humus will enhance the water retention of sandy soils and help to break down heavy clay soils. They need protection from hot dry winds and a position that gives winter sun and either full or filtered sun in summer. I have grown them successfully in an open, sunny position and also in filtered sunlight provided by overhanging eucalypts. These iris will grow very well in ordinary garden conditions as long as they get ample water in spring and summer. They should not be planted permanently in ponds or in permanently wet positions at the edge of ponds or streams. In these conditions they may survive one or more seasons, but will ultimately deteriorate. They need a rest period under normal garden conditions during the winter months.

In Australia we have reports of Japanese iris growing very well in the colder areas of Victoria and Tasmania, in subtropical Queensland, and they grow very well in both the humid coastal areas and the inland parts of New South Wales. They would seem to grow very well in any area where they are not exposed to extremes in temperature. As they are completely dormant in winter, frosts do not present any problems. Reports would indicate that they are also universally good growers throughout New Zealand, while from the USA Currier McEwen in *The Japanese Iris* reports that: 'Japanese iris are adaptable to a wide range of climatic conditions so long as their particular needs are met. They are extremely hardy to cold'. He goes on to say that 'Japanese irises can also be grown under semitropic conditions, but in hot, dry regions especially where the soil is alkaline, special methods are necessary'.

One such 'special method', and a very satisfactory way of growing these iris, is in large pots containing a mixture of coarse sand, garden soil, peat moss and cow manure in roughly equal proportions. The iris are planted with the crowns at soil level and must be left out of water for up to six to eight weeks while root growth is established. Immediate immersion will result in crown rot, lack of root growth and inevitable death. When the new shoots start to show in spring, a covering of 3–4 cm of compost or well-rotted animal manure can be added and the pots can then be placed in ponds, natural or artificial. Try to keep the water level 2 cm below the pot level so that the crowns of the iris are out of water. Small collections can be potted and the pots kept immersed in large plastic ice-cream containers during the growing season.

Japanese iris are best planted or divided in late autumn and care should be taken when dividing to ensure that plants are of a reasonable size to ensure new growth. Spring division is also acceptable, but plants divided in spring rarely perform to their full potential in the first bloom season. Because Japanese iris are such heavy feeders, they should be divided and replanted in good rich soil every three years. Plants in small pots should be potted on or divided each year, while those in larger pots can be left for two years. If the soil is not sufficiently acid it can be improved by the addition of agricultural sulphur.

Japanese iris can be propagated from seed and interesting seedlings usually result. It is not difficult to get a 'good one' from seed, but very difficult to get a new and worthy introduction sufficiently different from and an improvement on existing cultivars. Seed setting varies from season to season — some seasons even the bees have a great time while in others it is very difficult to obtain clean pollen to make a cross. Thrip and

'Gay Gallant' (Marx, 1961)

'Janet Hutchinson' (Grosvenor, 1994)

'Freckled Geisha' (Reid, 1981)

various other pollen-gathering insects will often strip flowers of pollen. We have found that the pod parent is most receptive one day after opening, so try to avoid freshly opened flowers or flowers that are in decline when selecting your pod parent. By contrast, the pollen is quite viable and fully mature one day before the flower opens so select an unopened bud for your pollen parent, open the flower and remove the pollen with a pair of thin pointed tweezers. Only a little pollen is needed for fertilisation, but we usually pollinate each of the three stigmatic lips and find that one anther can be used to pollinate several flowers. Crosses are best made in the cooler parts of the day, early morning or late afternoon; those made in the middle of the day are rarely successful. I prefer to work in the early morning and aim to finish between 10 a.m. and 11 a.m. Humid weather seems to increase the chances of success but wet flowers, either through rain or watering, rarely set seed. Sometimes the anthers are quite tight and reluctant to give up their pollen. A pair of thin-pointed tweezers is very useful in stripping pollen from tight anthers.

Once seed has set, the swollen ovary should be left until late summer when it will have hardened, browned off and be ready to split. The pods can be harvested, stored till autumn and the seed then planted in seed-raising mix, either in pots or the open ground. Germination is usually quick and easy and a fair amount of seedlings will appear before winter. These seedlings 'winter over' quite well and are best allowed to grow on for 12 months before planting out. Many will flower in that following summer. Care should be taken not to plant out the young seedlings until they are large enough to give them a good chance of survival.

Apart from pollen thrip and the ubiquitous snails and slugs, these iris are virtually pest and disease free. I have not observed Japanese iris suffering from fungal or viral diseases at any time. They are also extremely resistant to rhizome rot and as these are the main disease problems that iris growers face, it would be safe to recommend Japanese iris, together with Siberian iris, as the healthiest of all iris. The basic range of climatic conditions under which Japanese iris grow makes them ideal garden plants for those who are prepared to go to the added trouble of giving them their cultural requirements.

As distinct from the other popular types of iris, where great advancements have been made in recent years, the development of Japanese iris has not progressed at speed. There are fewer hybridisers working with Japanese iris, most of the work is confined to Japan and the USA, and new patterns and colours are difficult to obtain.

Recommended cultivars

Some recommended Japanese iris cultivars are included, primarily from personal experience in growing and flowering these iris. It is recognised that experiences will differ from place to place and from country to country and this long list can only be looked on as a guide for those interested in either growing a few or starting a collection of these wonderful plants. Because it is so difficult to classify to colour or pattern, these recommendations are given in alphabetical order. There is also considerable confusion as to hybridisers and year of introduction, primarily with the Japanese-raised cultivars, so information will be given only when ratified by registration (and introduction) through the American Iris Society.

Another major problem, because of the limited colour range, is to clarify in words the differences between cultivars. When preparing this list of recommendations I felt that many sounded very similar yet, in picturing the iris in my mind, I was aware of the sometimes subtle, sometimes immense differences between them. Mere words are not enough and there is a limit to the number of colour plates that can be provided. I have steered away from giving heights as no other iris are as dependent on cultivation for height of spike and diameter of bloom as the Japanese iris. Most cultivars reach 100 cm in height in our excellent growing conditions at Dural, and many will grow to 150 cm or more. In average conditions and well cared for, I would expect most Japanese iris cultivars to flower on spikes from 80 cm to 120 cm in height.

'Active Ayr' (Grosvenor, 1994) Double. Very large, wide, rounded and ruffled white. Tall, vigorous and prolific.

'Agrippine' (Innerst, 1981) Double. Large, full-flowered mid lavender-pink.

'Agrippinella' (Straw, 1980) Double. Dark rose-pink with a central white halo and ray pattern.

'Asato Biraki' (Hirao, 1969) Single. Blue standards edged violet and bright mid-blue falls with white rays. Styles are white with blue crests. Great!

'Asian Warrior' (Aitken, 1993) Single. Dark raspberry-red with white rays, white halo, white styles and red-purple crests.

'August Emperor' (Marx, 1962) Double. Red-violet with slight blue halo around yellow signals. Lighter styles with violet crests.

'Awaji Shima' (Mitsuda) Double. Ruffled blue-violet with lighter rays and halo. Styles are sanded violet with darker tips.

'Bellender Blue' (Bauer-Coble, 1993) Single. Tall, dark blue-violet of lovely colour. Early blooming.

'Beni Tsubaki' (Hirao) Double. Red-violet with white rays and white styles. Excellent quality.

'Blue Embers' (Bauer-Coble, 1993) Single. Pale blue standards rimmed violet. Light blue falls with a white halo and white rays. White styles, blue crests.

'Bluetone' (Payne, 1969) Double. Silver-blue-lavender with lighter styles and darker halo and veining. Large flowers.

'Butterflies in Flight' (Aitken, 1991) Double. White with blue veins and dark violet styles. Grows tall.

'Calamari' (Copeland, 1992) Single. Red-violet standards with white rims. White falls, violet veins. Red-violet styles with darker crests.

'Caprician Butterfly' (Marx, 1985) Double. White with dark purple veins and purple styles. This is a vigorous and very beautiful iris.

'Cascade Crest' (Aitken, 1990) Double. Ruffled white with a wide blue border and white styles with blue crests.

'Cascade Spice' (Reid, 1989) Double. Ruffled white with rosy violet borders, speckles and style crests.

'Cascade Springdress' (Reid, 1991) Double. Ruffled white with rosy violet edges.

'Centre of Attention' (Rich, 1986) Double. Silver ground with dark violet veining and sanding. Dark violet styles. Ruffled blooms.

'Chigogesho' (Seto, 1930) Double. White brushed rosy violet.

'Chiyo No Haru' (Hirao, pre-1980) Single. Purple standards with white rims. White falls, violet veins and violet sanded styles. Large flowers.

'Continuing Pleasure' (McEwen, 1982) Double. Light mid-blue with white rays and white styles.

'Crystal Halo' (Marx, 1959) Double. Red-purple gradually lightening to crystal white edges. Purple styles.

'Dace' (Copeland, 1980) Double. Pale blue buds open to white, ruffled flowers. Shorter growth and a long flowering period.

'Dancing Waves' (Payne, 1964) Double. Light base with a purple halo and veins. Mulberry-purple edges and large dark purple styles. White wire rim throughout. Lovely but not easy.

'Dappled Dragon' (Payne, 1969) Single. Red-violet with white splashes throughout. Very showy.

'Dramatic Moment' (McEwen, 1982) Double. Light ground with dark violet veining and shading and white rim edge.

'Ebb and Flow' (Hirao/Hager, 1989) Double. Mid-blue with violet shoulders and a lighter halo, dark blue centres and veins. White styles with blue crests.

'Electric Glow' (Aitken, 1982) Double. Ruffled blue-violet with light blue rays and red-violet edges. Dark violet style crests.

'Electric Rays' (Aitken, 1990) Double. Ruffled blue-violet with electric blue white rays in the centre of the falls.

'Enchanting Melody' (Rich, 1967) Double. Mallow pink with lilac styles. Ruffled flowers and probably the nicest pink of all.

'Extravagant Plumes' (Maddocks, 1978) Double. Plum red with a white centre and rays. White styles edged and tipped red-violet.

'Fairy Carillon' (Payne, 1969) Single. Blue-violet standards. White falls with light violet halo and veins. Blue-violet style crests.

'Fashion Model' (Payne, 1950) Double, peony form. Late flowering dark red-purple with layered petals (often nine) and black-purple styles.

'Flashing Koi' (Marx, 1978) Double. White with large red-violet halo and veins. Dark red violet styles.

'Freckled Geisha' (Reid, 1981) Double. White with wine-red freckles and edges. This is a vigorous and very beautiful iris.

'Frilled Enchantment' (Marx, 1959) Double. White with a narrow edge of rose red. Medium-sized, ruffled flowers but very beautiful and a great favourite.

'Frostbound' (Rich, 1971) Single. Deep plum-red with distinctive narrow white rim. Very attractive.

'Frosted Pyramid' (Marx, 1960) Double, peony form. Pure white with layers of petals (up to 12) all ruffled. Attractive but not easy.

'Galatea' (Marx, 1961) Double. Bright mid-blue with white rays and styles. Good grower.

'Garnet Royalty' (Reid, 1984) Single. Deep maroon-red self with white styles and maroon crests. Tall growing.

'Geisha Dance' (Marx, 1956) Single. White standards veined blue-violet. White falls with light blue sanded centres and white styles.

'Geisha Gown' (Maddocks, 1968) Double. White with red-purple halo, veins and styles. Vigorous and prolific.

'Geisha Mischief' (Maddocks, 1971) Single. Red-violet standards and red-violet falls splashed white. Blue halo. This is one of the nicest singles.

'Geisha Obi' (Rich, 1989) Double. Beet-red with white rays. White styles with red crests.

'Geisha Parasol' (Maddocks, 1968) Double. Orchid-pink with a blue halo, white edge and white styles.

'Glitter and Gaiety' (Payne, 1964) Single. Purple standards with a white rim. Red-purple falls shade out to white petal edges.

'Trance' (Warburton, 1979)

'Violet and Silver' (Payne, 1969)

'Yasaboshi' (Hirao pre-1980)

'Kalamazoo' (Hazzard, 1989)

'Le Cordon Bleu' (Swearengen, 1967)

'Glitter and Glamour' (Payne, 1969) Double. Light ground sanded and heavily splashed red-violet and blue violet. Sanded styles with blue-violet crests. Colourful.

'Good Omen' (Marx, 1956) Double. Deep red-wine self. Early flowering and easy growing.

'Gosan No Takara' (unknown but introduced in Japan pre-1940) Narrow petals are white with rose-violet edges and white styles tipped rose-violet. Can have three, four, five or six petals in single or double form.

'Grape Fizz' (Ackerman, 1981) Double, peony form. Grape red-purple with white and light violet splashes. Can have six or nine petals.

'Hagoromo' (Seiko-En, introduced in Japan pre-1940) Double, peony form. The king of all Japanese iris! Large, very double six to nine petalled white, often with blue-lavender brushing. Outstanding.

'Hakugyokuro' (Hirao, 1965) Double. Very large blooms of pure white.

'Harlequinesque' (Marx/Hager, 1986) Double. White centres with variable blue and red-violet splashes and violet borders. White styles, red-violet crests. Colourful.

'Haru No Umi' (Hirao, pre-1985) Single. Dark red-violet standards rimmed lilac. Falls are blue-violet halos, red-violet centres, lilac edges. Styles are red-violet rimmed lilac.

'Hatsu Kagami' (Hirao, 1966) Single. Ruffled pink with white styles and pink crests.

'Hekito' (Hirao,1958) Double. Cobalt blue with a few light blue veins.

'Hisakata' (Marx, 1950) Double. Very dark blue-purple. Beautiful flower.

'Hue and Cry' (Maddocks, 1970) Double. Red-purple with white halo and rays and white styles.

'Ike No Sazanami' (Hirao, 1956) Double. White brushed blue-violet. White styles.

'Izu No Umi' (Hirao, pre-1985) Single. Light blue standards edged darker. Mid-blue falls with white rays. White styles with blue crests.

'Janet Hutchinson' (Grosvenor, 1994) Double. White ground heavily margined and stippled dark pink to rose red. Very large blooms, rounded, very ruffled with tufted petaloids.

'Jewelled Sea' (Payne, 1969) Double. Dark blue with white halo and rays. White styles with blue crests.

'Jocasta' (Innerst, 1988) Double. Light ground with rosy-violet to red-violet veins, petal edges and styles. Blue-violet halo and white petal edges.

'Joy Peters' (Ackerman, 1990) Single. Pink with white styles and lavender crests.

'Joyous Troubador' (Payne, 1969) Single. Standards are white rimmed blue. Falls are white with dark blue stitched edges.

'Kalamazoo' (Hazzard, 1989) Single. Standards are white with a purple rim. Falls have purple centres lightening out to white edges. Styles are purple.

'Kozasa Gawa' (Hirao, pre-1980) Single. Lavender-violet standards edged lighter. Falls are pale blue with violet veins. Violet styles.

'Kumi' (unknown and unregistered) Double. Light lavender-mauve. Small flowers.

'Kyokko' (Tomino, 1957) Single. Light pink with darker halo and veins. Ise type.

'Lace Ruff' (Ackerman, 1986) Double, peony form. Ruffled white with violet veins and styles.

'Le Cordon Bleu' (Swearengen, 1967) Double. Dark blue centre shading to lighter edge. Dark blue styles.

'Leave Me Sighing' (Maddocks, 1964) Double. Bright lilac-pink.

'Lilac Peaks' (Vogt, 1987) Double. White with short lilac-lavender veins and styles.

'McKenzie Sunset' (Reid, 1989) Double. Ruffled violet with large white halo and white styles.

'Mai Ogi' (Hirao, 1957) Double. Dark blue-violet with white halo and rays. Large white styles with violet crests.

'Mai Shojo' (Hirao, 1965) Double. Very large red-purple, lighter in the centre.

'Midnight Stars' (Aitken, 1988) Double. Deep red-purple with a velvet sheen, bright yellow signals and black-red styles.

'Midsummer Reverie' (Marx, 1954) Double. White ground heavily and uniformly sanded and veined in rose-violet. White styles tipped rose.

'Miss Coquette' (Payne, 1969) Double. Red-violet with short white rays, white styles and crests with rose-violet edging.

'Mist o' Morn' (Payne, 1969) Double. White densely veined and sanded blue-violet.

'Mulberry Splendour' (Payne, 1969) Double. Light ground veined and sanded purple and shaded darker at the halo and edges. Lighter centres and purple styles.

'My Heavenly Dream' (Worley, 1965) Double. Rose-violet with darker halo and veins. Lighter edges.

'Nari Hira' (Hirao, 1960) Double. Deep velvet red-purple. Large flowers and excellent grower.

'Nemurijishi' (Seiko-En, pre-1940) Double, peony form. White, heavily splashed light blue-violet. It can have six or nine petals.

'Oriental Eyes' (Vogt, 1984) Double. Violet with a purple halo and lighter edges. Large yellow signals look like eyes. Well named.

'Oriental Fantasy' (Payne, 1969) Double. White with some lavender sanding, multiple cream styles and lavender crests.

'Over the Waves' (Marx, 1959) Double. White with blue-violet rays and edges. White styles with blue crests.

'Peacock Dance' (Marx, 1955) Single. Standards and styles are dark red-violet edged white. Falls are white with violet veins. Easy grower and a great iris.

'Peacock Strut' (Hirao/Hager, 1978) Single. Standards are white edged dark violet. Falls are white with blue-violet edges.

'Picotee Princess' (Reid, 1992) Double. White with blue-violet sanding and multiple dark-violet styles.

'Pink Frost' (Marx, 1955) Double. Light orchid-pink.

'Prairie Coquette' (Hazzard, 1976) Single. Violet standards, white falls with blue-violet veins.

'Prairie Fantasy' (Hazzard, 1981) Double. Large white with dark blue halo, dark blue veins and dark blue styles.

'Prairie Noble' (Hazzard, 1972) Double. Ruffled white with blue-violet halo and red-violet veins. Violet styles.

'Prairie Twilight' (Hazzard, 1977) Single. Standards and styles light red-violet. Falls silvery blue-violet to slate coloured, darker halo and veins.

'Prairie Velvet' (Hazzard, 1972) Single. Dark red-violet.

'Premier Danseur' (Payne, 1969) Single. Standards and styles red-violet with white rims. Falls red-violet with purple veins.

'Purple Parasol' (McEwen, 1977) Double. Dark blue-purple.

'Reign of Glory' (Marx, 1953) Double. White with blue-violet edges. White styles with blue crests. Very vigorous, easy grower. This is an all-time great.

'Rose Adagio' (Payne, 1969) Double, peony form. White with rose-violet stippled and sanded edges. Rose sanded styles with red-violet crests.

'Rose Prelude' (Marx, 1960) Double. Mid rose-violet with white halo and rays.

'Rose Queen' Incorrectly introduced as *I. laevigata* 'Rose Queen' in 1915. Single. Small-flowered pink.

'Rose Tower' (Marx) Ruffled rose-red-violet to near rose-pink with a white centre and orange signal.

'Rose World' (Reid, 1989) Double. Dark rose-violet with a white halo and white styles.

'Rosy Sunrise' (Vogt, 1992) Double. Ruffled lavender-pink with darker halo, veins and styles.

'Royal Crown' (Marx, 1961) Double. Dark beet-red with white rays, centres and halo. White styles and feathered red crests. Blooms through summer and autumn.

'Ruri Ugi' (Hirao, 1958) Double. Dark blue-violet with white halo and rays. White styles with dark violet crests.

'Sakurajishi' (Tomino, 1952) Double, peony form. Ruffled pink with darker styles and petaloids often forming a peony-type flower.

'Sea of Amethyst' (Rich, 1971) Double. White ground stitched and sanded rose-violet. White styles with rose crests.

'Silverband' (Bauer-Coble, 1989) Single. Small, dark wine-red flowers on plants with green and cream variegated foliaged.

'Skyrocket Burst' (Hirao/Hager, 1989) Single. Standards and styles white edged violet. Falls are white with dark violet edges.

'Snowy Hills' (Marx, 1954) Double. Quality white with large flowers of impeccable form. Excellent growth.

'Star at Midnight' (Rich, 1964) Double. Deep blue-violet with a white fleck and yellow star-like signal.

'Stranger in Paradise' (Hager, 1970) Single. Standards and styles are white edged with rose-violet. Falls are white with rose-violet rays and edges.

'Summer Storm' (Marx, 1955) Double. Dark ruffled purple with extra styles and petaloids. Easy growing, vigorous and floriferous variety.

'Swirling Waves' (Payne, 1951) Double. White with blue-violet veins, dark violet petal edges and white wire rims. Dark purple styles and petaloids.

'Taga Sode' (Hirao, 1957) Double. Red-violet with white rays and splashes and white styles.

'Taiko' (Hirao, 1960) Double. Deep beet-red with a white halo and rays, white styles and red crests.

'Temple Maiden' (Marx, 1953) Single. Pastel blue-lavender with white styles.

'Tender Trap' (Hager, 1965) Double. Soft mid-blue self shaded with lavender-blue edges.

'Mist o' Morn' (Payne, 1969)

'Flashing Koi' (Marx, 1978)

'Barbara's Kiss' (McCown, 1982)

'Custom Design' (Hager, 1981)

'Belise'
(Simonet, 1967)

'Thunder and Lightning' (Marx, 1954) Double. Dark red-violet with a blue-violet halo.

'Trance' (Warburton, 1979) Single. Standards and style crests are light blue with red-violet veins. Falls are white sanded light blue with violet veins. Style arms are white.

'Violet and Silver' (Payne, 1969) Double. Light ground with dark violet veined halo and petal edges. Dark purple styles.

'Warai Hotei' (Unknown, pre–1948) Double. Light ground with dark violet veins and edges and dark violet styles.

'Worley Pink' (Worley, 1966) Double. Lilac-pink with small blue halo. White styles and lavender crests.

'Yasaboshi' (Hirao, pre–1980) Double, peony form. Deep red-purple heavily splashed white. Styles are white sanded red-violet.

'Yuhi' (Miyazawa, 1920) Double, peony form. Small-flowered white with a pink wash and edge. White styles with pink crests. This often forms extra petals and/or petaloids.

'Yuki Chidori' (Hirao, 1969) Double, peony form. Large ruffled white with light blue brushing and layered petals, often nine to 12. Lovely.

'Yusho' (Hirao, 1980) Double. Mulberry-wine lightly veined white.

SPURIA IRIS

Spuria iris are widely distributed through Europe, North Africa and Asia Minor. They are readily distinguished from other iris by their fibrous rhizomes which grow on from the same point each season and their cylindrical seeds encased in a paper-like bag and contained in a tough, pointed seed pod. Once established, these iris are relatively easy-care and undemanding in soil and cultural requirements. They need sun and good drainage. Their main drawback is their resentment of being divided or transplanted and many spurias will not flower in the first season after being moved. This, in itself, makes them an iris only for those with patience (to wait for bloom) and foresight (to ensure they are planted in a permanent position).

The flowers of spuria iris resemble those of the Dutch and Spanish iris, but they are held on spikes which are usually taller with more flowers to the spike. Often, the spuria iris will open two or more flowers simultaneously. Their height, compactness of clump, graceful presentation of flowers and bloom production make them ideal specimens for the rear of the perennial border or for growing as individual clumps with shrubs as a backdrop and annuals in the foreground. Indeed the spuria iris form an invaluable garden perennial group as they are beautiful in flower and neat and tidy with attractive sword-like foliage at other times in the growing season. The foliage dies down in summer only to send up new clean shoots almost immediately in mild climates. The period of dormancy will depend on climate and water supply. Although these iris are from temperate areas and are thought of as iris suitable for warmer climates they are very cold hardy.

Modern spuria hybrids are bred mainly from *I. crocea* and *I. orientalis*. There are shorter spuria iris from other species suitable for the front of the border or display.

I. crocea is a native of Kashmir and is also known as *I. aurea*. It is a tall-growing iris reaching up to 140 cm in height and has stiff, sword-like leaves about 3 cm wide. Strong spikes carry four to five rich golden-yellow flowers clustered at the top of the spike and above the foliage. These large (12–15 cm) blooms have long, narrow standards with wider, longer falls somewhat pointed at the tip.

This iris requires an open position with full sun and good drainage for best performance. Like most spuria iris it resents being moved and will often skip a season for bloom after being divided and replanted. The bloom season is late spring into summer.

I. orientalis, also known as *I. ochroleuca,* is the best known and, by far, the most commonly grown spuria. It is found throughout Asia Minor and Syria.

This iris grows to 140 cm and has stiff, sword-like, dark green foliage. Flowering spikes are branched and carry several large (up to 12 cm) flowers which are white with a large yellow signal on the somewhat tucked-in falls. It grows naturally in areas that are wet in winter and spring but dry in summer.

Easy to grow, this iris enjoys an open, sunny position but is not particular as to soil conditions. It is slow to re-establish after planting or dividing. Bloom is obtained in late spring through early summer and the spikes make ideal, long-lasting cut flowers.

Both these species have a chromosome count of 2n=40.

I. carthaliniae is found naturally in Caucasia and Georgia. It grows 110–140 cm in height and has broad, grey-green foliage. The largish flowers with diameter 10–12 cm are clear blue with a yellow signal. There is a pure white form reported, but I have not seen it. Easy to grow, this iris blooms in late spring, through early summer.

I. demetrii and *I. klattii* are similar species from Caucasia. Each carries beautiful blue-violet flowers on spikes which reach 90 cm. There are three to five blooms per spike.

I. notha has larger flowers and reaches 110 cm in height. Blooms are carried three to the spike and in shades of blue to blue-violet. Flowering period is early summer.

I. halophila and the shorter *I. musulmanica* are native to central and south Asia, Romania and parts of the former

Soviet Union. *I. halophila* will grow to 80 cm and flowering spikes will carry six to eight flowers in shades of yellow, blue and white. This iris blooms early, usually with the tall bearded iris, and is a rewarding garden plant. The name 'halophila' means salt-loving and as these plants are found in soil which does contain some salt, they and their hybrids are somewhat salt tolerant.

I. monnieri probably comes from Asia Minor. It grows to 150 cm and carries dark green foliage and numerous soft yellow flowers. Bloom is quite late, coming in early to mid summer. There is confusion as to this iris' status as a species or natural hybrid and there are several different iris distributed under the name of *I. monnieri.*

I. spuria is very difficult to describe because of the diversity in height, bloom and colour found in various forms throughout Europe and Asia. Height ranges from 40 to 70 cm, colours are various shades of yellow, blue and white with spikes carrying up to four blooms which open sequentially. Bloom is in early summer following the tall bearded iris and this iris is easy to cultivate. Its chromosome count is 2n=38 while the other species noted have a chromosome count of 2n=44. All of these iris form what can be called a tall grouping of spurias. There is a shorter-growing series, referred to as the Gramineae series. I will restrict discussion of this group to the three most common species, *I. graminea, I. kerneriana* and *I. sintenisii,* all of which have claims to being of value as cultivated plants.

I. graminea has an extensive range throughout Europe and Caucasia and a wide variety of forms. It is typified by a dwarf habit, narrow grassy foliage and small flowers carried two to a spike. Height varies from 30 to 45 cm and the flowers are often hidden in the foliage. These flowers are coloured lilac to violet with shades of blue and have a sweet, fruity fragrance. *I. graminea* is very suitable for rock garden cultivation in full sun and acid soil. It is quick to multiply and easy to grow. It flowers in early summer with some autumn bloom.

I. kerneriana comes from Turkey. It has dull green foliage to 45 cm with spikes to 60 cm carrying two bright yellow blooms. After flowering it becomes completely dormant. It will bloom in late spring and is reasonably easy to cultivate.

I. sintenisii is more dwarf and compact than *I. graminea.* It is a native of Southern Italy and the Balkans and flowers profusely in late spring. Height varies from 25 to 35 cm and the glaucous foliage is evergreen. The small flowers, two to a spike, are blue-purple with white veins in the falls. This iris is excellent in rock gardens and is easy to grow once established.

As already stated, many of the early spuria hybrids were from the 40 chromosome species but hybridising in the second half of the 20th century has seen the introduction of blue, brown and cream to white varieties. There has been a steady, if not spectacular, development of colour patterns and we do have rich purples, rich orange-yellow and near-white cultivars, some very dark near-black and attempts to develop pink. Spuria iris do not command the commercial interest of the bearded iris and, by comparison, there are relatively few hybridisers working on them. Development from seed is slow as it usually takes four years from 'cross made' to 'bloom seen' and results in terms of improvements and colour breaks are also slow.

Increasing interest in spuria iris as cut flowers for the florist trade will see increased interest in these plants as garden subjects. As a cut flower the spuria iris surpasses all other iris. They are long-lasting, mostly double-socketed, tall and elegant. The colour range is good and the vase life exceeds that of most flowers. On the negative side, the plants usually take two years to acclimatise and growth is somewhat slow. Also, the control of virus diseases can present a problem. Once established, spuria iris are easy-care and a handsome return in terms of dollars/metre^2 can be expected with minimum effort.

In the home garden the foliage can be quite untidy following bloom, so to maintain their effectiveness in the landscape, spuria iris can be kept greener longer by maintaining water supply after bloom. These iris will relish copious watering as long as the drainage is good. Once the foliage starts to brown it is desirable to cut it off at ground level.

Recommended cultivars

'Amber Ripples' (Niswonger, 1981) has pale blue standards with an amber infusion at the midribs. The falls are amber with pale blue edges. This iris flowers mid season and reaches 95 cm.

'Barbara's Kiss' (McCown, 1982) has burgundy-mauve standards and light yellow falls with light burgundy-mauve veining. Flowers are ruffled and spikes reach 135 cm. Bloom is mid season.

'Blue Lassie' (Niswonger, 1978) is a light blue with some white in the falls. Bloom is mid season and spikes reach 100 cm.

'Bordertown' (Ghio, 1982) is a very dark brown with hints of black, and only a tiny yellow signal. It blooms mid to late season; to 80 cm.

'Bronzing' (Blyth, 1989) has blue-violet standards and similarly coloured falls with a glowing bronze area and overlay. Bloom is mid to late season; to 90 cm. This is an excellent cut flower cultivar.

'Capital Idea' (Ghio, 1987) is a ruffled blue-purple self. It grows to 100 cm and flowers mid season.

'Chestnut Chime' (Blyth, 1989) is a chestnut brown self with no signal. It blooms quite early, with the tall bearded iris, and continues through mid season. Spikes reach 90 cm and this cultivar is a very good cut flower.

'Adobe Sunset' (McCown, 1976)

'Dress Circle' (Hager, 1985)

'Forty Carats' (Ferguson, 1971)

'Look Lively' (Hager, 1988)

'Eleanor Hill' (Hager, 1980)

'Cinnamon Stick' (Niswonger, 1983) has cinnamon-red flowers with a gold overlay and speckling on the falls. It blooms mid season and reaches 100 cm.

'Diminuendo' (Hager, 1985) is a shorter-growing spuria with spikes reaching 75 cm. The early to mid season blooms are light lavender-blue.

'Dragon Rider' (Hager, 1983) is a rich chocolate-brown with small orange signals. Bloom is mid season and spikes reach 115 cm.

'Dress Circle' (Hager, 1985) has blue-violet standards veined white. Falls are yellow with a white band and narrow violet edge. It blooms mid to late season on spikes which reach 95 cm.

'Easter Colors' (Hager, 1991) has orchid standards and light yellow falls with orchid styles. It blooms mid season to 90 cm in height.

'Edith's Color' (Jenkins, 1992) has mauve-purple standards and gold falls with rims of white and purple. It flowers mid season; to 95 cm.

'Eleanor Hill' (Hager, 1980) has light-purple standards and bronze falls. Bloom is mid to late season on 95 cm spikes.

'Evening Dress' (Ghio, 1984) is a dark blue-purple with a black sheen. The mid to late season blooms are on spikes which reach 100 cm.

'Fixed Star' (Hager, 1990) is another of the new breed of shorter-growing spurias, reaching only 70–75 cm in height. It is a near white self with some lemon on the falls. Bloom is mid season.

'Follow Through' (Hager, 1981) blooms very late in the season on 90 cm spikes. It has a ground colour of pale blue with deeper blue veining and webbing to give a very blue effect.

'Forty Carats' (Ferguson, 1971) is an older cultivar still worth growing for its tall spikes to 135 cm and rich gold self colour. Flowering time is mid to late season.

'Full Sun' (Ghio, 1977) flowers late in a pure rich yellow on 115 cm spikes.

'Goldmania' (Blyth, 1989) is a pure rich golden-yellow self which flowers mid season on 105 cm spikes.

'Happy Choice' (Niswonger, 1977) is a ruffled pale blue with a gold signal. It blooms mid to late season on 105 cm spikes.

'Headway' (Hager, 1986) is an orange-yellow and a definite advance in the search for orange spurias. The large flowers are held on 105 cm spikes in mid season.

'Highline Amethyst' (McCown, 1976) is an older reddish purple with 105 cm spikes in mid season.

'Highline Halo' (McCown, 1982) is a rich yellow with a small white halo on the falls and style crests. It flowers mid season to a height of 100 cm.

'Ila Crawford' (Hager, 1976) was a great advancement with very ruffled white flowers and an orange-yellow signal. It flowers early to mid season with 90 cm spikes.

'Ila Remembered' (Hager, 1992), released 16 years after 'Ila Crawford', is bred from that great iris. It has pure white standards, styles and falls and a large dark yellow signal on the falls. The flowers are bigger, more ruffled and wider in form than its illustrious parent and it is proving to be a vigorous grower. Bloom is early to mid season; to 95 cm.

'In Depth' (Hager, 1988) is a rich deep blue-violet with only a tiny signal. Flowering spikes reach 90 cm in mid to late season.

'Janice Chesnik' (McCown, 1984) is a well formed, wide-flowered and lightly ruffled tawny gold. It is tall growing, reaching 140 cm, and blooms mid season.

'Lucky Devil' (Ghio, 1988) is a deep blue-purple with a black sheen. It flowers early to mid season on 90 cm spikes.

'Minneopa' (Ferguson, 1969) is an old variety, but is still a very worthy garden iris. The light blue flowers with a wide gold signal are particularly attractive and the iris blooms mid season to 105 cm.

'Missouri Gal' (Niswonger, 1976) is a pale to light blue with gold signals. It flowers mid season on 100 cm spikes.

'Respectable' (Ghio, 1988) is a very nicely formed violet self with a yellow signal. It blooms early to mid season on 90 cm spikes.

'Response' (Corlew, 1989) is an attractive iris for colour pattern. Standards are white with lemon veins, falls are yellow with a small white edge. This iris grows to 110 cm and flowers mid season.

'Social Circle' (Corlew, 1979) has long been a personal favourite with its white flowers, bright yellow signals and ruffled, picotee petal edges. The mid season blooms are on 95 cm spikes.

'Son of Sun' (Wickenkamp, 1983) is a brilliant yellow of good form and good growing habits. Spikes reach 115 cm and this iris blooms mid season. It is a top award winner in the USA.

'Twilight Mode' (Blyth, 1993) flowers early to mid season on 95 cm spikes. It carries navy blue standards with similarly coloured falls infused gold.

In the garden

Spurias can be used in mass planting in the home garden where they will provide colour for an extended bloom season in late spring and very attractive foliage accents for much of the year. They are easy-care and rewarding, but the foliage must be cut back hard in summer when they can look messy. Other than this one chore they are not demanding of attention.

The tall spikes of spuria iris make them an attractive feature plant for the back of the perennial border where they can be grown very successfully with other iris, other perennials or annuals. Because of their un-demanding nature spuria iris combine well with other iris species whose special needs can be catered for without creating any problems for the spurias. Their wide colour range ensures that there are spuria iris available for any colour plan. Emphasis can be on the warm colours of yellow, gold and shades of brown or on the cooler blues, mauves and purples. As yet there are no spurias in true pink tones, and red is just a dream.

A modern trend to shorter spikes and more compact plants will further enhance the value of these iris, both as feature plants and as companion plants.

Early planted petunias in the very wide colour range now available are excellent companion plants for spuria iris, particularly in the cooler shades, while marigolds are excellent companion plants in the warmer colours. As spuria iris flower late in spring, I find their use with early planted summer-flowering annuals more satisfactory than spring-flowering annuals.

The scope for using perennials as companion plants is as wide as the imagination allows, and personal choice is, of course, the determining factor. Although I have an unqualified love for lupins and would use them extensively with Siberian iris and to a lesser extent with bearded iris, I have never been happy with the combination of lupins and spuria iris. Equally, I have no great pleasure in combining spuria iris with Siberian iris. I am sure there are many who would dispute these very personal views, just as I am confident that talented landscape architects could devise plans for the use of spuria iris in many garden situations.

The added advantage of spuria iris is their unchallenged value as cut flowers. No iris, not even the celebrated bulbous iris, can match spuria iris for large cut-flower arrangements, either as vase companions for other flowers or sole occupants of vase space. The length of stem, positioning of buds, multibudded spikes and long vase life make them great for cutting and displaying. The new range of smaller-flowered, shorter-spiked cultivars will only add to their value as cut-flower specimens and there is a great future for these iris in the cut-flower trade.

OTHER BEARDLESS IRIS

To include or not to include, that is the question!

From the beginning it has been my wish that this book be a practical and primarily an enjoyable one. I have tried to avoid oblique references to rare and unobtainable species that neither I nor most other irisarians have ever seen, let alone grown. If one does not attempt to be comprehensive there is always the risk of finding (or not finding) the right cut-off point. With all of this in mind I wish to discuss some 'other beardless iris' while being aware that some, at least, could be offended by the omissions. My criteria for inclusion have been mainly: availability for gardeners; suitability for home gardens; and desirability as garden plants.

I. foetedissima could be listed in the 'to offend or not to offend' section as its name refers to the strong odour given off by the crushed leaves. The response to this odour varies and, as most gardeners do not go around crushing the leaves of their precious plants, it is incidental to the plant's value in the garden. *I. foetedissima* is a hardy iris, native of England, Europe and North Africa. It is easily grown in sun or shade, but is essentially a shade-loving plant and is much less attractive with increasing sunlight. Foliage of *I. foetedissima* is dark green, with linear veins, and reaches 50 cm in height. Spikes reach 60 cm, are unbranched and carry several blooms. These blooms are variable for colour from a dull greenish yellow to a somewhat dirty pallid lilac-mauve. They have little ornamental value in themselves and are, in form, similar to spuria iris. The blooms are followed by very attractive and ornamental seed pods which open to display rows of seed in colours of yellow, orange or red. These seed capsules can be cut and used for spectacular flower arrangements and, if sown, germinate quickly.

I. foetedissima is an easily grown plant, being easily pleased by soil conditions and not requiring large amounts of food or water. The rhizomes should be planted below the surface of the soil and can be left undisturbed for several years, during which time they will form large, attractive clumps. They are best divided or planted in autumn, but can be moved anytime in mild climates. As well as the green-foliaged plant, there is an attractive variegated form. *I. foetedissima* blooms in early summer.

I. unguicularis, also known as *I. stylosa,* is an undemanding, easily grown iris, native to Algeria, Crete, Greece, Syria and Asia Minor. It is hardy and adaptable and is the only true winter-flowering iris with blooms being produced intermittently from late autumn right through winter. This iris is also often called the 'Algerian Iris' or 'Winter Iris'.

Foliage can reach as high as 60 cm under good conditions, but flowering spikes reach less than half that

'Social Circle' (Corlew, 1979)

'Happy Choice' (Niswonger, 1977)

I. foetedissima

height, being hidden or partially hidden in the foliage. Plants are very cold hardy and frost resistant but are best grown in a semi-protected position, in well drained soil. They require ample water throughout the year except in summer, when they like to dry out.

Flowers vary in size and form, with standards about 2 cm wide and falls about 2.5–3 cm wide. These flowers come in shades of white, blue and violet and because of their habit of blooming on short stems in among the foliage, it is best to give this foliage a 'haircut' in autumn so that the blooms can be fully appreciated. This is a fault that I find hard to forgive as I believe the foliage should complement the flower, not hide it, and a flower with foliage cut back around it really looks out of place in the garden.

However, the iris is easy to grow, produces winter flowers and has a most pleasant perfume, particularly when cut for indoor decoration. As I sit writing this, in mid-winter, I can see and smell a vase of *I. unguicularis* in my office. It is forgiven all of its sins. This is a lovely cut flower.

This iris is best planted or divided after it has finished blooming in early spring. Care should be taken to use large divisions when replanting as small pieces often do not survive. They should be planted 1.5 cm below the surface and kept moist until re-established. Protection is always needed against snails and slugs, which find these flowers a real delicacy. *I. unguicularis* can be grown from seed, which should be sown immediately it is harvested. Good germination is obtained but seedlings develop slowly and may take three or four years to bloom. There are several named cultivars available, the best known of which are 'Mary Barnard' and 'Walter Butt'.

Longipetalae

The Longipetala series of iris is native to North America, particularly the USA, and is restricted to two species — *I. longipetala* and *I. missouriensis* — although there is argument as to whether plants known as *I. montana* and *I. arizonica* are true species or variants of *I. missouriensis*.

I. longipetala is found in coastal California, has green foliage that grows to about 60 cm with strong spikes, sometimes branched, and carrying up to six flowers. These spikes may reach 90 cm. Flowers are long and narrow with falls reaching 10 cm in length. Standards are violet, long and erect. Falls are white veined violet. There is some colour variation with white, blue and purple forms being found.

This iris is hardy and undemanding, performing best in full sun with adequate water in the growing season and a dry period after bloom. Foliage is evergreen.

I. missouriensis, as the name suggests, is found along the Missouri River, particularly in the high country of the Rocky Mountains. This iris resembles *I. longipetala* but is more slender in growth and appearance and less easily grown. Foliage grows to 40 cm and flowering spikes carrying up to three blooms reach 50 cm. The narrow falls are up to 6 cm long and 2 cm wide. Flower colourings are similar to *I. longipetala*. Foliage is dormant in winter.

I. montana, also known as *I. pelogonus* and *I. missouriensis* var. 'pelogonus' is probably a smaller form of *I. missouriensis* with foliage to 25 cm and bloom spikes to 30 cm. It has pale violet standards and lavender-blue veined darker falls.

I. arizonica, also known as *I. missouriensis* var. 'arizonica', is a taller growing variety with flowering spikes reaching 75 cm. The flower has white to pale blue-lavender base colour with heavy darker violet to purple veins. Blooms are small and of little interest to the home gardener.

I. verna is a native of the eastern states of the USA. It is a dwarf iris with deep green foliage reaching 14 cm in height, similar to a dwarf bearded iris but without a beard. Spikes are in the form of perianth tubes and flowers are among or slightly above the foliage. Blooms are lavender-blue with a gold median strip. There are other coloured forms ranging from white to violet. This iris is demanding in its cultural requirements — acid soil and part shade or dappled sunlight being prerequisites. It blooms in early spring and is a suitable rock garden or rockery plant.

CHAPTER 3

EVANSIA IRIS

Evansia iris are distinguished from other iris in having a crest of petaloid tissue running linearly on each of the falls. This crest can be described as fimbriated, serrated or toothed in different varieties and may be orange, yellow or white. Members of this group are often called crested iris. The Evansia iris are natives of Asia (China and Japan) and North America and form one of the most delicate and beautiful groups of the iris family.

All the Evansias have flat, strappy leaves which are usually broad.

The name Evansia was given to this section of iris to honour Thomas Evans, who introduced the first known species to England in 1794. The name will continue to be attached to this section by common usage, although they are now classed under the subgenus *crossiris*.

Evansia iris are quite varied in size and height, but fall broadly into two quite distinct groupings, the hardy temperate species which are dormant in winter and come mainly from North America, and the tender subtropical species which are evergreen and come mainly from Asia.

Hardy crested iris

I. cristata is a beautiful miniature iris from the eastern states of the USA, where it grows right up to the far north. Flowering spikes reach only 12 cm in height and this is the height of the foliage at bloom time, although it may continue to grow to nearly double this height later in the season. The small, slender rhizomes increase rapidly and form a mat with hairy roots coming from each growing point. The colour of the foliage varies from light green in full sun to a rich dark green in semi-shade. The foliage is strappy and broad.

Flowers are flat, up to 5 cm in diameter, and come in soft lavender-blue colouring with a small white signal edged deeper blue. The crests are white, tipped gold. There is a rare and difficult white form of *I. cristata*.

These iris like a rich, deep, acid soil and prefer partial shade, particularly in areas with intense summer heat. They require good drainage and appreciate a mulch of compost.

Propagation by division is best done immediately before flowering, which is early spring or immediately afterwards.

While *I. cristata* will survive in full sun it is essentially a woodland plant, preferring semi-shade and protection from the hot afternoon sun. It is a beautiful plant in a rockery if a suitable position can be found.

I. lacustris is the smallest of the Evansias and very similar to *I. cristata* except in size. Dykes considered this iris another form of *I. cristata,* and it is identifiable as a miniature *cristata* with foliage to about 7 cm. This iris is native to the central and north-eastern states of the USA and into Canada, where it is found around the shores of the Great Lakes. It is not as vigorous as *I. cristata,* but requires similar growing conditions to that iris.

I. tenuis occurs naturally in Oregon USA, and is quite similar to *I. cristata* but is taller. Flower form and colour are very similar but this iris is less hardy.

I. gracilipes is a native of China and Japan and one of the most attractive of all iris. Foliage is narrow and upright for 15 cm, then gently weeping in habit to allow the 30 cm flowering spikes to be appreciated. This grassy foliage is light green in spring, turning yellow in autumn. Flowers are 3–4 cm in diameter, a light lavender blue in colour with a large, feathered, white signal and a tiny orange crest. They come in sprays on well-branched spikes. In its natural setting, it grows in moist soils with a cool aspect on wooded slopes so is best grown in semi-shade with protection from hot afternoon sun.

Division or planting is best done in early spring or immediately after flowering in mid spring. There is a very attractive white form, but it is less vigorous than the blue form.

These iris are ideal rockery plants as long as their preference for woodland conditions can be accommodated.

Subtropical—evergreen Evansias

This section of iris includes the beautiful Japonica series of evergreen and somewhat cold-tender iris. In mild temperate climates these are superb iris for landscaping in protected semi-shaded positions.

I. japonica is also known as *I. fimbriata* and *I. chinensis.* It is a native of China and Japan where it grows in woodland settings. This iris revels in a rich, slightly acid soil in a sheltered, semi-shaded position. It needs protection from frost and hot afternoon sun so is best naturalised under trees. Given these conditions, it grows vigorously and increases quickly.

The foliage is rich dark green, evergreen and fan-like in growth. It reaches 60 cm in height and hangs gently at the tips. Spikes can reach 80 cm in height in ideal conditions, are multibranched and multibudded with 30 or more flowers to a spike, and five or six flowers open simultaneously. The flowers are up to 8 cm in diameter, rounded and ruffled with a fringed edge. They are pale blue-lavender with orange markings on a white ground edged and dotted with a darker lavender blue. Each flower is delicately frilled and ruffled, hence the name *fimbriata*.

Bloom period is late winter through early spring and, when happy, this iris will produce a mass of bloom over a five-week period. In colder climates this iris can be grown in greenhouses or under glass.

I. japonica is a gross feeder which responds to being fertilised and mulched. Good drainage is essential for optimum results as poor drainage leads to fungus disease.

In temperate climates, *I. japonica* grows beautifully with azaleas and late-flowering camellias to present a landscape spectacle. These are ideal companion plants that require similar position and culture.

Other forms of *I. japonica* (and hybrids):

'Ledgers Variety' from England has darker foliage and more deeply coloured flowers.

'Nada' is a smaller, paler near-white hybrid from *I. japonica* crossed with *I. confusa.*

'Darjeeling' is from 'Nada' self-crossed and is darker than 'Nada' but paler than *I. japonica,* which it resembles in shape and size.

'Fairyland' is a miniature *I. japonica* in pale blue colouring. This is a most attractive garden subject.

I. japonica 'Variegated' has variegated foliage which is more sun tolerant than the green-leaf form. Flowers are similar in colour, slightly smaller as grown here in Sydney, and difficult to obtain. While the foliage has its attraction the reluctance of this iris to bloom casts doubt on its value as a garden plant. Unlike many variegated foliaged plants, this iris is a very vigorous grower.

'Japo-Watt' is a hybrid of *I. japonica* and *I. confusa,* somewhat confusing as *I. confusa* was being grown at the time under the name of *I. wattii* (hence the misnomer). This is an outstanding cultivar with taller foliage, larger and somewhat darker coloured flowers than *I. japonica*.

I. wattii is a native of Yunnan and the tallest growing of the Evansias with luxuriant, rich green, fan-like foliage that reaches 160 cm in height and sometimes more in ideal conditions. In late winter and early spring long slender flowering spikes, multibranched and carrying up to 50 blooms, emerge. The flowers are 10 cm in diameter with standards held at 30° and falls slightly reflexed. The frilled and ruffled flowers are lavender blue with darker spots on the falls and an orange crest. The profuse bloom lasts from eight to ten weeks in most seasons, sometimes even longer.

I. wattii is a rapid increaser, quickly developing into a large clumps but always remaining neat and tidy. It makes a beautiful landscaping plant if given protection from sun, wind and frost.

I. confusa was originally introduced into England as *I. wattii* and when the real *I. wattii* was brought into the country it was renamed — hence the confusion, hence the name. The two species are very similar, but *I. confusa* is much paler in colour, almost white with no blue markings but has yellow crests. This iris does not grow as tall as *I. wattii* and the flowers are much smaller. It is said to be hardier in cold climates than *I. wattii*.

Two hybrids worthy of note are 'Queen's Grace' bred in New Zealand by Jean Stevens from seed set on *I. wattii,* probably with *I. tectorum* as the pollen parent, and 'Bourne Graceful', bred in England by Dr Ellis from *I. japonica* 'Ledger's Variety' and *I. japonica* 'Capri Form'.

'Bourne Graceful' is one of the loveliest of all iris and a superb Evansia. It is similar in habit to *I. japonica* but the flowers are more heavily fimbriated with a large yellow area surrounding the white crests. This area is in turn

I. tectorum

I. japonica

I. milesii

edged in white and then in a rich blue-violet, much darker than the basic lavender-blue colour of the petals.

I. formosana is a native of Taiwan and is very similar to *I. japonica* but is larger in flower size and lighter in flower colour. The blooms are white, suffused blue sometimes with yellow spots on the falls. This iris does not seem to be in cultivation.

I. speculatrix is a native of Hong Kong. It has very dark green foliage more heavily substanced than other Evansias and evergreen. Slender spikes 25 cm in height carry only two flowers 4 cm in diameter. These flowers are light lilac-purple in colour with a yellow area around the crest. It seems to grow quite well in full sun but has not proven hardy in cold climates. This iris is rarely in cultivation, although Jean Stevens grew and distributed it in New Zealand.

I. milesii comes from the eastern Himalayas near Burma and south-western China. The foliage is bright green, wide and heavily ribbed. It reaches 90 cm but dies down in winter. Tall spikes are multibranched and carry small, frilled blooms of lilac-purple with darker spots and a fringed orange crest. Although the small flowers seem out of proportion with the foliage this iris has garden value because of its extended bloom season of ten weeks or more from late winter right through spring. It requires acid soil and good drainage.

I. tectorum is a native of central and south-west China and has achieved fame by virtue of its use by the Japanese, who, in some parts of their country, have grown it on the ridges of the roofs of thatched houses. Two explanations for this practice have been given, the first being that in a long-ago time of famine no soil was allowed to be used for anything else but growing food. The Japanese women made a face powder from the roots of the plant and, rather than do without the face powder, were forced to find an alternative place to cultivate it. The other explanation is that the iris roots were found to be an excellent medium to bind together the thatch and wet clay used to complete the thatching process. Take your pick.

The foliage of *I. tectorum* is broad, shining and light green in colour. Flowering spikes are 45 cm in height, poorly branched and carrying three to four blooms 10 cm in diameter. These flowers are a dark blue-lavender with deeper mottling on the falls and a prominent white crest. There is also a very beautiful but less vigorous white form, *I. tectorum* 'alba', with yellow crests.

This iris is vigorous, hardy and adaptable but requires protection from frost to perform at its best. Conditions similar to *I. japonica* are required; this iris is also a gross feeder which will quickly exhaust the soil unless it is heavily fertilised and kept well mulched. It requires plentiful water in the growing season and can easily be grown from seed, which sets readily. Because of its hungry habits, *I. tectorum* is best divided after three years.

Hybrids from *I. tectorum*

'Paltec' is the best known hybrid of *I. tectorum*, variously reported as being a cross with *I. pallida* or the bearded iris 'Edina'. It has the growing habits of *I. tectorum*, but produces lilac-blue flowers on short stems similar to an intermediate bearded iris. As the blooms age they open wide to resemble *I. tectorum*.

There are reports of crosses between *I. tectorum* and both *I. gracilipes* and *I. cristata* as well as another interspecies cross with a bearded iris, 'Cengialti'. All of these hybrids are sterile.

For those who can give these beautiful iris their climatic and positional requirements, the Evansias are highly recommended garden plants. A small planting of *I. japonica* in any of its forms can give a multitude of flowers over an extended bloom period. I have used *I. japonica* with pink camellias for a very satisfying landscape effect. Coordinated bloom can be obtained with late-flowering *Camellia japonica* or early flowering *Camellia reticulata* cultivars. I can envisage the Evansia iris being used very well with small to medium flowered camellias in tones of white or pale pink. No doubt, late winter and early spring flowering azaleas would also give beautiful results, but they would require far more effort than the easy-care Evansia iris and camellias.

I have been tempted to try Evansia iris with cinerarias but have always backed off at the last minute. It is probably worth trying for effect. One very beautiful companion plant is the delightful *Primula obconica*, which takes on new appeal with the newer, more user-friendly strains available. While I have never had any personal misadventure, I have heard of gardeners developing severe skin irritation and rashes from handling *Primula obconica* in the past. These primula are such beautiful plants in late winter, early spring that I have always felt they were worth growing, but now they are a plant for anyone to use.

Many daisies come into flower with the Evansia iris and although they require more sunlight they are valuable companion plants. The highlight of bloom in the late winter, early spring garden is thought by many to be the gorgeous wisterias with their soft delicate blooms in white, blues and pinks. Evansia iris are excellent companions for wisterias, each of which compliment the other when in flower while the wisteria canopy once it comes into leaf can be used for protection of the delicate Evansia foliage. The ease of cultivation of Evansia iris makes them ideal companion plants for so many different shrubs, perennials and annuals and they are deserving of far more extended use in the landscape.

CHAPTER 4

BULBOUS IRIS

Bulbous iris are easily distinguished from all other iris in that they will flower year after year, going through a dormant and an active period annually. Most bulbous iris will die down in summer, after spring bloom, and will re-emerge either in autumn or spring of the following season. Increase is by way of bulblets, taken from the parent plant, and these bulblets will normally flower in two years and be true to the parent plant. While many bulbs can be left in the ground for several seasons, they all should be lifted at least in alternate years to ensure healthy, vigorous growth. Annual lifting and replanting will ensure better growth and faster multiplication. The exception to this rule is the Juno group of iris which prefer not to be disturbed, and hence should be left in the ground for four years.

BULBOUS SPECIES OF THE SUBGENUS XIPHIUM

By far the best known and most commonly grown bulbous iris are derivatives of *I. xiphium*. Those iris known to us as Spanish, Dutch and English iris are all derivatives of *I. xiphium* in one way or another. Their common names have no bearing on their natural habitat.

I. xiphium is native to the western Mediterranean region of Europe and adjacent areas in North Africa. It is found naturally in Spain, southern France, Portugal, Algeria, Morocco and Tunisia. Extensive plantings have also been located in Italy and Sicily.

These bulbs grow naturally in hot, dry summer conditions and unless you can provide soil that is hot and dry in summer and not overly cold in winter, the bulbs should be lifted and stored once the foliage has died down in mid-summer. They are best stored in a cool dry situation or bedded in sand for a month to six weeks before replanting. A free passage of air is essential, but bulbs should never be stored in direct sunlight.

I. xiphium will grow best in a heavy soil with good drainage. It is advisable to use sand to lighten, or humus such as compost or well-rotted manure to enrich inappropriate soil. They enjoy an alkaline soil so the addition of lime or dolomite to the soil will improve performance. Bulbs should be planted 8–10 cm below the surface and at a distance apart consistent with the display desired. Obviously, if bulbs are planted closely together they must be lifted after flowering, but great garden displays can be achieved by planting as close as 5–6 cm apart without any sacrifice of quality. Newly acquired bulbs are best planted in early autumn and while planting can continue until the end of autumn, performance will be less satisfactory with later planting. These iris do not require a lot of fertiliser and will thrive with a dressing of bulb fertiliser or blood and bone given when the new shoots appear.

'Apollo'

Dutch iris

'Viscount'

Dutch iris seedling

To ensure maximum increase, the small bulblets should be replanted soon after lifting and planted separate from the parent stock. Sufficient room should be left to ensure adequate and quick growth. Increase will be aided by providing rich soil and clean cultivation. Under good culture, bulblets should reach flowering size in two years from planting.

The parent bulbs can be cleaned three to four weeks after lifting, and prepared for planting in another three to four weeks. This is the best time to remove bulblets — replant them immediately. The parent bulbs are best placed in a dry, well-ventilated position, covered with dry sand or vermiculite and periodically dusted with a fungicide and sprayed with an insecticide. This will help to control shrivelling, mould and aphids.

The foliage is thin and reedy on young and newly planted bulbs, thickening and broadening as maturity is reached. It is blue-green in colour and part, or all of it, should be left attached to the bulb if flowering spikes are picked or cut. The flowering spikes should not be cut too low as this can also damage or remove foliage, necessary for the maturity of the bulb and the development of next season's bloom.

Probably the greatest single problem in growing the Xiphiums is their susceptibility to virus diseases which infect the bulbs. These weaken the iris, causing streaking and distortion of flowers and foliage and resulting in a deterioration and possible eventual death of the bulb. There is no cure and infected bulbs should be burned.

Prevention is the only answer and this starts with the acquisition of clean, healthy stock. Bulbs should be purchased only from reputable nurseries with a history of supplying healthy stock. Packaged bulbs which may have been on the shelf for a long time and 'backyard specials', while seemingly good value can, at times, be exactly the opposite. Once good stock has been obtained it should be planted in ideal conditions, as described earlier, to ensure good growth and prevent disease. Bulbs should never be planted in soil where infected bulbs have been grown previously. As virus diseases are transmitted by aphids, these pests must be controlled. Regular spraying, preferably with a systemic spray to give long-term protection, is recommended. Mustard seed fungus can be a problem in warm, humid weather and again, prevention is better than cure. The best prevention is good growing conditions and soil preparation with the incorporation of aureomycin or terramycin in the soil before planting.

Xiphiums lend themselves to pot culture and for those who wish to grow only a few bulbs, there is no better way to grow them. They require a fertile, well-limed potting mix, readily obtained as 'bulb raising mix'. Bulbs can be planted close together and about 5 cm deep with five to ten bulbs in a 20 cm pot. Pretty floral pictures can be painted by mixing these bulbs with other bulbs or annuals.

All the Xiphiums can be grown easily from seed but seed is not readily available and the most reliable source would be from that collected yourself. It will take four years from seed collection to flowering. Germination in a seed-raising mix is easy and seed from commercially available cultivars will not be true to the parent.

Some of the Xiphium species worthy of special mention are:

I. boissieri, I. filifolia, I. fontanesii, I. juncea, I. latifolium and *I. tingitana*.

I. boissieri is a rare and somewhat difficult bulb from the Gerex Mountains of Portugal. It is distinctive, in that the summer-blooming flowers have yellow, hairy appendages ('beards') on the inner half of the signal on the falls. This is the only known 'bearded' bulbous iris.

The foliage is fine and reedy, dull blue-green in colour and grows to 40 cm in length. Flowering spikes are 30 cm or more in height, and carry two rich blue-violet flowers with red-violet at the base of the standards and red-violet styles.

The bulbs are small and readily produce seed which is slow to germinate and then takes up to three years to bloom following germination. Bulbs require alkaline soil and excellent drainage with sand added to heavy soil. They do well in light soil in a warm, sunny position.

I. filifolia is a small and somewhat difficult bulb from Gibraltar and Southern Spain. It is distinctive by way of the mottled sheaf which protects the new growth. This foliage is fine, reedy and somewhat lax. Flowering spikes are 30 to 45 cm and carry two rich purple flowers with a blue margin to the orange signal on the falls. Bloom period is late spring and cultural requirements are similar to *I. boissieri*.

I. fontanesii is a native of North Africa and although similar to *I. tingitana* is inferior to that iris in plant habits and quality of bloom, but far more reliable in flower production. The foliage is somewhat broad and silvery green, reaching upward of 60 cm. Flowering spikes can reach up to 120 cm and carry two to three flowers in shades ranging from pale to rich blue violet in late winter, early spring.

Seed is readily produced and will flower three to four years after germination. This iris is not cold-hardy.

I. juncea is a native of North Africa and Sicily, and has distinctive bulbs with hard, dark brown skin, fibrous at the neck. The rounded rush-like foliage is dull blue-green. Flowering spikes reach 40–70 cm in height and carry two bright, vivid, golden-yellow flowers. Some seedlings have brown veins radiating from the gold signals. Standards are pointed and falls pendent, lacking substance.

Increase is not easy except in near-perfect conditions, but seed is easily raised and will bloom four years after germination. This iris is not cold-hardy and not easy to grow. It prefers a sandy, gravel soil, has cultural requirements similar to *I. boissieri* and blooms in late spring, early summer.

I. tingitana is a native of Tangiers and a most beautiful but frustrating iris to grow. I can well remember growing the most delightful flowers from bulbs which, I believe, came from New Zealand some fifteen or more years ago. They had their one season of glory for I was never able to coax them to repeat that performance and this is an experience shared by many gardeners as *I. tingitana* is, to describe it kindly, very erratic in its flowering.

Foliage is broad, heavily channelled, blue-green in colour and silvery on the upper surface. Flowering spikes, up to 100 cm in height in good conditions, carry two buds which open to lavender-blue flowers, very much richer on the edges of the falls, and carrying large gold signals.

Cultural requirements are rich, well-drained and limed soil, a hot sunny position and protection from frost. A supply of potash in the growing season is beneficial. Bulbs can be planted less deeply than most others, about 3–4 cm below the surface and given sufficient room for optimum growth. They benefit from being placed on a bed of sand and also covered with a layer of sand.

The huge bulbs, more the size of a daffodil than the typical iris, are best planted in early autumn and can be left in the ground after bloom except in areas with wet summers. Production from seed is not difficult and flowering-sized bulbs are produced in four years.

I. latifolium is a native of the damp, alpine meadows of the Pyrenees. These meadows are snow-covered in winter and melting snow in summer and autumn, coupled with rain, maintain moist soils. *I. latifolium* requires a damp soil that is never completely dry, but drainage should be good.

The distinctive foliage is rigid with deep green channelled leaves, smooth and green-white on the inside. Inner leaves are finer and follow the rather thick fleshy growth tips which do not emerge until well into spring. Flowering spikes reach 70 cm in height with two flowers having short, rounded standards and falls, narrow at the haft, broadened and more rounded blades. The flowers are dark blue-violet with a thin central yellow line.

Cultural requirements are to give these bulbs as near as possible their natural conditions. Seed is easily produced and takes four to five years to develop into flowering-size bulbs.

English iris are derivatives of *I. latifolium* and make large bulbs which should be planted to a depth three times their length and left undisturbed as long as possible, as the bulbs are easily damaged and deteriorate quickly if left out of the ground. They flower quite late in the season, usually towards the end of spring, early summer. English iris are not suitable for temperate climates as they need winter cold and are equally unsuccessful in climates with hot dry summers. If given cold, wet winters with moist soil in the summer they will thrive and make excellent cut flowers. There are named cultivars in the trade but they are not readily available and English iris are usually sold according to colour in white, and all shades and combinations of blue and purple. I have heard of lavender and pink cultivars, but have not seen them.

NAMED CULTIVARS

'Flower Dream' — pure white with a yellow signal.
'Blue Rain' — rich dark blue with a yellow signal edged white.
'Summer Sky' — sky blue with a yellow signal.

Hybrids from the xiphiums

Other than the English iris, those iris known to us as Dutch and Spanish iris are derivatives from the *xiphium* species. The Spanish iris come directly from *I. xiphium* while the English iris come from *I. latifolium*. Most of the Dutch iris are derivatives of *I. xiphium*, *I. tingitana*, *I. filifolia*, *I. fontanesii* and possibly other species. These iris are now so interbred that unless flow charts and family histories were plotted it would be difficult to determine their exact ancestry. It is probably sufficient to say that hybridisers have given us a multitude of outstanding garden and cut flower bulbs which far surpass the species for performance and reliability.

Until around 1960, Spanish iris had been a significant cut flower and a favourite garden bulb throughout the world. Derived mainly from *I. xiphium* with naturally occurring colours of white, purple, blue and yellow and combinations of these colours, they were made to order for hybridisers to develop. These iris flower in mid spring and carry small to medium sized blooms. While now surpassed and supplanted by the Dutch iris as cut flowers for the trade, these iris do have significant value as garden plants and for floral decoration as cut flowers.

Dutch iris have been developed by intercrossing various *xiphium* species. Various accounts of hybrids developed by crossing *I. xiphium* with *I. tingitana*, *I. filifolia* and *I. fontanesii* are documented and there is evidence to support the use of *I. boissieri* as well. The earlier raised hybrids have been used to produce many newer and often more spectacular flowers while colour breaks have enlarged the colour range.

Jean Stevens in her book *Iris and Its Culture* reports that the very popular bronze-toned Dutch iris were probably obtained from a bronzed purple toned Spanish iris called 'Thunderbolt'. In more recent times, clean bronze flowers without the dull purple influence have been developed. She also reports that 'Wedgewood', an early and most successful Dutch hybrid, was developed from crossing *I. xiphium* and *I. tingitana*. As 'Wedgewood' is in the parentage of so many modern Dutch hybrids, this would enable breeders to trace right back to the original species.

Dutch iris flower earlier than Spanish iris, have larger flowers, are easier to cultivate and have a greater colour range. Hybridisers have been able to lengthen and extend the blooming period and by forcing and holding methods, bloom is now available throughout the year. These are the most successful commercial cut flower iris and such is their popularity that, to many, they are the only known iris. Their popularity is justified as fresh Dutch iris can have a vase life of from one to two weeks in good conditions.

They are also good garden subjects, requiring much the same cultural practices as the species but being far more easy and rewarding in cultivation. New bulbs can be produced from bulblets which are true to the parent stock and take two years to reach mature flowering size. New bulbs can also be produced from seed but these bulbs will not be true to the parent.

For those gardeners wishing to grow bulbous iris, I strongly recommend the Dutch iris hybrids for all-round performance in all but the coldest climates. In very cold climates where they are less successful in the garden they can be grown successfully in greenhouse or glasshouse conditions. They also make excellent pot plants which can be brought into the house at bloom time if the grower does not wish to cut them. They can be grown very successfully with other bulbs which bloom simultaneously and spectacular displays can be obtained by combining Dutch iris with suitable spring-flowering annuals.

Recommended cultivars

The following list of 20 named cultivars gives a good selection of older and some more recent additions in an excellent colour range. There are many others, some of which, no doubt will surpass those listed here for some gardeners in some situations. Those of you who become collectors will be able to enlarge your collections through contact with specialist growers.

'Apollo' A distinctive true amoena with white standards and primrose-yellow falls. The slightly darker signal is hardly noticeable. Flowers are well formed, growth is vigorous.

'Blue Magic' Blue-violet self with a yellow signal edged in white.

'Bronze Queen' One of the best of the bronze-toned iris, this has blue-bronze standards and darker bronze falls with an orange signal. Well formed, medium-sized flowers and the bulbs are relatively vigorous and disease free.

'Golden Harvest' Somewhat small but perfectly formed rich golden yellow self with only the slightest signal noticeable. While not the tallest or largest in this colour range, it is the best. Standards are held in perfect 120° gap position and do not twist as many cultivars are prone to do, while the balance between standards and falls is perfect. This iris flowers mid season, is very vigorous and very healthy. I strongly recommend this outstanding cultivar.

'H C van Vliet' This is a bitoned blue iris with mid-blue standards and lighter blue falls with a small orange signal. Mid season bloom.

'Ideal' Rich lobelia blue with a yellow signal, this iris is similar in form and growing habits to 'Wedgewood' and is possibly a sport of that cultivar.

'Imperator' Mid-blue edged deeper and one of the best cut flowers, being one of the longest lasting of all Dutch iris once cut. Blooms later than most other cultivars.

'Lemon Champion' More cream in colour than lemon, with a deep yellow signal.

'Mariner' Soft light blue, yellow signal.

'Marquette' Slightly darker than 'Apollo' and in the amoena pattern. Standards are creamy white, falls are yellow with an orange signal. Good quality.

'Professor Blaauw' One of the more vigorous cultivars, but comes on shorter spikes and has a shorter shelf-life. The rich, dark velvety gentian blue colour is gorgeous and set off by a yellow signal. Blooms are quite large and flowering is mid to late season.

'Purple Sensation' The rich violet-purple flowers are set off by yellow signals with a blue rim. This is a very good cultivar with mid-season bloom.

'Telstar' Attractive deep blue with a yellow signal.

'Viscount' Very large and tall growing blue purple with a yellow signal.

'Wedgewood' (also often listed in catalogues as 'Wedgewood Blue'). Always one of the first to bloom, this is one of the great Dutch iris. It is a cross of I. xiphium and I. tingitana and has all the beauty of I. tingitana coupled with superb all-round performance. The flowers are light sky blue with a yellow signal. Growth is vigorous and bloom is prolific and reliable. This is a healthy variety and an excellent parent. It is the Dutch iris most widely sold as a cut flower.

'White Cloud' Although called white, this iris has slight blue shadings giving it a pallid appearance.

'White Excelsior' Pure white with a small yellow signal, the flowers are smallish but bloom early in the season.

'White Perfection' Outstanding pure white with high-quality, large blooms on tall spikes. Excellent cut flower and the best available white.

'White van Vliet' Tall, high-quality white with good all-round performance.

'White Wedgewood' This is really a white to cream bitone. The standards are creamy white, falls are grey white with yellow signals. Good quality.

Some newer cultivars to the Australian market available since 1994 are:

'Blue Star' dark blue. Said to be an improved 'Professor Blaauw'.

'Casablanca' white.

'Gipsy Beauty' violet standards, tan to light brown falls, yellow signals.

'Hildegarde' lovely sky blue of impeccable form.

'Majestic Beauty' blue with a bronze-veined signal.

'Oriental Beauty' light blue standards, yellow falls darker signal.

'Paris' violet.

'Saturnus' white standards, yellow falls.

BULBOUS IRIS IN THE GARDEN

Whole books have been written on gardening with bulbs and bulbous iris would rate highly with anyone interested in growing bulbs. Probably the single most important factor in the use of any bulbs in the garden is the awareness of the bulbs' appearance in the garden and cultural requirements before and after flowering.

Soil and climate conditions will determine whether bulbs need to be planted and lifted each year and all bulbs need a rejuvenating period immediately after flowering, whereby the bulb uses nutrients from the foliage to build up to flowering size for the following season. Bulbs can therefore look untidy in the garden, particularly after flowering. For this reason many gardeners prefer to grow their bulbs in pots.

DUTCH IRIS FOR THE CUT-FLOWER TRADE

The production of Dutch iris for the cut-flower trade is a multimillion dollar world-wide business. These iris can be purchased from florists virtually any time of the year and even allowing for the import and export of iris between southern and northern hemispheres, this requires quite a bit of manipulation by the growers.

A Dutch iris spike can be cut for sale in anything from eight to 14 weeks after planting and the successful production of iris year-round depends on the grower planning a planting strategy and either forcing or retarding bulbs for bloom. Bulbs are stored in cool-room conditions to induce dormancy and can then be grown in greenhouses, under glass or under normal field conditions to induce bloom at the desired time. This 'forcing' process is very satisfactory for obtaining early spikes. Bulbs that have been lifted late can be stored at high temperature (30°C) for an additional period of inactivity during which there is no growth. Staggered holding from four to six weeks is then followed by six weeks of cooling as a minimum and the retarded bulbs are then planted to extend the bloom season well beyond that of the normal field-grown bulbs. While timing for 'spot on' daily production would be critical, the sheer magnitude of the operation of producing millions of cut flowers and the fact that flowering spikes can be held in cool room conditions for five to 10 days without deterioration makes the timing less critical. Control of heat and light throughout the operation is critical and, as is to be expected, there are some cultivars which respond better than others to this form of culture.

Cultivars used extensively in the cut-flower trade for 'out of season' production include 'Wedgewood', 'H C van Vliet', 'Imperator', 'Professor Blaauw', 'Ideal', 'Golden Harvest' and 'White Excelsior'.

BULBOUS IRIS OF THE SUBGENUS IRIDODICTYUM

These are the well-known small bulbs of the 'Reticulata' group of almost stemless irises with distinctive four to eight ribbed rounded leaves and bulbs with netted tunics. These iris are native to Iraq, Iran, Syria, Lebanon, Turkey, Turkestan, Israel and Russia. They require a cold winter and hot dry summers for optimum growth. They like a rich, well-composted, heavy, alkaline soil with good drainage and need to be planted in full sun, preferably with some shelter.

The flowers resemble small Spanish iris but only one flower is produced on a very short spike. They seem to relish some early summer rain, but prolonged summer rain is detrimental to their performance and under these conditions they should be lifted and stored. Bulbs are best planted to a depth of 5 cm in late summer and should be well watered in winter and spring. Early planting is essential for good performance. These bulbs are subject to a fungus disease, commonly called black spot or ink spot, owing to the black spots which form on the diseased bulbs. They can be kept clean by dipping in any of the commercial fungicides before planting, with the possible need of a follow-up spray.

Some of the more important species are *I. reticulata, I. histrio, I. histrioides, I. danfordiae, I. vartanii,* and *I. bakeriana.*

I. reticulata is a native of the Caucasus. It is the tallest of these species and produces 5–6 cm blooms on spikes up to 18–20 cm in height. Flowers are violet with a gold stripe on the falls and are of narrow form. The scented flowers are often hidden by the foliage. It is easily raised from seed, taking three to four years to mature. There is a darker red-purple form collected from the wild and known incorrectly as *I. krelagei*.

I. histrio is a variable species found naturally in Syria, Turkey, Lebanon, Armenia, through the region once known as Asia Minor. Flowers are smaller and appear earlier than *I. reticulata,* often blooming in early to mid winter. It is less robust than *I. reticulata* and is unscented. Colours range from blue to violet to purple, each flower carrying a gold signal stripe surrounded by veins and flecks of a darker blue than the ground colour. These iris require good drainage and do best in a rich, light soil.

I. histrioides is a native of northern and eastern Asia Minor through to Iran. It is the most attractive of the reticulatas with rich blue flowers, dotted deeper blue around the white hafts and with a yellow median stripe. The 10 cm diameter flowers are carried singly on 10 cm spikes and single bulbs will often carry multiple flowers, all of which precede the foliage. The large somewhat untidy foliage does not interfere with bloom. This iris requires full sun and good drainage for best performance and the foliage needs to be left until it dies off to ensure good production for the following season. Easy to grow and multiply and easy to produce from seed, this iris is a garden gem in winter.

I. danfordiae is also a native of eastern Asia Minor. The foliage consists of slender four-ribbed spikes and while it does appear before the flowering spikes, bloom is above the foliage which later becomes quite long (up to 40 cm). Flowering spikes 8–10 cm high carry single 5 cm flowers which are greenish yellow in bud and open bright yellow. The standards are short and inconspicuous, and the falls carry an orange stripe and are dotted green at the hafts. This iris requires a rich, light soil and excellent drainage for best results. Even then, the parent bulb, having flowered, will often split into bulblets which take three or more years to again reach flowering size. Bloom period is late winter and bulbs should be lifted each year.

I. vartanii is a native of Palestine and carries small white to slate blue flowers with a yellow median stripe on 10 cm spikes. This iris is delicate and difficult, but will flower in early winter if successful. It is probably of interest only to collectors, its main claim to fame being its almond-scented blooms.

I. bakeriana comes from Iran, Iraq, Syria, Turkey, Armenia and is a somewhat rare and distinctive species with slender eight-sided leaves. The small 5 cm flowers are produced on 10 cm spikes and have light to mid blue standards and darker blue violet falls with a white signal patch surrounded by blue violet dots and a yellow median line. It can be grown well in light sandy soil but is demanding in culture and not particularly vigorous.

Commercial cultivars

Bulbs of *I. histrioides major,* a large, rich blue flower with thick foliage that follows the bloom are often available and are of garden value and easy to cultivate. There are also quite a few interspecific crosses resulting in named cultivars. All of these grow to about 15–20 cm in height.

'Cantab' is a selected pale blue form of *I. reticulata* and a proven performer.

'J.S. Dijt' is an easy growing, taller, deep red-violet.

'Natascha' is ivory white with green veins and a yellow blotch.

'Harmony' is a rich sky blue of quality.

'Joyce' is also sky blue, but flowers later than 'Harmony'.

Many newer cultivars have come onto the market in recent years and I was able to see a large display of new and older cultivars when visiting the Floriade in Holland in 1992. Most are in various shades of blue-violet and purple, but white and yellow flowers and associated shades are available and in specialist catalogues.

BULBOUS IRIS OF THE GENUS JUNO

There is debate as to whether this group of bulbous iris from the Mediterranean area of Sicily and Spain, the near east, Iraq, Iran, Turkestan, Afghanistan and parts of what was the USSR should be given separate generic status or be recognised as a subgenus of the genus iris. For many years they have been recognised as iris and I see no great harm in continuing to do so.

The foliage of this group of 60 or so species is distinctive and plants, in growth, resemble dwarf or miniature maize or corn. Flower buds are produced from the axils of the leaves and blooms are also easily distinguished from 'other iris'. Most of the species are difficult to grow and of little garden value. They are thick-necked large bulbs and develop large, white, fleshy roots which resemble long radishes and they send out fibrous roots when actively growing. Care must be taken not to damage these roots in storage or transportation.

Junos require a rich, alkaline soil with good drainage, a sunny position and hot dry summer for best performance. Most are not cold-hardy. Once established, they like to be left undisturbed. Increase and multiplication is not easy and although seed is readily set it will take four to five years to develop into mature bulbs.

In describing the species I will adopt that which is common terminology and include them in the genus

Iris, although there is strong argument to separate them completely from the iris into the genus *Juno.*

Some species worthy of special mention are: *I. aucheri (I. sindjarensis), I. bucharica, I. caucasica, I. graeberiana, I. magnifica, I. orchioides, I. persica, I. planifolia (I. alata), I. postii, I. rosenbachiana, I. stocksii,* and *I. warleyensis.*

I. aucheri, also known as *I. sindjarensis,* comes from Iran, Iraq, Jordan, Syria and Turkey. It has bright green foliage and spikes that grow to 30 cm and carry up to six pale to light blue flowers, 6 cm in diameter, recurved and sweetly perfumed. It prefers a lighter soil than most junos and flowers in late winter.

I. bucharica is the best known and easiest juno to grow. It is native to Bukhara and has bright, shiny, light green foliage with flowering spikes reaching 45 cm or more. The tiny horizontal standards are white and the rounded falls bright yellow with white crests and styles. Up to eight blooms are produced from the large, floriferous bulbs. This is a vigorous grower that will make good-sized clumps in a sunny position in the garden.

I. caucasica is native to the Caucasus, Turkey and Iran. It is a miniature species with fan-shaped blue-green foliage. The 20–25 cm spikes carry up to four pale yellow translucent flowers.

I. graeberiana is native to Turkestan and has spreading, upright green foliage. The 30 cm spikes carry four to six rich blue, slightly bitone flowers. It is spring flowering, free of bloom, and relatively easy to cultivate in a warm, sunny position with well drained soil.

I. magnifica, also known as *I. vicaria,* is native to Turkestan. The blue-green foliage gives rise to somewhat tall spikes up to 60 cm, which carry up to seven blooms. Blooms range from white to lilac to lavender and appear in spring. It is relatively easy to grow and maintain and is easily raised from seed.

I. orchioides, often confused with a yellow form of *I. bucharica,* is a native of Turkestan. Broad green foliage supports 30–40 cm spikes of deep, pure yellow but often with some green at the haft. Blooms are 6 cm or more in diameter and carried up to six on a spike. This iris is reasonably easy to grow and is free flowering.

I. persica is a native of Iran and Turkey and, although quite rare, is available commercially. The 6–7 cm flowers are produced on 20 cm spikes which carry two greenish blue flowers and a yellow line signal. Foliage is narrow and ribbed. Flowers are produced in late winter and spring. This iris requires a dry summer for adequate performance and is not easily grown and maintained. There are many colour variations known with flowers in white, yellow, grey-blue, red-purple and violet. Classification is difficult.

I. planifolia, also known as *I. alata,* is widely distributed naturally in Spain, Portugal, Sardinia, Algeria, Libya, Sicily and into Malta. Foliage is maize-like and two to three flowers 10 cm in diameter are produced on spikes which reach 20 cm. The fragrant blooms come in shades of blue with an orange line signal and are ruffled. This iris will bloom from autumn into winter. It is not easily maintained. Another difficult juno, *I. postii* is similar to *I. persica* but distinguished by its long slender roots. It hides its 4 cm blooms in the foliage and is of little garden value.

I. rosenbachiana is a native of Turkestan and Bukhara. The crescent-shaped dark green leaves are short during the bloom period and this adds to its value as a garden subject. The 15 cm spikes carry up to three blooms 6 cm in diameter. There is much colour variation in shades of violet and purple with yellow signals and white dots. Blooms appear in winter and early spring.

I. stocksii is similar to *I. caucasica* but has a silver margin to the foliage and purple blooms.

I. warleyensis is a native of Bukhara. It has narrow, drooping foliage and 30–40 cm spikes which carry up to five mauve to red-violet flowers with an orange signal surrounded by white. This spring blooming iris is hardy.

Moraea — 'Lousberi'

Neomarica caerulea

D I E T E S

Dietes bicolor

Dietes grandiflora

CHAPTER 5

IRIS THAT ARE NOT IRIS

When discussing iris it is probably beneficial to mention some of the 'non–iris' which are often referred to as iris, purely by common usage. Such terms as 'snake's head iris', 'butterfly iris', 'peacock iris' and 'sisyrinchium' have been in common use for many years and will continue to be used both by home gardeners and in the trade.

I have no real problem with this as long as the common names used are uniform both in usage and acceptance. One can, of course, open a can of worms and eventually find the list growing and growing as gladiolus, crocus, freesia, babiana, ixia, sparaxis, laperouisia and all the other Iridaceae come under notice. That is not intended for this book and I will restrict mention to those plants commonly referred to as iris.

Hermodactylus tuberosus is also known as *I. tuberosa* and snake's head iris and is very similar in flower shape to a reticulata, as is the foliage, which is four-sided, narrow, green and lax in habit. It is a native of Greece and Sicily. The very weak spikes grow to 30 cm and are often found bent over or prostrate in the garden after wind or rain. The 5 cm flowers, one or two per spike, have green-yellow standards and velvety black-purple falls with green styles and crests. The bloom is unusual, dull but not unattractive and sweetly perfumed. It grows from fat, white tubers, flowers in winter and is easily cultivated.

MORAEA

The genus *Moraea* consists of over 80 different species, mainly from South Africa, but some from more tropical parts of that continent. Although strictly not an iris but a member of the Iridaceae, there are some species which are commonly called peacock iris. Moraeas are easily grown from corms in frost-free, temperate climates. They are not particular about soil but do require a sunny position. In cold climates they need greenhouse or glasshouse protection. In suitable conditions, multiplication of corms is quick and production from seed is easy with corms reaching maturity in three years from planting.

These corms are easily grown in containers, which can produce a magnificent display in full bloom.

M. aristata, also known as *M. candida* and *M. glaucopsis,* and regularly called peacock iris, grows to 45 cm and has pure white flowers, with a deep blue spot at the base of the outer petals.

M. bipartita, also known as *M. polyanthos,* grows to 60 cm and comes in blue-purple shades with yellow at the base.

M. neopavonia, also known as *M. pavonia* and *I. pavonia,* grows to 50 m in shades of orange to red with black or blue 'eyes'. There is a yellow form known as *M. neopavonia lutea.*

M. villosa is often regarded as another variation of *M. neopavonia.* Flowers are in the blue-purple shades with an iridescent central eye zone. This *Morea* has been much hybridised with *M. neopavonia* with a resulting large colour range of cream, yellow, orange to red, blue, mauve and purple. Many of the *M. neopavonia, M. villosa* hybrids, as well as the species, are referred to as peacock iris.

M. vegeta, also known as *M. juncea* and *M. tristis,* grows to 30 cm and has buff-coloured flowers with yellow markings edged in maroon.

M. spathulata, also known as *M. huttonii* and *M. spathacea,* produces long slender leaves and tall slender spikes to 120 cm with several iris-like, golden-yellow flowers with darker markings.

DIETES

The genus *Dietes* is not iris, but these plants are also members of the Iridaceae. Like most iris, they do grow from rhizomes. *Dietes* are native to South Africa and Australia and have flowers very similar to *Moraea*. Unlike *Moraea* they have evergreen foliage, long, broad, stiff and pointed. They are often known as butterfly iris.

Dietes are tough, undemanding, easily grown plants in warm, temperate climates. They will thrive in most soils if kept well watered, but will survive drought. Their toughness and ease of cultivation has earned them a solid position in the landscape trade.

Once established, the rhizomes will multiply quickly and can be lifted and divided in late summer or autumn. They grow easily from seed and produce mature plants in one to two years. All *Dietes* seem pest and disease free.

D. bicolor, also known as *I. bicolor, M. bicolor,* peacock flower, butterfly flower and butterfly iris, is a native of South Africa. Foliage is long, 5 cm wide, pointed and a dull green colour. It forms a fan shape at the base from which come tall spikes to 120 cm with many cream flowers, each with a brown 'eye'. The prolific bloom, in temperate climates is through spring with spot bloom in summer. Flowers are 5–6 cm in diameter.

D. grandiflora develops tall foliage similar to *D. bicolor,* but wider and very tall spikes to 120 cm and more. Flowers are 6 cm in diameter, white with an orange signal (or eye). This is a delightful plant which will bloom throughout spring and into summer.

D. iridioides, also known as *D. vegeta, M. iridioides* and *M. vegeta,* is a native of South Africa. It is often referred to as the butterfly flower, butterfly iris and peacock iris,

all giving rise to a great deal of confusion. Foliage is basal and very fan-like, up to 45 cm in length, dark green, leathery and pointed. Flowering spikes reach 90 cm in height and are produced from early spring, through summer and into autumn in temperate climates. The somewhat thin spikes carry many light blue-white flowers with orange-yellow signals and lavender to purple styles. This is an outstanding plant for massed effect as it is long flowering and attractive when not in bloom.

GYNANDRIRIS

There are seven species in this genus, but one of these, *G. sisyrinchium,* has been known for many years as *Iris sisyrinchium* and will continue to be known as such for many more years.

Gynandriris sisyrinchium is a native of the Mediterranean and grows from a corm. It has tiny, iris-like flowers in shades of blue and violet with yellow or white signals on the falls. Spikes can reach up to 40–50 cm and the fleeting blooms are produced in spring. It is frost tender but in a mild, temperate climate will multiply very quickly and can become invasive.

The other species of *Gynandriris* are from South Africa, more attractive but less well known. I have grown a white *sisyrinchium* which is an unknown hybrid, vigorous and prolific but of little garden value.

TUBEROUS IRIS — NEPALENSIS

In the iris family the majority of species develop from rhizomes, with some bulbous members.

The subgenus *Nepalensis* has one species, *I. nepalensis,* also known as *I. decora,* which grows from a tuberous rootstock similar to that of a daylily (*Hemerocallis*). This iris is native to the Himalayas, particularly Nepal (as the name would indicate) and is of interest more because of its classification than any other feature. The short-lived flowers are lilac in colour and the iris is not known to be in commerce.

Other iris given species status as *I. collettii* and *I. staintonii* are possibly only other forms of *I. nepalensis.* All would be of interest only to collectors.

CHAPTER 6

LIVING WITH IRIS

LANDSCAPING WITH BEARDED IRIS

Bearded iris are very versatile plants in the landscape as long as their basic cultural needs of full sun, good drainage and neutral to alkaline soil are provided. Many gardeners like to grow their iris in a separate iris garden where their cultural needs can be provided without interference from other plants, but tall bearded iris can usually be planted in the general garden.

Massed displays of iris bursting into bloom simultaneously are easy to accomplish and most appealing to the eye, but have the disadvantage of a short blooming season. Most tall bearded iris spikes are attractive in the garden for two weeks, maybe a little more, and it is a long wait for the next bloom. A mass planting of the one cultivar is absolutely spectacular in bloom but as most spikes of the one cultivar of tall bearded iris grown in the same garden flower simultaneously, the beauty is short-lived. 'Lady Friend' (Ghio, 1981) is of particular interest for massed display, not only for its garnet red colour but for its all-round garden performance. This is one iris that does not mind being moved around, will put on an outstanding display each year even on first-year plants and is clean, healthy and attractive. In one season (1995 bloom) at Dural this

iris was planted in five different locations and each of the five had a different bloom period so that a succession of bloom was obtained throughout the whole season. 'Lady Friend' is one bearded iris which performs well in warmer, more humid climates where some bearded iris fail and it is outstanding in cooler climates. Spectacular effects have been achieved in our plantings with the white-edged blue plicata 'Rare Treat' (Schreiner, 1987), 'Lady Friend' (Ghio, 1981) and the white-edged lavender-blue-violet plicata 'Jesse's Song' (Williamson, 1983). These are three great iris with excellent bud count and bud placement and so lend themselves to a massed display where other iris without these attributes would be less spectacular.

Some Australian-raised iris which have given startling massed colour effect are: 'Alpine Journey' (Blyth, 1984); 'Aztec Burst' (Blyth, 1993); 'Azure Angel' (Grosvenor, 1994); 'Bahloo' (Caldwell, 1986); 'Blues Brothers' (Lesley Blyth, 1989); 'Close Your Eyes' (Blyth, 1989); 'Dance Man' (Blyth, 1989); 'Divine Duchess' (Blyth, 1990); 'English Charm' (Blyth, 1989); 'First Movement' (Grosvenor, 1993); 'High Waters' (Blyth, 1989); 'In Town' (Blyth, 1988); 'Liqueur Creme' (Blyth, 1989); 'New Tune' (Grosvenor, 1996); 'Pemcaw' (Harding, 1994); 'Ribands' (Grosvenor, 1994); 'Royal Honey' (Blyth, 1992); 'Temptone' (Grosvenor, 1994); 'Words and Music' (Grosvenor, 1984); and 'Lilac Lustre' (Donnell, 1984). All can be stunning in large solo clumps. Others of outstanding quality for massed display are 'Just

‘Mary Frances’ (Gaulter, 1973) — Courtyard at
Rainbow Ridge

Sunset at Hillview—‘Planned Treasure’ (Burger, 1985)

Intermediate bearded iris at Rainbow Ridge

Louisiana iris at Rainbow Ridge
Nursery featuring ‘Ann Chowning’,
‘Mrs Ira Nelson’, ‘Edith Fear’

Iris at Hillview, 1992

Iris at Hillview — mass of Tall Bearded 'Cycles' (McWhirter, 1986) in the foreground

Magic' (Blyth, 1990), 'Latin Lark' (Blyth, 1988) and 'Lipstick Lies' (Blyth, 1985).

When one starts thinking about massed displays of the one cultivar it is really the same as selecting the top garden varieties and what greater recommendation can one give than to say they have seen or would like to see a massed display of a given cultivar in all its glory. Undoubtedly, I have just given a list of my top 20 Australian-raised cultivars that are readily available in large quantities. As newer cultivars come onto the market each year and those that are now available become better established there is little doubt that a list would change, just as there is little doubt that a list would change from year to year according to performance in that year.

In evaluating imported iris or iris that I have seen on my travels it is obvious that 'Lady Friend', 'Jesse's Song' and 'Rare Treat' rate very highly. Others that come readily to mind are — 'Silverado' (Schreiner, 1987), 'Beverly Sills' (Hager, 1979), 'Portrait of Larrie' (Gaulter, 1979), 'Skating Party' (Gaulter, 1983), 'Dusky Challenger' (Schreiner, 1986), 'Breakers' (Schreiner, 1986), 'Classic Look' (Schreiner, 1992), 'Mystique' (Ghio, 1975), 'Cheerful One' (Hamner, 1989), 'Blenheim Royal' (Schreiner, 1990), 'Indigo Princess' (Schreiner, 1992), 'Bogota' (Ghio, 1989), 'Goddess' (Keppel, 1981), 'Snowbrook' (Keppel, 1981), 'Social Event' (Keppel, 1991), 'Honkytonk Blues' (Schreiner, 1988), 'Hello Darkness' (Schreiner, 1992), 'Rustler' (Keppel, 1988), 'Santiago' (Ghio, 1989) and 'Sweet Musette' (Schreiner, 1986).

You can see from the above selection the influence that the iris from Schreiner's Gardens has had on me. Over the years they have produced an abundance of superb quality iris, particularly in blue, purple, neglecta and blue-on-white plicata patterns. Both their 'red' and their 'black' breeding lines also lead the world in their fields.

To visit the display garden of Schreiner's Iris Nursery in Salem, Oregon, USA is an awe-inspiring experience. There, beautifully laid out gardens display iris grown to perfection in all kinds of colour combinations. Any attempt to replicate the display can lead to frustration as those iris that grow well in the north-western USA may not grow as well in warmer parts of the country and there is a further problem when importing iris from other countries as plants may not acclimatise. My personal experience with the Schreiner irises has been very rewarding and I find their rigorous culling and selection processes work well in the interests of the purchasing public. If, however, you wish to produce landscape scenes similar to the display gardens at Schreiner's it is advisable to seek the assistance of the expert staff available from that nursery or your local iris specialist nursery. Equally inspiring is the spectacular display garden in Cooley's Nursery, Silverton, Oregon, USA.

One could go on and on and it soon becomes clear that personal preference for colour and pattern dominate the selection process. An even greater influence is the performance of particular iris under your own growing conditions and this can only be developed by growing the iris — a sort of catch-22 situation. Very often you can learn by observing those iris that grow well in your area, by discussion with neighbours, by joining an iris society or garden club or, most likely, by seeking advice from a specialist nursery.

Very often the exact effect you wish to produce can be achieved in your particular situation by varying the choice from that which you see on display. The performance difference of particular cultivars from one area to another and from one garden to another never ceases to amaze me.

There are many varieties which vary considerably in performance while there are those universal favourites which never fail to please. Apart from the Schreiner irises I have a particular affection for the iris bred by Keith Keppel, and Joe Ghio, the two American iris hybridisers with whom I have established a long friendship. Their irises together with those hybridised in Australia, particularly by Barry Blyth, form the basis of my extensive collection.

Another means of massing bearded iris for display is in colour groupings, with colours blending and harmonising or contrasting for effect. The possibilities are endless and the choice of colour combinations personal, but before embarking on such a venture gardeners should spend time researching the bloom period so that the colour display is simultaneous. Many early flowering cultivars are finished or almost finished bloom by the time late flowering cultivars are beginning to bloom and so are not suitable for planting together for a massed display, but are very suitable for obtaining a continuous display. A combination of dwarf, intermediate and tall bearded iris is excellent for continuity of bloom over an extended period but not suitable for a massed effect. Knowing what you want and taking care in your selection is the key to success. If you don't know exactly what you want, seek assistance from a specialist iris nursery.

Some landscaping ideas

◆ Massed beds of one cultivar.
◆ Collections of colours or colour patterns, blended or contrasted, e.g., a blue bed — 4 different shades of blue; a blue and white bed; a group of three or four or more — blue, purple, white, amoena (white/blue) or neglecta (blue/purple).
◆ A collector's garden — no attempt at colour combination. Grow them for individual beauty and satisfaction.

- A hybridiser's garden — rows and rows of seedlings and/or a section set aside with cultivars to be used in hybridising.
- As an extended border in front of trees and shrubs.
- In pockets as highlights in front of trees and shrubs.
- As highlights in a perennial garden.
- Edging a driveway or path.
- Around a pond or water feature.
- As a specimen clump — surrounded by annuals or ground covers.
- As a feature iris garden — surrounded by annual or ground covers.
- As a supplementary planting to a feature such as a fountain, bird bath, etc.
- In pots or tubs.
- As a bearded iris garden for continuous bloom (tall bearded, IB and SDB).
- Rockeries, both SDB and IB iris are beautiful in rockeries, while TB iris would only be satisfactory in very large rocky outcrops.
- Ribbons of colour can provide brilliant visual effects, either as a massed iris display or within a tree and shrub setting.

Companion planting

It is difficult to advise on companion planting as iris will grow under such diverse climatic conditions. They will be far more adaptable than many of the companion plants that would attract gardeners. Most gardeners are aware of those plants that grow well in their area and assistance will always be available from local nurseries.

Care should be taken when selecting companion plants to avoid the pitfalls.

- Select plants which require the same soil conditions and culture as your iris.
- Select plants which are proven in your particular climate and growing conditions.
- Take care to ensure that the companion plants do not encroach upon the iris.
- Allow adequate spacing for your iris and your companion plants to grow.
- Ensure that your iris are not dominated by the companion plants if you intend the iris to be the feature.

I can remember visiting Chatsworth House in England and seeing the magnificent lupin garden which was surrounded by a planting of tall bearded iris. Here the lupins were the dominant and featured plant while the iris were an interesting accessory. At Schreiner's Gardens, lupins are used in spot planting to accent the iris. Here the tall bearded iris were the dominant and featured plant while the lupins were an interesting accessory. Both gardens were outstanding in their own way and each was completely successful.

- Take care in selection for height and spread of companion plants to ensure the desired visual effect is achieved.
- Give careful consideration to bloom period for companion plants. Do you want to achieve a massed colour effect? — plant for similar bloom timing. Do you want a succession of bloom whereby companions precede or follow the iris? — plant for diverse blooming.
- Be careful with colour schemes if you are looking for a massed display. One of the great joys of using iris is that you can virtually select any colour scheme you desire. Similar care should be taken with companion plants to reinforce desired results.
- If using annuals, give careful thought to the timing of your planting of seedlings or sowing of seed. Remember that tall bearded iris flower towards the end of spring, so, if using spring annuals for a massed effect they need to be planted late while summer annuals would need to be planted very early. Don't forget that IB iris flower earlier than TB iris and dwarf bearded iris earlier still.

Some personal preferences for perennial companion plants that flower with bearded iris are: russell lupins; delphiniums; daisies of various types; verbena; gauera; diascia; and liatris.

There are many trees and shrubs which flower in mid to late spring and a personal choice should be made from those suited to your climate. Most of the early spring flowering trees will coincide their bloom with that of the dwarf bearded iris while the crab apples and flowering cherries bloom with the tall bearded iris.

I have a particular affection for the crab apples and two, in particular, are worth a place in any garden. They are *Malus floribunda* 'Hillieri' and the later flowering *Malus ioensis*.

Another flowering tree well worthy of a position in any garden is the Manchurian pear, *Pyrus ussuriensis*. Bloom is early, before tall bearded bloom, but this is a tree of quality throughout the year.

Roses bloom at the same time as tall bearded iris and enjoy the same climatic and soil conditions. Many people do not like to grow roses with companion plants just as many prefer to grow their iris in solitary confinement and many who grow both roses and iris like to keep them separate, but they do flower at the same time of the year. I have a particular affection for Rugosa roses which have softer, more welcoming foliage and are excellent companion plants for iris. The Rugosa roses have a strong perfume and are outstanding landscaping plants in any garden.

Louisiana iris at Rainbow Ridge Nursery featuring 'Bit o' Blue'

Sunset at Hillview—'Fortunata' (Ghio, 1985)

Sunrise at Cooley's Gardens — 1994 Convention

First in the fields — early morning at Cooley's Gardens — 1994 Convention

Commercial fields — Cooley's Garden

LANDSCAPING WITH BEARDLESS IRIS

While most of what has been written for bearded iris will also apply to beardless iris in terms of general rules for landscaping and companion plants, the beardless iris have the advantage of even greater flexibility as many can be grown in damp or wet conditions, while Californian iris are ideal in rockeries and Evansia iris love woodland settings with a semi-shaded situation and are therefore ideal for naturalising. Bulbous iris are part of the main early spring display and the Dutch iris combine readily with other spring bulbs while reticulata bulbs are beautiful in suitable climates. The winter-flowering *I. unguicularis (I. stylosa)* has a special part to play in the winter garden while *I. foetedissima* has the special attribute of being shade-loving.

Many daffodils flower earlier in spring than the Dutch iris and their use together could be a failure on two counts — different bloom periods and uniquely formed elegant flowers competing for attention at approximately the same height could be seen to be a distracting sight. For a similar reason, I would not see the use of Dutch iris and hyacinths together as being a perfect combination, but I am sure many beautiful pictures have been and will continue to be painted with combinations of these flowers.

For those who wish to make the 'timing' easier, it is rewarding to plant iris bulbs with long-flowering annuals such as violas, primula or alyssum. Violas have a distinct advantage as there are so many colours in the same hues as the Dutch iris available. Here the main concern is with height as violas grow and bloom quite low while well grown Dutch iris can be quite tall. A gradation for height could be worked using the ground cover alyssum in white, coloured violas, taller primula in white and Dutch iris to colour as the tall focus.

Figure 12. Iris in various garden settings

(a) Japanese-style water garden

(b) Rows of different colours

(c) Drift or massed bed

Iris at Tempo Two featuring 'Elegant Blue' (foreground) and 'Liqueur Creme'

Siberian iris and lupins at Hillview

Cooley's display garden—1994

Cooley's display garden—1994

Cooley's display garden—1994

Cooley's display garden—1994

(d) Specimen clump

I love the gaudy colours of sparaxis, but doubt that they could be used with anything but the yellow or bronze Dutch iris while the blue and purple-toned babianas would be ideal with the similarly toned iris.

All of these and of course many other combinations of plants, be they bulbs, annuals or perennials, can be worked in pots, tubs or in massed garden displays.

The earlier flowering reticulatas are beautiful little bulbs in suitable climates and can be most attractive in combination with other low-growing plants.

Perhaps the most satisfying way of growing bulbous iris for massed display is in rockeries where so many blendings and contrastings of foliage can really enhance the iris. There are many perennials that provide gorgeous foliage throughout the year with the added bonus of flowers in season. The reticulata iris poke through cold winter soil and come into bloom as harbingers of spring. There are few perennials which will flower at this time, but the beautiful plant habit of the sedums and small geraniums enhance a rockery display featuring these iris bulbs.

(e) Edging pathways

(f) In pot

(g) Highlights in front of shrubs and trees

One of the highlights of my visit to the Floriade in Holland in 1992 was to see massed displays of *Iris reticulata* bulbs set out in a landscaped situation. These tiny bulbous iris flowered on spikes 10–20 cm in height. The blue-violet *I. reticulata* was blended with the sky blue of 'Harmony' and 'Joyce', the red-purple of 'J.S. Dijt', the ivory-white of 'Natascha' and all was lit up with the bright yellow of *I. danfordiae*. Clumps were from 12 to 20 blooms in a small area less than one square metre and the effect was stunning.

Louisiana iris are outstanding for massed display in damp, boggy or wet positions. They revel in standing water but it should never be forgotten that they are equally outstanding plants for the 'normal' garden if they are kept well watered. Their great attribute is their versatility, but they should not be grown in the same garden as bearded iris because of their different cultural requirements.

These iris are excellent for growing in a pond but there are a few rules to be followed for complete success. As the rhizomes are large, Louisiana iris need a minimum 20 cm

(h) Dwarf iris in rockery

'Rapture in Blue'
(Schreiner, 1990) and
'Dusky Challenger'
(Schreiner, 1986)

Schreiner's display garden —
1994

Schreiner's display garden —
1994

Massed iris, Schreiner's Gardens — 1994

Row of convention guest iris, Schreiner's Gardens — 1994   Convention garden guests, Schreiner's Gardens — 1994

pot. For clump effect, a tub 25 cm or more would be desirable. The potting mix should be about one-third garden loam, one-third peat and one-third compost or well-rotted animal manure. The mix must be acid (pH 5 to pH 6 is desirable) and the pot should be half to three-quarters full before planting. Once the rhizome is planted, a teaspoon of eight to nine month slow release fertiliser should be added and the pot left in a cool position. Water regularly, but do not keep the mixture 'wet' until new growth commences. This will usually take about three weeks and is observed as new green foliage emerging from the centre of the fan. A mulch of compost or well-rotted manure and a layer of pea gravel or some stabilising material can then be added and watering can be increased. After about five weeks the plant should be quite green and the pot can then be immersed in water to water level or thereabouts. Water level depth can be controlled by using inverted pots or rock mounds for deeper water. Immersion of plants before the rhizome shows visible signs of growing can result in loss through rhizome rot as the plant has not had sufficient time to re-establish its root system. The only other major problem experienced at potting time is the possible loss of the rhizome through rot if it is exposed to direct contact with animal manure. As is always the case with Louisiana iris, the initial establishment is somewhat slow but this is then compensated by rapid growth when established. Once immersed in water, the Louisiana iris can be left for two or three seasons before dividing, or they can be divided of potted on whenever the pot is overcrowded.

Treatment of *Iris pseudacorus* and its hybrids is similar, but *I. pseudacorus* is really too vigorous for anything other than large expanses of water. Treatment of *Iris virginica*, *Iris versicolor* and hybrids is similar, but these are smaller growing than most Louisiana iris and are more suitable for small ponds.

Iris ensata (Japanese iris — Kaempferi) can be grown in pots in ponds but care needs to be taken to remove the pots in late autumn as the iris die down, and to replace them in late winter-early spring when the new shoots start to grow. For all of these iris the potting mixture recommended and the cultural requirements are similar to those for Louisiana iris.

Siberian iris are excellent in damp positions, but they will not tolerate growing in wet conditions for an extended period of time. Laevigata iris can be treated exactly the same as Louisiana iris — the only major difference being that the Laevigata iris are dormant in winter while Louisiana iris are evergreen. It should also be remembered that both the Japanese and Siberian iris are dormant in winter and should therefore be used appropriately in the landscape or aquascape.

With these principles firmly established, the beardless iris can be used in much the same way as bearded iris with the added advantage that they can be used in water. There are many suitable bog and/or water plants which can be used as companion plants for beardless iris, and once again I suggest that satisfactory results will be most likely obtained by consulting an iris specialist nursery in your area or your local nursery. If the nursery is responsible in approach, 'availability' should be indicative of 'suitability'.

Waterlilies, both hardy and tropical, are regularly grown in conjunction with the water-loving beardless iris and there is a wide colour range of these beautiful plants available. Other recommended water-loving companion plants are:

- Astilbe for damp, semi-shaded positions.
- *Lobelia cardinalis* for damp, sunny positions.
- Any of the decorative rushes.
- Green goddess and white arum lilies for bog or standing water.
- Water hibiscus for standing water.

POTTED IRIS

Bulbous

Iris grown solely for cut flowers can be mass planted in pots and then the pots or cut flowers brought into the house at bloom time. Adequate slow-release fertiliser should be added to the potting mix to enable the bulb to reach flowering and then build up for the following year. Care needs to be taken to supply adequate water without overwatering. After bloom, the foliage should be allowed to die back naturally. Quality bulbous iris are easy-care potted plants.

For a massed bulb display, large pots and tubs can be used in the garden. Unfortunately many home gardeners get it all wrong by using mixed bulbs which do not complement one another or by using bulbs which do not flower simultaneously. Care should be taken to judge bloom period, compatibility for cultural requirements and the effect required. Much has been written in the 1990s on colour coordination and what colours go well together in planning colour schemes and themes. I am firmly of the belief that whatever gives pleasure to the gardener is right. I can fully appreciate the trend towards blending of colours, but find that sharply contrasted groupings are also very attractive. I would find a large tub with the blue iris 'Wedgewood' planted in the middle with the smaller yellow 'Golden Harvest' surrounding it a most attractive picture. Be careful though — 'Wedgewood' is early and 'Golden Harvest' is mid season for bloom. An equally attractive 'picture' could have 'Professor Blaauw' replace 'Wedgewood'. Again be careful — 'Professor Blaauw' is late while 'Golden Harvest' is mid season. As the seasons overlap, the picture could be very attractive either way.

Bearded

Growing bearded iris in pots has not been popular with gardeners or nurserymen, but there is now a definite trend in this direction. For the home gardener with limited space, terrace or patio gardens or easy-care gardens, potted bearded iris have come into their own as a specialist plant.

For the non-specialist nurseryman, potted iris in spring form an alternative to autumn bare-rooted rhizome sales. Bearded iris should be potted in summer and autumn for bloom in the following spring. Dwarf and median iris can be potted into 15 cm pots while tall bearded iris require a 20 cm pot as a minimum. The potting mix should be open and neutral to alkaline in pH (i.e., pH 7–8). A mixture of sand, soil, vermiculite with a minimum of manure or compost is ideal. The main issue is to ensure good drainage and supply adequate nutrients.

Potting should be completed in late summer–early autumn to ensure rhizome establishment and bloom. Place the rhizome at soil level in a pot two-thirds to three-quarters full of mix. Ensure that the fan is at the centre of the pot so that the toe is at the edge and foliage will fill from the centre outwards. Add a teaspoon of eight to nine month slow-release fertiliser at planting time.

Position the pots in full sun so that they are exposed to summer/autumn 'baking' and winter cold. They should not be grown under shadecloth or in protected positions. Pots should be regularly watered but never wet and sodden. Once flowering spikes appear the plants will appreciate protection and can be developed under shadecloth. They must be protected from snails and slugs. Use snail bait pellets or mesurol spray.

Beardless

Most of the beardless iris are very satisfactory plants for pot culture, but care must be taken to ensure that the potting medium is of the right acidity. Optimum pot size will be determined by the size of the rhizome and aftercare should be in alignment with the plant's cultural needs.

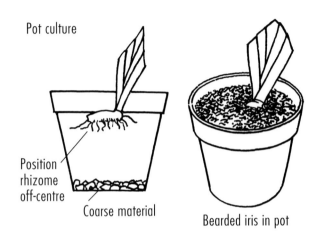

Pot culture

Position rhizome off-centre

Coarse material

Bearded iris in pot

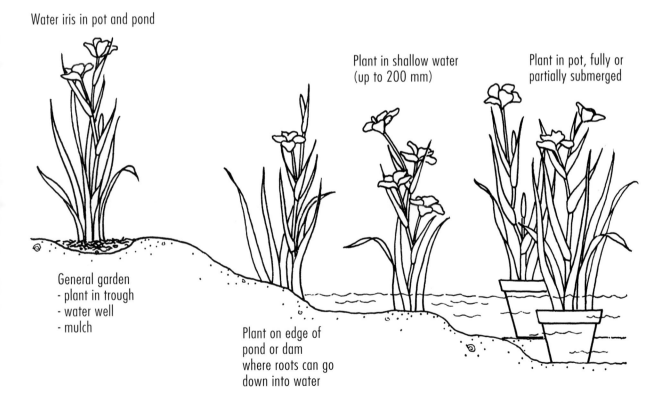

Water iris in pot and pond

General garden
- plant in trough
- water well
- mulch

Plant on edge of pond or dam where roots can go down into water

Plant in shallow water (up to 200 mm)

Plant in pot, fully or partially submerged

Figure 13. Bearded iris potted. Water iris potted

An arrangement of tall bearded iris from Rainbow Ridge Nursery

Louisiana iris as cut flowers on display at Rainbow Ridge Nursery

Vase of Californian iris seedlings

Californian iris and Evansia (crested) iris should therefore be grown under shadecloth. Both are very good for pot culture.

Japanese iris make excellent potted plants in a potting mix with a pH of about 5. After they are established, they can be placed in standing water to the level of the pot or else they will need watering twice a day to maintain the moisture content.

Louisiana iris require much the same approach. Both Japanese and Louisiana iris can be grown in large pots or tubs and they provide a wonderful display if several rhizomes of the one cultivar are planted in the same container.

Laevigata iris and the American natives, *I. versicolor* and *I. virginica,* are all excellent for pot culture either immersed in water or not.

I have not grown Siberian iris in pots but there is no reason to suspect that they would be anything short of excellent because of their ease of cultivation.

Spuria iris are easy plants for pot culture, the only drawback being that the pots need care for a long time before bloom is obtained. Beware of using the species *I. pseudocorus* in pots in water as it is vigorous and can overrun or burst the pots. The variegated and other forms are better subjects for pot culture.

IRIS AS CUT FLOWERS

Iris are essentially garden plants, but flowers may be cut for indoor decoration or flower arrangement, for the cut flower trade or for exhibition at iris shows and displays. The 'average' iris bloom under 'average' weather conditions will live for three days. Dwarf bearded iris, some Japanese iris and quite a few species will not live as long, while the fleeting *I. pseudocorus* will only last one day. Modern *pseudocorus* hybrids such as 'Roy Davidson' and 'Come in Spinner' will last three days. Cutting the blooms has little or no effect on life expectancy and iris are particularly attractive for floral display. Of particular interest are the bulbous Dutch iris and the spuria iris, both of which are ideal cut flowers. Dutch iris cut fresh will keep a week or more while spuria iris can last up to five days. Most iris have back-up buds and it is not unusual to obtain from one to two weeks of indoor bloom from a spike of iris. Spikes should be cut and recut to obtain maximum life and there are good reports of increased life expectancy with the addition of chemical preservatives sold commercially.

Massed displays of iris, in particular large vases of the same cultivar of both tall bearded and Louisiana iris are spectacular. Bearded iris in large vases are beautiful for three to four days, but lose their appeal as they age. People are enthralled by large displays of blue-on-white plicatas and I can remember a large vase of 'Rare Treat' that we displayed at a show creating a sensation. Equally fascinating are mixed vases with contrasting colours. A large display of the reblooming iris 'Harvest of Memories' (yellow) and 'Feedback' (blue-violet) in the one arrangement was very well received at an autumn display. Everyone loves a large display of blue iris and the dark blue 'Breakers' and soft silvery-blue 'Silverado' have both provided us with brilliant vases for display. Both of these Schreiner irises have wonderful form, colour, buds and branching — all attributes that are desirable for special arrangements. Smaller arrangements of three to four spikes can also be spectacular, particularly if displayed with a good balance of buds and open flowers and if associated with the attractive foliage of conifers or complementary flowers and foliage such as the variegated weigelia.

I have seen some wonderful floral arrangements at shows under the direction of the NSW Region of the Iris Society of Australia where for many years the floral art arrangements have been a highlight. Such classes as — Weather Forecast, Solitude, Midnight Drama, Tall and Free, Some Like It Hot, Bright and Cheery, Elegance, Gone with the Wind, By the Lake, Rhythm and Blues, Play it Cool, Dinner for Two, A Movie Title, My Favourite Song, Duet, Simplicity, A Spring Bouquet, Tall and Eloquent, Blue Moon, Purity, Down to Earth, Hello Dolly, Reflections, Dinner by Candlelight, Bold and Brazen, One of a Kind, Morning, Noon and Night, Upward Trend, In the Mood, Tall and Stately, Down Memory Lane, Old South, On the Move, Aspirations, On the Edge, and a variety of themes on spring — have inspired the most beautiful work with iris of all types.

Of all the iris for cut flower arrangements, it is the Louisiana iris that command most attention. These iris are excellent in the garden and in water features but, when cut and exhibited in mass display, are absolutely breathtaking. The vibrancy of the colour, the lush green of the foliage and the spectacular form make them cut flowers supreme. A large urn filled with mixed Louisiana iris arranged by my wife Helen is always a highlight for visitors to our nursery in bloom season. In massed, mixed display the Louisiana iris far outshine the bearded iris, which are better in single-colour displays.

On a smaller scale but equally colourful, a massed, mixed display of Californian iris is spectacular. With their intricate patterns and veinings, the Californian iris blend beautifully together to present vases of real distinction.

More subdued in colouration, taller in stature but equally beautiful are massed displays of Siberian iris or Laevigata iris. These iris combine beautifully with pebbles or smooth rocks and I have seen gorgeous displays where mirrors are laid horizontal and edged with white sand to provide reflection and a waterscape effect.

Prized in their native country for floral display, the Japanese iris are a favourite with Ikebana enthusiasts, who delight in using the partly opened flower. Because of their huge size, the Japanese iris do not lend themselves to large displays as effectively as bearded or Louisiana iris. They are, however, most beautiful when used with restraint. The use of iris for floral arrangement is limited only by the imagination. They are as exciting indoors as they are in the garden.

The use of Dutch iris in the cut flower trade is well known and many people without gardens who love flowers in the home think only of Dutch iris when they think of iris. In the 1990s this is changing and there are many growers who are now allocating areas to spuria iris, Louisiana iris and tall bearded iris for the cut flower trade. Of these, the spuria iris are natural success stories for those with the resources and the patience to plant a crop which will give no return for two years. Once established, spuria iris are easy to grow and prolific to bloom. Flowers are long-lasting and command a premium price. They are also held close to the stem, making them easy to handle and market. They are an excellent cut flower. Louisiana iris have many desirable traits as cut flowers and are increasing in popularity. Their one big drawback is that they do take up a lot of garden space with limited return, but increasing interest will lead hybridisers to develop plants with more compact clumps and an increased yield per square metre. Already cultivars such as the white 'Dural White Butterfly', blue 'C'est la Mote', and yellows 'Dural Charm' and 'Koorawatha' have met the criterion and are very successful cut flowers.

Tall bearded iris have been slower to take off as cut flowers. I feel this is because of their apparent fragility and the wide branching so much preferred for garden display and show bench judging, which has been in evidence. If cut as the terminal flower has reached the 'pencil stage' where it has one day to opening, the tall bearded iris will transport very easily and withstand reasonably rough treatment. Many of the cultivars available do have close or tight branching and once growers discover the suitable cultivars and a demand is created, hybridisers will respond to the call. I feel there will be an increasing demand for bearded iris as cut flowers. Someone will make the big discovery, others will wonder why they didn't think of it earlier. An acre of TB iris can produce 50 000 to 60 000 spikes, which if well grown could give an annual return of $50 000 or more if properly marketed. Why, you ask, don't you, the author, do it? Answer — I love my iris too much to cut and sell them and I have enough irons in the fire right now!

IRIS SHOWS, DISPLAYS, SOCIETIES AND AWARDS

To a large extent I have already dealt with iris displays, but competitive iris shows fall into another category altogether. Once you are growing your iris and growing them well it is very natural for many people to wish to display them at iris shows. What motivates growers will differ from one person to another. Many will have the ultimate pleasure in taking their precious blooms to a central point (the show) where they can share their pleasure with others. Many will have a genuine interest in promoting the flower — why shouldn't other people have the iris thrust at them as a plant to be enjoyed? Others (and I must confess to being one of these) have that innate competitive streak and want to prove that they can do it (in this case grow and show iris) better than anyone else.

Whatever the motivation for the contributors, iris shows are wonderful experiences. They act as a meeting place for the 'true believers', many of whom travel great distances; they bring together people from all walks of life with this one great mutual interest; they bring out the best and worst in people; and they introduce the iris to many who would never otherwise be exposed to its beauty. Iris shows are great levellers and great ego boosters. I never cease to be amazed by the number of people who had the grand champion yesterday and/or would have had it tomorrow but had nothing today. I never cease to be amazed by the number of people who can walk around a show bench with the identical comment 'I/we have better ones than that at home in the garden'. I never cease to be amazed by the number of hail storms, wind storms, sudden downpours and attacks by all kinds of predatory beasts, including the neighbours' children and dogs, that beset unsuspecting 'would-be exhibitors' on the day before show day. No matter what the stories are, nor what the motivations are, there is a buzz about an iris show. I have exhibited for decades and have judged both in Australia and overseas and I just love iris shows.

Exhibiting iris

There is an art to exhibiting iris, but there is far more to this art than simply cutting a spike, a bloom or a collection of spikes and putting them in a container in a hall on show day. Successful exhibiting begins with successful growing and the first requirement is to grow your iris well and hence have quality spikes and quality blooms for the show bench.

Preparation for a successful day on the show bench begins about one week before show day. A walk around

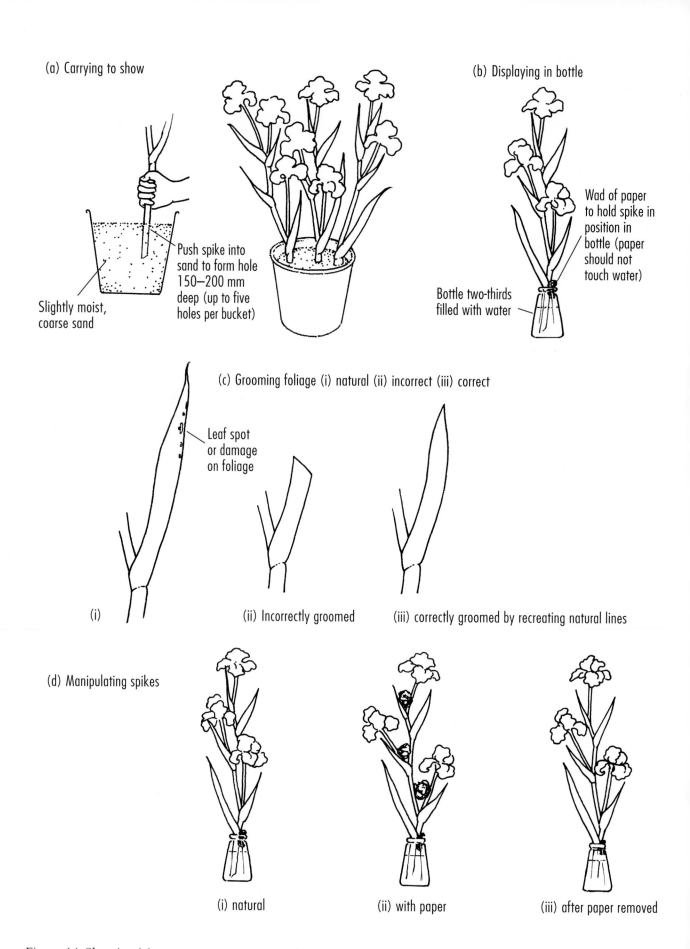

(a) Carrying to show

Push spike into sand to form hole 150–200 mm deep (up to five holes per bucket)

Slightly moist, coarse sand

(b) Displaying in bottle

Wad of paper to hold spike in position in bottle (paper should not touch water)

Bottle two-thirds filled with water

(c) Grooming foliage (i) natural (ii) incorrect (iii) correct

Leaf spot or damage on foliage

(i)

(ii) Incorrectly groomed

(iii) correctly groomed by recreating natural lines

(d) Manipulating spikes

(i) natural

(ii) with paper

(iii) after paper removed

Figure 14. Showing iris

Bearded iris on display at Swane's Nursery, Dural

Vase of Louisiana iris from Rainbow Ridge Nursery on display at Swane's Nursery, Dural

EXHIBITING IRIS

John Taylor with 'Koorawatha' (Taylor, 1987) — the champion spike at the Sydney Convention Show 1988

Graeme Grosvenor with a champion spike of 'Wedding Vow' (Ghio, 1972)

the garden will enable the exhibitor to choose those spikes with exhibition potential. How to make this possible choice will be learned with experience and will quite often be as a result of miscalculation and failure. The road to success is often a rocky one! The next step is to mark and stake, if necessary, the selected spikes. Keep the potential show spikes well watered but avoid overhead watering, which could mark the flowers. Make sure there is adequate protection from snails and slugs and then be vigilant. Observe the daily progress of the spikes, listen to weather reports and delay cutting the spikes as long as possible. Ideally spikes should be cut the day before show day, but the iris are not always cooperative and it is important that blooms be allowed to open inside. If all is going to plan spikes should be cut, bottled and kept in a cool part of the house. To speed up those buds which do not look like opening in time, the spikes can be left in a bathroom with hot water filling a bath to provide a steamy warm atmosphere and lights left on at night. To hold up those buds which look like opening too early, the spikes can be kept in a cool room (approximately 4°C is the preferred temperature) or the buds can be gently and loosely wrapped in tissue paper to prevent them opening and spikes kept in the coolest possible place. Remember that each flower will reach its peak one day after first opening.

After all the care and anguish of the week preceding show day there is always some relief when time for transportation arrives. Before taking exhibits to the show, make sure that you have read your show schedule carefully and have complied with entry procedures of the organising body. Also ensure that you know which classes you intend to enter. If any identification cards need to be filled in it is a good idea to have all the paper work done before setting out for the hall. The actual management of transportation can be difficult, as the iris are fragile when opened and any damage will result in a deduction of points. The means of transportation will be determined by what is available but care must be taken to ensure that blooms do not rub against one another or against parts of the vehicle.

I have found a very satisfactory means of transportation. It involves the use of large buckets (preferably with vertical sides) and damp sand. Spikes can be placed in the sand by first punching a hole and then firmly holding the spike in place with the packed sand. Five or more spikes in fully open state can be transported in each bucket if you have a van or similar vehicle able to accept the height of the spikes. Careful driving has ensured that we have rarely had a spike lost or even damaged.

It is remarkable the distances that exhibitors can travel and arrive at the show with spikes in perfect condition. In exhibiting days, we regularly transported spikes nearly 500 km with little or no problem.

Handling iris in and out of buckets and in and out of vehicles requires care and patience. The top flower of

that precious 'champion' is always vulnerable in the hands of the careless or the impatient.

Once the exhibits are at the show hall and the registration entry ritual has been completed, it is time to bottle the spikes and display them on the show bench. Spikes should be placed in containers so that they are displayed to best advantage.

Try to position the spike so that the distance from the top of the container to the bottom branch is equal to the spacing distance between the branches.

Ensure that the bottle is not overfilled with water but that the spike is in the water and then pack the spike firmly with butcher's paper or whatever is provided, while ensuring that the spike is vertical and firmly held.

Once the spike is positioned in the vase it should be groomed. Any spent flowers should be removed as should any flowers which will die before judging. Here experience and knowledge of your iris are both important. Any unsightly or diseased foliage should be removed or trimmed. If trimming foliage, ensure that the natural lines of the leaves are maintained.

Sometimes flowers are held too close to the stem for perfect display and the spike can be greatly improved by padding out the offending branch(es) using butcher's paper. Care must be taken to ensure that the branch is not broken and it is essential that the paper is removed before placing the spike on the bench. Failure to do so will result in penalty and possible disqualification. When the paper is removed the branch will move back towards the stem but will be better situated than originally.

Finally the moment of truth! When placing the spike on the show bench ensure that it is displayed to its best advantage. Flowers should face the judge and any labelling that may be required should be completed.

Do not expect to get it all right at your first attempt. Remember that the first major requirement is to grow quality plants. Enter iris shows for the fun of it — if it is a chore or is a stressful activity, leave it to others. Be prepared to give it your best shot and then be prepared to learn by your mistakes, by talking to other exhibitors, by watching the best exhibitors operate and by talking to and seeking help from the judge(s). Most judges are only too happy to give advice or constructive criticism if approached in a friendly way. No one reacts kindly to an abusive or confrontational approach so even if you think you should have won and didn't, remember to ask in a reasonable manner and you will undoubtedly learn. Most important of all is to enjoy what you are doing — and remember that any spike on the show bench is a better exhibit than all the spikes still in the garden.

Iris shows are usually organised by regional iris societies or affiliated societies and provide an excellent opportunity for members of the public to view the iris grown by others, to meet people with similar interests and to gain information about iris.

Iris societies fulfil all of the above functions but can provide much more for those with sufficient interest.

There are iris societies in most of the countries where iris are grown and the cost of membership is, in general, very reasonable for the benefits provided. These benefits can involve publications on iris, monthly meetings and excursions, trading tables where iris can be exchanged, rhizome sales where iris can be purchased for a nominal charge, seed pools where seed is distributed or exchanged, 'round-robins' whereby people can form smaller groups and interchange information on a rotational schedule and, above all, the bringing together of people with a common interest. This is often done by running iris conventions in bloom time.

Many iris societies provide additional opportunities for those with special interests. Foremost among these is the establishment of a system for trialling and evaluating iris. Once this structure has been established, there is the encouragement given to enthusiasts to hybridise and have their iris seedlings evaluated, there is the establishment of an awards system for the garden performance of iris — as distinct from the show bench performance and there is the encouragement given to those with special attributes to be trained and to become judges of the society.

The ultimate award that an iris can obtain and the award to which all hybridisers aspire is the Dykes Medal. At the time of writing, this medal is awarded by the British Iris Society to one iris hybridised in Britain each year, to one iris hybridised in the USA each year and, in alternate years, to one iris hybridised either in Australia or New Zealand. The award honours the famed English irisarian William Rickatson Dykes and before an iris even becomes eligible for consideration it will have gone through a rigorous evaluation over some years. This evaluation differs slightly in each of the four countries, whose iris societies make the final recommendation to the British Iris Society as to which iris is most deserving of the medal, but it is sufficient to say that an iris awarded the Dykes Medal has proven itself as a quality garden iris.

I do not wish to pursue all the stepping stones that an iris needs to cross to achieve this illustrious award, but do wish to point out that iris are usually evaluated in the first place as unnamed seedlings. A preliminary award, if given, will encourage the hybridiser to name the iris, release it for sale and hence ensure distribution. The iris will then be further evaluated by society judges and if further awarded, may eventually be eligible for consideration for the Dykes Medal.

Of particular significance to the British Iris Society are the Trial Gardens at Wisley and it is an honour for an iris to be selected for trial at Wisley. Here an iris can receive a certificate of preliminary commendation, then be highly commended, receive an award of merit and a first class certificate.

In the USA, Australia and basically in New Zealand, eligible iris receive a highly commended certificate followed by an honorable mention certificate and then an award of merit.

There are special awards, usually named in honour of irisarians who have made a significant contribution to developing and furthering the iris cause, and these are often given in special categories of iris or as personal honours to individuals. In general, these special awards are limited to iris or irisarians from the country giving the awards, but there are two international awards worth a special mention.

The Italian Iris Society holds an international competition for bearded iris at its trial garden in Florence. Hybridisers from all over the world are invited to submit their iris in two categories — tall bearded iris and border bearded iris — for evaluation three years after entry. Judges from all over the world are invited to judge the iris over a one-week period in May each year. Awards are made on an overall basis and in special categories and this is a most prestigious competition.

The NSW Region of the Iris Society of Australia holds a similar competition for Louisiana iris. This competition is called the Sydney Louisiana Iris Spectacular and is judged, in Sydney, during October/November each year.

PURCHASING IRIS

Successful gardening is, to a large extent, about planning, although many of us amble along with moderate success without ever giving thought to any kind of plan. Iris plants are not cheap, although there is an argument to support the case that, in terms of their growth and development, they are not as expensive as many shorter-lived garden subjects. New-release bearded iris in the USA are costing between $US35 and $US45 while in Australia new releases are $A30 or more in 1997. Many beardless iris are first released at prices up to $50 and there is an upward trend in pricing for both bearded and beardless iris. Import and export costs between these countries, and between all other iris-growing countries, are high and the nurseries which export and import can expect to pay for Agriculture Department inspection, health certificates, quarantine and growing-on fees, freight and packing and health checks. On top of that there is always the likelihood of plant losses, lack of or delay in acclimatisation, or general unsuitability of the plant. Many plants can survive all of this and grow on vigorously only to bloom-out in the first year and leave no increase.

Hybridising is also very expensive as much land has to be prepared and maintained and many seedlings have to be planted and developed and evaluated over a three to five year period before release. When all of this is considered, there is much to suggest that new release iris are 'reasonably priced'.

Iris plants are one of the few plants, or any other commodity for that matter, which progressively decrease

'Azure Angel' (Grosvenor, 1994)

'Town Clown' (Blyth, 1987)

'Rococo Valley' (Johnson, 1972)

'Shiralee' (Blyth, 1988)

'Alpine Journey' (Blyth, 1984)

in price over the years. As nurserymen build up stock the price of an iris decreases accordingly, and an iris which costs $30 in one year may be down to $20 or $25 the following year and cost as little as $10 to $15 the following year. Price is determined by supply and demand and iris which command high prices after their introductory year are either in very high demand or are very slow growers, or a combination of both. After a few years on the market most iris will cost somewhere between $5 and $10 and there are many superb quality iris in that price range. A gardener with an interest in iris would be well advised to 'cut their teeth' on the older, well-established cultivars and then build up a collection as interest increases. It should be noted that irisarians are generous people and there is usually a gift or bonus of some kind with each order supplied by specialist iris nurseries.

In planning an iris planting, you should make yourself aware of the suitability of the type of iris you like for your climate. This can be done by reading literature (iris catalogues are fun), by visiting gardens, shows or nurseries or by contacting specialist growers.

Much of the selection progress then comes down to what to get and from where to get it, and herein lies the question of personal choice. I recommend that gardeners new to iris growing should purchase, initially, proven, well-established reliable iris. There is always a little adventure in us and often the expensive new releases are a temptation too difficult to resist. I can remember purchasing 'Mary Frances' as a new release many years ago! It was a temptation too difficult to resist and proved an excellent investment. 'Mary Frances' was an instant success and remains a personal favourite to this day. I further recommend that you purchase only from a reputable nursery, or an agent acting for a specialist and always remember that a cheap, poor quality or inferior plant takes up as much room in the garden and requires as much care as a top quality plant. It never ceases to amaze me that people will not pay $20 for an iris that they really love yet will spend the $20 by purchasing at $10 each two iris, both of which are of minor interest. I suppose we all like to think we are getting value for money and there is some safety in quantity.

Iris should be ordered early in the season to ensure complete satisfaction. Late ordering of popular varieties will often result in disappointment if they are sold out. Early planting ensures a good start for the following season and specialist nurseries send out their best plants to fill the first orders. Most specialist iris nurseries give a guarantee that plants are true to name and will survive the first season and they will willingly replace any failures or mistakes. If you have doubts, ask!

Most iris nurseries work on a mail order or pick up service of bare-rooted ex-garden rhizomes. The plants you receive should be large, firm and disease-free. Depending on the time of purchase there should be

signs of increase for the following season. Large, well matured rhizomes in good condition should show increase in the following autumn while undersized plants may take months to reach full size. Remember that the size of a mature rhizome will vary from one cultivar to another and that a full-size rhizome of one cultivar may be more than twice the size of a mature rhizome of a different cultivar. The rhizomes of tall bearded iris such as 'Lilac Lustre' or 'Polished Amber' are huge while a mature rhizome of 'Marriage Vows' is quite small.

Rhizomes planted in summer or early autumn should flower the following spring. Later planting diminishes the chances of the rhizome flowering in its first year. There are some particular cultivars which skip a bloom season while others, like 'Lady Friend' seem to be able to be moved anytime and then flower with ease. Remember that spuria iris will rarely flower in the first season after being replanted and that all perennials are at their best in second or subsequent years after initial planting.

There is a definite trend in Australia for nurseries, both specialist and non-specialist, to pot iris for sale in spring in flower. This trend in marketing iris follows the trend in marketing roses. I can remember a time when roses were sold only as bare-rooted plants from late autumn through to late winter, early spring. Now roses can be purchased in pots throughout the year. There is little doubt that more and more iris will be marketed as potted plants in the future, but it is doubtful if the mailorder marketing of iris rhizomes will be unduly affected. Purchasing iris as potted plants in flower has the decided advantage of customers seeing exactly what they are getting and not relying on catalogue descriptions and photographs. The obvious disadvantage is the considerably higher price that has to be paid for a potted plant that has been grown on for several months and brought to flower.

Care always has to be taken in purchasing unlabelled and unnamed potted plants or 'backyard specials' where people are removing old or unproductive plants or nurseries are looking for some return for their seedlings which, in reality, should be discarded if they are not up to a standard warranting naming and introduction. Quite often that which appears to be a bargain is not really a bargain at all. For those who really want a bargain and are not particular as to what they get, the best value is usually to be obtained by purchasing from sales initiated by specialist nurseries at the close of the digging season in autumn. From these sales you will often obtain the very best growers and quickest increasers as this is usually the reason that the nursery has excess stock.

Another excellent source for iris is at trade stalls run in conjunction with iris shows. At these stalls you are often able to purchase the best of iris, grown and donated by iris society members, and available at very reasonable prices. Iris societies, as already stated, can also give you access to the awards that iris have received and lists of recommended cultivars. These could be invaluable for gardeners purchasing their first iris or wishing to enlarge their collections.

A NOTE ON THE PHOTOGRAPHY BY JIM FRAZIER

Most of the photographs in this book are either my work or that of the author, world-renowned iris breeder and outstanding photographer of his favourite flower. I would also pay tribute to the contributions of another noted flower photographer, my partner Densey Clyne.

For myself, I am very proud that some of the pictures in this book introduce an entirely new style of deep-focus photography. The technique was originally devised by me for a very different purpose. It has given me much pleasure to apply it here to the photograph of flowers, in particular to the delicately beautiful flowers of the genus *Iris*.

You might think of flower photography as an easy kind of assignment. And for me, used to filming and photographing small wild animals, perhaps it was a little easier in some ways. For one thing, unlike a butterfly, a flower is not likely to take off at the very instant of sharp focus; and unlike a spider it's fairly certain not to bite you.

The truth is, though, that the perfect flower shot is just as elusive as that of any more mobile subject. The problems are just a little different — wind for instance. For my technique to be effective — to gain maximum depth of focus — long exposures are essential. And a long exposure in even the slightest breeze means a blurred image. So you just have to wait for a lull. A split second will do — but it means a lot of patient waiting with your trigger finger ready and no time to blink.

Twenty-five years ago when I took up the macro-cinematography of small, very active invertebrate animals, I found formidable problems. Simply keeping your subject in focus was hard enough, but to tell a scientifically accurate story while bearing in mind the visual aesthetics was daunting, to say the least.

That necessity is the mother of invention has been literally true in my case. Over the years, to do what I envisaged in my mind's eye, I found it necessary not only to develop special techniques, but to invent special equipment, including lenses.

Knowing nothing of the theory of optics, I started playing around with bits of optical glass, stacking them together in various configurations. My object was to obtain a depth of focus impossible with any commercially available lens, that is, a sharp focus from macro to infinity.

Somewhere about this time I heard someone mutter that the inverse square law of optics makes infinite depth of focus impossible in any lens system. But I knew nothing of the accepted theory of optics. I simply persevered and eventually came up with the results I wanted. Ignorance can sometimes be bliss.

To be honest, although I know the difference between a positive lens and a negative one, I still do not understand the physics of it all. But I have learned, after much trial and error, that if you put certain lenses together in a certain way, you *can* gain extra depth and a very different perspective from that obtained with conventional lenses.

My original requirement was for cinematography — moving pictures of wildlife. Building lenses and successfully using them for cinematography is one thing. For still photography it's a very different matter. I built many lenses before I got them to work satisfactorily for use with a normal 35 mm still camera. When I finally got the effect I was looking for, I started trials in earnest. It took a long time, but the result is a unique lens system now the subject of a patent application.

Creating the lens was one thing. Now I had to work out the best method of using it. I virtually had to develop a whole new style of photography. Not for me the luxury of throwing the background out of focus, showing the subject against a beautifully muted backdrop. No, I had to examine critically everything I could see in the viewfinder for balance, colour and overall composition.

When everything is in focus, a shot can be ruined by a garden hose, people, powerlines, any small object like a plant label showing up in the picture. The camera captures it all. For the multiple iris shots in this book it was sometimes necessary to deadhead every spent flower in the background. No convenient throwing out of focus to lose distractions in the general haze of disinformation.

In using this lens, the placement of the camera in relation to the desired foreground and background is critical. A tiny movement of the camera is enough to affect foreground balance. Lining up foreground and background correctly can sometimes be a headache.

Wherever possible I find it essential to include a strong mid-ground element in the composition. There are two reasons for this. Firstly, it helps to correct perspective; secondly, it overcomes the illusion that your principle foreground subject is a giant model! In other words, you need a receding image, a gradual movement back from foreground to background.

Foreground, middle ground and background must be lined up to give a natural-looking perspective. It's a matter of trial and error, but you know when it looks right.

One of the benefits of having everything in focus is that your viewers are never under any illusions. They have unrestricted viewing of any part of the picture.

'First Movement' (Grosvenor, 1993)

'Jesse's Song' (Williamson, 1983)

The background creates the environment while the foreground subject is there, prominent and clearly identifiable. From a publisher's point of view this means getting two shots for the price of one, and saving a lot of space.

To sum up. With regular macro or close-up shots, it is usually only possible to have one or two flowers in focus and even then parts of those flowers may be out of focus. A deep-focus lens such as mine can keep all the flowers in focus, and at the same time give an overview of the whole scene.

At the time of writing, my lens has not yet reached the production stage, but I hope it will become available to all photographers in the not too distant future.

In the meantime, those of you who simply want to take happy snaps of your flowers and gardens already have access to a range of reasonably adequate equipment. You don't have to be a professional photographer with state-of-the-art equipment to obtain pleasing pictures.

However, when it comes to 'instant auto-everything' cameras, there are limitations to bear in mind, particularly limitations on close-ups. If you try to get closer to your subject than the minimum distance stated in the camera's instruction book, two things will happen. One, the flower or other subject will be out of focus. Two, it won't be in the centre of the picture or wherever you planned it to be. The first happens because these cameras are technically unable to focus at close range. It's one of the prices you pay for simplicity.

The second happens because when you look through the camera's viewfinder you don't see exactly what the lens sees. The lens is below the viewfinder; light comes into it at a slightly different angle; the closer you are, the greater the angle. Get too close and your flowers can all but disappear out of the top of the picture.

If you're serious about close-up flower photography get a single lens reflex (SLR) camera. It overcomes both the above problems. Firstly, SLRs have a mirror inside them that reflects into the viewfinder exactly the same scene as the lens sees. So what you see is what the camera gives you.

Secondly, with an SLR camera the lenses come as separate units and you can buy yourself a macro lens that specialises in close focus. And that's what I recommend if you're really serious about close-ups. A macro lens gives you infinity at one end of the focusing range, and, in some cases, a full, life-size image at the other.

'Bahloo' (Caldwell, 1986)

'Santiago' (Ghio, 1989). Through the eye of the iris

Beyond that again there are tubes and supplementary lenses that let you get even closer, but it must be said that once you get beyond life-size, or 1:1 magnification as it's called, the problems, both technical and otherwise, increase proportionately.

I'll say something now about matters that relate less to the equipment than to the way you use it. And also about a nasty habit the weather has of thwarting your plans.

A very important decision is whether or not to use a tripod. While it's easy and convenient to hand-hold your camera, this doesn't necessarily yield sharp photographs.

Hand-holding a camera while a flower is blowing in the breeze means you have two moving objects, the camera and the flower. Not so bad when the light is so bright you can use a fast shutter speed, but shutter speed is related to depth of focus. When one goes up, the other goes down. So slow shutter speeds are the rule rather than the exception for close-up work, if you want your flowers in focus from front to back.

Stand with your legs braced, they say; hold your arms against your body; take a deep breath. Well it can work sometimes, but even a single heartbeat can ruin a slow shot when you're in macro mode. A tripod is safer; it doesn't have to breathe, it hasn't a heart, and it's got three legs. No-one wants to carry it around, but the results will speak for themselves.

Now to weather and the elements. Are you about to rush outside with your camera because the sun's shinning from a cloudless sky? Don't — it can be a recipe for disaster! Photographic film can record only a given range of brightness; on sunny days you risk getting overexposed highlights and black shadows. Choose a day with soft, even light from cloud cover, particularly hazy cloud; this natural lighting will do justice to the delicacy of your flower subjects.

Having said that, there are some simple ways of overcoming the contrasty lighting of bright sunshine. One way is to carry your own cloud with you — in other words, a diffuser. All you need is a sheet of some translucent white material to hold between the sun and your subject. Held very close to your flowers it will bathe them in a flattering glowing light, but be careful not to let the diffuser stray into the shot.

Another way to overcome contrast is to lighten the dark shadows with a reflector. A piece of white cardboard will do. Hold it near the lens at an angle to reflect the sun onto your subject. This won't affect the highlights, but it will lighten the shadows, reducing the contrast your film has to cope with.

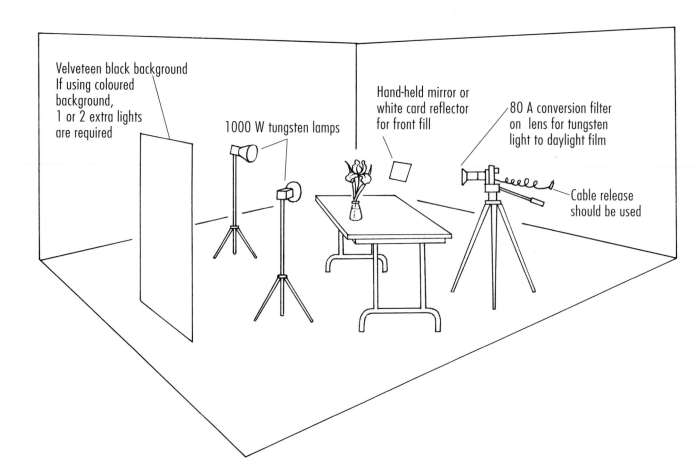

Figure 15. Simple studio set-up for recording high-quality flower portraits

A word about the use of flash. Out of doors I generally avoid it as being unflattering to flowers. It can, of course, be used to fill in shadows, but for fill flash — as it is called — it is necessary to reduce the flash output so that the ambient light is not overpowered. There are ways of doing this automatically with some flashheads, but there is still a certain amount of guesswork involved. With a reflector, on the other hand, you can see exactly what you're getting.

On the whole, the use of flash out of doors can be risky. Perhaps the only proper place for it is in a studio set-up with cut or potted flowers, using several flash heads and diffusers. However, this is not for the faint-hearted; studio work takes a lot of expertise, and can only be learned by experience.

When it comes to indoor work I prefer to use the main studio light as a backlight, and use reflectors to provide the front lighting. A simple set-up is illustrated in figure 15. It gives excellent results and seems to make the flowers come alive. Backlighting takes advantage of the translucency of petals, making their colours glow. Front lighting tends to flatten, and reduces the rich colours.

I use a black velvet background to enhance the colours. If you prefer a coloured background you will need one or two additional lights to direct onto it and care should be taken that no light spills from these on to the flowers.

Finally, whatever techniques or equipment you use, a little extra attention to detail can mean the difference between a wasted film and a lasting memento of the flowers you love.

'Better Believe It' (Taylor, 1998)

CHAPTER 7

HYBRIDISING
IRIS

The mechanics of hybridising most plants is easy and iris are no exception. All you need to know is the basic plant and flower structure and how to get the pollen on to the stigma.

Remove the anthers from the flower by using a pair of tweezers. The anthers hold the pollen at the end of the filaments. Gently pull back the stigma from the style crests and rub the pollen across the inside of the stigmatic lip.

It is desirable but not essential to put pollen on each of the three stigmatic lips and it is desirable to remove the standards, and possibly the falls, and then cover the pollinated floral parts to ensure that insects do not confuse the issue by adding other pollen. Label each cross with a swing tag or plastic label. Evidence of success, if any, will be available within a week as the ovary swells noticeably. If the cross has not taken, the floral parts will shrivel and fall off.

Once a 'take' has been identified it is important to keep the developing pod free from damage by insects, birds, grubs or the weather. We have found it desirable to cover the pod with stocking or 'Evolution Cloth' and tie firmly to the spike. This also ensures that if the pod ripens and seed is spilled before having been harvested, it will be collected in the stocking or cloth. Pods will take from 60 to 90 days to ripen. This depends upon the type of iris, the particular cultivar and the weather conditions. I have used a tall bearded flower to illustrate the process, but it is much the same for all types of iris.

For maximising your number of 'takes', here are a few hints.

◆ Select as the pod (female) parent a flower which has been open for one day.
◆ Select pollen only from young flowers — less than a day old. Viable pollen can be obtained by opening some unopened buds.
◆ Do your crosses early in the morning or in the evening. Avoid extreme heat and avoid rain or using flowers wet with dew or watering. I like to start early in the morning and finish between 10 a.m. and 11 a.m.
◆ Some pollen is difficult to obtain from the anthers and may have to be scraped using tweezers.
◆ Some stigmatic lips are damaged by weather or insects and should be rejected in favour of those that are firm, clean and intact.

Once the seed has been obtained there are differing views as to when is the best time to plant. Much depends on climate and it is important that seed not be allowed to dry out once planted. I have found the best results are achieved by holding seed until mid autumn and then planting in the open garden. There are arguments for earlier planting and arguments for planting in containers. If planting in containers, use seed-raising mix as a medium. Germination can be erratic and is dependent on a variety of factors. I have

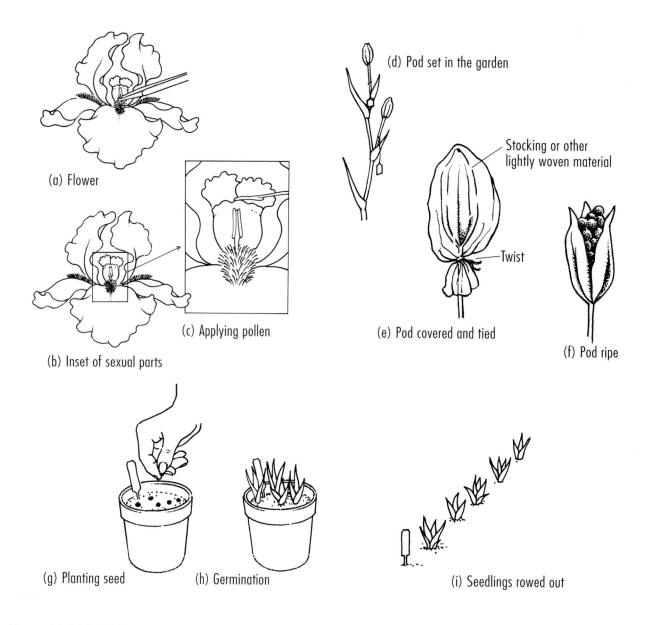

(a) Flower

(b) Inset of sexual parts

(c) Applying pollen

(d) Pod set in the garden

Stocking or other lightly woven material

Twist

(e) Pod covered and tied

(f) Pod ripe

(g) Planting seed

(h) Germination

(i) Seedlings rowed out

Figure 16. Hybridising

had seed germinate within a month, but usually there is an eight-week wait for some germination and this germination may continue until the following spring. To obtain bloom in the second season from making the cross, it is important that seedlings be set out in permanent positions by early summer. As this often can not be achieved for a variety of reasons, I like to delay planting out until after the heat of summer if I cannot achieve my prime aim of early planting. This inevitably results in delaying flowering until three years after making the cross instead of the usual two years.

While the mechanics of a cross are relatively easy, the success rate can be highly variable. If you follow the advice given above, you will maximise your success rate. Many hybridisers are quite happy to splash a little pollen around and hope for some success. The initial approach for most is to look to see what is in bloom and then see if you can set seed.

All of the peculiarities of the iris plant can be learned by consulting literature, talking to (and listening to) those people with experience, observation and experimentation.

Some hybridisers will not proceed any further than making random crosses, and will be happy with any success. This success will be measured by succeeding in setting a pod, harvesting a pod and sowing seed, and germinating the seed, growing the seedlings on and seeing them bloom.

Random crosses will not usually result in any great advancement and, for some hybridisers, the next step is to develop a hybridising philosophy whereby objectives are set. Once you reach that stage, you can be considered a serious hybridiser.

OBJECTIVES

The objective or objectives of a hybridising campaign can be very personal and can be motivated by various factors. The objectives may be simple or highly complex. Motivation may be personal interest, precipitating a need, financial gain, marketing or competitive factors. Objectives can vary to encompass some or all of the following.

- Improved form, substance, texture or an overall improvement in flower quality.
- Improved flowering habits — more flowers, better-displayed flowers, bloom at different times, in and out of season.
- Improved health, vigour, disease and pest resistance, i.e. better plant habits.
- Varied growth habits, e.g. miniatures, compact clumps, suitability for specific or more general climates.
- Varied growing conditions, e.g. pot culture.
- New colours or patterns.

Many hybridisers are unambitious in their aims and are therefore easily satisfied. If you are ambitious, your ambition needs to be coupled with patience. Most projects cannot be achieved in a single iris generation and several generations can take a long time. Annuals and some perennials will flower from seed on a one-year cycle. Iris will take a minimum of two years from seed setting to seeing the results of the cross. Once a breeding program is in full swing, new results of hybridising efforts will be seen on a yearly basis, but a change in direction or implementing new insights can be a long-term mission.

I must admit that many of my objectives in breeding have been unimaginative. I have set out to improve flower form and quality and develop iris with better flowering habits and better plant habits. Too many iris come on to the market as 'unfinished' products and too many are suitable only for very narrowly defined climates. I have deliberately set out to produce iris that will be of good form with good growth habits that will prosper in diverse growing conditions. These objectives were and are fuelled by the temperate, humid climate of Sydney where (I was told more than thirty years ago) tall bearded iris would not thrive and there were few other types of iris suitable for Sydney and similar climates. With the introduction and development of Louisiana iris, the introduction and development of the Japanese iris (hybrids of *Iris ensata)* and a determined hybridising and evaluation of tall bearded iris of my own and an equally determined evaluation of bearded iris introductions from other hybridisers, both Australian and foreign (mainly from the USA, but some from UK, France and other European countries) I feel confident that a large range of suitable iris can be grown in Sydney and places of similar climate.

Above all though, the objective of most serious hybridisers is to develop new colours and colour patterns, and I quote from correspondence with famed Australian hybridiser Barry Blyth:

'I would say that the number one driving force in breeding iris with most people is new colour patterns . . . It certainly is the most important thing with my breeding and rates number 1 in my iris fantasies. The next nearest number would be about 10 in importance for a motivation force. Other realities come in, but if all iris were yellow or all were blue and nothing else showed up, there would be no hobby or business in breeding iris, or many other things. Have you noticed a thriving breeding program in Sprekelias?'

In developing a hybridising program there are many pitfalls, many disappointments and much hard work. I have already stressed the need to know what you hope to achieve and this is a great help, but there are many sidetracks.

Barry set out many years ago in pursuit of a pink amoena — an iris with pure white standards and pure pink falls. He has still not achieved his objective, but in the process has developed the most outstanding collection of bicoloured tall bearded iris in the world. The search for the elusive pink amoena goes on, but the nearest that Barry has got is the beautiful 'Magharee' with white standards and a pink flush and pink falls with a white rim. Other hybridisers have used the Blyth iris in an attempt to produce a pink amoena and have also been unsuccessful, but there is little doubt that it will eventually be produced. Barry has found that most of his success in producing quality bicolours has been obtained not as expected, by crossing bicolour x bicolour, but by crossing bicolour x self colour, or self colour x bicolour, where the self-coloured iris had bicolour iris in its parentage. This is not a hard and fast rule, but a general observation he has made from years of experience. What I want to stress is the need of experience and, even more important, the ability to observe what is happening and then be able to rationalise why it is happening.

When a hybridiser is working for colour breaks (i.e. developing iris in new colours or colour patterns) there is always the dilemma as to what to name and release and what to withhold for further development.

The dilemma occurs when the iris lacks perfection in some way but has many desirable attributes. It is easy to be trapped into releasing every new colour as an 'advancement' and equally as easy to 'hold off' until deficiencies have been improved in future generations only to find that you end up never naming or releasing anything.

Over many years I have observed the development of Barry Blyth's line of bicolours and seen the remarkable development both in terms of the innovative colours and patterns and the improvement in flower form and plant quality which have accompanied this development. I have observed many fascinating colour breaks that have never made it into commerce and had the frustration of

Spuria seedling (Helen Grosvenor)

Grosvenor seedlings — Japanese iris

Grosvenor seedlings — Japanese iris

Grosvenor seedlings — Japanese iris

Grosvenor seedlings — Japanese iris

UJ5-13 'Memorial Tribute' x 'Janet Hutchinson'
(Grosvenor)

UJ7-7 'Mist o' Morn' x 'Memorial Tribute' (Grosvenor)

growing others only to be disappointed in performance under my conditions. I have come to recognise the great dilemma that a hybridiser faces when one cross produces so many good things that selection is so difficult as to be well nigh impossible and other crosses produce beautiful colours with no 'finished products' among them. To name and introduce or not to name and introduce? I suppose the answer, in general, is 'if you have doubts, don't!' But here is the real dilemma. Where is the cut-off point? Should a hybridiser name and introduce 'unfinished plants'? For the 'Yes' case, there is always the chance that others will do the hybridising to produce a finished product. There is also the argument that many people want only the new colours and patterns and do not care for the 'finished product'. For the 'No' case, there is always the argument that you will be better known for your failures than your successes. I must confess to having regrets about some cultivars named and released for sale and even greater regrets for encouraging my brother-in-law, John Taylor, to introduce some of his Louisiana iris against his better judgement.

A most important part of any hybridising campaign is the selection process. A good hybridiser needs a good eye for selecting those seedlings with which to continue and those worthy of naming. Many hybridisers get too close to their work and become over critical or, even worse, too enthused about their own seedlings. It is often beneficial to get help in assessing your seedlings and the best help is someone who is knowledgeable and honest, even if their honesty is not always appreciated. Our partnership has always been fortunate in that John and I assess each other's seedlings and my wife Helen, with her intuitive eye, is the best selector of the lot and probably the most critical.

I could ramble on at length on my own and other people's breeding campaigns. There are so many little hints and ideas; mostly they work, but mostly you have to find out for yourself.

I could advise you not to cross two iris from the same hybridiser as, no doubt, the cross would have been done before by that hybridiser and you would only be reinventing the wheel. Then I could confess that I crossed 'Silverado' (Schreiner) with 'Dusky Challenger' (also Schreiner), both great iris, both Dykes Medal winners (USA) and I obtained 'Temptone', different from either parent and a Dykes Medal winner in Australia.

I can remember talking to Keith Keppel about one of his iris and how I could see it as a potentially good parent but I was reluctant to use it because, no doubt, he had. He hadn't. After all there are only so many that you can use and if you decide to use them there are many inhibitors which may result in you not getting the cross made that you want.

These are all little things that you learn as you go along, so the best advice is to decide on what you want to do and go for it! Learn from your mistakes and enjoy your successes.

DOS AND DON'TS

1. Do be observant.

2. Do evaluate your plants and flowers to be aware of their good and bad points. What is desirable is a question of taste, but there are usually 'standards' that have been set and developed long before you were involved. However, you should be prepared to challenge existing paradigms.

3. Don't be a know-all. It is important that you learn all you can about your subject, but never be frightened to learn from others. The more you learn the more you will know how little you know. Above all, be tolerant of the views of others and take interest in what others in your field are doing, even if all you learn is what not to do. Barry Blyth reports that the most important part of his learning has been observing, both on paper and in gardens, what other hybridisers are doing.

4. Do plan your crosses.

5. Don't be inflexible. Be prepared to vary what you want to do or how best to go about achieving it. Very often you can achieve the same, similar or even better results by using alternative but available parents if your plans are frustrated by: lack of pollen; poor pod setting; inappropriate weather; failure of a desired plant to bloom; or bloom occurring out of sequence.

6. In planning and executing your crosses, don't ever use two parents with the same fault. The progeny will only have the same fault emphasised.

Example: If you cross an iris with poor flower substance with another poorly substanced iris, the children *will* have poor substance. If, however, you use a poorly substanced iris with an iris of good substance the progeny (or some of them) *may* have good substance.

The genetic make up of the children is a result of the genes contributed equally by both parents. If both parents contribute genes for poor substance the result can only be poor substance. Where one parent has poor substance and one parent has heavy substance, the progeny will have substance dependent on the dominance of one over the other. This leads to dominant v. recessive traits, which will be discussed later.

7. Do be scientific in your approach. Remember the scientific method — observation; form hypothesis; test hypothesis; evaluation — and then, if necessary, repeat the process or go from further observation to form a new hypothesis. You don't have to be a scientist to be a leader in your field of plant development, but you should be scientific in you approach. Part of this is keeping good records for future reference.

8. Do use your intuition. Some of the best plants have been developed by the hybridiser 'feeling' that this would go well with that. If you want to do something wild, do it — the worst result is disappointment, but you will learn from every experience.

9. Do be critical. Many hybridisers fall into the trap of not being able critically to evaluate their own seedlings.

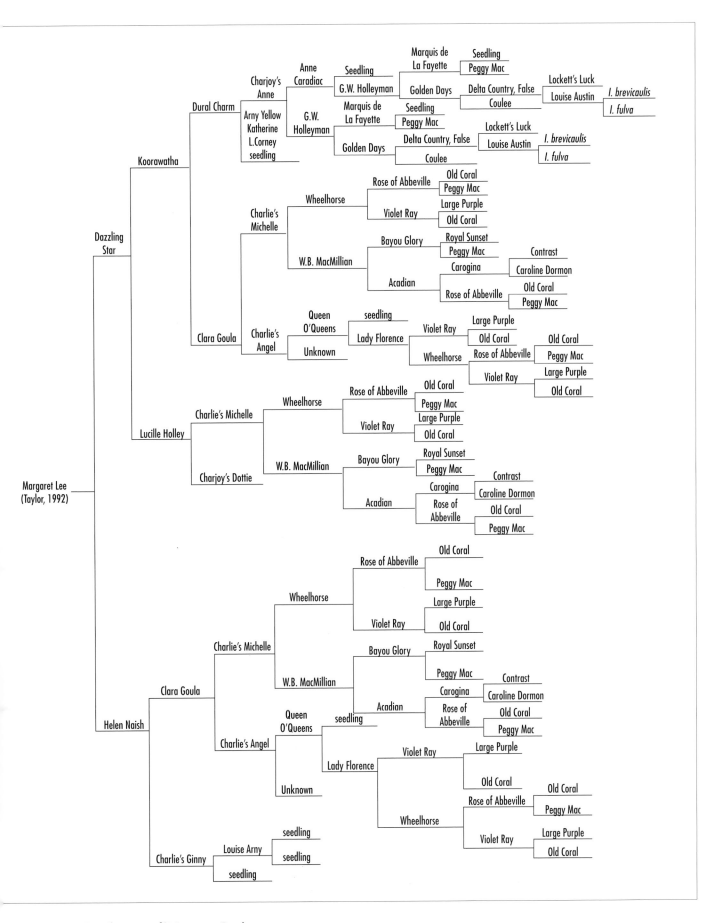

Figure 17. Family tree of 'Margaret Lee'

'Antique Doll' (Taylor, 1998)

'Undercover' (Taylor, 1998)

'Insider' (Taylor, 1998)

'Magnetic' (Taylor, 1998)

'Roman Warrior' (Taylor, 1998)

'Totally Wild' (Taylor, 1998)

Try not to be too critical, but, above all, be prepared to discard those plants which do not reach a satisfactory level. You don't have to achieve exactly what you set out to do, but a minimum standard of retention must be set if you are to be a hybridiser of worth. Try to find someone who will evaluate your plants honestly with you and give a balanced opinion. The balance is important as you want neither a person who finds no good nor a person who finds no fault in your work.

10. Above all, do be patient, resourceful and resilient. You can hope for immediate success but, in reality, success will only come when you have mastered your art. This mastery will, to a large extent, be as a result of experience and this experience is only achieved by doing. All the disappointments that a hybridiser experiences only help to develop the ultimate talent. Even though you may not think so at the time, you will learn as much, if not more, from your failures as from your successes.

DOMINANCE AND RECESSIVENESS

When two parents are used to produce progeny, they contribute genes equally for every trait in the make-up of the product. If the genes differ, then the result in the progeny will be as a result of dominance of one parent's genes over the other's. While this is simple, in itself, there is need for great depth of research to determine the likely results of any cross. You need to know, not only parents but grandparents, great grandparents etc. for many generations. Even then you will be often amazed by what happens. With relatively undeveloped plants, family histories will not be available and all your knowledge will have to be learnt from experience.

Let me use a human example to explain. In humans, brown eyes (Br) are dominant over blue eyes (Bl), so the simplistic answer is that if you cross a brown-eyed person with a blue-eyed person you will get brown-eyed progeny as brown will dominate blue. Not so! It will depend on the parents of the parents.

1. If the brown-eyed person is from a line of all brown-eyed people, then the only gene in that make up is for brown eyes so crossing Br x Bl = Br.

2. If the brown-eyed person is from a line of brown and blue eyes, where the brown has dominated, there is the possibility that the blue factor carried through in the brown-eyed person will produce blue eyes when crossed with blue eyes, so

Br x Bl = Br (some)
Br x Bl = Bl (some)

The progeny from parentage of brown eyes and blue eyes will depend on the genetic make-up of the dominant (brown-eyed) parent.

Now, two other possibilities should be considered.

3. Bl x Bl = Bl. Blue eyes x Blue eyes must produce blue eyes.

4. Br x Br = Br Brown eyes x Brown eyes must produce brown eyes if either parent is from pure brown lines, but if both are from Br x Bl lines then some Bl may occur.

The only way to avoid confusion is to plot family trees and by going back sufficient generations, you can make more accurate predictions.

Mendel's laws

Mendel observed that in plants that bred true for a certain trait (such as self colour or plicata pattern) both factors of the pair were identical (homozygous) — either two 'self' factors or two 'plicata' factors.

However, if these two types were crossed and the F1 (first generation hybrids) showed only one character, e.g. self colour even though one factor of each type was present (heterozygous), this characteristic was called the dominant characteristic. The one not expressed, e.g. plicata, was called the recessive characteristic.

This is a useful tool in hybridising and very helpful in planning crosses and predicting expected results. It must be stressed that this terminology has never been technically correct, and it is frequently confusing. Experiments with many different species have shown that dominance does not always occur and is only a relative phenomenon, not an intrinsic property of the factors themselves. For example, the plicata pattern in irises is recessive to self colour, but dominant to one type of white. Thus dominance is a statement about the relationship between a particular heterozygous genotype and the phenotype it demonstrates.

Further reading on the genetics of plants in which you are interested would equip you with sufficient knowledge to form the basis of a breeding program.

RECORDING RESULTS

This leads to the issue of accurate keeping of records. Keeping accurate records is time-consuming, but essential for the serious hybridiser. This is the way to learn and to have at your fingertips your accumulated knowledge about:

◆ Sterility (complete)
◆ Pollen sterile/pod sterile
◆ Fertility — seed production
◆ Value of plants (pod parents v. pollen parents)
◆ Good proven parents
◆ Poor parents

- Germination (chlorosis and other problems)
- Productivity
- Dominance
- Unusual (unexpected) results.

Each pod set should be labelled in the garden (with swing tags) and cross-referenced to a recording book in case of a garden mishap.

Means of recording results

Most hybridisers keep a hybridising book. In addition, I cross-reference my seedling numbers with a colour transparency to make record keeping easier. A typical entry in a hybridising book could read:

Cross	Parents	Seeds	Plants
A1	'Silverado' x 'Snowbrook'	36	36
A2	'Sea of Joy' x 'Silverado'	35	18
A3	'Bubbly Mood' x 'Titan's Glory'	24	6

'A' represents the year. A1 is the first cross made in that year, A2 the second, etc. The cross A2 'Sea of Joy' x 'Silverado' indicates that 'Sea of Joy' is the pod parent and that pollen from 'Silverado' was used. The pod parent is always recorded first. From the cross A2, I may decide to further evaluate seven seedlings. These would be labelled A2–1, A2–2, A2–3, A2–4, A2–5, A2–6, A2–7 and would be photographed. The other 11 plants from the cross would be disposed of and the seven to be kept grown on for another year.

If they continue to show promise, they would be entered in Trial Gardens (official) or sent to trusted friends for further evaluation.

From any one cross it is possible to obtain many 'look alikes', nothing of any value, or one outstanding plant. You can hit the jackpot and get great diversity of high-quality plants, but this is the exception rather than the rule.

Each numbered seedling must then be labelled in the garden (beware of children, dogs and other natural disasters — keep a plan to back up your labelling).

Line breeding

From an initial cross, let us assume you have kept seven seedlings, all with varying admirable qualities but none of absolute perfection. We will use the A2 cross as an example.

Let us assume
A2–1 has beautiful form, colour not exactly what you want and ordinary branching
A2–2 has poor form, great colour, great branching
A2–3 has good form, different colour, average branching

A2–4 has excellent form, good colour, poor branching, and so on

To try to achieve the 'ultimate iris' there is a variety of approaches that can be taken to improve your result.

At your disposal you have 'Sea of Joy' (SOJ), 'Silverado' (S) and the seven children, A2–1 to A2–7. The possibilities are vast.

1. You can intercross the children:
A2–3 x A2–1
A2–1 x A2–3
A2–7 x A2–2, etc.
This is called pure-line breeding.

2. You can cross back to the parents:
SOJ x A2–3
A2–3 x S
S x A2–3, etc.
This is called back-crossing.

3. You can cross the seedlings with themselves:
A2–3 x A2–3
This is called selfing.

4. You can cross the seedlings to named varieties (bringing new blood into your line)
A2–3 x A1–3, or
A2–3 x 'Snowbrook'
'Snowbrook' x A2–3, etc.
This is called outcrossing.

Modified line breeding consists of crossing seedlings with other seedlings having only one common parent. Some observations on the above.

1. If you have one outstanding seedling from a cross, there is little to be gained from intercrossing this with siblings (seedlings from the same cross).

2. Selfing is of little value unless you have lost one very valuable trait, but otherwise have a perfect seedling. Even then it is usually better to cross back to whichever parent is nearest to what you want in that lost trait. Barry Blyth reports, 'Selfing in my experience is usually a disaster and can be very frustrating. Iris seem to have an in-built inhibitor to selfing in that usually seed will not germinate, or if it does, the seedlings are weak and often die out.' He goes on to say 'Close line breeding can also do the same with seedlings just sitting for two to three years with no increase and when something does flower and is any good it often has no increase. I stopped a very colourful line breeding program for tangerine factored dominant pink amoenas and pink bicolours some 15 years ago because of this factor causing no increase despite some marvellous colours showing up. I threw them all out.'

3. Modified line breeding is often very valuable and can lead to all kinds of diversification or intensification of desired traits.

UL20-5 'Switched On'
(Taylor, 1998)

Black tall bearded seedling C39-J

Keppel tall bearded seedling 91-77D

Shoop tall bearded seedling 86-12

Schreiner tall bearded seedling DD 975-1

Schreiner tall bearded seedling CC 758-B

Keppel tall bearded seedling 91-111B

Schreiner tall bearded seedling BB 326-1

4. Outcrossing is valuable to develop a new line or to incorporate other outstanding plants into your own line.

5. Continuous line breeding can result in loss of vigour in further generations. Foliage becomes very poor, leading to the iris being poor garden subjects. This has been a problem in both pink and brown breeding lines in particular.

6. It is always desirable to do reverse crosses, if possible, i.e. do A2–3 x A2–1 and A2–1 x A2–3. Barry comments that 'This is a point that many hybridisers do not emphasise enough. Despite what science says, i.e. it doesn't matter which parent is used as pod and which is used as pollen, I have found from many instances that from a cross not one seedling is picked while from the reverse cross 8 or 10 or more can be marked for future evaluation'.

PHILOSOPHY

To become involved in hybridisation is to separate yourself from other gardeners, other plant people. In becoming 'creative' you will observe your plants in another light, each plant, each flower will not only be looked at for its own worth, but will be observed as to how it can be improved, how it can be used; what its potential is. You cannot describe, outline or establish hybridising goals without taking aesthetic considerations into account, and there cannot be aesthetics without judgement. Hybridising methods depends on what nature will allow us to do and only on that — it is not a question of what we should or should not do, but what we can or cannot do. This requires scientific thinking and experimentation, but does not require a scientific background. The scientific method has nothing to do with aesthetics. You must not confuse the two issues of scientific method and aesthetics or your efforts are doomed before you start.

By making random crosses, a hybridiser may grow hundreds, even thousands of seedlings of no particular value. If, by chance, there is a quality seedling in the patch and this line is pursued without giving any thought as to why it occurred, 'luck' will eventually run out. Too many hybridisers rely on 'luck' and even though luck may continue, they (and others) learn nothing about why it happened. There is a need for observation, a need for thinking about results, a need for formulating, testing and evaluating hypotheses. It is essential that our aesthetic goals and our objective methods are clearly separated from each other without minimising either.

CHAPTER 8

THE FUTURE — 2000 AND BEYOND

If anyone had told me 30 years ago what iris we would be growing now, there would have been exclamations of disbelief. Oh to be here and part of the developing iris scene in 30 years' time because I have no doubts that progress will continue at an ever-increasing rate. After all, progress in the last 10 years has far outstripped that in the previous 20 years and there is no evidence of any slowing down. Indeed, progress is escalating.

Who could have envisaged the standard to which Joe Ghio has taken the Californian iris, Robert Hollingsworth has taken the Siberian iris, Lorena Reid has taken the Sino–Siberian iris and John Taylor has taken the Louisiana iris.

Who could have envisaged the creativity and imagination to develop the colour patterns in tall bearded iris exemplified in the creations of Barry Blyth and Keith Keppel. Who could have envisaged the quality of form and colour shown in the originations from Schreiner, Joe Ghio and Ben Hager.

It is interesting to read the writings over the last 50 years, where experts in the field predict that progress will be slow or will even cease to happen. An optimist by nature, I think that there will continue to be overwhelming development. It may not be along the lines that I predict or that I hope, but it will happen.

The main thrust of development will be with the tall bearded iris. They are the most popular iris, the most commonly grown and hold most influence over hybridisers. I have long been an advocate of improving the tall bearded as a garden subject for performance in the landscape throughout the year. In recent years too much emphasis has been placed on producing pretty flowers at the expense of other desirable attributes. This will not change completely and there will continue to be an emphasis on new colour patterns, but gardeners will become more demanding of a product that is healthy, vigorous, floriferous and an all-round performer. There has always been the feeling that iris bloom for too short a period in the year and so there will be an increased interest in reblooming iris and extended season iris. Already there is a move towards rebloom and the quality of the reblooming iris has improved in form and general appearance. This trend will continue. There will also be an extension of interest in iris which have a higher bud count and those that have an extended bloom season by throwing up spikes over a longer period in the bloom season.

Health and vigour will become major factors. Emphasis will need to be placed on producing a plant which is resistant to the two greatest problems found in iris — bacterial soft rot and leaf spot — and other associated fungal diseases. Perhaps this will be achieved by genetic engineering, perhaps disease resistance will be bred into future iris. There are many new iris released which just do not make the grade as garden subjects. These iris will often perform well in the microclimate in which they are developed but perform

Tall bearded iris of the future

Tall bearded iris of the future

Tall bearded iris of the future

Tall bearded iris of the future

rather poorly when distributed. I have often heard it said that iris are temperamental and one of the joys of growing them is their uncertainty of performance. Quite frankly, this is just not good enough! There are 'temperamental' iris and there are many, many fine iris that are good all-round performers. There is a feeling that poor growers and 'temperamental' iris should never be named and released for sale, but we must appreciate that bearded iris will grow in such diversity of climatic conditions there are certain to be some cultivars which fail in some climates.

If a hybridiser has doubts, then the iris in question should be subjected to further testing and wider distribution pre-release. No matter how meticulous any hybridiser is, mistakes can be made but there are too many mistakes for a feeling of comfort and I believe that a more discerning and more demanding purchasing public will ensure a much greater degree of attention to health and vigour in the future.

But what, do you ask, about the flowers?

I cannot see any likely trend away from the very popular ruffled and laced cultivars of generous size. Hopefully, there will be a more universal acceptance of iris that are not exhibiting the largest, most ruffled flowers because there is an attractiveness about the simplicity of less extravagant blooms as long as they have good substance. I believe there is a market for a variety of forms. The so-called 'space age' iris with horned or spooned beards and other appendages will become more popular as people seek something different. Likewise the traditional requirement of 'closed' or touching standards will be relaxed and blooms will be accepted with open standards so that you will be able to see right into the flower. I do believe that there will continue to be an expectation of good substance whereby the standards will need to hold firm. Floppy, poorly substanced blooms will not come into favour. Blooms with wide falls, dished at the hafts, have become very popular and I find this form particularly attractive. I both hope and believe that more emphasis will be placed on achieving this most pleasant effect. A criticism of many modern tall bearded iris is that the falls flare too much and the iris clump loses its definition from a distance. I believe there will be a continuing interest in flared falls but many people will seek iris with gently arched falls for long-distance visual effect. There will always be interest in both flared and semi-flared falls.

And what about colours and patterns?

In my experience in the industry, I have found pink, blue and white self-coloured iris to be the most popular with customers, in that order. There is huge interest in black iris in the late 1990s and I believe that this will continue. Fashions change! I can remember when we had great difficulty in marketing orange or purple iris,

but at the time of writing these colours are very popular. I can see no reason to expect the great developments in the popular self colours to stop or even slow down. There are so many subtle variations in colour or shade of colour, in form, in beard colour and so many other facets that interest will not wane in the popular colours.

True red will probably only come as a result of genetic engineering. I do not know enough about the scientific requirements to engineer a red iris, but if it can be done it will be done! Hybridisers will continue to work towards this elusive goal. Without some intervention I do not feel it will be achieved. A true green iris is probably easier to achieve and will come. Meanwhile, there will be all kinds of variations in shades of selfs and coloured beards to blend or contrast.

In recent times there has been a great interest in iris with broken colour patterns where blooms are streaked, lined or blotched in another shade or colour. There will always be a market for such novelty and this pattern will be pursued, successfully, by a small band of hybridisers. I do believe the 'novelty' will wear off and while enthusiasts will be happy to have one or two of this type of iris, I cannot see a major development in this area. Likewise, there will always be 'some' interest in plants with variegated foliage but only as a novelty. In recent times we have experienced beards in two or more colours and even bearded iris without beards. Beard colour will always be of interest and there will be much work done in special areas, e.g. a black iris with a red beard.

The great advance over the last 20 years has been in the bicoloured and bitoned iris. In this grouping I include the 'plicata' pattern which has reached new heights through intercrossing with the bicolours so that we now have all kinds of bicolour plicatas. The two great hybridisers in these fields have been Barry Blyth in Australia and Keith Keppel in USA, and each has brought his individual flair into operation to provide the iris world with iris of unbelievable beauty and distinction. While Barry has worked primarily with bicolours and Keith has worked primarily with plicatas, their work has overlapped to such an extent that the new bicolour plicatas are somewhat difficult to classify. With both these leaders in their field comparatively young (each is in his 50s at the time of writing) and showing no diminution in enthusiasm we can look forward to an ever increasing range of colour combinations and patterns. Remembering also that there are several other very talented hybridisers working in this field and that interest grows each year, I feel the future is very bright.

I can predict that there will be amoenas (white standards) with falls of virtually every colour. Already we have blue amoenas and purple amoenas and yellow amoenas and apricot amoenas and brown amoenas. The elusive pink amoena, that Barry Blyth has sought, is very close to being achieved and some already are close enough to be called pink amoenas. I believe that a black amoena will be produced and that 'red' amoenas, true orange amoenas and green amoenas will be developed. With the excellent work being done on reverse amoenas (coloured standards, white falls) already, there will be further development of this pattern.

We already have available bicolours which combine yellow/blue, pink/purple, yellow/'red', yellow/brown as well as other combinations. The well-known neglecta pattern features shades of blue and purple and there are many beautiful combinations already available in these shades, including the blue/black combination. Within the next 20 years there will be a huge range of colour combinations in true bicolours.

And then there are the plicatas!

With white ground stitched in various colours, yellow ground stitched in various colours and now shades of pink stitched in various colours, where does it end? I don't think it will. The base colouring will be enlarged as will the stitched colour. It will become close to 'design an iris'. Already there are plicatas with the standards stitched a different colour to that of the falls, already there are plicatas with standards a solid colour and falls stitched (the amoena plicatas and bicolour plicatas), already there are iris with a base colour and three different colours in standards and falls. The variations and improvements will continue to come. I have wandered in awe in the great seedling patches of the world's leading hybridisers and I can only enthuse about the future of tall bearded iris.

In the other types of bearded iris there are different colour patterns to those in tall bearded iris. I believe that these patterns will continue to be worked in the smaller iris and that popularity will continue steadily with the dwarf bearded.

It is in the domain of intermediate iris that I feel a growing excitement. There is a move towards smaller gardens and patio gardens in units. The intermediate bearded iris are less dependent on cold winters than the dwarf bearded, are closer in stature to the tall bearded and since they have tall bearded 'blood' can combine the patterns of both the tall and dwarf strains. A major restriction in their development has been the 'dead-end' hybridising of obtaining a sterile intermediate bearded by crossing a tall bearded with a dwarf bearded. Light at the end of the tunnel came with the release of Barry Blyth's 'Zing Me' — a fertile intermediate bearded carrying genes for the spot pattern so admired in dwarf bearded iris. Barry has already produced and released iris bred from 'Zing Me'! Pandora's Box!

When the spot pattern is extended into the tall bearded range another pattern will be there for the hybridisers of the world to explore.

I feel there will be some interest in the arilbred iris and the infusing of aril 'blood' into other bearded lines, but this work will be confined to a limited number of enthusiasts.

And what do others think?

Barry Blyth believes that we will obtain plicatas in reverse patterns, i.e. with blue base colour stitched white, brown base colour stitched yellow, etc. and this colour pattern will come through working with luminatas and glaciatas. Glaciatas, now predominantly in shades of pink, will be available in white, lemon, cream, yellow and pure pink and luminatas, now in violet and mauve blue, will have the colour range extended.

Plicatas will be available with vibrant red or rose colouring on different ground colours.

Bicolours, available now, will be reversed with reverse variegatas, reverse plicata bicolours and flowers with rose pink or red standards over blue falls, pink standards over blue falls, blue standards over orange falls, orange standards over blue falls and so it goes on.

Beards will play a prominent part in variations on colour themes. There will be white beards on black falls, purple beards on pink or yellow or white falls and black beards on pink falls.

Pink breeding will intensify to produce darker shades of rose and cerise leading towards red, while the blue effect on pink will be pursued to give blue standards over pink falls and pink standards over blue falls.

Metallic or 'shot' effects will be enhanced in iris both in self colours and bicolours. This area is where colours we are not yet aware of will come into being and then all we need do is blend in the colours we have already and add the metallic effect.

Brown is a colour where a good range is more or less unique to iris. It will be an area in which it is easy to gain new patterns and tones and improve form if the two inhibiting factors of poor seed germination and a tendency for brown iris to overbloom or increase poorly can be overcome.

And what of our cover photo?

Alas, it is only in the artistic mind of Jim Frazier, who worked his skill and imagination into its production.

And the Louisiana iris?

There has been a steady increase in interest in the beardless iris over recent years and in particular a real upsurge in interest in the Louisiana iris. Development of interest has a flow-on effect in the production of new colours and patterns and it is in the Louisiana iris that the greatest advances have been made. In particular, there has been great advancement in substance and bud-count and this has resulted in the Louisiana iris becoming a much more desirable garden plant. This has been amplified by the introduction of healthier plants with smaller, more compact and less invasive rhizomes. Of equal importance has been the improved bud placement which enables the flowers to open freely. I believe all these attributes will become essential ingredients before a new cultivar is accepted.

Tall bearded iris of the future

Louisiana iris of the future

Louisiana iris of the future

Louisiana iris of the future

The trend towards ruffled, rounded blooms will continue. One of the great attributes of the Louisiana iris is the variety of acceptable forms and hybridisers will continue to look for diversity in this area. However, there will be added interest in the development of cultivars with shorter flowering spikes.

There is now evidence of rebloom in Louisiana iris and this will become an area of increasing importance as will season extenders with early or late blooming habits and multibudded spikes. Gone are the days of acceptance of four or five flowers on a spike as adequate, and with the arrival of the great yellow iris 'Koorawatha' (Taylor, 1987) with its 12–15 buds per spike, when well grown, we are in a new dimension of Louisiana iris growing. A modern Louisiana iris is expected to bloom over an extended period with well-substanced blooms to withstand the vagaries of the weather. With the introduction of 'Dural White Butterfly' (Taylor, 1990) we have a pristine white iris, compact, multibudded and an awe-inspiring sight when in full bloom. The superb garden qualities of these great irises will be developed across the full colour range.

Many older Louisiana iris had weak stems which would not withstand difficult weather conditions. There has been great improvement in the strength of stem and its ability to hold the flowers erect and this is a facet which will continue to improve.

Louisiana iris, once thought to be a semi-tropical plant, have shown their ability to flourish in cold climates and, in time, a completely cold-hardy range will be available.

And what of colours and patterns in Louisiana iris?

White and yellow Louisiana iris have reached a very high level. I believe that this will continue with a particular interest in the development of 'greener toned' iris from both the white and yellow sides. This will be achieved as much by the emphasis on green styles and signals as by the actual 'greening' of the petals.

There are many good violet and purple Louisiana iris available but, strangely, quality blue iris are at a premium. This is a colour which will be greatly developed in the near future. The same can be said of pink Louisiana iris which until recently have lacked form, substance and clarity of colour. All of these areas are being addressed and a whole range of quality pink iris will soon be available. Black is very much an 'in' colour and top-quality black Louisiana iris are starting to come on the market. There is little doubt that the 'red' Louisiana iris are the 'most red' of all iris and this is another colour which will be enhanced. I doubt the arrival of a pure red, but the 'reds' will get 'redder'. Although there are approaches to orange in Louisiana iris, a true orange has yet to be developed. It should not take long. There are already quality brown and tan toned Louisiana iris and these will be improved more as an offshoot of orange and red breeding.

Perhaps the most appealing attribute of Louisiana iris is their wide colour range (and the vibrancy of the colours). There are bitones, bicolours, blends and fancies of great diversity. I predict that this colour range will be greatly enlarged with hybridisers working towards a true plicata pattern as found in the bearded iris and much work being done to develop blending and contrasting styles and signals. There will be more distinct bicolours and bitones, an ever-increasing array of iris with rims, edges and reverse colours to emphasise edges. There will be increased interest in double and multipetalled flowers. Already the star pattern of signals on all floral parts has given us several iris of great beauty and this pattern will be more and more in evidence in the future. By contrast, there will be cultivars with little or no signal. There will be different coloured signals, other than the traditional shades of yellow and green.

And then there are the tetraploids! Tetraploid Louisiana hybridising has been pioneered by Joe Mertzweiller in the USA and there is a limited range available. Progress has been slow but as soon as someone undertakes to convert and use the Taylor diploids, a much wider field will be opened. The opportunities are there for someone with the patience and the enthusiasm.

And other beardless iris?

Siberian iris retain modest popularity despite a limited colour range and a dependence on winter cold to flourish. I am sure that their popularity would increase if cultivars less dependent on very cold winters were developed. Some cultivars such as the older 'Caesar's Brother' and the more recent 'Emma Ripeka', bred in New Zealand by Frances Love and a Dykes Medal winner, are more tolerant of mild winters so the basis for a hybridising campaign is there. I feel confident that the rounded, ruffled cultivars as typified by Robert Hollingsworth's 'Strawberry Fair' will come into vogue and this form will be extended to the full colour range. Fancy signals and markings on the falls will become popular and the search for a pure yellow will continue. I believe that a pure yellow will be developed and that the colour range will be extended. Only time will tell if the brief bloom period can be extended.

It is unfortunate that the 40-chromosome Siberian iris are so demanding in their climatic requirements and it is to be hoped a more tolerant strain can be developed. Already Lorena Reid has developed hybrids of outstanding beauty, diversity of colour and diversity of pattern. If these iris can be grown more readily, no doubt there will be more hybridisers and more development.

Californian iris are colour gems, rivalled only by the Louisiana iris in diversity. Joe Ghio has developed these iris in a myriad of colour patterns with an emphasis on round, ruffled form. They are outstanding garden plants once established. I hope that work can be done to develop cultivars which will transplant more readily.

Perhaps this will be achieved by Thomas Tanberg, the great German hybridiser who has achieved so much in inter-species crosses. We already have Cal-Sibs from crossing the 40-chromosome Siberian iris with the Californian iris and it is through this avenue of breeding that I hope a beautiful strain of easily managed garden hybrids can be developed. I believe that it is possible — and can but hope that more hybridisers take up the challenge.

Spuria iris are easy to grow and set seed easily, but development over recent years has been slow. The colour range is limited to white, yellow, shades of blue and purple, shades of orange and brown. It seemed as if a pink spuria was on the way in the 1970s/1980s but little has eventuated and few hybridisers are working on them. I believe a pink spuria is possible.

I. ensata (Japanese iris) have a limited colour range in shades of white, blue, purple, pink and a variety of patterns but progress in their development has been very slow. There have been interspecies crosses with *I. pseudacorus* to produce yellow (but alas sterile) hybrids. The door as yet is unopened although I feel confident that there is a key both to improving the colour range and the variety of patterns. Very much the same can be said for the laevigata iris but, once again, the opportunities and possibilities are there.

You will, I feel, observe that I am optimistic about the future development of iris. This is an optimism dimmed only by my concern about an ever-changing world. It is my observation that most of the great hybridisers have been 'pollen daubing' for many years and most started when very young. My only pessimism is that there are too few young people involved actively in hybridising, because it is the young hybridisers who are active now that will be the great hybridisers of the 21st century.

GLOSSARY

amoena a bearded iris with white standards and coloured falls.

anther the tip of the stamen where the pollen is found.

apogon rhizomatous iris with no beard or crest; beardless iris.

aril the white collar surrounding the hilum of a seed.

arilmed a median iris from aril breeding.

bee pod seed set naturally.

bicolour an iris with standards one colour and falls a different colour.

bitone an iris with standards and falls different shades of the same colour.

blend a flower showing both blue/purple and yellow/pink pigments.

bulb an underground fleshy storage organ with leaves modified for storage and attached to a basal plate of solid tissue. Bulbs go through a life cycle of flower production, replenishment of tissue and then flower the following season.

chromosome the darkstaining body in the nucleus bearing genes in a linear order. The number of chromosomes is constant for a species or variety.

clones a population of individual plants obtained by vegetative reproduction from a single ancestor.

crest the ridge on the haft of the falls of evansia iris flowers.

cross see **hybrid**; **hybridisation**.

cultivar a variety of cultivation as distinct from a botanic variety or species.

diploid a plant with two sets of chromosomes.

domed standards of an iris flower when rounded and closed.

dominance the quality of one of a pair or series of genes that masks or suppresses expression of others.

embryo the rudimentary plant within the seed.

eupogon a true bearded iris.

factor hereditary unit or gene that determines the inherited characteristics of an organism.

falls the flaring or drooping floral parts which form the outer series of petals.

fertilisation the union of the sperm and egg to form the zygote from which the embryo develops.

filament the stalk of a stamen.

form the shape of a flower.

gene a unit of heredity.

genus the taxonomic group between family and species, including one or more species with characteristics in common.

germination the beginning of growth by a seed.

glaciata a recessive clear-coloured white, citron or pink iris from plicata breeding but without plicata markings.

haft the constricted part of the standards (petals) and falls (sepals) near the centre of the iris flower.

heredity the sum of the qualities and potentialities genetically derived from ancestors.

hybrid the offspring of genetically unlike parents.

hybridisation the formation of offspring between unlike parents.

inhibitor a gene that inhibits (or stops) the action of another gene.

line breeding intercrossing seedlings from the same or closely related crosses in order to improve certain qualities of a particular iris pattern.

luminata an iris with an all-over washed plicata pattern usually with a lighter edge around a darker colour on the falls.

median a collective term for those bearded iris whose height lies between that of the standard dwarf bearded and that of the tall bearded, i.e. any bearded iris of height greater than 40 cm and less than 70 cm.

neglecta an iris pattern in two shades of blue or purple with the standards lighter in colour than the falls.

ovary the ovule-bearing structure at the base of the iris flower which develops after fertilisation into the seedpod containing seeds derived from the ovules.

ovule the egg-containing organ within the ovary of the flower that develops into a seed after fertilisation.

petal one of the inner series of perianth parts (standards) of the iris flower.

pH designation for acidity or alkalinity: 7 indicates neutral, lower than 7 acidity, higher than 7 alkalinity.

plicata a pattern of a base colour stitched, dotted and edged in a different colour.

pod parent the female parent used in a cross, i.e., the iris onto which the pollen of another iris is placed.

pogon bearded.

recessive a trait suppressed by dominance.

rhizome a horizontal underground stem.

sanded a pattern peculiar to the Japanese iris whereby a base colour has an allover sprinkling of another colour or shade, usually in the form of dots or short lines.

scape a leafless flowerstalk arising from basal leaves.

self (colour) an iris flower with standards and falls of the same colour.

self (pollination) placing pollen of a flower on its own stigma.

sepals the falls of an iris flower.

sheath the base of a leaf that wraps around the stem.

sib (sibling) offspring from the same parents.

sibcross a cross between iris from the same mating.

spathe a bract or modified leaf subtending a flower or group of flowers.

species generally undefinable but in practice a plant found naturally-developed without human interference.

sperm the mature male sex cell.

spoons extended appendages (in the shape of a spoon) to the beards of bearded iris.

stamen the pollen-bearing structure of the flower, consisting of a filament and an anther containing the pollen grains.

standards the upper, usually broad and erect, petals that form the inner series of the perianth of which the flaring or drooping falls (sepals) form the outer series.

stigma the portion of the pistil receptive to the pollen. In irises it has the form of a ridge or lip projecting from the inner surface of the style branch of the flower.

stolon an elongated creeping stem on the surface of the ground.

style a narrow prolongation of the ovary which bears the stigma.

style crest a projection of the style branch.

substance the characteristics of the petals to determine their strength, firmness and flexibility, hence their ability to withstand water, wind and heat.

tetraploid having four sets of chromosomes.

triploid having three sets of chromosomes.

tuber a short, thick, swollen underground storage organ usually capable of producing shoots.

variegata the name of a diploid species with yellow standards and falls with reddish veining. Now used to describe garden varieties with yellow standards and darker (usually redbrown) falls.

variety a cultivated plant (cultivar) with an identifying common name.

virus submicroscopic particles that reproduce only within host cells.

BIBLIOGRAPHY

American Iris Society. Bulletins of AIS.

Baldwin, John O. *Iris Pioneers and Personalities of Australia.* J Baldwin, Melbourne. 1987.

Caillet, Marie, Mertzweiller, Joseph K. *The Louisiana Iris.* Texas Gardener Press, Waco. 1988.

Cave, N. Leslie. *The Iris.* Faber and Faber, London. 1950.

Dykes, William Rickatson. *The Genus Iris.* Dover, New York. 1913.

Grosvenor, Graeme. *Growing Irises.* 2nd edn. Kangaroo Press, Sydney. 1992.

Kohlien, Fritz. *Iris.* Timber Press, Portland. 1987.

McEwen, Currier. *The Japanese Iris.* University Press of New England, Hanover and London. 1990.

Price, Molly. *The Iris Book.* Dover, New York. 1973.

Stevens, Jean. *The Iris and its Culture.* Lothian, Melbourne.

Valette, Wilma L. *Iris Culture and Hybridising for Everyone.* Adams Press, Illinois. 1961.

Waddick, James, Zhao Yu Tang. *Iris of China.* Timber Press, Portland 1992.

Warburton, Bee (editor). *The World of Irises.* Wichita, KA: American Iris Society, 1978.

GENERAL INDEX

INDEX OF IRIS SPECIES

INDEX OF CULTIVARS

INDEX OF CULTIVARS CONTINUED

Watercolor of 'Dural White Butterfly' (Taylor, 1990) by Australian artist Darryl Trott. © Darryl Trott